THE CATHOLIC CHURCH IN THE CONTEMPORARY MIDDLE EAST

Studies for
The Synod for the Middle East

edited by
Anthony O'Mahony
and
John Flannery

MELISENDE

The Catholic Church in the Contemporary Middle East:
Studies for The Synod for the Middle East
First published 2010
by Melisende
London
e-mail: melisende@btinternet.com

ISBN 978 1 901764 61 1

Melisende, London
and
Rimal Publications, Nicosia

For information on our publications, visit our website
www. melisende.com
and for
Rimal Publications, Cyprus, www.rimalbooks.com

Editor: Leonard Harrow
Printed and bound in Malta at the Gutenberg Press

CONTENTS

CONTRIBUTORS

Antoine Audo SJ is Chaldean Bishop of Aleppo. Born in Aleppo in 1946 he entered the Jesuits in 1969. Ordained a priest 1979, he commenced his academic formation with a *Licence de lettres arabes*, University of Damascus, 1972; followed by a doctoral thesis, Paris III, Sorbonne, 1979. He completed his philosophical and theological formation with Biblical studies at the Pontifical Biblical Institute (Rome), and was for a time professor in Biblical exegesis at Université Saint-Joseph and Université Saint-Esprit (Kaslik). His publications include a study on the Syrian Alawite and political thinker, *Zakî al-Arsouzî un arabe face à la modernité*, Université Saint-Joseph, Faculté des lettres et des sciences humaines, Collection Hommes et Sociétés du Proche-Orient, Dar el-Machreq, Beyrouth, 1988; 'Approches théologiques du récit de Joseph dans Gn. 37-50 et Coran sourate 12', *Proche-Orient Chrétien* (Jerusalem), Vol. 37, 1987, pp. 268-281; 'Isaac de Ninive, Jean de Dalyatha et la spiritualité orientale', *Mélanges en mémoire de Mgr Néophytos Edelby (1920-1995)*, Damascus, 2005; 'Storia e prospettive dei cristiani in Iraq', *La Civiltà Cattolica* (Rome), no. 3787, 2008, pp. 85-93.

Frans Bouwen M.Afr, born in Belgium in 1938, is a member of the Society of Missionaries of Africa (White Fathers). After his ordination to the priesthood in 1963, he completed his studies in Eastern theology, ecumenical relations and Islam in Rome and Athens, before moving to Jerusalem in 1969, where he has since been living at St Anne's Church in the Old City. For many years he has been the editor of the review *Proche-Orient Chrétien*, specialising in the history, theology, liturgy and present-day life of the Churches of the Middle East, with a particular emphasis on ecumenism and Christian-Muslim relations.

He is a consultant to the Pontifical Council for Promoting Christian Unity, a member of the International Joint Commission for Theological Dialogue between the Roman Catholic Church and the Eastern Orthodox Church, and of the International Commission for Theological Dialogue between the Catholic Church and the Oriental Orthodox Churches. He has taken an active part in several meetings and commissions of the Middle East Council of Churches, and at present is also vice-moderator of the Commission on Faith and Order of the World Council of Churches. In Jerusalem, he is active in ecumenical and interreligious relations and was for many years the president of the Justice and Peace Commission of the Catholic Churches.

Sebastian Brock, Oriental Institute, University of Oxford: a leading expert on Syriac Christianity, he has written a series of important publications on the subject including *Syriac Perspectives on Late Antiquity*, 1984; *Studies in Syriac Christianity: History, Literature, Theology*, 1992; *From Ephrem to Romanos: Interactions between Syriac and Geeek in Late Antiquity*, 1999; *The Luminous Eye: The Spiritual World Vision of Saint Ephrem*, 1992; *The Wisdom of Saint Isaac the Syrian*, 1997; 'The Syriac Churches in Ecumenical Dialogue on Christology,' in *Eastern Christianity: Studies in Modern History, Religion and Politics*, edited by A O'Mahony, London, Melisende 2004, pp. 44-65; 'The Syriac Churches and Dialogue with the Catholic Church', *The Heythrop Journal*, Vol. 45, 2004, pp. 466-476; 'The Syrian Orthodox Church in the Twentieth Century', in *Christianity in the Middle East: Studies in Modern History, Theology, and Politics*, edited by A O'Mahony, London, Melisende 2008; 'The Syrian Orthodox Church in the modern Middle East', in *Eastern Christianity in the Modern Middle East*, (eds) A O'Mahony and E Loosely, London, Routledge, 2010.

Najla Chahda began working full-time for Caritas Lebanon in 1988, serving vulnerable people in the Lebanon. Najla became a trained professional social worker in 1991. She holds a Master's Degree in Development and Community Action, a Master's in Psychosocial Issues in War-Torn Societies, and the Master's in Business Administration/Enterprise (EMBA). In 1994, Najla was charged with running Caritas' newly-created Migrant and Refugee Center. Under her management, the Center has expanded from two to over 100 staff members, increasing the number of migrants it helps and the services provided to them, as well as its geographical presence. It currently aids Iraqi refugees, domestic workers from different nationalities and other immigrants in Lebanon. Najla successfully managed the Caritas Lebanon Migrant Center during several major disasters, including the July/August 2006 conflict in Lebanon. In 2002, the Center began implementing programmes addressing migrant workers, refugees and asylum-seekers, with a special focus on victims of trafficking. As a result it was possible to assist the hundreds of victims who were identified, sometimes rescuing them from their abusers' homes. Under Najla's guidance, CLMC aims to provide prevention services in country of origin and re-integration assistance, in addition to the multi-faced assistance afforded in Lebanon. Additionally, as of 2003, Najla represents the Migrant Center in Caritas Europa's pilot project COATNET (Christian Organizations Against Trafficking NETwork). She is the Focal Point on Migration in the MENA Region, and has been invited to intervene as an expert in trafficking on several occasions (among others by UNODC). As a result of initiatives undertaken, in 2006 the Lebanese Government created a National Steering Committee to combat Trafficking in Persons. CLMC, represented by Najla, is the sole NGO represented on this Committee. Throughout the years, Najla has endeavored to establish a network of partners in countries of origin with the aim of ensuring a holistic approach to migrants, especially victims of trafficking.

Michel Cuypers LBJ is a priest and brother of the Little Brothers of Jesus, who take their inspiration from Charles de Foucauld, and a senior member of L'Institut Dominicain d'Etudes Orientales in Cairo. His academic research on the rhetorical analysis of the Qur'an, *Le Festin. Une lecture de la sourate al-Mâ'ida*, Collection Rhétorique Sémitique n° 3, Lethielleux, Paris, 2007, has been published in English as (tr. Patricia Kelly) *The Banquet. A reading of the fifth sura of the Qur'an*, Convivium Press, Miami, 2008. In 2009, this book was granted the 'World Prize for the Book of the Year', awarded by the Ministry of Culture and Islamic Guidance of the Republic of Iran as 'one of the best new works in the field of Islamic studies'. Other publications include, 'Une lecture rhétorique et intertextuelle de la sourate al-Ikhlâ', *Midéo*, 25-26 (2004); 'Structures rhétoriques des sourates 105 à 114', *Midéo*, 23 (1997); 'Structures rhétoriques dans le Coran', *Midéo*, 22 (1995); 'Une rencontre mystique : 'Alī Sharī'atī-Louis Massignon', *Midéo*, 21 (1993); and numerous scholarly papers in *Annales Islamiques* (Cairo-Paris) and *Luqman* (Tehran-Paris).

John Flannery. Originally from the English Lake District and educated in Scotland, he established and managed a printing company in East London for many years before undertaking studies in theology at Heythrop College,

University of London. The award of a Diploma in Theology in 2000 was followed by an MA in Christianity and Interreligious Dialogue in 2003, with a dissertation on the first Jesuit missions to Tibet by the Portuguese Jesuit, António de Andrade (1624-1635). In 2009 he successfully defended his doctoral thesis on the relations of the Catholic Church with Shi'a Islam and Eastern Christianity, as illustrated by the religio-diplomatic missions of the Portuguese Augustinians in early 17th century Persia. From 2004-2009 he was Projects Administrator for the Centre for Christianity and Interreligious Dialogue, Heythrop College, University of London, and is now Executive Administrator of the College's Centre for Eastern Christianity.

Publications include 'The martyrdom of Queen Ketevan in seventeenth century Iran: an episode in relations between the Georgian Church and Rome' in *Sobornost* 27/1 (2005); 'Through a Glass Darkly: the Jesuit Encounter with Buddhism in Tibet' in Anthony O'Mahony and Peter Bowe OSB (eds), *Catholics and Interreligious Dialogue: Studies in Monasticism, Theology and Spirituality*, Gracewing, Leominster, 2006; 'The Syrian Catholic Church' in Anthony O'Mahony (ed.), *Christianity in the Middle East: studies in modern history, theology and politics*, Melisende, London, 2008; 'The Martyrdom of Queen Ketevan of Georgia: an Episode in the Relations between the Church of Rome and the Georgian Church' in *Chronos: Revue d'Histoire de l'Université de Balamand*, 17 (2008); 'Christianity in Sudan' in A O'Mahony and E Loosley (eds) *Christian Responses to Islam: a global account of Muslim-Christian relations*, Manchester University Press, Manchester, 2008, 'Religião, comércio, política, apostasia e polémica: uma visão geral da missão persa dos agostinhos portugueses (1603-1747)' in *Oriente* (Lisbon), no. 19 (2009). Two papers recently presented to international conferences: 'The Augustinians and the Mandaeans in 17th century Mesopotamia', and 'For the Redemption of Captives—The Trinitarians and Islam: an Episode in Muslim-Christian Relations in the Medieval Mediterranean' are to be published in *ARAM: Society for Syro-Mesopotamian studies* (Oriental Institute, University of Oxford), and *Al-Masaq: Islam and the Medieval Mediterranean* (Institute of Arab and Islamic Studies, University of Exeter), respectively. A further paper, 'Dom Frei António de Gouveia OESA, missionary-ambassador, bishop in partibus infidelium, and Apostolic Visitor to Persia (1575-1628)', will be published in the forthcoming collection, Nicolas Balutet *et al.* (eds), *Contrabandista entre mundos fronterizos: Hommage au Professeur Hugues Didier*, Publibook, Paris, 2010.

Current research interests include the history of Frei Valentim da Luz, Augustinian prior of the Convento da Graça in Tavira, Portugal, condemned to death by the Inquisition in the fifteenth century, and the 'lead books' of Sacromonte, a series of messianic and millenarian forgeries, probably of morisco origin, discovered by treasure-hunters on the outskirts of Granada, and purporting to date from apostolic times.

Robin Gibbons (Father Robert-Philip Gibbons) is Fellow and Dean of Studies of Foundation House,Oxford, and Alexander Schmemann Professor of Eastern Christianity. He was professed as a Benedictine Monk at St Michael's Abbey Farnborough in England in 1973 and ordained priest in 1979. It was there that he became introduced to the Eastern Church, especially the Byzantine tradition. He is also an iconographer and one of his major works can be found in the Monastery of Christ in The Desert (Abiquiu, New Mexico). He later transferred to the Eastern Rite (Greek Catholic). Dr Gibbons studied Theology at the University of Kent, doing his Master's in Theology and his Ph.D. in Liturgy at Heythrop College, University of London, later taking a Master of Studies (M.St.) degree in Reformation history at Cambridge (Trinity Hall). He is also a member of the Academy of Teaching and Learning, a Fellow of the College of Preceptors and a Fellow of the College of Preachers. He has specialized in three related areas, liturgy, the art and architecture of the Christian Church and Eastern Christianity, and has taught (and still teaches) in these areas in several universities (London, Surrey, Cambridge and Oxford) as well as in seminaries and other academic institutions in the UK. He acted as monastic *formator* in two monastic communities in the United States. Dr Gibbons has written many articles and been a contributor to several books, in 2006 publishing a small monograph, *The Eastern Church*, and a major work on Christian space, *House of God: House of God's People*. At present he is engaged in writing a book on liturgical formation. He is currently Director of Theology and Religious Study Programmes and Departmental Lecturer in the Oxford University Department for Continuing Education. He is also Associate Director of the Oxford University Theology Summer School and Assistant Pastor for the Greek Catholic Melkite Church in London and Great Britain. Dr Gibbons has been named the Administrative Director of the Centre for the Study of Religion in Public Life, Kellogg College, Oxford University.

Professor Sidney H Griffith, Institute of Christian Oriental Research, Catholic University of America, Washington DC. He is a Roman Catholic priest who has a special research interest in Arabic and Syriac literature, especially its encounter with Islam; see *Arabic Christianity in the Monasteries*

The Catholic Church in the Contemporary Middle East

of *Ninth-Century Palestine*, Collected Studies Series 380, Variorum, 1992; *The Beginnings of Christian Theology in Arabic: Muslim-Christian encounters in the early Islamic period*, Collected Studies Series 746, Variorum, 2002; 'Faith Adoring the Mystery': Reading the Bible with St. Ephraem the Syrian*, The Père Marquette Lecture in Theology, 1997, Marquette University Press, Milwaukee, WI, 1997; *A Treatise on the Veneration of the Holy Icons Written in Arabic by Theodore Abu Qurrah, Bishop of Harran*, Eastern Christian Texts in Translation 1, Peeters, Leuven, 1997; 'Theology and the Arab Christian: the Case of the "Melkite" Creed,' in *A Faithful Presence: Essays for Kenneth Cragg*, (ed.) D Thomas with C Amos, Melisende, London, 2003, pp.184-200; *The Church in the Shadow of the Mosque: Christians and Muslims in the World of Islam. Jews, Christians, and Muslims from the ancient to the modern world*, Princeton University Press, Princeton, NJ, 2007. He also has a strong interest in modern Catholic theological encounter with Muslim thought, see in particaulr, 'Bediüzzaman Said Nursi and Louis Massignon in Pursuit of God's Word: A Muslim and a Christian on the Straight Path', *Islam & Christian-Muslim Relations*, Vol. 19 (2008), no. 1, pp. 5-16; 'Mystics and Sufi masters: Thomas Merton and dialogue between Christians and Muslims', *Islam & Christian-Muslim Relations*, Vol. 15 (2004), no. 3, pp. 299-316; 'Sharing the Faith of Abraham: The "Credo" of Louis Massignon', *Islam and Muslim-Christian Relations*. 8 (1997), pp. 193-210.

Leonard Marsh is an Anglican priest to a London parish. He has a specialist interest in contemporary theological (especially Liberation theology) and political movements within the Palestinian Christian community in Jerusalem and the Holy Land. He undertook postgraduate research and study at the School of Oriental and African Studies, University of London, and has published many articles on contemporary Palestinian Christianity and theology including 'Palestinian Christianity: A Study in Religion and Politics', *International Journal for the Study of the Christian Church*, Vol. 5, no. 2 (2005); 'Palestinian Christians and Liberation Theology', in A O'Mahony (ed.), *Christianity and Jerusalem: Studies in Modern Theology and Politics in the Holy Land*, Gracewing, Leominister, 2010.

David Neuhaus SJ is Latin Patriarchal Vicar for Hebrew-Speaking Catholics in the diocese of Jerusalem. He was born in South Africa and lived for many years in Jerusalem. He received a PhD in political science from Hebrew University and studied theology at the Jesuit faculty, Paris. He has published widely on various aspects of the religious history and contemporary situation of Christianity in the Holy Land and Christian-Jewish relations in Israel, including, with Alain Marchadour, *The Land, the Bible and History*, Fordham University Press, 2007; 'L'idéologie judéo-chrétienne et le dialogue juifs-chrétiens', *Recherches de Science Religieuse*, Vol. 85/2 (1997), pp. 249-276; 'A la rencontre de Paul. Connaître Paul aujourd'hui: un changement de paradigme?', *Recherches de Science Religieuse* (2002); 'Jewish Israeli attitudes towards Christianity and Christians in contemporary Israel', in (eds) A O'Mahony and M Kirwan, *World Christianity: Politics, Theology, Dialogues*, Melisende, London, 2004, pp. 347-369; 'New Wine into Old Wineskins: Russians, Jews and Non-Jews in the State of Israel', *Journal of Eastern Christian Studies*, Vol. 57, 3/4 2005, pp. 207-236; 'Moments of Crisis and Grace: Jewish-Catholic relations in 2009', *One in Christ: a Catholic Ecumenical Review*, Vol. 43, no. 2 (2009), and in reviews such as *Al-Liqa, Pastoral Psychology, Proche-Orient Chrétien, Mishkan*.

Anthony O'Mahony is Reader in Church History and Theology, Director, Centre for Eastern Christianity, Heythrop College, University of London. He was a founding member of Heythrop College Centre for Christianity and Interreligious Dialogue, and Director until 2009. He has published a number of studies on the modern history and theology of Eastern Christianity and Catholic relations with Islam, including: (ed.) *Palestinian Christians: Religion, Politics and Society in the Holy Land*, Melisende, London, 1999; (ed.) *The Christian Communities of Jerusalem and the Holy Land: Studies in History, Religion and Politics*, University of Wales Press, Cardiff, 2003; (ed.) *Eastern Christianity: Studies in Modern History, Religion and Politics*, Melisende, London, 2004; (ed.) *Christianity in the Middle East. Studies in Modern History, Theology and Politics*, Melisende, London, 2008; (co-ed. with Emma Loosley) *Christian responses to Islam: Muslim-Christian relations in the modern World*, Manchester University Press, Manchester, 2008; (co-ed. with Emma Loosley), *Eastern Christianity in the modern Middle East*, Routledge, London, 2010; (ed.) *Christianity and Jerusalem: Studies in Modern Theology and Politics in the Holy Land*, Gracewing, Leominister, 2010; 'Pilgrims, Politics and Holy Places: the Ethiopian Community in Jerusalem until ca. 1650', in Lee I Levine (ed.) *Jerusalem: Its Sanctity and Centrality to Judaism, Christianity and Islam*, Continuum, New York, 1999, pp. 467-481; 'Christianity in Modern Iraq', *International Journal for the Study of the Christian Church (IJSCC)* Vol. 4/2, 2004, pp. 121-142; 'The Chaldaean Catholic Church: the politics of church-state relations in modern Iraq', *Heythrop Journal* 45, 2004, pp. 435-450; 'Coptic Christianity in modern Egypt' and 'Syriac Christians in the Modern Middle East', in *The Cambridge History of Christianity. Volume 5: Eastern*

Christianity, Cambridge University Press, Cambridge, 2006, pp. 488-510 and 511-536; 'The Vatican, Jerusalem, the State of Israel and Christianity in the Holy Land', *IJSCC*, Vol. 5/2, 2005, pp. 123-146 ; 'Tradition at the Heart of Renewal: the Coptic Orthodox Church and Monasticism in modern Egypt', *IJSCC*, Vol. 7/3, 2007, pp. 164-178; '"Between Rome and Constantinople": the Italian-Albanian Church: a study in Eastern Catholic history and ecclesiology', *IJSCC*, Vol. 8/3, 2008, pp. 232-251 ; 'The Influence of the Life and Thought of Louis Massignon on the Catholic Church's Relations with Islam', *The Downside Review,* Vol. 126, no. 444, 2008, pp. 169-192 ; 'Louis Massignon, the Melkite Church and Islam', *Aram: Society for Syro-Mesopotamian Studies,* Vol. 20, (2008), pp. 269-297; 'Catholic Theological Perspectives on Islam at the Second Vatican Council', *New Blackfriars,* Vol. 88, No.1016, 2007, pp. 385-398. Forthcoming: 'Between Rome and Antioch: the Syrian Catholic Church', Nicolas Balutet *et al.* (eds), *Contrabandista entre mundos fronterizos: Hommage au Professeur Hugues Didier,* Publibook, Paris, 2010

Suha Rassam was born into a medical family in Mosul, Iraq, in 1941. She studied medicine at the University of Baghdad, where she obtained a postgraduate degree in internal medicine in 1969, and then practised as a physician in the city. She was assistant professor of medicine at the University of Baghdad when she came to England in 1990 to undertake further research. She has since worked in London hospitals, and studied Eastern Christianity at London University. The year 2005 saw the publication of her *Christianity in Iraq,* Gracewing, Leominster, outlining the history of Christianity in Iraq from its beginnings until the present. Following this, she has lectured in a number of venues in order to bring the plight of Iraqi Christians to the attention of the British public. A new and updated edition of *Christianity in Iraq* was published in 2010, devoting a supplementary chapter to the situation of Iraqi Christians between 2005 and 2010.

Archbishop Louis Sako: Born in Zakho in the north of Iraq in 1949, he has lived mostly in Mosul. He was educated at the St John Seminary run by the Dominican fathers. Ordained priest 1 June 1974, he obtained a MA in Islamic Studies from the Pontifical Institute for Arabic and Islamic studies (PISAI) in Rome, 1984; a PhD in Christian Oriental Studies, with a thesis entitled, *Lettre Christologique du Patriarche syro-oriental Iso'yahb II de Gdala (628-646),* from the Pontifical Oriental Institute, Rome in 1983; and a PhD in history on *Le rôle de la hierarchie syrique orientale dans les rapports diplomatiques entre la Perse et*

Byzance aux Ve-VII siècles, from the Sorbonne in Paris, 1986. He served as a priest of the Mosul diocese from 1986 until 1997, and was then appointed Rector of the Major Seminary in Baghdad, until 2001. He also lectured at Babel College (Faculty of Theology) in Baghdad. Archbishop Sako is a well-known scholar in Christian Oriental and Arabic studies, and has published a number of significant and important books and articles. Ordained Bishop on 14 November 2003 he was subsequently appointed Archbishop of Kirkuk, Iraq, a senior Episcopal See in the Chaldean Catholic Church. He is a member of the foundation PRO ORIENTE, Vienna, for dialogue with the Syriac Churches, and a senior consultor to the Pontifical Council for Interreligious Dialogue at the Vatican.

Fadel Sidarouss SJ is a Coptic Catholic and Jesuit from Egypt in the Near East Province. He wrote his doctorate on Coptic Christianity and ecclesial renewal in the Coptic Orthodox Church at Université Saint-Joseph (Beirut), which was published as 'L'Eglise copte et monde moderne', *Proche-Orient Chrétien*, Vol. 30, 1980. He currently teaches theology at the Catholic theological school in Cairo. Publications include a translation of Ignatius' Autobiography and Spiritual Exercises into Arabic; 'Eglise Copte et Monde Moderne', Thèse de Théologie Pastorale, présentée à la Faculté de Sciences Religieuses de l'Université Saint Joseph, Beirut, 1978. Cf. résumé in *Proche-Orient Chrétien*, Vol 30, 1980, pp. 211-265; 'Les nouveaux courants dans la communauté copte orthodoxe' (in collaboration with P M Martin and C Van Nispen), *Proche-Orient Chrétien*, Vol 40, 1990, pp. 245-257; 'L'Egypte Chrétienne—Traditions, Défis et Espérances', *Eglises au Moyen-Orient: défis et espérance*, Cahiers de l'Orient chrétien N° 3, CEDRAC, Beirut, 2005, pp. 15-31; 'Pour une Théologie Contextuelle dans l'Orient Arabe Contemporain', in *Quo Vadis, Theologia Orientalis?*, Actes du Colloque 'Théologie Orientale: contenu et importance' (TOTT), Ain Traz, April 2005, Textes et Etudes sur l'Orient Chrétien N° 6, CEDRAC, Université Saint Joseph, Beirut, 2008, pp. 215-237.

Constantin Simon SJ: Professor of Church History and Vice Rector, Pontifical Oriental Institute, Rome. A member of the southern Belgian Province of the Society of Jesus, he recently published his monumental *Pro Russia. The Russicum and Catholic Work for Russia*, Orientalia Christiana Analecta 283, 2010. His research has concentrated on modern Eastern Christian Church history and especially encounters and contact with the Catholic Church, see in particular, 'Benedict XV's Church Politics towards the East and its

Repercussions on the Foundation of the Pontifical Oriental Institute', in *Da Benedetto XV a Benedetto XVI. Atti del simposio nel novantennio della Congregazione per le Chiese Orientali e del Pontificio Istituto Orientale*, Orientalia Christiana Analecta 284, Rome, 2007 (2010); 'A Romanian proposal for Church Unity—Rome, 1937', *Orientalia Christiana Periodica*, Vol. 70, no. 2 (2004), pp. 359-430; 'Alexis Toth and the beginnings of the Orthodox movement among the Ruthenians in America', *Orientalia Christiana Periodica*, Vol. 54, no. 2 (1988), pp. 387-428; 'Europe and America: the Ruthenians between Catholicism and Orthodoxy', *Orientalia Christiana Periodica*, Vol. 59, no. 1 (1993), pp. 169-210; 'The First Fifty Years of Ruthenian Church Life in America', in *Orientalia Christiana Periodica*, Vol. 60, 1994, pp. 187-232; 'L'Église orthodoxe russe à la fin XIXe et au début du XXe siècles: isolement et intégration', *Histoire du christianisme des origines à nos jours*, Vol. XI, 1995. He is a regular contributor to *La Civiltà Cattolica* (Rome), *Diakonia* and *Plamia* (Paris).

Dominique Trimbur: Senior Researcher at the Centre de recherche français de Jérusalem, and chargé de mission 'la Fondation pour la Mémoire de la Shoah', Paris. His doctorate examined the diplomatic reconciliation between the West German state and the State of Israel after 1948, and was published as *De la Shoah à la réconciliation?—La question des relations RFA/Israël (1949-1956)*, Centre de recherche français de Jérusalem, Collection 'Hommes et Sociétés', vol. 7, Paris, CNRS Éditions. He has a special expertise in the history of Catholic approaches to Judaism, Zionism and the State of Israel, see his contributions, *Une École française à Jérusalem—De l'École pratique d'Études bibliques des Dominicains à l'École Biblique et Archéologique Française de Jérusalem*, in *Mémoire dominicaine*, V, Éd. du Cerf, Paris, 2002; 'La Shoah dans la mémoire religieuse juive' in Bruno Béthouart, François Ars, *Christianisme et lieux de mémoire* (XVème université d'été du carrefour d'histoire religieuse contemporaine), Les Cahiers du Littoral–2–n° 6, 2008, pp. 195-205; 'Les missions des Assomptionnistes en Terre Sainte', in Bernard Holzer, AA (dir.), *L'aventure missionnaire assomptionniste*, Rome, (coll. Recherches Assomption, n° 1), 2006, pp. 205-240; 'Les Assomptionistes de Jérusalem, les Juifs et le sionisme', in *Tsafon-Revue d'études juives du Nord*, n° 38, hiver 1999-printemps 2000, pp. 71-111; 'Des catholiques français et les débuts du sionisme', in Sobhi Boustani, Françoise Saquer-Sabin (eds), *Nationalisme juif et environnement arabe*, Université de Lille 3 (Collection UL3: travaux et recherches), 2005, pp. 109-133; 'L'Église catholique et le sionisme au temps de Theodor Herzl, 1897-1904', in *Mélanges de Science Religieuse*, Université catholique de Lille, tome 61, n° 4, octobre-décembre 2004, pp. 19-34; 'Entre rejet et respect—Les communautés catholiques françaises de Palestine, les Juifs et le sionisme, 1880-1939', (eds) Ilana Y Zinguer and Sam W Bloom, *L'antisémitisme éclairé—Inclusion et exclusion depuis l'Époque des Lumières jusqu'à l'affaire Dreyfus/Inclusion and Exclusion: Perspectives of Jews from the Enlightenment to the Dreyfus Affair*, Brill (Brill's Series in Jewish Studies, 34), Leiden, 2003, pp. 369-396; (eds) D Trimbur and Ran Aaronsohn, *De Bonaparte à Balfour—Les puissances européennes et la Palestine, 1799-1917*, CNRS-Éditions, Paris, 2008 (collection 'Mélanges' du CRFJ, vol. 3—1ère édition: 2001); (eds) D Trimbur and Ran Aaronsohn, *De Balfour à Ben Gourion—Les puissances européennes et la Palestine, 1917-1948*, CNRS-Éditions, Paris, 2008 (collection 'Mélanges' du Centre de recherche français de Jérusalem, Vol. 5).

John Whooley is a Catholic priest of the Diocese of Westminster. Publications include 'The Armenian Catholic Church: A Study in History and Ecclesiology', *The Heythrop Journal*, Vol. XLV (2004), pp. 416-434; 'The Armenian Catholic Church: a modern history until the Synod of Rome 1928', in A O'Mahony (ed.), *Christianity in the Middle East: Studies in Modern History, Theology and Politics*, Melisende, London, 2008, pp. 263-327; 'Armenian Christianity: An historical and Theological Overview', *One in Christ: a catholic ecumenical review*, Vol. 45. no. 4, 2004; 'The Mekhitarists: Religion, Culture and Ecumenism in Armenian Catholic Relations', in A O'Mahony (ed.), *Eastern Christianity: Studies in Modern History, Religion and Politics*, Melisende, London, 2004, pp. 452-489; 'The Armenian Church in the Contemporary Middle East', A O'Mahony and E Loosley (eds), *Eastern Christianity in the Modern Middle East*, London, Routledge, 2010.

Dietmar Winkler: Professor of Patristic Studies and Ecclesiastical History at the Catholic Theological Faculty of the University of Salzburg, Director of the Mayr-Melnhof Institute of Eastern Christian Studies, Salzburg; Member of the board of directors of the PRO ORIENTE Foundation (Vienna) and scientific director of 'Pro Oriente Studies in the Syriac Tradition'; Consultant to the Pontifical Council for Promoting Christian Unity. Publications include: *Ostsyrisches Christentum. Untersuchungen zu Christologie, Ekklesiologie, und zu den ökumenischen Beziehungen der Assyrischen Kirche des Ostens*, Studien zur Orientalischen Kirchengeschichte 26, LIT Verlag, Münster, 2003; 'The Current Theological Dialogue with the Assyrian Church of the East', *Symposium Syriacum VII,* Orientalia Christiana Analecta 256, Rome, 1998, pp. 158-173; Wilhem Baum and D Winkler, *The Church of the East: a concise history*, London,

RoutledgeCurzon, 2003; 'East Syriac Christianity in Iraq', in (eds) Dietmar Winkler and Li Tang, *Hidden Treasures and intercultural Encounters: Studies on East Syriac Christianity in China and Central Asia*, LIT Verlag, Vienna and Berlin, 2009, pp. 321-36; 'Between Progress and Setback: The Ecumenical Dialogues of the Assyrian Church of the East', *Syriac Dialogue* 4, PRO ORIENTE, Vienna, 2001, pp. 138-151.

Petrus (Pierre) Yousif is a priest of the Chaldean Catholic Church, Paris, and lecturer in Liturgical Theology at the Pontifical Oriental Institute, Rome. He was born in 1936, in Karmleis, Northern Iraq. He studied theology and philosophy at the Urbaniana, Rome; Diplome Supérieur d'Etudes bibliques, at the Catholic Institute Paris (1978); Doctorate in patristic theology, University of Strasbourg, 1979, published as, *L'Eucharistie chez saint Ephrem de Nisibe*, Orientalia Christiana Analecta, no. 224, Rome. Since 1981 he has taught at the Pontifical Oriental Institute, and between 1991-2000, lectured in Eastern Christian Liturgy at the Catholic Institute, Paris. He has directed some 29 doctoral theses at the Oriental Institute, and has published many articles on theology and liturgical studies, including, 'Marie, mère du Christ dans la liturgie chaléenne', in *Études mariales*, Vol. 39, 1982; 'La célébration du marriage dans le rite chaldéen', in: *Studia Anselmiana*, Vol. 93, 1986; 'The Divine Liturgy according to the Rite of the Assyro-Chaldean Church', in J Madey (ed.), *The Eucharistic Liturgy in the Christian East*, Paderbron, 1984; 'An Introduction to the East Syrian Ecclesial Spirituality', in A Thottakkara (ed.), *East-Syrian Spirituality*, Rome-Bangalore, 1990; and a memorial on Chaldean Catholic scholarship in 'Remembering Fr Joseph Habbi (1938-2000): A Bio-bibliographical Report', *Orientalia Christiana Periodica* 69, 2003, pp.7-28.

PREFACE

The Synod of Bishops Special Assembly for the Middle East called by Pope Benedict XVI in Rome in 2009 is a significant event for the Catholic Church in the Middle East. The Synod is also, however, an important event for the wider Christian Church (both in the region and in the West) and for the Christian tradition as a whole. The Conference, 'The Synod for the Middle East: Catholic Theological and Ecclesial Perspectives', 9-11 June 2010, held at the Centre for Eastern Christianity, Heythrop College, University of London, was organized with the intention of making a fraternal engagement with the preparations for the Synod, seeking to honour the importance of the event. We have sought to gather as wide as possible a cross section of contributors from a broad spectrum and with different backgrounds. The Conference was not seeking to be comprehensive, as this would not have been possible in the time available, but sought to cover the principal themes. We are aware, however, that many important subjects and ecclesial communities have not been represented, which we regret. Nor, sadly, were all those who had been invited able to be attend. What the Conference attempted to do was to engage with various aspects of the Synod agenda and to give a supporting witness.

We would very much like to thank all who supported and assisted in the preparation of the Conference, especially CAFOD (London) and the staff of Heythrop College.

Anthony O'Mahony and John Flannery
Heythrop College
August 2010, London

1

Note

This volume contains contributions from authors from a number of different academic disciplines and traditions. Whilst there is a general uniformity in the style of presentation of the material, it has seemed wise to the editors to allow individuals some leeway where their background has influenced any transliteration system used, and in the spelling of proper names in particular. Although most inconsistencies have been addressed, a number of idiosyncracies doubtless remain.

FOREWORD

Archbishop Louis Sako

CHRISTIANS IN THE MIDDLE EAST SHOULD REMAIN IN THEIR LAND TO
CONTINUE THEIR PRESENCE AND UPHOLD THEIR HERITAGE AND WITNESS

The Middle East is the cradle of Christianity; Christianity was born in Palestine
and rapidly spread to Syria, Lebanon, Iraq, and Egypt. The Churches of the
Middle East are repositories of ancient Christian traditions: Syrian, Copt,
Greek, Armenian, Latin and Arabic. Their liturgy, spirituality, monasticism
and ecclesiastical discipline and canons have great importance for the whole
Church. Their way of understanding the message of the Gospel, of living it
and explaining it in a multicultural context is truly authentic. Even today their
Muslim neighbours show appreciation for their skills and the openness which
characterises them, with an expectation that they will witness to their Christian
values. The migration of Christians from the Middle East is thus a great loss
for both communities. In time Christians in the diaspora will lose their Eastern
identity through integration into Western society and culture, and this is a
significant challenge for all the Eastern Christian Churches. In the Middle East,
Muslims, and Islamic society and culture, will lose the presence of Christians,
with their commitment to open-mindedness and their engaged skills.

Before the coming of Islam, Christians formed a major part of the
population. During the first centuries of Islam, especially under the 'Abbasid
caliphate, many Christians worked in the royal palace as scholars, doctors,
scribes, translators, philosophers and astronomers. Their contributions
were highly focused and helped give Arabic language and culture a rich and
textured voice in the world. In modern times also Christians in the Middle
East were pioneers in education, medicine, culture and political thought, in
the formation and development of their respective countries in the Middle
East. It is a tragedy that Christians should be leaving their homelands to go
into the lands of exile and emigration.

In the early twentieth century the Christians of these countries were 20 percent of the population, but today they account for less than 10 percent. In Iraq, their number was estimated at between 800,000 and 1,000,000 people, but because of frequent wars and the deterioration of the security situation following the US-led invasion in 2003, the number has decreased significantly, leaving only 400,000 to 500,000. This is a matter for concern, and led to the requesting of a Synod for the Churches in the Middle East, to be held from 10-24 October 2010.

Because of the importance of this opportunity for these Churches, and focusing on the importance of supporting their millennial presence, a conference on 'The Synod for the Middle East: Catholic Theological and Ecclesial Perspectives' was organised by the Centre for Eastern Christianity, Heythrop College, University of London, on 9-11 June, 2010. Here Church representatives and eminent scholars and experts including Sebastian Brock, Herman Teule, Sidney Griffith, and Dietmar Winkler, to name but a few, discussed at length the issue of the situation of Christians in the Middle East, and their historical, liturgical, and spiritual presence there, now threatened by so many challenges.

I would like to thank Anthony O'Mahony, Reader in Church History and Theology, Director of the Centre for Eastern Christianity, Heythrop College, University of London, for establishing this initiative and for his concern to support the Christians of the Middle East in a practical way.

The Churches of the Middle East should take advantage of this veritable impulse of the Spirit which the Synod represents to rediscover their identity of unity-communion and mission-witness. They must speak with deep courage and profound objectivity. We need to focus on a number of important tasks:

1. Liturgical and pastoral practice should be effectively reformed, responding to the needs of our faithful today, while at the same time reminding faithful to our Tradition. The Churches should find new ways of pastoral engagement to give hope to their communities and develop a sound and appropriate theological language which can help non-Christians to understand the evangelical message. A Church without mission is an impoverished Church!

2. Reform of the structure of the Eastern Churches: dioceses, institutes, and religious congregations, in order to respond to the reality of today and not to the contexts of the past.

3. Unity with Sister Churches. It is important to restore unity between Orthodox and Catholics, particularly since they are united dogmatically. We are small Churches, and without unity there will be no future for us! We need a real and effective ecumenism with courageous and robust initiatives. Time is wasted through formality and the making of fine speeches. To remain as separate and vulnerable Churches weakens communion and witness. Muslims do not always understand the denominations and divisions of Christians. Communion and Witness are the themes of our Synod, let them also become a living reality of our ecclesial life in the Middle East.

4. The migration of Christians. A haemorrhaging of humanity is threatening Christian presence in the area. This is a disaster, since with them will depart their history, heritage, liturgies, spirituality and witness. Consequently, it is a matter of utmost urgency for both the Church in the West and for Muslims to keep these Christians in their homelands, to help them to live in dignity and harmony, and to enable the continuation and development of these great Christians traditions and cultures which have such long and rich histories, so that they may be a true spiritual force, a positive factor in real progress towards a joint future. Dialogue with Muslim leaders and governments is therefore the only way to restore security and stability. The openness of Christians, their individual qualities and personal skills and expertise are essential in this urgent process.

We hope that the Eastern Churches may profit from this special Synod by experiencing 'a new Pentecost' restoring unity and giving renewed vigour and strength to their mission of bearing the Gospel of Jesus Christ in their region.

INTRODUCTION
Christianity in the Middle East

Anthony O'Mahony

The ecclesial context for Middle Eastern Christianity is one of great complexity. Its origins are those of Christianity itself. The Churches of the Middle East can be grouped into five families—Oriental Orthodox; Eastern Orthodox; Oriental and Eastern Catholic; Anglican and Protestant; 'Assyrian' Church of the East. Even if it cannot be summed up in figures, the reality of Christianity in the modern Middle East is first of all one of numbers. The number of Christians, unfortunately, is very difficult to discern. For some decades, there have no longer been confessional censuses in the countries of the Middle East, where governments are concerned with veiling the multi-confessional nature of their societies. However, the Middle Eastern Church families represent about 30-35 million Christians, of whom approximately 15 million reside in the Middle East. The Middle Eastern Christian diaspora in North and South America, Australia and Europe is an important and dynamic reality for all the Churches. This diaspora reality contributes to making Christian identity in the Middle East often a contested one; caught between an 'Arab' Christian identity and an 'Eastern' Christian identity. The jurisdiction of each Church normally corresponds to a definite territory, but emigration of numerous faithful has also given it a personal character. The Churches have responded by creating numerous ecclesial structures in the West to help retain the link between the land of origin and these new Middle Eastern Christian spaces. This renewed ecclesiological link overcomes geography in this case, and the Eastern Churches, with regard to their respective diasporas, behave as though they were independent structures, constituting distinct episcopacies on the same territory.[1]

To break down the five families of Churches in the Middle East, there are:

1. The Oriental Orthodox family comprising:

---

1   Frans Bouwen, 'The Churches in the Middle East', (ed.) Lawrence S Cunningham, *Ecumenism. Present Realities and Future Prospects,* University of Notre Dame Press, Notre Dame, 1998, pp. 25-36.

- The Armenian Orthodox Church
- The Syrian Orthodox Church
- The Coptic Orthodox Church
2. The Eastern Orthodox family comprising:
- The Greek Orthodox Patriarchate of Jerusalem
- The Greek Orthodox Patriarchate of Antioch
- The Greek Orthodox Patriarchate of Alexandria
- The Greek Orthodox Patriarchate of Constantinople
3. The Catholic family: six Oriental, one Latin, one Hebrew, comprising:
- The Latin Patriarchate of Jerusalem (restored in 1847), which includes a small Hebrew Catholic expression mainly located in the modern State of Israel.
- The Greek Catholic Church
- The Maronite Church
- The Syrian Catholic Church
- The Armenian Catholic Church
- The Chaldean Church
- The Coptic Catholic Church
4. The Evangelical and Anglican-Episcopal family comprising:
- The Anglican and Episcopal Church (in Jerusalem and the Middle East)

There are various Protestant, Presbyterian and Lutheran Churches throughout the Middle East, which have emerged from Eastern Christian communities or from converts from Islam to Christianity.

5. The fifth family is, in terms of independent history, one of the oldest and most self-contained of the Middle Eastern Churches: the Assyrian Church of the East. Sometimes identified by its historical tradition as the Church of the 'East Syrians' or the Church of Persia. Its Catholic counterpart is the Chaldean Catholic Church, mainly found in Iran, Iraq, Syria and Lebanon.

THE ORIENTAL ORTHODOX CHURCHES

The largest groupings of Christians in the Middle East are those belonging to the Oriental Orthodox Churches. The doctrinal position of these Churches is based on the teachings of the first three ecumenical councils: Nicea (325), Constantinople (381) and Ephesus (431). They have traditionally rejected the Council of Chalcedon (451). The Armenian Apostolic Church governs a community of some five million people, scattered, like all the Armenians, across the globe. The Armenian Church is represented today by two Catholicosates: Etchmiadzin, which has primacy in the Caucasian and diaspora region, and Sis which has authority over most of the Orthodox Armenians of the Middle East; and two Patriarchates: Jerusalem and Constantinople. The Coptic Orthodox Church, whose current Patriarch Shenouda III lives in Cairo, traditionally had a close relationship with the Ethiopian Church, which is the largest of the Oriental Orthodox family with 30 million members. The Syrian Orthodox Church, numbering up to 400,000 at home and in the diaspora, whose Patriarch Ignatius Zakka I Iwas is based in Damascus, is today connected to the many millions of Syriac Christians in India through the Malankara Orthodox Syrian Church. From the point of view of numbers of Christians of the Middle East—Coptic Christians, numbering up to ten million, are dominant, with almost 60-70 per cent.

Too often Christianity in the Middle East is obscured from view, especially in the West. The Oriental Orthodox Churches have been depicted in Western and Byzantine Church history as isolated from the rest of the Christian world and concerned with mere survival. This was, to a certain extent, true. A significant feature of Oriental Orthodoxy has been persecution and genocide suffered under Byzantine, Muslim and Ottoman powers. On the whole, relations between the Oriental Orthodox Churches and the Latin Crusader states were good, which encouraged at times important ecclesial and theological dialogue. The Oriental Orthodox Christian tradition has been marked by this suffering—leaving a permanent 'wound' on its life, witness, theology and spirituality.

Another reason was the Christological controversies of the fifth and sixth centuries, producing a three-way split among the Christian Churches which still continues to this day, although it is only among the Churches of Syriac liturgical tradition that all three doctrinal positions are represented. These controversies were originally over how best to describe the relationship between the divinity and the humanity in the incarnate Christ—for the Orthodox and Catholic (and derived Reformed) traditions, the Council of Chalcedon had settled the matter in 451. The Arab invasions and the rise of Islam in the seventh century effectively fossilized this division. Since the 1960s, these Churches began a process of rapprochement with both the Catholic and Orthodox Churches which has significantly altered this situation. This has led in turn to an extremely important ecumenical theological dialogue on Christology and ecclesiology. Caused perhaps by misunderstandings created by differences of language, the Christological quarrels have today been overcome, and nearly all the pre-Chalcedonian Churches recognise themselves to be in communion of faith, at least in this area, with Rome and Constantinople. Pope John Paul II and representatives of the Syrian, Coptic and Armenian Orthodox Churches have signed 'Common Declarations of Faith' on the nature of the Incarnate Word. In fact, one of the most significant events in the history of the present-day ecumenical movement, and one of the richest promises for the future is, beyond any doubt, the Christological consensus that has emerged in the course of the last decades, between the Churches that recognized the Council of Chalcedon and those that did not. However, in terms of faith, it is not quite true to say that nothing separates or distinguishes them, for, beyond the Christological splits of the early centuries, division led to further areas of doctrinal divergence, each Church having followed its route apart from the others and not having subscribed to the new 'dogmas' proclaimed by Councils following the break of unity.

THE EASTERN ORTHODOX CHURCHES

The Eastern or 'Byzantine' Orthodox Church in the Middle East is composed of the four ancient patriarchates of Constantinople, Alexandria, Antioch and Jerusalem. These are autocephalous Churches, each independent and self-governing. The independence between the four Churches is administrative; some pre-eminence is given to the ecumenical patriarch of Constantinople but it 'is one of honour and not authority,' however, each patriarchate has its own metropolitans, bishops and synod. The four patriarchates have a shared identity based upon doctrine, patristic theology, liturgy, ecclesiology and canon law. The Churches of the Orthodox communion define themselves in dogmas formulated by the first seven ecumenical Councils, and their theology remains that of the Fathers of the Church, particularly the Greeks: that is, essentially, as it was fixed during the first few centuries and has scarcely evolved since.

The following common challenges have been posed by history for Eastern Orthodoxy in the Middle East: relations to Islam, relations to Russian Orthodoxy and the Russian State, relations to Rome and Eastern Catholicism, relations to Protestantism—European then American, friction and conflict among the four sees, and the problem of relations between the Greek Hierarchy and the Arab Orthodox. Eastern Christianity in the Middle East had often to face these challenges within the context of Islamic conquest, conversion and settlement, the long centuries of Ottoman rule in which the only difference that really mattered in religious terms was the Muslim one, and an emerging modern synthesis between Orthodoxy and nationality, which was in turn a Christian 'revivalist' response to political domination in the late Ottoman period.

From the point of view of structures, Orthodoxy is divided between the four Patriarchates, one of which, Antioch, which has authority over the Orthodox communities in Syria and Lebanon (Arabic-speaking) as well as their diasporas, represents on its own nine-tenths of the faithful (900,000) in the Middle East. As such, this is the real face of the Arab Orthodox community. Its leader, today Patriarch Ignatius IV Hazim, who resides in Damascus, can be considered to be the leader of the Orthodox in the Arab Middle East. In the diaspora, Eastern Orthodox Christians who originate from the Middle East number at least 500,000, two-thirds of whom are in South America (Brazil and Argentina) and the rest in North America. These expatriate communities come almost exclusively under the Patriarchate of Antioch

The Patriarchate of Jerusalem leads a community of about 70,000 faithful divided between Israel, Palestine and Jordan, Arabic speaking, but the senior clergy, including the Patriarch are Greek; its *raison d'être* is above all the exercise of Orthodox rights in the Holy Places. However, this is supplemented by large numbers of Orthodox Christians now living in the State of Israel, either as migrant workers, for example, until recent times 70,000 Romanians, or the many tens of thousands of Orthodox who arrived among the large wave of Russian 'Jewish' migration in the last two decades of the twentieth century.

The small Greek Orthodox Patriarchate of Alexandria, some 300,000 faithful mainly in Africa and only 3,000 in Egypt, is led by a Patriarch who lives in Alexandria or Cairo. Confined for a long time to the Greek-speaking community in Egypt, which has significantly declined over the twentieth century, it has renewed its vocation by developing missions in Africa, where there are not the same prohibitions with regard to proselytism as in the Muslim world. Thus this Patriarchate is no longer greatly 'Middle Eastern'.

The same is true of the Ecumenical Patriarchate of Constantinople. The current incumbent, Patriarch Bartholomew, lives in Istanbul, which has primacy of honour among the Orthodox, but whose real jurisdiction, reduced to the smallest part by all the autocephalous Patriarchates which have appeared in the Balkans since the nineteenth century, is today over communities in northern Greece, the islands of the Aegean, Turkey, and (extremely importantly in contemporary terms) for Orthodox Churches emerging in

Western and newly independent states of Eastern Europe. However, the significance of the Ecumenical patriarchate for the global Orthodox Church cannot be underestimated.

THE EASTERN CATHOLIC CHURCHES

The Eastern Catholic families of Churches, as with their Orthodox counterparts, represent an extremely complex ecclesiology, which, however broadly, reflects that of their sister-Churches of the same rite, each denomination of which it mirrors. There are six patriarchal Churches: Latin, Melkite, Syrian, Armenian, Coptic and Chaldean. The emergence of Hebrew Catholicism in the modern state of Israel might be seen as the most recent expression of Eastern Christianity in the Middle East. Eastern Catholics in number are far from negligible: approximately three million across the Middle East, or a fifth of Middle East Christians. However, this excludes the many millions of Roman Catholics who live and work in the Arabian Gulf states, or who are refugees or foreign workers in the wider Middle East.

The Maronite Church, which has its origins in the fourth or fifth century, has no Orthodox equivalent. The Maronite Church has approximately one million members in Lebanon but up to three million faithful scattered throughout the world. It emerged gradually over many centuries in the province of the Patriarchate of Antioch, from a small rural Syrian community quite distinct from the rest of the Chalcedonian Church, which was then in real decline. Maronite identity is complex: accepting the Council of Chalcedon, Syriac in rite, and Catholic in its faith and discipline, and in union with the See of Rome. The future of the Maronite Church, although it does not bring together all the Christians of the Lebanon, has been largely confused with that of Lebanese Christianity, even that of Lebanon itself, whose spirit of survival through difficult times it incarnates. Its leader, Patriarch Nasrallah Pierre Sfeir, lives in Bkerke, north of Beirut.

The other Oriental Catholic Churches are all branches from the Orthodox and pre-Chalcedonian Churches. The oldest is the Chaldean Catholic Church, formed in 1553. Because of the dispersed population after the First World War, and then following the massacre of 1933 in Iraq, today it is more numerous than its equivalent—the 'Assyrian' Church of the East. It has about 700,000 members, principally living in Iraq, with minorities in Iran, Lebanon, Syria and Turkey. Its leader, the 'Patriarch of Babylon of the Chaldeans', Emmanuel

III Delly lives in Baghdad. Like other Syriac Christians of the region, the Chaldean Church is linked to India through the Catholic Malabar Church of India, which has over four million members.

Three small Oriental Catholic Churches have come from the Oriental Orthodox tradition. The Syrian Catholic Church, with only 150,000 faithful, was formed following a schism in the Syrian Orthodox Church in 1663 but was not definitively established until the end of the eighteenth century. Mostly represented in Syria and the Lebanon, it is led by a 'Patriarch of Antioch and the East of the Syrians'. The current leader of the Syrian Catholic Church is Patriarch Ignace Joseph III Younan, based in Beirut. A Coptic Catholic Church, tiny in comparison to the Orthodox Patriarchate (250,000 compared to up to ten million) also exists in Egypt, but only since the end of the nineteenth century. Its leader is the 'Patriarch of Alexandria of the Copts', Antonios Naguib, living in Cairo. The Armenians also, since the 18th century, have had a Catholic branch, called the 'Patriarchate of Cilicia of the Armenians' which brings together 550,000 faithful living both in the Middle East and the rest of the world. Their patriarch is Nerses Bedros XIX Tarmouni, who lives in Beirut.

Of a totally different importance, both because of its numbers and its role in local religious and political life, the Greek Catholic 'Melkite' Church was born in the eighteenth century following a schism in the Antioch Patriarchate of the Greek Orthodox Church. With nearly a million and half members it is as large as its Orthodox equivalent, but fewer than half are still living in the Middle East (mainly in Syria and Lebanon). This Church, Byzantine in rite and Arabic-speaking, only has one Patriarchate, of 'Antioch, and all the East, Jerusalem and Alexandria', Gregory III Laham, who resides in Damascus.

THE ASSYRIAN CHURCH OF THE EAST

The Assyrian Church of the East is one of the oldest Christian Churches in existence, founded on the eastern marches of the Byzantine Empire and in Persia following the condemnation of 'Nestorianism' by the Council of Ephesus. Church membership is under 400,000. It might be considered the national Church of Iraq and Iran, which, along with an important diaspora, are its most important settlements in the Middle East. In 1964 it was split into two branches, one of which, the 'Catholicosate of the East of the Assyrian Church of the East' is led by Mar Dinkha IV, who lives in Detroit and the other, the 'Catholicosate of the East of the Old Catholic and Apostolic Church' has Mar Addai II, who lives in Baghdad, as its leader of under 50,000 members. The Church of the East, after many centuries of isolation from the rest of the Christian world, has emerged renewed in the latter part of the twentieth century, with ecumenical dialogue as an essential element of that revival. Mar Dinkha IV met Pope John Paul II in 1984 and signed a 'Common Declaration of Faith' in 1994. An unprecedented Eucharistic sharing agreement signed in 2001 in the Vatican between the Church of the East and the Chaldean Catholic Church crowned these achievements. Benedict XVI and Mar Dinkha IV held an historic meeting in Rome in June 2007 to discuss the future of their relations and the current situation of Christianity in Iraq after the fall of the Baathist regime in 2003.

CURRENT SITUATION AND FUTURE OF CHRISTIANITY IN THE MIDDLE EAST

It is all too easy to be the bearer of bad news about Christianity in the Middle East. The last hundred years of their history has witnessed a profound series of crises. These have overtaken Middle Eastern Christianity in modern times. Displacement by war, genocide and interreligious conflict, leading to loss, emigration and exile, would seem to be the main experience of Christianity in the modern Middle East. Against this background of displacement, when allowed, Christians have sought to resettle and build anew. They have been able to make a significant cultural, political and economic contribution to Middle Eastern society. Some observers have suggested that there is a 'Christian barometer' which provides the world with an accurate measurement of the political atmosphere in the Middle East. Progress toward freedom, particularly religious freedom, in the Middle East can be gauged by focusing on the status of the large Christian minorities. Most are highly educated and multilingual and have studied and worked in Europe and North America, where they also have a large diaspora. The theory goes that as the Middle East becomes more free and prosperous, linked to the West and hospitable to minorities and women, the higher the probability that the Christians will continue to live and even return from abroad to countries like Lebanon, Egypt and Syria. And vice versa, if Christians sense that things are getting worse, and if the Middle Eastern countries they live in are losing their commitment to political, economic and religious freedom, they would tend to emigrate from the Middle East.

After the fall of the Baathist regime in 2003, the Christians in Iraq became 'the canaries in the coal mine' for the greater Middle East. The extent to which they are tolerated in the new Iraq is being watched closely by the Maronites of Lebanon, the Copts of Egypt and other non-Muslim populations of the region. The Christians in Iraq are deeply troubled by the rise of radical Islamic tendencies in both the majority Shi'ite and the former ruling class, the Sunni minority. For Iraqi Christians, the continuing spectre of growing insecurity, which has led to church bombings, kidnapping and assassinations, has created a situation which has caused them to leave in large numbers. Maybe as many as 300,000 have left Iraq never to return. Others are refugees in the region: in recent years some 150,000 in Syria and maybe up to 40,000 in Jordan. Some states have welcomed these newcomers and hope that they will stay, bringing their skills, and some hope that their presence will add to a diversity in society which in turn will help support 'moderate' politics. In fact, previous generations of displaced Christians, particularly Armenians and other Oriental Christians, arrived in Lebanon and made that country (before the Civil War 1975-1990) a leading cultural and economic space for the region.

The twentieth century was a period of conflict, which has not left the Churches of the Middle East untouched. Ecclesial institutions that may have been settled in one place for many centuries have been displaced. For example, the Syrian Orthodox Patriarchate, which was located at the Monastery of Mor Hananyo (Deir as-Za'faran) near Mardin since the thirteenth century, was transferred to Homs in modern Syria in 1923, and to Damascus in 1950 due to the destruction of the Syrian Orthodox community at the end of the Ottoman Empire and the foundation of the Turkish Republic. The Chaldean Patriarchate moved from Mosul to Baghdad in 1950. With the ongoing conflict in Iraq and the difficult security situation in Baghdad, it might be set to move again.

The long centuries of Ottoman domination fossilized the Churches in their division. Initially these Muslim rulers centralized all Christian authority within the Patriarchate of Constantinople (followed a few years later by an Armenian Patriarchate). It was not until the nineteenth century that reformist measures allowed these ancient Churches to be formally recognized. Modern crisis and contemporary ecumenism are beginning to bring down the barriers. In the course of the last decades, remarkable developments have taken place in the ecumenical relations between Churches in the Middle East, both on bilateral and multilateral levels—agreements that allow partial mutual participation in sacraments, formation of future priests, and catechesis. Three main factors can be identified as being responsible for these developments: the ecumenical movement of the twentieth century and the establishment (in 1948) of the World Council of Churches, the Second Vatican Council, and the large-scale emigration from the Middle East to Europe, the Americas and Australia.

Although this large-scale emigration has in general been disastrous from the point of view of the life of the indigenous Christian Churches in the Middle East, there have at least been two good consequences: emigration to Western countries has provided the possibility of publication without censorship, and it has brought the existence of these non-Chalcedonian Churches more into the awareness of the Western Churches—thus providing an opportunity and incentive for theological dialogue. Christian theologians have been calling for a new discernment to evaluate the theological and ecclesiological meaning of this new form of communion that is growing among Churches of the Middle East. The Christian Churches have become part and parcel of each other in some mysterious way.

Modern times have brought about a profound change in the configuration of Christian presence in the Middle East. In the last days of the Ottoman Empire, Christians made up 20-30 per cent of the population. The Armenian genocide, the massacre of the Syriac Christians and the exchange of populations between Greece and Turkey (there is still debate about numbers, but approximately a million and half Orthodox Christians and half a million Muslims) had a radical impact. Today there are barely 200,000 Christians in a population of seventy million in the modern Turkish republic, although there might be up to two million people of Armenian descent who issue from the large numbers of Christians taken as slaves or forced into Islam at the fall of the Ottoman Empire. A number of these each year re-trace steps to their (often grandmothers') original Christian faith. Christians in Syria are down from 20 percent before the Second World War to fewer than ten per cent (800,000). During the Lebanese Civil War, some 670,000 Christians were displaced, as opposed to 160,000 Muslims. Lebanon always had a Christian majority, but no longer. This has allowed the Shia community to emerge as the majority community and its political organizations, such as Hezballah, to try and capture the state and challenge traditional Maronite Christian dominance. Since the beginnings of the 1960s and the internal Kurdish-Iraqi war, some one million Christians have left their northern Iraqi mountains and homelands to go into the lands of emigration. During this period Baghdad gained large numbers of Christians, and the Chaldean patriarchate relocated there in 1950. Although several hundred thousand of mainly Greek, Armenian and Syrian Christians left in the 1950s, the large Coptic Christian population in Egypt has traditionally not undertaken emigration until very recent times. One estimate is that perhaps twelve per cent of Copts now live abroad. Since 1948, some 230,000 Christians have left the Holy Land. The Christian population of Jerusalem may be down from 30,000 in 1948 to 5,000 today. There may be fewer than 150,000 Christians left in Iran, many having departed after the 1979 Islamic revolution.

The Christian communities have inevitably lost many of their young and most educated members. The Churches thus not only lose part of their future, but also the potential leadership that should be charting the communities' fortunes. In some communities, this has seen more men leave then women and has changed the gender balance. Christian women marry Muslim men and this fractures the Christian population and diminishes it, with implications for property rights and the education of children.

All are aware that the Churches have lost many millions of their people to emigration, and that their diaspora communities have grown correspondingly, but the question of presence is a dynamic one. Today, large numbers of non-indigenous Christians, brought by the global economy, have come to live and work in the region. 250,000 Christian workers are estimated to be in Israel, and have been there for some time. These are made up of Eastern European and Asian workers. There are large numbers of Filipinos, and increasingly Sri Lankans, Indians and Africans in the region, for example approximately 140,000 Asian workers in Lebanon, eighty per cent of whom are women. At times the traditional Churches are slow to provide for them.

In this changing situation, patterns of authority have altered. Somewhat marginalized by secular politics, the patriarchs of the different Churches have emerged as significant voices for Christianity in the political 'public square'. In the context of profound social and economic dislocation created by modernity, leading to political upheaval and lack of 'legitimate' political structures, religious revival has brought these traditional loci of authority to the fore. We think of the public role of the Coptic Patriarch Shenouda in Egypt, the Maronite Patriarch Sfeir in Lebanon, Michel Sabbah, the former Latin Patriarch in the Holy Land, the Melkite Patriarch in Damascus, to name but some.

To sum up, Christianity originated in the Middle East. The Christian presence there today bears witness to the global Church of the unity of its origins and the diversity of its expression. Christians also help maintain and sustain the diversity in the Middle East. However, there has been large-scale flight from the Middle East and this has implications for those left behind. Christianity in the Middle East has a witness beyond itself: let us hope that the Churches of East and West rise rapidly to this challenge, for the key to the future of this important region may lie with the few. [2]

---

2   See the following studies on Christianity in the Modern Middle East: Sidney H Griffith, *The Church in the Shadow of the Mosque: Christians and Muslims in the World of Islam,* Princeton University Press, Princeton, 2008; John Binns, *An Introduction to the Christian Orthodox Churches,* Cambridge University Press, Cambridge, 2002; Michael Angold (ed.), *The Cambridge History of Christianity: Volume Five—Eastern Christianity,* Cambridge University Press, Cambridge, 2006; Suha Rassam, *Christianity in Iraq,* Gracewing, Leominister, 2005 (revised ed. 2010); A O'Mahony (ed.): *Palestinian Christians: Religion, Politics and Society in the Holy Land,* Melisende, London, 1999; A O'Mahony (ed.), *The Christian Communities in Jerusalem: Studies in History, Religion and Politics,* University of Wales Press, Cardiff, 2003; A O'Mahony (ed.): *Eastern Christianity: Studies in Modern History, Religion & Politics,* Melisende, London, 2004; A O'Mahony (ed.): *Christianity in The Middle East: Studies in Modern History, Theology and Politics,* Melisende, London, 2008; A O'Mahony (co-ed), *Eastern Christianity in the modern Middle East,* Routledge, London, 2010; A O'Mahony (ed), *Christianity and Jerusalem: Studies in Modern Theology and Politics in the Holy Land,* Gracewing, Leominister, 2010; A O'Mahony (co-ed), *Christian Responses to Islam and Muslim-Christian Relations in the Modern World,* Manchester University Press, Manchester, 2008.

EASTERN CHRISTIAN IDENTITY:
A CATHOLIC PERSPECTIVE

Antoine Audo

In order to speak about Christian identity in the modern Middle East we will first consider in parallel two eminent figures of the Eastern Churches, Mgr Néophyte Edelby and Father Afif Osseïrane. Their characteristics as twentieth-century sage and prophet respectively will enable us to illustrate certain of their personality traits and the message they have for us.

Secondly, having listened to the replies of the Christians of Aleppo to the questions put by the *Lineamenta* of the Synod for the Eastern Catholic Churches, we will summarise their questions and expectations on three important points, illustrating the salient features and expectations of these Christians.

Finally, by way of conclusion, in the third section we will make five suggestions for a way forward for the Eastern Churches, as well as for the Arab and Muslim world. Identity is always complex and elusive: it seeks to express itself through various figures, histories and perspectives, and it is this that we will seek to delineate.

TWO VISIONARY AND PROPHETIC SPIRITUAL FIGURES:
MONSIGNOR NÉOPHYTE EDELBY AND FATHER AFIF OSSEÏRANE

On 19 September 2010, Pope Benedict XVI convoked a Special Assembly of the Synod of Bishops for the Middle East. In these difficult times, the Eastern Churches feel encouraged to seize their destiny, to redefine their identity, and to witness to their faith. In the introduction to the *Lineamenta*, we read:

> The synod also offers us the opportunity to assess the social
> as well as the religious situation, so as to give Christians a clear
> vision of the significance of their presence in Muslim societies
> (Arab, Israeli, Turkish or Iranian), and their role and mission
> in each country, and thereby prepare them to be authentic

witnesses of Christ where they live. Accordingly, this involves
reflecting on the current situation, which is a difficult one of
conflict, instability and political and social evolution in the
majority of our countries.

One way of preparing for the Synod is to put questions, in one way or
another, to those who have preceded us, and whom we have known: those
who have navigated complex situations, but who have succeeded in living in
communion and in being witnesses to reconciliation.

I had the good fortune to be close to one of the finest figures of the
Church in Aleppo in modern times, the late Monsignor Néophyte Edelby,
and to have twice met Father Afif Osseïrane, a Shi'ite Muslim converted to
Christianity, in 1945 in the Lebanon. It would clearly be difficult, in a short
paper such as this, to go into all the details of the intellectual scope and
Christian and social engagement of two such complex personalities. What
we can attempt, twenty-five years after their passing, is a re-reading of their
journeys in the service of the Church and of their country. Such a re-reading
is only possible through the questions we put to them and the responses
which they themselves offer us.

We will employ a comparative method to evaluate the salient aspects
of their lives in order to better put into relief these two figures, who have
left traces in the milieu in which they lived. We will proceed in three stages:
to begin with, since both lived at almost the same time—Mgr Edelby,
1920-1995, and Father Osseïrane, 1919-1988—we can look for points of
similarity in their spiritual and human experience. Then, since both had
their own particular spiritual and social background, our approach will be
more to consider the differences between the figures of sage and prophet.
Finally, we will be able to hear the message which each of them addresses
to Christians and Muslims today.

Similarities

Mgr Edelby and Father Osseïrane were, as we have said, contemporaries.
They appeared just as the Ottoman Empire and the French Mandate in Syria-
Lebanon were ending. They witnessed the accession of their countries to
independence, as well as the creation of the State of Israel, the Six Days' War,
and the drama of the Lebanese War. As Christians and churchmen, each was
affected, in his own fashion, by the renewals of the Second Vatican Council.
While coming from different cultures and environments, both Edelby and

Osseïrane were rooted in Arab Muslim culture, in which they lived, taught and wrote. Mgr Edelby had a perfect grasp of literary Arabic which he spoke with simplicity and elegance. For Father Osseïrane too, Islam and Arabic formed an integral part of his personality. No-one reading his translation of the Psalms, written in a Qur'anic style, can fail to admire his complete mastery of Arabic and the language of the Qur'an.

Furthermore, in addition to their in-depth philosophical and theological studies, we may note that both made full use of modern languages, both classical and foreign. Mgr Edelby, who was completely fluent in French and Italian, also had Greek and Latin, while Father Osseïrane knew French and English, as well as Hebrew and Persian. In describing their intellectual status, we must emphasise the part played in their lives by university teaching, particularly in the fields of Islamology, philosophy and theology. Both concentrated on the study of Islam, but, apart from this, Mgr Edelby was more interested in liturgy and canon law, while Father Osseïrane taught philosophy and Muslim mysticism.

The names of both Mgr Edelby and Father Afif Osseïrane, in their own way, immediately inspire respect, affection and respect. To conclude this first section it will suffice to give two quotations describing them. During a celebration in homage to the deceased bishop, Patriarch Maximos V said:

> We will limit ourselves to saying that Mgr Edelby was among those whom God has given the gift of a penetrating intelligence, an iron will, and an excellent character. He made use of these talents, each of which was multiplied tenfold. He excelled in knowledge of languages, and his knowledge of philosophy, theology and canon law shone forth. He was also a likeable man, a zealous preacher and a holy bishop. We shall remember him always.

The second quotation is similarly taken from a homily given by Father Youakim Moubarak during a Requiem Mass for Father Osseïerane:

> Afif sought to show, through a humble but active and inventive exercise of everyday charity, that far from removing him from his own, his membership of the Church brought him even closer. It made him an even more closely attached member of his Muslim family, due in fact to his exceptional generosity, to live out his Christian difference in their midst.

Differences

The life of faith of these two religious men of the twentieth century has enabled us to demonstrate what united them. But the originality of faith, lived, as the Christian tradition teaches, in a personal relationship to God, is capable of illuminating the particularity, or the originality even, of every person.

I would immediately say that Mgr Edelby was the sage *par excellence*, while Father Osseïrane was the prophet. But before going on to illustrate what I have just suggested through example, quotations, and personal witness, let us turn for a moment to Biblical teaching on the three figures of priest, prophet and king.

In effect, exegesis informs us that the Hebrew Bible is divided into three parts: *Law, Prophets and Writings.* Three personalities correspond to these texts:

> Law is taught by the priest
> Prophecy is proclaimed by the prophet
> and Wisdom belongs to the king. And the king is, in fact,
> Solomon.

If one figure comes to the fore in a particular case, the other two are not excluded. In support of our proposition, we would say that while Mgr Edelby and Father Osseïerane were both priests, one was more the sage and the other more the prophet. Furthermore, we know perfectly well how Christian theology has applied these three figures of priest, prophet and king to Jesus Christ, based on a reading of Scripture.

Having qualified our two personalities as sage and prophet, we must now set out the salient characteristics of their lives in order to read there the signs of wisdom *(sagesse)* and prophecy.

All who knew Mgr Edelby, both during his life and after his death, described him as a sage. It is certainly a quality which generally corresponds with the Eastern temperament. We see how he was described by his Vicar General, Archimandrite Ignace Dick, in a speech given on February 22 1987 on the occasion of Mgr Edelby's episcopal jubilee:

> You were born into the environment of the people. You have loved the poor without paternalism, but you have shown no rancour towards the rich. You have known how to gain the esteem and friendship of all, without flattery or compromise. There has been no contradiction in your relations with rich and poor, the great and the simple ... In you we see greatness and simplicity, reason and feelings, WISDOM and good taste,

love of the religions and openness to worldly things, the spirit
of the East and openness to world culture, an attachment to
patrimony and an aspiration to progress and inculturation. You
meet everyone at their own level, you wish to please everyone,
to sadden no-one, and to refuse no-one, something which is
not always possible, and which causes you pain.
(*Mélanges en mémoire de Mgr Néophytos Edelby (1920-1995)*,
Damascus, 2005, p. 26)

Having heard the witness given by this close collaborator with Mgr
Edelby, we must also mention a text broadcast over Syrian radio by the
Metropolitan of Aleppo on September 10 1972. Mgr Edelby had entitled
this speech *The Virtue of 'moussayara'*. The author began by saying that his
behaviour, his way of life, in short 'his secret', could be explained by this
virtue of *moussayara*. He recalled having searched in vain for an explanation
of the term in both Arabic and foreign dictionaries. And yet it is, he said,
a fundamental virtue of our Eastern and Arabic patrimony, and one of
the traits honoured in the Gospel. He continued: did Christ not say in
Matthew's Gospel: 'He who brings a case against you in order to take your
tunic, give him your cloak also. And he who requires you to go one mile,
go with him two miles'?

Before explaining Mgr Edelby's thinking, we should say that the root of
the word *moussayara (musāyara)* is *s.y.r*, 'to walk'. The word is based on a verbal
form meaning 'to walk in company with'. It signifies the fact of being two
and of acting together, to be 'with' and to walk 'with'. This is what gives the
word *moussayara* its force. Such attempts to translate the term as 'conviviality'
or 'empathy', or the act of 'putting oneself in tune with someone' or 'putting
oneself in harmony with someone' fall short of the Arabic expression
which Mgr Edelby explains with great conviction and passion, since it is a
fundamental trait of his personality:

> It is the feeling of profound, complete, concrete charity
> towards everyone, as brothers and sisters in humanity. It is the
> determination of a well-anchored conscience, which drives one
> to care for the well-being and interests of their neighbour just as
> they would care for their own well-being and their own interests.
> I would even say: to prefer the well-being and interests of their
> neighbour over their own interests. '*Moussayara*' is an attitude
> of welcome, of patience, of balance. The WISE man does all
> he can to distance himself from harsh and violent positions ...

Through a special grace, Mgr Edelby was filled with that wisdom which, with no tension whatever, renders people both great and simple at the same time.

While the personality of the sage tends towards harmony, moderation and serenity, the figure of the prophet reveals contrasting traits, ways of behaving different to those of common mortals.

After his conversion, and at the moment of his priestly ordination, Father Osseïrane chose the name Paul. Converted like Paul, he remained profoundly attached to his Shi'ite Muslim tradition. How can we explain his characteristics as prophet through his life, his interventions, and the witness of those who knew him?

Firstly, his conversion was somewhat paradoxical. Originating in a well-known Shi'ite family, the Osseïranes of Saïda, as the son of parents of integrity who followed the precepts of the Muslim religion, Father Osseïrane encountered Christ in a private vision and was baptised on 10 February 1945, at the age of 26.

The second paradox in Father Osseïrane's life was his fidelity to his family, to his birthplace and to Islam. His conversion did not prevent him from maintaining an incarnation of the Gospel in his Islamic milieu. The rupture of a conversion such as that lived by Father Osseïrane remains extremely radical, but its authenticity is measured by the quality of his fidelity to his family and his Islamic environment. As a consequence, until the end of his life, Father Osseïrane enjoyed the respect of both Christians and Muslims.

He unwittingly showed himself a prophet in becoming a baker and a garbage-man at Saïda! He insisted strongly on the witness of life, of gestures, of action, of life alongside the poor. Finally, instead of choosing a career solely in teaching, he preferred to dedicate his life to delinquent children, living in poverty with them and seeking to assure them of a future worthy of their humanity.

The aspect of the life of this mystic which most demands respect is that he never sought to exploit his vocation in any way, whether with Christians or Muslims. For him it was sufficient to be a servant of Jesus Christ.

Two men of God, two men of prayer. 'Tell me how you pray and I will tell you who you are'; here is a proverb which can guide us in our approach to these two figures, in the knowledge that prayer can be the criterion for all that is at the same time the most subjective and the most objective in someone's personality.

All those interested in the activities of Mgr Edelby soon became aware of the care which he devoted to Byzantine liturgy. Following his studies at the major seminary of Saint Anne in Jerusalem, directed by the White Fathers, he deepened his knowledge of the various subjects taught there and was a valuable collaborator with Father Jean-Baptiste Darblade in his research in the fields of Byzantine liturgy and Melkite canon law.

His bibliography, edited by Father Pierre Masri, also testifies to his joint interest in liturgical questions and canon law.

Some liturgical experts have a tendency to concentrate on rubrics, and spend a great deal of time in defending the origins of such and such a prayer or gesture. However, we find no such ideological positions in the intellectual approach of Mgr Edelby. The liturgy exists to aid us in praying worthily to God.

So it was that, in his liturgical prayer, he distinguished himself both by the majesty of the Byzantine liturgy which introduces us into the mystery of Christ, Lord and Master, and the modesty of the sinner who prostrates himself before his God. Tested by illness during the last ten years of his life, Mgr Edelby became increasingly silent, listening to God and welcoming him into his life.

In the context of his country, a man of such intellectual stature could easily fall into an ideological way of speaking, with a constant tendency to affirmation and exaggeration, with no concern for the dichotomy between words and action. But Mgr Edelby earned respect through the authenticity of both his way of life and his manner of speech. He was the image of his Master.

While a young religious in the Maronite Antonine Order, Father Louis Al Ruhban had known Father Osseïrane at the convent of Mar Achaya, near Broumanna, in Lebanon. He provides useful evidence for a deeper understanding of the make-up of this priest as regards prayer. In a collection of accounts of Father Osseïrane published in Arabic, he writes:

> What struck me, and what drove me to admire what distinguishes Afif, is his spirit of prayer … It is this that made me love Islam. For me, the first time that I knew Islam was through Afif Osseïrane. In my opinion, Afif has returned to us what preceded Islam, and that which it took from Christianity, that is to say, adoration. Adoration, for us as for them, is … 'annihilation' in the presence of God. It is an expression of an intense feeling of the grandeur and beauty of the Creator and of the nothingness … of man before him. The theology of prostration, the theology of annihilation, are a patrimony

common to Syrian Christianity and to Islam. And Afif Osseïrane is the inheritor of this double legacy.

All who knew Father Osseïrane were struck by the amount of time this young religious spent in adoration before the Blessed Sacrament. In fact, his integrity of life, his total availability in the service of the poorest, the peace and joy he radiated, and the quality of his friendships, can only be understood through this profound communion with Jesus Christ, who had made him a man of silence and adoration.

I personally had the pleasure to meet Father Osseïrane at his training centre for young delinquents, when I accompanied a group of young people on retreat there. After an evening Mass he rejoined us in the church, and began to recite the Beatitudes, using a Qur'anic melody. Through this gesture, prophetic in itself, he sought to communicate a message to these young Christians in a way which could not but give rise to respect and admiration.

Any description of Mgr Edelby's rich personality would be seriously incomplete if we failed to give due attention to the part that Vatican II played in his life. Consecrated bishop in 1962, and named by Maximos IV as his auxiliary, Mgr Edelby played a very active part in the Council, along with his patriarch, who was famous for his interventions in favour of the Eastern Catholic Churches and the Orthodox. To fill out this page from the history of Vatican II, we must turn first to the historian's view, that of Professor Andrea Riccardi in the introduction to the book *Recollections of the Second Vatican Council*, first published in Italian in 1996, and then in French in 2003. In his richly observant introduction on the situation of Eastern Christians, Professor Riccardi wrote as follows:

> The bishop of Aleppo, as a man of different worlds, the Eastern Christian world, Catholic and Arab, in contact on the one hand with Islam and with the West on the other, has experienced the event of the Council with a great engagement with respect to new possibilities. His intellectual finesse, his capacity to develop friendly relations, and his interest in other worlds were forcibly displayed.

In this brief passage, Professor Riccardi has succeeded in combining Mgr Edelby's very diverse characteristics, showing us a personality at once harmonious and controlled. By qualifying him as 'of Aleppo', Professor Riccardi, a fine observer, pays homage to the rich history of Aleppo, of which Mgr Edelby was the product *par excellence*. The same author goes on to emphasise that the bishop belongs fully to the Eastern Church and to the

Catholic Church. He is, furthermore, well-lettered and capable of developing friendly relations.

This double fidelity to the Eastern and Catholic Churches, to Eastern and Arabic culture and to the West, this intellectual capacity for research, his simple homilies which constituted teaching for the people, all in a certain manner, explain the Christian and human qualities of this man. Fifteen years after his death, he is able to deliver his message to us who are also Middle Eastern Arabs and Christians.

Father Osseïrane also experienced, in his own way, the grace of Vatican II. He was ordained priest on 21 April 1962, in the Maronite diocese of Beirut, and his bishop, Mgr Ignace Ziadé, authorised him to exercise his apostolate in the education of young delinquents. Father Afif sought to live with and for the poor, free of any clericalism which claims rights and privileges. From his youth, he possessed a charismatic temperament, searching, able to leave the beaten path, to find new summits to climb. Even before choosing Christ as his Master and companion for life, he distinguished himself by a desire to be himself and to affirm himself as such, within a peaceable and believing Muslim family.

Examining his career closely, we must recognise that the spirituality of Charles de Foucauld influenced him profoundly. In the interviews given by Father Osseïrane he recalled his period of formation with the Little Brothers of Jesus, but never made explicit mention of this spirituality: he lived it. I believe that there is a kind of mysterious connection between Charles de Foucauld, recalled to the Christianity of his childhood on seeing Muslims at prayer in the desert, and Father Osseïrane, a convert from Islam to Christianity and remaining the friend of both Christians and Muslims. Father Osseïrane is in some way a new Foucauld, a Foucauld become Arab and Eastern Christian.

We may end this section with a nicely-related anecdote from Mme Zahita Osseïrane, Father Osseïrane's cousin. She relates:

> The family loved him so much that it received its blessing because of his attitude, completely characterised by humanity. At first, my elderly and rather uncultured aunt covered her face whenever Afif appeared, since he had become a Christian. But when she saw his good deeds she abandoned this habit of covering her face in front of him.

Disinterested charity, acceptance of the other just as they are, are the road to reconciliation and peace.

Their Messages

Having reached the end of our reflection on these two contemporary spiritual figures rooted in the Catholic Church and Middle Eastern society, we now ask what message they offer us on the eve of the Synod of Bishops, '*The Catholic Church in the Middle East: communion and witness.*'

In view of the distinct origin of each, Mgr Edelby, an Arab Christian of Syrian origin, and Father Afif Osseïrane, originating from Lebanon, and a Muslim who became a Christian, our desire is that they might speak to us today. It is possible that the message of Mgr Edelby will resonate more in the heart of Muslims, while that of Father Osseïrane will touch Christians more closely.

The figure of the sage which we have emphasised, together with the bishop's capacity to be himself, without any ideological alienation, and to integrate several identities (Arab, Eastern, Byzantine, and Catholic), is the bearer of a call to communion in respect of difference. Pope Benedict XVI, in his latest encyclical *Caritas in Veritate*, also directs our search towards an authentic communion between truth and love. He says:

> Through this close link with truth, love can be recognized as an authentic expression of humanity and as an element of fundamental importance in human relations, including those of a public nature. *Only in truth does love shine forth*, only in truth can love be authentically lived. Truth is the light that gives meaning and value to love. That light is both the light of reason and the light of faith, through which the intellect attains to the natural and supernatural truth of love: it grasps its meaning as gift, acceptance, and communion. (§ 3)

Dialogue between reason and faith, communion respecting difference, a flight from violence in order to affirm trust in oneself and in others, these are demands which challenge our intellect as Christians and Muslims in search of peace and justice.

As to Father Osseïrane, it is clear that through his spiritual experience, he lived out a life within the Catholic Church in profound communion with Jesus Christ. He influenced many Muslims around him, but without any tendency to proselytism or fanaticism, as many Muslims who were close to him have borne witness. However, in a paradoxical way, we would affirm that it is Christians in general, and the Christians of the Middle East in particular, who need to pay him greater heed. He tells them, in effect, not to be afraid of 'political' Islam, but to appreciate its mystical and humanist dimensions.

In this, he calls them to give witness in a Muslim environment through their prayer life and an attitude of adoration, which can transform them into living icons transfigured by the mystery of God. In addition, they can equally, while engaging seriously in politics, infuse it with the grace of love which liberates it from its instinct for power and possession, and founds it on justice.

Finally, another quotation from Benedict XVI helps to clarify all that Mgr Edelby and Father Osseïrane strove to say through their life and teachings. In the same encyclical, *Caritas in Veritate*, the Pope says:

> *Development needs Christians with their arms raised towards God* in prayer, Christians moved by the knowledge that truth-filled love, *caritas in veritate*, from which authentic development proceeds, is not produced by us, but given to us. For this reason, even in the most difficult and complex times, besides recognizing what is happening, we must above all else turn to God's love. Development requires attention to the spiritual life, a serious consideration of the experiences of trust in God, spiritual fellowship in Christ, reliance upon God's providence and mercy, love and forgiveness, self-denial, acceptance of others, justice and peace. (§ 79)

A Number of Points from Responses to the *Lineamenta* from the Catholic Church in Aleppo

To return to the present, we present a number of essential points arising from responses to the *Lineamenta* drawn up by the Catholics of Aleppo. They are given as complementary or contrasting pairings, and reflect the daily lives of these Christians, faced as they are by numerous religious and social challenges.

Double Affiliation to the East and to Christianity

The Christians of the Middle East have a strong sense of belonging to the East. They are proud of its qualities of hospitality, of human warmth, of a trusting abandonment to God. They aspire to be recognised as such, and wish to keep their specificity and their identity. This translates equally into the social domain and daily life and into the religious sphere. In the religious category, Eastern Christians are attached to their liturgical patrimony and to

29

the mosaic of ritual which enriches the entire Church. As this religious reality is unfortunately little known in the West, they seek to witness it, both at home and in the countries to which they emigrate.

On the other hand, these Christians have a sense of being 'strangers', 'intruders', 'isolated', forceful expressions which describe their feelings of disarray and fear, confronted by an ever-more invasive Muslim majority. Despite their attachment to their own countries, they also feel more and more drawn to 'the West' (Europe, USA, Australia).

The reasons for emigration are economic, religious and political. It is equally the consequence of fears for the future of the Middle East, and especially that of Christians as such.

This attraction to the West is sometimes rather utopian and illusory, as if all the problems and difficulties experienced by the emigrants in their own country would find ready-made solutions in the countries which accept them.

However, despite this attraction to the outside, there is often regret, a nostalgia for the 'mother-country', a desire to return when things improve.

And, thank God, not all Christians are tempted to emigrate, and many among them wish to remain in their own country, whatever the cost, in order to testify to their message of faith in Christ.

Integration, Incarnation / Community Spirit and Individualism

Eastern Christians have by their very nature a communitarian spirit. They have a sense of welcome, of openness, of interest in others. They are realists, and seek to live firmly integrated within their country and their Church, thus following the example of their ancestors, rooted in the East from the beginnings of Christianity.

A spirit of initiative is not lacking in the ecclesial domain, and there are numerous movements which seek to incarnate the faith in the life and social situation of each person.

But, at the same time, faced with the concrete reality of social and political life, they are often forced to make individual decisions (particularly as regards emigration, where each family feels responsible for its future).

Those Christians who remain in their own country are sometimes tempted to turn in on themselves, to closure to the other, to distrust. Fear of disappearance, or of not being recognised, can reinforce this attitude or make them give up hope.

There are, however, some movements, groups, or individuals who seek dialogue, reconciliation, and social interaction, three qualities generally inherent in the Eastern soul (cf. in the Old Testament, the history of the Hebrew people, incessantly confronted by pagan nations and tempted to imitate them, to allow themselves to be absorbed by them, and to lose their faith in the one God). In the long term, it is the solution of dialogue which appears best. It is, in any case, an authentically Christian witness: the Church, with all its members, clergy and laity, seeks to live like Christ, trying to love and to understand the other right to the end, even if that may lead to the Cross and to martyrdom (unfortunately, there is no shortage of examples of this in Iraq, in Egypt and elsewhere).

To live out this dialogue, Christians seek to engage politically, socially and culturally, and are encouraged in this approach by their pastors. This political witness can have a more visible and lasting effect, and even influence decisions or civil laws (e.g. the autonomy of the Catholic Church as regards marriage and inheritance).

As to relations with Islam, these are a secular and daily reality. Much unites Christians and Muslims: country, language, culture, certain social habits, and so on. All this works in favour of social interaction.

Inter-religious encounter takes place especially at the level of work, of personal relationships, of day-to-day social life. But dialogue in depth often appears difficult, since it touches on highly personal and delicate religious experiences and realities. How far can we go in dialogue without damaging the respect due to the other and their freedom?

In order to truly live out in depth this dialogue with Islam, Christians need to feel themselves more united, and supported by the pastors of the entire Church, Eastern and Universal.

An experience of life with God and with other Christians is fertile soil for an ever-greater openness to the 'brother or sister' who differs in their faith and in their manner of translating it into a way of life.

Activism and Prayer/ Popular Devotion and the Deepening of Faith

The engagement of Christians in ecclesial, social and political life, while extremely desirable, possesses, nevertheless, the danger of activism. In the purely ecclesial sphere, groups and movements are extremely numerous: scouts, choirs, camps, catechesis …, and risk exhausting the resources of priests and committed lay-people.

Confronting this risk, there are, in Aleppo, more and more groups for prayer and adoration, and charismatic movements (within the Church or privately), which provide the counterpart to this activism. The Eastern spirit, being by its nature contemplative (cf. the example of frequent and public Muslim prayer calling to mind the greatness of God), Eastern Christians live out their double affiliation, Eastern and Christian, through participation in such meetings for prayer.

In order not to remain at the level of sentiment, all of this needs to be entered into more deeply. What strikes Western Christians when they arrive in the East is the external vitality of the Church, a reality of which they are often totally unaware. At first glance, this Christianity seems to them a popular religion, strongly anchored in the heart and soul of the people. Various devotions, especially in Holy Week and the month of Mary, form an integral part of the normal religious landscape.

But this external devotion is felt by more and more Christians to be good but insufficient, and they insist on a deeper understanding of doctrine and practice. Priests are aware of their teaching responsibility, expressed through consistent homilies and a serious catechesis adapted to the needs of the faithful of the countries of the East.

The faithful equally feel a need for personal meetings with their bishops and priests, and the visits made by them to their families are considered extremely important in aiding them to grow in faith and to trust in the Church.

PERSPECTIVES

Having sketched a portrait of two Arab Christians, Mgr Néophyte Edelby and Father Afif Osseïrane, and having set out the most significant hopes and fears of the Christians of Aleppo through examining their responses to the *Lineamenta* of the next Synod of the Catholic Church in the Middle East, we arrive at the final part of our presentation, that is to say an attempt at describing Eastern Christian identity on the eve of the Synod soon to be held in Rome.

We must recognise from the start that speaking about Eastern Christian identity is a delicate and complex undertaking. In effect, sketching the portraits of two very specific personalities, and outlining the main features of the attitude of Christians in a town such as Aleppo, remains an enterprise limited in both time and space. But to speak of Eastern Christian identity from the perspective of the Catholic Church bears considerable risk. For this reason, everything to be proposed in this third section is no more than an attempt to express this identity through a search for 'communion' and 'witness' in the context of the Middle East and at the heart of the Muslim Arab world.

In order to avoid affirming identity through ideological characteristics, at a time when the whole world mistrusts ideology, and to escape the impasse of discouragement and despair in the face of certain fundamentalisms which strive to empty the Middle East of Christians, we will propose a number of characteristics with respect to the identity of these Christians.

Above all, this identity is a living reality, in search of communion and in the spirit of service, in the Muslin and Arab world.

The communion which Eastern Christians seek is based primarily on a double denial; a refusal to consider themselves as *dhimmi*, under Islamic protection, and a refusal to set themselves above Muslim society in the name of a superiority of faith or of civilisation, automatically identifying them with the West or with globalisation.

This double denial leads them to an affirmation that assists them to derive their identity as Eastern Christians from Arab culture. In fact, no-one is ignorant of the intrinsic link between Islam and the Arabic language, to such an extent that for Muslims one can speak of an identification between Islam and being Arab. However, when Arab Christians take Arab culture seriously as humanity, a way of living in the world and speaking of God as Absolute, they cannot but introduce difference into that culture. It is no longer, for Christians, a question of immediate identification between Islam and being Arab, but rather of an opening to difference and hence to the universal. Christians, by means of a serious and respectful approach to Arab culture, can, through the human sciences, contribute to the modernisation of Islam, and facilitate a positive and critical approach to modernity. To be different is a path of humility for Eastern Christians, something which liberates them from fear, from closing in, from discouragement and from emigration, as well as from the desire to identify themselves with Western power, unconditional and irresponsible superiority and security.

A re-reading of the contribution of Eastern Christians to the development of Arab and Muslim civilisation allows us to envisage ways of openness, trust, and conversion. We cannot, in the restricted framework of this brief presentation, detail the contribution made by Arab Christians in the Umayyad (640-750) and 'Abbasid (750-1258) periods, or finally in the 'Renaissance', *Al-Nahda*, of the nineteenth and twentieth centuries. In this great debate between faith and reason, between Islam and culture, Christians did not have the last word—who could?—but they did open up spaces, within the fabric of Muslim-Arab culture, spaces of freedom and communication between faith and reason. Arab culture, which directly identifies itself with Qur'anic revelation, must be approached with great respect and seriousness, allowing the opportunity, in the fullness of time, to speak a word of truth and to create authentic paths to the universal.

This difference, seen as a dynamic of liberty distinguishing itself both from an attitude of *dhimmitude* and from a complex of superiority and alienation *vis-à-vis* the West, is, in itself, a place of dialogue and not of conflict. In fact, Muslims, especially those given to philosophy and theology, find in this Eastern and Arab Christianity a space within which to consider their own faith and Qur'anic tradition. In contesting our 'falsified' Scriptures, in examining the historical context of Qur'anic texts taken from the Old Testament and the Gospels, they cannot avoid rational criticism. Finally, this Christian difference, rather than being provocative, 'infidel', 'associationist', can become an experience at once spiritual and human.

Some Muslims may be troubled by the existence of this Arab Christianity which has proved resistant since the coming of Islam in the seventh century. Others, more numerous, are attracted to an Arab Christianity which witnesses to a personal relationship between humanity and God, and among humanity itself, a relationship rooted in the Gospels. Has not the mystical tradition of Islam also sought, beyond all dogmatism, to encounter God, so also becoming a place of dialogue and communion?

In conclusion, starting from a Catholic perspective, while seeking to respect all the Eastern Churches, we can sketch out certain traits of this Middle Eastern Christian identity. Having broadly outlined the three parts of our presentation, we offer five propositions:

1) It is clear that, in the face of modernity and globalisation, the Arab Muslim world feels threatened and lacking in confidence with regard both to itself and to others. In this context, Eastern Christians, instead of marginalising themselves and choosing emigration as a way out, are called, through re-reading their history, to discover paths to confidence for themselves and for their societies, thereby refusing all closing-in on themselves in a psychology of 'victimhood'. To do so, they must set aside their fears and demonstrate their sincerity as regards their relations with Europe and the USA, seeking to explain Muslim concerns to the West, and the problems of rational modernity to Islam.

2) This leads us to say that we, as Christians, must not, first of all, invent strategies which resist the development of Islam. Rather, in multicultural societies, it makes sense for us to create pluri-dimensional dialogues and to engage effectively, in a spirit of friendship and trust, in the evolution of Islam and its modernisation. However, this socio-cultural evolution can only be realised in a spirit of cooperation.

Finally, true Islam must understand that it will not be able to modernise itself without there being peace with Christians. This road to peace will lead it to be liberated from all its complexes of fear of the other.

3) Eastern Christians can, with Muslim thinkers, re-read the history of Arab philosophy, recognising its rational and critical dimension. Through this work of the Spirit, to which many Christians have contributed, the Muslim world can recover its national and universal unity, which will help it to free itself from fundamentalism and the call to violence leading increasingly to death. We have, in the history of the Chaldean Church and the Society of Jesus, such eminent figures of the Arab Renaissance as Father Louis Cheikho (1859-1927) and Father Paul Nwiya (1925-1980).

4) Eastern Christians can contribute to the achievement of a pluri-religious society by encouraging dialogue and allowing an objective understanding of the religion of the other. In this way, through the use of a new language, that of a 'civilisation of life in common', Muslims and Christians can together seek a lay democracy.

5) From all that we have proposed, the vocation of Eastern Christians will be to become a bridge, or better, a model of communion between the Christian West and the Muslim world.

TOWARDS A SPECIAL ASSEMBLY OF THE SYNOD OF BISHOPS FOR THE MIDDLE EAST
From the announcement of the Synod to the promulgation of its *Instrumentum laboris*

Dietmar W Winkler

On 6 June 2010, in the context of a Eucharistic celebrationin Nicosia (Cyprus),[1] Pope Benedict XVI presented the *Instrumentum laboris* of the 'Special Assembly of the Synod of Bishops for the Middle East' This paper will provide information about the synodical process and the work of preparation. It will include an introduction to the *Lineamenta* and relate them to the work of the PRO ORIENTE Foundation, before finally giving a brief introduction to the *Instrumentum Laboris*, the document which provides the basis for the discussions of the Synod.

THE SYNODICAL PROCESS AND PREPARATORY WORK

Whilst in Rome in January 2009 for the official dialogue between the Oriental Orthodox Churches and the Catholic Church,[2] I met the Chaldean Archbishop of Kirkuk, Iraq, Mar Louis Sako, who was there for the *ad limina* visit of the Chaldean Synod. Sitting together in the evening, he said to me: 'Tomorrow I will meet the Pope, and I will suggest to him that he should convoke a Synod for the Middle East.' The suggestion was obviously taken seriously by His Holiness Pope Benedict XVI.

---

1   Cf. *Instrumentum Laboris*, Synod of Bishops, Special Assembly for the Middle East: The Catholic Church in the Middle East: Communion and Witness. 'Now the company of those who believed were of one heart and soul' (Acts 4:32), Vatican City 2010, http://www.vatican.va/roman_curia/synod/documents/rc_synod_doc_20100606_instrumentum-mo_en.pdf.

2   Cf. Sixth Meeting of the International Joint Commission for Theological Dialogue between the Catholic Church and the Oriental Orthodox Churches, Rome, Italy, 26-30 January 2009, in *The Pontifical Council for Promoting Christian Unity*, Information Service No. 131 (2009/I-II), pp. 28-29.

Announcement of the Synod

During his visit to the Holy Land in May 2009 Pope Benedict was able to form his own impressions of the Middle East. Four month later, in a meeting with the patriarchs and major archbishops of the Eastern Catholic Churches in Castel Gandolfo on 19 September 2009, he announced the 'Special Assembly of the Synod of Bishops for the Middle East', and revealed the topic of the Synod as 'The Catholic Church in the Middle East: Communion and Witness', to which was added a phrase taken from Acts 4:32: 'Now the company of those who believed were of one heart and soul.'

In his address, Pope Benedict XVI said to the patriarchs and major archbishops who were present:

> For my part, I feel it is my main duty to encourage the synodality so dear to Eastern ecclesiology and acknowledged with appreciation by the Second Vatican Ecumenical Council. I fully share in the esteem that the Council showed your Churches in the Decree *Orientalium Ecclesiarum* which my venerable Predecessor John Paul II reaffirmed in particular in his Apostolic Exhortation *Orientale Lumen*. I also share in the hope that the Eastern Catholic Churches will 'flourish' in order 'to fulfill with new apostolic strength the task entrusted to them', so as to foster 'the unity of all Christians, in particular of Eastern Christians, according to the principles laid down in the decree of this holy Council, 'On Ecumenism'" (*Orientalium Ecclesiarum* nn. 1, 24).' The ecumenical horizon is often connected with the interreligious outlook. In these two areas the whole Church needs the experience of coexistence, which your Churches have developed since the first Christian millennium.[3]

The topic of the Synod, combined with the motto taken from Acts, clearly expresses the intention of the Synod. Communion *and* witness go together, because only through common witness can the gospel be effectively proclaimed. Therefore 'one heart and soul' is needed, firstly among the various Eastern Catholic Churches themselves, and secondly in unity with all the Christian Churches of the region.

---

3   Benedict XVI, 'Address to the Eastern Catholic Patriarchs and Major Archbishops', Castel Gandolfo, 19 September 2009. http://www.vatican.va/holy_father/benedict_xvi/speeches/2009/september/documents/hf_ben-xvi_spe_20090919_patr-arciv-orient_en.html.

For regional Synods of Bishops, the 'Special Synods', the Catholic Church has an established organizational process. The 'Synod of Bishops' is a permanent institution, with its own *dicasterium* in the Vatican, established by Pope Paul VI in 1965, in response to the desire of the Fathers of the Second Vatican Council (1962-65) to keep alive the spirit of collegiality engendered by the conciliar experience.[4]

The preparation for a synod is itself supposed to be part of the synodical process.[5] Before the announcement, several consultations take place in a climate of collegial communion. The first official step would in fact be a process of consulting the Eastern Catholic Churches *sui iuris*, Episcopal Conferences, departmental heads of the Roman Curia, and the Union of Superiors General for suggestions on possible topics for a synod. Among other things, the bishops are asked to bear in mind the following criteria: (a) the topic should have a contemporary character and urgency, in the sense that it has the capacity to excite energies and movement in the Church towards growth; (b) it should have a pastoral focus, as well as a firm doctrinal basis; (c) it should have feasibility, which means that the topic must actually have the potential to be accomplished.

Such a procedure has certainly been the case regarding the Middle East Synod, with the suggested topic being submitted by the Council of the Synod of Bishops to the Holy Father, who officially made the final decision on the theme and announced the synod.

The 'Pre-Synodal Council'

The next step was the formation of a 'Pre-Synodal Council for the Middle East', composed of six Patriarchs of the Eastern Catholic Churches, the Latin Patriarch of Jerusalem, two presidents from episcopal conferences and four heads of dicasteries of the Roman Curia:[6]

His Beatitude Cardinal Nasrallah Pierre Sfeir, Patriarch of Antioch of the Maronites

His Beatitude Cardinal Emmanuel III Delly, Patriarch of Babylon of the Chaldeans

---

4   Cf. Paul VI, 'Motu Proprio *Apostolica solicitudo*', 15 September 1965.

5   Cf. *Ordo Synodi Episcoporum, Code of Canon Law* c. 242-248, *Code of Canons for the Eastern Churches* c. 46, http://www.vatican.va/roman_curia/synod/.

6   Cf. First Meeting of the Presynodal Council for the Middle East, Rome, 21 and 22 September 2009, http://www.melkite.org/Patriarch/PA24.htm.

His Beatitude Antonios Naguib, Patriarch of Alexandria of the Copts

His Beatitude Ignace Youssif III Younan, Patriarch of Antioch of the Syrians

His Beatitude Gregory III Laham, Patriarch of Antioch of the Greek-Melkites

His Beatitude Nerses Bedros XIX Tarmouni, Patriarch of Cilicia of the Armenians

His Beatitude Fouad Twal, Patriarch of Jerusalem of the Latins

Archbishop Ramzi Garmou of Tehran of the Chaldeans, President of the Iranian Episcopal Conference

Bishop Luigi Padovese OFM. Cap., Apostolic Vicar of Anatolia, Turkey[7]

Cardinal Leonardo Sandri, Prefect of the Congregation for the Oriental Churches

Cardinal Walter Kasper, President of the Pontifical Council for Promoting Christian Unity

Cardinal Jean-Louis Tauran, President of the Pontifical Council for Inter-religious Dialogue

Cardinal Ivan Dias, Prefect of the Congregation for the Evangelisation of Peoples

The first meeting of the Pre-Synodal Council took place in Rome on 21-22 September 2009, only two days after the announcement of the Synod. Those present included Professor Fr Samir Khalil Samir SJ as expert.[8] The

---

7   Bishop Luigi Padovese was murdered in Turkey on 3 June 2010, only a few days before the visit of the Pope to Cyprus. Benedict XVI remembered him especially, when he presented the *Instrumentum laboris*: 'Before I begin, it is only fitting that I recall the late Bishop Luigi Padovese who, as President of the Turkish Catholic Bishops, contributed to the preparation of the *Instrumentum laboris* that I am consigning to you today. News of his unforeseen and tragic death on Thursday surprised and shocked all of us. I entrust his soul to the mercy of almighty God, mindful of how committed he was, especially as a bishop, to interreligious and cultural understanding, and to dialogue between the Churches. His death is a sobering reminder of the vocation that all Christians share, to be courageous witnesses in every circumstance to what is good, noble and just.' Cf. Benedict XVI, 'Address—Consignment of the *Instrumentum laboris* of the Special Assembly for the Middle East of the Synod of Bishops ', Nicosia/Cyprus, 6 June 2010, http://www.vatican.va/holy_father/benedict_xvi/speeches/2010/june/documents/hf_ben-xvi_spe_20100606_instr-laboris_en.html.

8   Also present were Revd Mgr Alberto Ortega Martín (Counsellor of Nunciature, Second Class, Second Section, Secretary of State, Vatican) and His Exc. Mgr Jules

members gave a brief and comprehensive review of the socio-politico and religious situation in the Middle East, in order to decide the main topics to be dealt with in the forthcoming synod, and this meeting and its discussions led to the drafting of the *Lineamenta*.

The Work on the Lineamenta *and the* Instrumentum Laboris

Though the drafting of the *Lineamenta* would represent the combined work of the Pre-Synodal Council members, expert theologians, and the staff of the General Secretariat which co-ordinates the various efforts, it was in fact Fr Samir Khalil Samir SJ (Beirut), who was the main drafter of the *Lineamenta,* in close co-operation with Archbishop Nikola Eterović, the General Secretary of the Synod of Bishops. After studying the draft text and making the necessary revisions, the Pre-Synodal Council created a final version of the *Lineamenta* which was submitted to the Holy Father for his approval. The document was then translated into Arabic, English, French and Italian.

In January 2010, the *Lineamenta* were sent to the Churches.[9] It was intended that the Patriarchs and the episcopate would generate study and discussion at the local level regarding the topic of the synod. Thus, each chapter of the *Lineamenta* is followed by a set of questions designed to initiate such a discussion. The *Lineamenta* are by their nature very broad in scope and are meant to elicit a broad range of observations and responses. Though the first and authoritative recipients of the *Lineamenta* are obviously the bishops and the bishops' conferences, they have full liberty to broaden the basis of their consultation—whether they choose to do so or not.

The responses to these questions were to be sent to the General Secretariat of the Synod of Bishops by Easter, i.e. 4 April 2010.[10] The Pre-Synodal

---

Mikhael Al-Jamil (Archbishop of Takrit of the Syrians, Procurator and Apostolic Visitor for Western Europe). The latter replaced his Patriarch for the first meeting, but was designated by Ignatius Youssif III Younan to be his substitute.

9   Cf. *Lineamenta*, Synod of Bishops, Special Assembly for the Middle East, The Catholic Church in the Middle East: Communion and Witness. 'Now the company of those who believed were of one heart and soul' (Acts 4:32), Vatican City 2009, http://www.vatican.va/roman_curia/synod/documents/rc_synod_doc_20091208_lineamenta-mo_en.html.

10   On 14 May 2010, PRO ORIENTE organized a panel on the Middle East Synod at the 'Ökumenische Kirchentag' in Munich Germany, where I moderated a discussion on the *Lineamenta* with Fr Samir Khalil Samir, Prof Elias Kattan (Münster; Orthodox Patriarchate of Antioch) and Bishop Armash Nalbandian (Damascus, Armenian

Council then met again on 23 to 24 April in Rome, during which time[11] it worked on an outline of the *Instrumentum laboris*—in a plenary session and in three groups—seeking to integrate into an organic scheme the vast number of contributions comprising responses from eparchies, institutions and religious to the questions of the *Lineamenta*.

In the days following, the main drafter of the *Instrumentum laboris* was again Fr Samir Khalil Samir, aiming to include and synthesize the responses on the basis of the guidelines of the Pre-Synodal Council in order to create a more substantial document. Having finished his work, he consulted further, asking some five additional experts for any additions, contributions and suggestions thought necessary. At this point the draft, then a mixture of Italian, French and English was submitted on 5 May to Archbishop Nikola Eterović of the General Secretariat of the Synod of Bishops. There the last work of revision took place, and it was again sent to the members of the Pre-Synodal Council for a final examination. The members were asked to reply with comments to the Synodal Office as soon as possible.

In the second half of May 2010, the Synodal Office produced the final version of the *Instrumentum laboris*, and, after approval by Pope Benedict, the document was translated into the official languages of the Synod. All the members of the Pre-Synodal Council were invited to participate in the Eucharistic celebration presided over by Benedict XVI in Nicosia for the presentation of the document.[12]

The *Instrumentum laboris*, although made public, is only a provisional text, a study document, which forms the basis and reference-point for the synodal discussion. The document is not a draft of the final conclusions, but only a text which aims at helping to focus discussion on the synod's topic. Since 1983 the *Instrumentum laboris* of a given synodal assembly has been made public in order to receive wide circulation. The bishop-delegates and members are supposed to read the document in order to familiarize themselves with the contents,

---

Apostolic Church). On that occasion, Fr Samir provided the information that about 300 pages of responses had been returned by the bishops. This demonstrates the lively interest and robust discussion on the topics of the Synod.

11   Cf. Third Reunion of the Presynodal Council for the Middle East, Rome, 23-24 April 2010. Report by Patriarch Gregorios III of the Melkite Greek Catholic Church, http://www.melkite.org/Patriarch/PA35-SynodMiddleEast.htm.

12   Cf. Benedict XVI, 'Homily—Holy Mass on the occasion of the publication of the Instrumentum laboris of the Special Assembly for the Middle East of the Synod of Bishops', Nicosia, Cyprus, 6 June 2010, http://www.vatican.va/holy_father/benedict_xvi/homilies/2010/documents/hf_ben-xvi_hom_20100606_instr-laboris_en.html.

which will then be discussed at the synodal assembly. It is envisaged that, as a result of preparatory work in the local Churches based on the *Lineamenta* and the *Instrumentum laboris*, the bishops will then be able to present the experiences and aspirations of each community as well as the fruits of the preliminary discussions of the episcopal conferences.

THE *LINEAMENTA*

We will look first at the *Lineamenta,* since it has largely the same structure as the *Instrumenum laboris*. The document has an introduction, three main chapters and a conclusion.

The *Introduction* outlines the aim of the synod. The ecumenical and inter-religious context of the region is mentioned there:

> Our Catholic Churches are not alone in the Middle East. There are also the Orthodox Churches and the Protestant communities. This ecumenical aspect is basic, if Christian witness is to be genuine and credible. 'That they may all be one, *so that* the world may believe' (Jn 17:21). Thus, communion has to be deepened at all levels: within the Catholic Churches in the Middle East themselves, among all Catholic Churches in the region and in relations with other Christian Churches and ecclesial communities. At the same time, we have to strengthen the witness we give to Jews, Muslims, believers and non-believers.[13]

The first main chapter *(I: The Catholic Church in the Middle East)* focuses on the situation of Christians in the Middle East (A), the challenges facing Christians in the region (B), the Christian response in daily life (C). The brief historical sketch outlining unity in diversity in section A is followed by the very fact of the apostolicity and important witness of the Church, especially in this region where revelation took place. The role of Christians in society, despite their small number, is mentioned, as well as problems of political conflict, freedom of conscience and religion, developments in contemporary Islam, and emigration as well as the immigration of Christians from throughout the world.

The second main chapter *(II: Ecclesial Communion)* has the Catholic Churches at its centre. It addresses the problem of ecclesial communion

---

13   *Lineamenta,* §§ 2 and 3.

among bishops, clergy and laypeople within the various Catholic (eastern and Latin) Churches of the Middle East.

It is interesting to note that several statements of the *Lineamenta* were not included in the *Instrumentum laboris*. Here we quote only one paragraph, which, since it mirrors a reality of daily life, deserved to remain:

> Furthermore, the attitude of the two apostles, James and John, who asked Jesus to grant them the first places at his right and his left (Mk 10:35-37), can still be detected, posing difficulties among the brethren. Instead of coming together to face difficulties in common, we sometimes argue among ourselves, counting the number of faithful in our Churches to ascertain who is the greatest. This spirit of rivalry destroys us. Instead, emulating each others' good practices in spiritual and pastoral service can stir our creativity in serving others. Consequently, emulation of what is best in our services must be encouraged. At the same time, our Churches, like all Churches in the world, are in need of continuous purification. This Synod can provide the occasion for a sincere examination of conscience to ascertain, on the one hand, the strong points for promotion and development, and, on the other, the weaknesses to be courageously faced and corrected.[14]

The third main chapter (*III: Christian Witness*) focuses on collaboration in catechesis and works (A), on common witness with and of all the Christian Churches (B),[15] on the particular relationship to Judaism (C) and relations with Islam (D) as well as to the contributions of Christians to society (E), including Church-State relations. This chapter ends with a conclusion on the specific and irreplaceable contributions of Christians in the Middle East (F).

The *Conclusion* seeks to see what lies ahead for Middle Eastern Christians and what they should hope for:

> We must make a firm decision for the future, which will be shaped by how we manage to treat others and forge alliances with people of good will in our society. We need a faith which becomes involved in the life of society, a faith which serves to

---

14   *Lineamenta*, § 43.

15   It is a source of pride that the ecumenical work and endeavors of the PRO ORIENTE foundation are specifically mentioned in the *Lineamenta*: 'From time to time, the *Pro Oriente* Foundation of Vienna gathers together the Catholic and Orthodox Churches of the region for theological and ecumenical reflection.' (*Lineamenta*, § 56)

remind the Christians of the Middle East of the inspirational words: 'Do not be afraid, little flock!' (Lk 12:32). You have a mission, you are to fulfill it and assist your Church and your country to grow and develop in peace, justice and equality for all citizens.[16]

SOME CONTRIBUTIONS OF PRO ORIENTE:
THE SECOND COLLOQUIUM SYRIACUM IN VIENNA/AUSTRIA
AND THE STUDY SEMINAR IN SULAYMANIAH/IRAQ

It became clear from various announcements, from the time of the preparatory work, that Orthodox, Muslim and Jewish observers were supposed to be present. Nevertheless, since PRO ORIENTE had been informed by the (Oriental) Orthodox and Assyrian Churches that the invitations to 'non-Catholic' observers had not yet been sent in May 2010, the foundation took the initiative and sent a letter, signed by its President Johann Marte to Archbishop Nikola Eterović, which stated that, from 'the perspective of PRO ORIENTE, from the experience of our work and in the ecumenical spirit of the II Vatican Council, we would like strongly to suggest that observers of the Christian Churches of the Middle East—Orthodox, Oriental Orthodox (Coptic, Syrian, Armenian) and Assyrian as well as representatives of the Middle East Council of Churches (MECC)—get invited to the Special Assembly for the Middle East in October 2010'.[17] Attached to the letter was the Final Report of the *Second PRO ORIENTE Colloquium Syriacum*, which took place in Vienna, November 2009.[18]

From its beginnings in 1964, PRO ORIENTE—as a foundation of the Archdiocese of Vienna (Austria) and therefore in the context of the Latin Catholic tradition—has focused not only on the (Byzantine) Orthodox Church but has also included the Christian traditions of the Orient. Since the early 1970s the Foundation has maintained close contact with Oriental (Orthodox) Christianity.[19]

---

16 *Lineamenta*, § 88.
17 Cf. Johann Marte, 'Letter to Archbishop Nicola Eterović', 20 May 2010 (Archive Pro Oriente Vienna).
18 See Appendix I.
19 Cf. especially the non-official Consultations between Theologians of the Oriental Orthodox Churches and the Roman Catholic Church, published in *Wort und*

For more than a decade, PRO ORIENTE has also been facilitating mutual exchange between the Syriac Churches through its former 'Syriac Dialogue' (with six non-official Consultations, 1994-2005) and has therefore contributed to a better understanding of the spiritual, liturgical, patristic and theological treasures that derive from their sacred tradition. These non-official consultations focused mainly on Christology and its historical contexts, and on the *raze/roze*, i.e. the Sacraments of the Syriac Churches.[20]

In the context of a changing ecumenical landscape and several ecumenical problems concerning the family of Oriental Orthodox Churches of the Middle East and the Assyrian Church of the East, PRO ORIENTE decided to start a new endeavour called *PRO ORIENTE Studies of the Syriac Tradition.* For these studies PRO ORIENTE has formed a *Forum Syriacum*, a team of representatives and expert scholars in Syriac studies and from Syriac Churches, who commit themselves to the promotion of the Syriac heritage, mutual enrichment, and better understanding within their Churches. This *PRO ORIENTE Forum Syriacum* advises and consults the Foundation in order to develop appropriate studies and helps to coordinate research projects. Within the *PRO ORIENTE Forum Syriacum* there is also an exchange of current developments of the Syriac Churches to learn about their sufferings and successes, and to strengthen the solidarity of those who belong to the Syriac tradition.

Since this new approach, two *PRO ORIENTE Colloquia Syriaca* have taken place: the first on the topic 'Syriac Churches encountering Islam: Past Experiences and Future Perspectives' in Salzburg (14-16 November 2007)[21]

Wahrheit. Revue for Religion and Culture Supplementary Issue 1-5 (1971, 1973, 1976, 1978, 1988). For a comprehensive analysis cf. Dietmar W Winkler, *Koptische Kirche und Reichskirche. Altes Schisma und neuer Dialog.* Mit einem Vorwort von Franz Kardinal König (*Innsbrucker theologische Studien* 48). Innsbruck, Tyrol, 1997, esp. Part C. *Idem*, 'Die altorientalischen Kirchen im ökumenischen Dialog der Gegenwart', in Christian Lange/Karl Pinggéra, eds., *Die altorientalischen Kirchen. Glaube und Geschichte*, WBG, Darmstadt, 2010, pp. 89-122.

20   Cf. Sebastian P Brock's contribution in this volume. For a comprehensive analyses cf. Dietmar W Winkler, *Ostsyrisches Christentum. Studien zu Christologie, Ekklesiologie und zu den ökumenischen Dialogen der Assyrischen Kirche des Ostens* (Studien zur orientalischen Kirchengeschichte 26), Lit, Münster, 2003; *idem.*, 'Dogmatic and Historical Results of the first three Pro Oriente Syriac Consultations', in PRO ORIENTE, ed., *Syriac Dialogue 4*, Vienna, 2001, pp. 121-137; *idem*, 'Between Progress and Setback: The Ecumenical Dialogues of the Assyrian Church of the East', in PRO ORIENTE, ed., *Syriac Dialogue 4*. Vienna, 2001, pp. 138-151.

21   Cf. Dietmar W Winkler, ed., 'Syriac Churches Encountering Islam: Past Experiences

and the second one on 'Syriac Christianity in the Middle East and India today: Contributions and Challenges' in Vienna (4-6 November 2009). It was in the context of the latter meeting that PRO ORIENTE decided, on the invitation of Archbishop Mar Louis Sako, to hold the next meeting in Iraq and to combine this with a study seminar on the Middle East Synod. However, the Second *Colloquium Syriacum* had already picked up many of the themes and challenges which were now mentioned in the *Lineamenta* of the Special Synod,[22] and it therefore seemed highly appropriate to send the joint results, which were discussed in the ecumenical context of all the Syriac Churches, i.e. Assyrian and Ancient Church of the East, the Syrian Orthodox and Malankara Orthodox Churches and the Eastern Catholic Churches of the Syriac tradition (Maronites, Chaldeans, Syrian Catholic, Syro-Malabar and Syro-Malankara Churches), to the General Secretary of the Synod of Bishops.

The study seminar on the Middle East Synod took place on 26-27 May 2010, in Sulaymaniyah, Iraq. Along with expert scholars from PRO ORIENTE, Archbishop-Metropolitans, Bishops, and Reverend Fathers of all the above mentioned Churches participated, with the exception of the Malankara Orthodox Churches and the Syro-Malankara Catholic Church, who were prevented from coming to Iraq. The Pontifical Council for Promoting Christian Unity were also represented, and with a letter of 17 May 2010, signed by Archbishop Cyril Vasil SJ and Mgr Maurizio Malvestiti, the Congregation for the Eastern Churches apologized for not being able to send a participant, but expressed its lively interest in the results of the study seminar.[23] The final report[24] has been sent to the members of the pre-synodal Council and to the General Secretary of the Synod.

Since this study seminar was the only ecumenical preparatory meeting for the Middle East Synod, it is evident that some points were seen in a wider perspective. The first three points of the final report are therefore worth mentioning:

> The Special Assembly of the Synod of Bishops for the Middle East is characteristically different from similar Synods concerning different geographical areas. In the Middle East, we are faced with the unique ecclesiastical situation that the Catholic Oriental Churches, with the exception of the Maronites, have a long common spiritual and liturgical tradition with their

---

and Future Perspectives', *Pro Oriente Studies in the Syriac Tradition* 1, Gorgias, Piscataway, NJ, 2010.

22 Cf. Appendix I.

23 Oriental Congregation, Letter to Dr Johann Marte, 17 May 2010 (archive PRO ORIENTE).

24 Cf. Appendix II.

Orthodox Sister-Churches. For this reason we believe that the invited persons from the Orthodox Churches should be present at the Synod not only as fraternal delegates, but should be able to fully participate in the various activities during the Synod. In general we are concerned about the constant ecumenical dimension of the whole synodal process in its different stages. For instance we would have liked that the Orthodox Churches had been invited to take part at the preparatory stage and we hope that they will also be able to participate in the implementation of the decisions and recommendations of the Synod. The challenges put to the Eastern Catholic and Orthodox Churches are common, a supplementary reason for close cooperation. This is particularly true of the burning issue of massive emigration from the Middle East.[25]

THE *INSTRUMENTUM LABORIS*

With some fifty pages the *Instrumentum laboris* is a more voluminous and much more substantial document than the *Lineamenta*, since it integrates the reactions of the bishops, bishops' conferences and religious institutions of the Catholic Middle East. The structure remained more or less the same, with minor corrections, especially in Part III, concerning Christian witness.

The first chapter better elaborates the necessity of catechesis and properly prepared members of faithful. The chapter in the *Lineamenta* called 'Witnessing together with other Churches and Communities' is now named 'Ecumenism', which is rather more precise; the chapters on relations with Judaism and Muslims become somewhat stronger. In the chapter on witnessing in society, the paragraphs on the problems dealing with 'Modernity' are more specific.

Some points should be highlighted: in the preface Archbishop Nikola Eterović underlines that for many 'the present-day situation in the Middle East is much like that of the primitive Christian community in the Holy Land', which had to face difficulties and persecution.

---

25   PRO ORIENTE Final Report Study Seminar, Sulaymaniah (Iraq), pp. 1-3.

Lineamenta	Instrumentum Laboris
PREFACE	PREFACE
INTRODUCTION	INTRODUCTION
A. The Aim of the Synod	A. The Goal of the Synod
B. A Reflection Guided by Sacred Scripture	B. A Reflection Guided by Holy Scripture
Questions	
I. THE CATHOLIC CHURCH IN THE MIDDLE EAST	I. THE CATHOLIC CHURCH IN THE MIDDLE EAST
A. The Situation of Christians in the Middle East	A. The Situation of Christians in the Middle East
1. An Historical Sketch: Unity in Diversity	1. An Historical Sketch: Unity in Diversity
2. Apostolicity and Missionary Vocation	2. Apostolicity and the Missionary Vocation
3. The Role of Christians in Society, Despite their Small Number	3. The Role of Christians in Society, Although a Small Minority
B. The Challenges Facing Christians	B. The Challenges Facing Christians
1. The Political Conflict in the Region	1. Political Conflicts in the Region
2. Freedom of Religion and Conscience	2. Freedom of Religion and Conscience
3. Christians and Developments in Contemporary Islam	3. Christians and the Evolution of Contemporary Islam
4. Emigration	4. Emigration
5. The Immigration of Christians to the Middle East from the World Over	5. The Immigration of Christians to the Middle East from the World Over
C. The Christian Response in Daily Life	C. The Response of Christians in Daily Life
Questions	
II ECCLESIAL COMMUNION	II. ECCLESIAL COMMUNION
A. Introduction	
B. Communion within the Catholic Church and between the Various Churches	A. The Communion in the Catholic Church and Among the Different Churches
C. Communion among Bishops, Clergy and the Lay-Faithful	B. The Communion among the Bishops, Clergy and Faithful
Questions	

III. CHRISTIAN WITNESS

A. Witnessing to the Gospel within the Church: Catechesis and Works

B. Witnessing Together with other Churches and Communities

C. Particular Relations with Judaism

D. Relations with Muslims

E. The Contribution of Christians to Society

1. Two Challenges for Our Countries

2. Christians at the Service of Society in their Countries

3. State-Church Relations

F. Conclusion: The Specific and Irreplaceable Contribution of the Christian

Questions

III. CHRISTIAN WITNESS

A. Witnessing in the Church: Catechesis

1. A Catechesis for Our Times, by Properly Prepared Members of the Faithful

2. Catechetical Methods

B. A Renewed Liturgy Faithful to Tradition

C. Ecumenism

D. Relations with Judaism

1. Vatican II: The Theological Basis for Relations with Judaism

2. The Present-Day Magisterium of the Church

3. The Desire and Difficulty of Dialogue with Judaism

E. Relations with Muslims

F. Witnessing in Society

1. The Ambiguity of 'Modernity'

2. Muslims and Christians Must Pursue a Common Path Together

G. The Specific and Unique Contribution of Christians

CONCLUSION

What is the Future for Middle Eastern Christians? 'Do not be afraid little flock!'

A. What Lies Ahead for Middle Eastern Christians?

B. Hope

CONCLUSION

What does the Future hold for Christians in the Middle East? 'Do not be afraid, O little flock!'

A. What Lies Ahead for Middle East Christians?

B. Hope

The introduction underlines the principal aims of the Synod: These are firstly 'to confirm and strengthen the members of the Catholic Church in their Christian identity, through the Word of God and the Sacraments,' and secondly 'to foster ecclesial communion among the *sui iuris* Churches, so that they can bear witness to Christian life in an authentic, joyous and attractive way.'[26]

The first part focuses on the *Catholic Church in the Middle East*, recalling that all the Churches in the world 'trace their roots to the Church of Jerusalem.'[27] It also recalls that the Churches of the Middle East are apostolic in origin and that it 'would indeed be a great loss for the universal Church if Christianity were to disappear or be diminished in the very place where it was born.'[28] Here lies the 'grave responsibility ... to maintain the Christian faith in these holy lands.'[29] According to the *Instrumentum laboris*, Christians, despite their 'low numbers', 'are entitled to be a part of the fabric of society and identify themselves with their respective homelands.'[30] Their disappearance would mean a loss in the pluralism of the Middle East. Catholics are called to promote the concept of 'positive laicity' of the state to 'eliminate the theocratic character of government' and allow 'greater equality among citizens of different religions, thereby fostering the promotion of a sound democracy, positively secular in nature, which fully acknowledges the role of religion, also in public life, while completely respecting the distinction between the religious and civil orders.'[31]

The document then underlines the fact that regional conflicts make the situation of Christians even more fragile. 'The Israeli occupation of Palestinian Territories is creating difficulties in everyday life, inhibiting freedom of movement, the economy and religious life (access to the Holy Places is dependent on military permission which is granted to some and denied to others

---

26 *Instrumentum laboris*, § 3.
27 *Instrumentum laboris*, § 4. In the English text of *Instrumentum laboris* 15 and 16 it should be 'Oriental Orthodox' rather than 'Eastern Orthodox'. In *Instrumentum laboris*, p. 17, it would be historically more correct to read 'Later, from the 11th century onwards, the Great Schism occurred ... rather than 'Later, at the beginning of the 11th century, the Great Schism occurred ...'
28 *Instrumentum laboris*, § 19.
29 *Ibid.*
30 *Instrumentum laboris*, § 24.
31 *Instrumentum laboris*, § 25.

on security grounds).'[32] Christians are the main victims of the war in Iraq.[33] 'In Lebanon, Christians are deeply divided at the political and confessional level ... In Egypt, the rise of political Islam on the one hand, and the disengagement of Christians (forcefully at times) from civil society on the other, lead to severe difficulties ... In other countries, authoritarianism or dictatorships force the population, Christians included, to bear everything in silence so as to safeguard the essential aspects of living. In Turkey, the idea of "secularism" is currently posing more problems for full religious freedom in the country.'[34]

Christians are exhorted to remain strong in their commitment to society, despite being tempted to discouragement. 'In the Middle East, freedom of religion customarily means freedom of worship and not freedom of conscience, that is, the freedom to believe or not believe, to practise openly one's religion, privately or publicly, or to change one's religion for another. Generally speaking, religion in the Middle East is a social and even a national choice, not an individual one. To change one's religion is perceived as a betrayal of the society, culture and nation, which are founded, for the most part, on a religious tradition.'[35] For this reason 'conversion to the Christian faith is perceived to be from self-interest and not authentic religious conviction. Oftentimes, the conversion of Muslims is forbidden by State law.'[36] In the meantime, Islamic extremism continues to grow in the entire area creating 'a threat to everyone, Christians and Muslims alike'.[37] In this context of conflict, economic difficulties and political and religious limitations, Christians continue to emigrate. 'International politics often times pay no attention to the existence of Christians, and the fact that they are victims, at times the first to suffer, goes unnoticed. This is also a major cause of emigration.'[38]

Part two is again dedicated to Ecclesial Communion, but above all communion among the various Catholic Churches of the Middle East. It shows a classical Catholic ecclesiology: 'Communion within the universal Church is principally manifested in two ways: in the first place, through Baptism and the Eucharist, and, secondly, through communion with the Bishop of Rome, the Successor of St Peter, chief among the Apostles, "permanent and visible source and foundation of the unity of faith and

---

32 *Instrumentum laboris*, § 32.
33 Cf.. *Instrumentum laboris*, § 33.
34 *Instrumentum laboris*, § 34.
35 *Instrumentum laboris*, § 37.
36 *Instrumentum laboris*, § 38.
37 Cf.. *Instrumentum laboris*, § 41.
38 *Instrumentum laboris*, § 43.

communion."[39] Communion among the various members of the same Church or Patriarchate is based on the model of communion with the universal Church[40] and the successor of St Peter, the Bishop of Rome. At the level of the Patriarchal Church, communion is expressed by a Synod which gathers the bishops of an entire community around the Patriarch, the Father and Head of his Church.'[41] Christians are called to see themselves as members of the Catholic Church in the Middle East and not simply as members of a particular Church.

Part three deals with the theme of Christian Witness, reiterating the importance of catechesis in knowing and transmitting the faith. A new chapter on the liturgy was included: 'In this regard, many responses express a desire for liturgical renewal, which, while remaining firmly grounded in tradition, takes into account modern sensibilities as well as present-day spiritual and pastoral needs.'

The urgent need for ecumenism, overcoming prejudices and mistrust through dialogue and collaboration is emphasized. The document rejects 'a proselytism' which employs means not in keeping with the Gospel. 'Ecumenism calls for a sincere effort to overcome prejudices in order to work for a better mutual understanding, so as to attain the fullness of visible communion in the faith, sacraments and the apostolic ministry. Ecumenical dialogue is marked by a common quest for truth, particularly concerning the Church.' *(Ut unum sint)* This dialogue takes place at various levels. On the official level, the Holy See has taken initiatives with all the Churches in the Middle East, in collaboration with the Catholic Churches. On the unofficial level, the *Pro Oriente* Foundation of Vienna has brought Eastern Catholics and Orthodox together for an ecumenical, theological reflection, which has already produced many fruits in the areas of Christology and ecclesiology.'[42] 'An essential instrument of ecumenism is dialogue, which should take place in a positive atmosphere so as to increase mutual understanding, overcome suspicion and work in defence of religious values, collaborate on projects for the benefit of society, foster understanding among the faithful in each country and better their living conditions. Given a history of misunderstandings, a *healing of memories* is necessary to free souls from various prejudices through accepting one another and working together for things in common.'[43]

---

39   *Instrumentum laboris*, § 55.
40   *Instrumentum laboris*, § 71.
41   *Instrumentum laboris*, § 57.
42   *Instrumentum laboris*, § 78.
43   *Instrumentum laboris*, § 80.

With reference to the theological basis to be found in Vatican II, relations to Judaism are also elaborated. Dialogue with the Jews is defined as essential, though at times not without its obstacles, being affected by the Israeli-Palestinian conflict.[44] The Church hopes that 'both peoples may live in peace in a homeland of their own, within secure and internationally recognised borders.'[45] The document firmly rejects anti-Semitism, underlining that 'current animosity between Arabs and Jews seems to be political in character' and therefore foreign to any ecclesial discussion. Christians are asked 'to bring a spirit of reconciliation, based on justice and equality of the two parties. The Churches in the Middle East also call upon all involved to take into account the distinction between the religious reality and the political one.'[46]

The Catholic Church's relations with Muslims also have their foundation in Vatican II, and are mentioned in the *Instrumentum laboris*. 'Oftentimes relations between Christians and Muslims are difficult, because Muslims make no distinction between religion and politics, thereby relegating Christians to the precarious position of being considered non-citizens, despite the fact that they were citizens of their countries long before the rise of Islam. The key to harmonious living between Christians and Muslims is to recognise religious freedom and human rights.'[47] Christians are called upon not to isolate 'themselves in ghettos and a defensive and reclusive attitude which is sometimes seen in minority groups.'[48] To work together for peace, social justice and freedom the younger generation especially has to become well educated in schools and universities. 'To do this, some responses suggest that educational texts be revised, especially materials for teaching religion, so as to eliminate all prejudices and stereotypes concerning others.'[49]

The document also analyses the strong impact of 'modernity', which 'to most Muslim believers is perceived to be atheistic and immoral and a cultural invasion, threatening them and upsetting their value-system.'[50] 'At the same time, "modernity" is the struggle for justice and equality, the defence of

---

44   Cf. *Instrumentum laboris*, § 89.
45   *Ibid.* With reference to Benedict XVI, *Discourse at Ben Gurion Airport Tel Aviv (11 May 2009)*.
46   *Instrumentum laboris*, § 90.
47   *Instrumentum laboris*, § 96.
48   *Instrumentum laboris*, § 97.
49   *Instrumentum laboris*, § 98.
50   *Instrumentum laboris*, § 104.

rights.'[51] In that sense Christians and the Churches have a special contribution to make in the area of justice and peace. It is the Christian duty, 'which implies the double obligation of fighting the evils in our society, be they political, juridical, economic, social or moral, and contributing to the building of a more just, sound and humane society.'[52]

The document then examines the topic of evangelisation, which in a Muslim society can only happen through witness. The charitable activities of Christian communities 'towards all without distinction, to the poorest and those pushed to the periphery of society, represents the clearest way of spreading the Christian message.'[53]

In its conclusion, the document points out the 'great concern for the present difficulties Christians are facing,' yet, at the same time express 'a hope, founded on the Christian faith … For decades, the unresolved Israeli-Palestinian conflict, disregard for international law, the selfishness of great powers and the lack of respect for human rights have disrupted the stability of the region and subjected entire populations to a level of violence which tempts them to despair. Many—Christians for the most part—are emigrating elsewhere. In the face of this challenge and sustained by the universal Christian community, Christians in the Middle East are called to respond to their vocation of service to society.'[54] The *Instrumentum Laboris* finally quotes Lk 12.32: ' "Do not be afraid, little flock." You have a mission; the growth of your country and the vitality of your Church depend on you. This will only be achieved with peace, justice and equality for all citizens!'

The Middle East Synod will hopefully raise awareness through the press and media in a wider public of the sincere challenges and profound contributions of Middle Eastern Christianity, and have an impact on the Middle Eastern states to contribute to justice and equality for the Churches in that troubled region.

---

51 *Instrumentum laboris*, § 103.
52 *Instrumentum laboris*, § 106.
53 *Instrumentum laboris*, § 115.
54 *Instrumentum laboris*, § 118.

APPENDIX I

PRO ORIENTE
Second Colloquium Syriacum
'Syriac Christianity in the Middle East and India today:
Contributions and Challenges'
Vienna, 4-6 November 2009

FINAL REPORT

1. With its *Studies in the Syriac tradition* PRO ORIENTE intends to facilitate mutual understanding and exchange as well as to promote the common heritage of the various Churches belonging to the historical Syriac tradition. In continuation of the former 'Syriac Dialogue' (1994-2005), the *PRO ORIENTE Forum Syriacum* was formed in October 2006 to face the challenge of an ecumenically changing context and to find practical ways for fruitful exchange on issues of common concern. The *Forum Syriacum* aims, in a true ecumenical spirit, to learn about the achievements and sufferings of the respective Churches and to strengthen the solidarity among, and with, those who belong to the Syriac tradition.

2. The PRO ORIENTE Forum Syriacum therefore decided in its meeting in Aleppo on July 1-2, 2008, to organize the *Second PRO ORIENTE Colloquium Syriacum* on the topic 'Syriac Christianity in the Middle East and India today: Contributions and Challenges.' The Middle Eastern countries under consideration were Iran, Iraq, Turkey, Syria and Lebanon.

3. At the inaugural session, Wednesday morning, November 4, 2009, the Archbishop of Vienna, H. E. Cardinal Christoph Schönborn, presided over the opening prayer and cordially welcomed the participants. He recalled the spirit and vision of the founder of PRO ORIENTE, the late Cardinal Franz König, whose life was devoted to dialogue and a profound love for Oriental Christianity. A greeting of Cardinal Walter Kasper, President of the Pontifical Council for Promoting Christian Unity, was read. He expressed his deep hope that the studies of the PRO ORIENTE Colloquium Syriacum, highlighting the urgency of religious freedom and pluralism, will contribute to a strengthening of ecumenical dialogue. Further, he encouraged the participants to reflect together on the motives and the impact of emigration for the future of Christianity in the Middle East. PRO ORIENTE President Johann Marte welcomed the participants, who came from India, Lebanon, Syria, USA, Great Britain, France, Austria, Germany, the Netherlands, Italy.

4. For spiritual guidance, participants prayed together the Morning Prayers according to the East Syriac (Hudra) and West Syriac (Sh'imo) liturgy.

5. On the evening of November 5, a public panel was held at the Diplomatische Akademie on the topic 'Israel, Palestine and Jordan: Perspectives after the visit of Pope Benedict XVI to the Holy Land'. The main speakers were: Martin Tamcke (Göttingen, Germany), Anthony O'Mahony (Heythrop College, University of London) and Fr Frans Bouwen (Jerusalem). The participants were also invited for a reception by the Apostolic Nuncio Archbishop Peter Zurbriggen in the Apostolic Nunciature in Vienna, and welcomed for a dinner-reception by the Ambassador of the Republic of Iraq, Mr Tariq Aqrawi. The participants want to thank the staff of the Pallottihaus for their generous hospitality.

6. The study days of the *Second PRO ORIENTE Colloquium Syriacum* were structured according to the following topics: In its first part, the *contributions* of Syriac Christians to their societies in the fields of culture, education and civil society throughout the history in the Middle East and India were taken into consideration. In its second part, the Colloquium focused on the main present *challenges* of living and professing the Christian faith in a multi-religious and diverse society, with special attention to religious freedom, education and personal status. The final session was devoted to the vital question of continuous *emigration* of Christians from India and the Middle East.

7. The following ten papers were presented:

Christianity in the Middle East: Some historical Facts and demographic Figures (Dietmar W Winkler, Salzburg, Austria)

Cultural, social and educational Contributions of Syriac Christianity in South India (Baby Varghese, Kottayam, Kerala, India)

Christians in Iran and Iraq: Which Contribution to Society? (Herman Teule, Nijmegen, The Netherlands)

Cultural, social and educational Contributions of Syriac Christianity in Syria and Lebanon (Karam Rizk, Kaslik, Lebanon)

Religious Freedom, Education, Pluralism, Personal Status of Syriac Christianity (Family Rights) in India (Philip Nelpuraparambil, Changanassery, India)

The Church-State Relations in Modern Iraq (Anthony O'Mahony, Heythrop College, University of London)

Religious Freedom, Education, Pluralism, Personal Status of Syriac Christianity (Family Rights) in Syria and Turkey (Mar Gregorios Yohanna Ibrahim, Aleppo, Syria)

The Contribution of the Syriac Family to the Experience of the Islamo-Christian

Co-existence in Lebanon (Mar Paul Matar, Beirut, Lebanon)
Emigration of Syriac Christians moving from India—Motives and Impact (Mar Kuriakose Theophilose, Ernakulam, India)
Emigration of Syriac Christians moving from the Middle East—Motives and Impact (Martin Tamcke, Göttingen, Germany)

8. On the basis of these studies and after extensive discussion and exchange, the following points were emphasized:

On Contributions of Syriac Christians

(a) In India the contribution of the Syriac Christians to the cultural and social life of Kerala, in particular in relation to education, in schools for both boys and girls, in the areas of journalism, literature, political life, economic development, and industry have been significant. Although the Christian communities compose only a small percentage of the population, they have been a leaven in the society of Kerala as a whole. For instance, in the area of banking, one particularly valuable contribution has been in the development of micro-financing.

(b) Syriac Christians in India have been especially active in the development of Malayalam as a literary and cultural language in Kerala. Early on, the *Peshitta* (the canonical Syriac version of the Bible) was translated into Malayalam. Since the 1890s there have been continuing projects to translate the *Peshitta* into Malayalam, particularly the Gospels. Furthermore, in the early years of the nineteenth century, under the influence of the British, Bible translations were made from English versions of the scriptures translated from the original languages, Hebrew and Greek.

(c) In Iran the number of Christians is extremely small and the impossibility for them to have access to public functions makes it impossible to play a significant role in the society. Nevertheless the Assyrians, Chaldeans and Armenians are maintaining their own schools and are recognized as distinct ethnic identities.

(d) In Turkey, especially in the region of Tur 'Abdin, Syriac Christians have suffered periods of difficulty and hardship. In recent times, one can perceive a change in the attitude towards Christians in some academic and political circles. This development notwithstanding, a number of problems, such as integration into society and recognition of some juridical rights have not yet been resolved.

(e) Currently in Iraq the situation of Christians is in transition and extremely complex. The present plight of the indigenous Christians of the 'Cradle of Civilization' should be of urgent concern for the international community at large. Today's five autochthonous Syriac Churches have witnessed to Christianity in its Mesopotamian homeland since ancient times and long before the rise of Islam. Since the times of early Christianity these Churches have contributed to shaping and molding the Middle Eastern societies in intercultural exchange. Their impact on cultural, literary, social and political life throughout history should not be underestimated. Furthermore, today Christians in Iraq are a reminder that a society and a culture can never be monolithic, uniform or mono-religious (which is a temptation for some Islamic societies).

(f) Recently the situation of Iraqi and Iranian Christians has been complicated by the activity of some evangelical movements undertaken to the detriment of the autochthonous communities.

(g) There was much discussion of the proposed autonomous region for Christians in the Nineveh Plain in Iraq. Some advocate a 'soft autonomy' that would take into account the shared history of the Christians, as well as their cultural and national concerns; and the need to feel at home in their country. It was pointed out that this last suggestion should not be easily rejected. Rather, one must consider it within the perspective of justice for ethnic and religious particularities in the country; it is not a matter of proposing a Christian ghetto. As a matter of fact, the idea of a homeland for indigenous Christian groups, such as the Assyrians, goes back to the end of the First World War. Fears were also expressed in regard to the future of religious minorities in Iraq in general and in this region in particular. The Assembly of the Catholic bishops in Iraq stated on 29 October 2009 that 'the Iraqi Christians are an indigenous component of the Iraqi nation and that their loyalty is to Iraq. They want to continue to live in collaboration with their brothers and sisters in good and in bad and to strengthen the harmonic conviviality. They do not want to live isolated from them in any way.'

(h)   The beautiful monuments of Christian art and monasticism in Syria and Lebanon witness to the spiritual power of Syriac Christianity throughout history. Within their genuine homeland, these Syriac churches as well as Christians individually have engaged themselves in the educational sector, in the domain of literature, arts and administration.

(i)   In Lebanon the Christian communities, especially the Maronites, have contributed essentially to the various aspects of the socio-cultural and political life of the nation, especially in the area of education with the foundation of a number of schools and of well known universities. Their social and political contribution is shaping the country significantly in matters of freedom, human rights and dialogue of cultures.

On Challenges

(j)   Concerning challenges there is a sharp contrast between the Indian and Middle Eastern situation. The basic reason for this is the difference in the respective constitutions of the Nation-States and the embedding in different cultures.

(k)   The Indian Constitution specifically protects and safeguards the rights of religious and other minorities, this is also the case of the Lebanese Constitution. Though provisions for a protection of religious minorities are not absent from the constitutions of some Middle Eastern states, their application on the local level is often not acknowledged.

(l)   The question of identity is a complex one. Plurality of identities applies to every individual in every society, depending on different contexts: this only becomes a problem when the wider society does not accept, or does not allow for one or more of these identities. In India the axiom 'Christian in religion, Indian in culture, and Eastern in worship' expresses the situation accurately. Here an important factor is that Indian culture is seen as a cultural mosaic where all have a place: unity lies in diversity. However, recent politicization of religion among certain sections of Hindu society, leading on occasion to open conflict and violence committed against religious minorities, as well as the emergence of certain propaganda within the Communist government of Kerala aimed at interfering with Christian educational institutions, are serious threats to the Indian culture of religious tolerance and freedom.

(m) In the Middle East the problems of identity, and especially Christian identity, are very different. What is lacking in many places is an acceptance of cultural diversity, and of some basic human rights involving a religious and cultural freedom to partake and play a role in the wider society.

(n) In order to promote human rights in the Middle East, there is an underlying essential need to achieve peace, justice and stability in this region as a whole.

(o) The situation of Christians in Syria is considerably better than in other Middle Eastern countries apart from Lebanon. For example, the government provides land for building places of worship, helps the churches as well as mosques in many other ways. Over a century ago, legislation allowed for the establishment of private schools belonging to churches or to certain religious orders. However, recent legislation has made it no longer possible for Churches as institutions to own schools.

(p) Despite the comparatively good situation for Christians in Syria, considerable numbers are leaving due to the sense of unease and the increasing marginalization which is experienced by Christians as extremist ideas increasingly make their presence felt, not only in the wider society, but also in some government circles.

(q) An essential topic was raised concerning conversions, which are only possible in one direction, with no possibility for return allowed. In mixed marriages the woman can keep her religion, but the man has to convert to Islam, and all the children will be raised as Muslims.

(r) The situation for Christians in Lebanon is in marked contrast to that elsewhere in the Middle East. Only here is there a widespread feeling of mutual respect and equality, leading to the possibility of effective dialogue on practical matters. The main reason for this is the large number of Christians and of Christian educational institutions where many Muslims are educated. Likewise the freedom of press and other media allows for the possibility of informing public opinion.

(s)   The situation of Syriac Christians in the Middle East remains fragile and unstable, and will do so as long as the wider political problems, above all the Israel/Palestine question, remain unresolved. If only a real peace could be achieved, then the whole situation for Christians and other minorities in the Middle East would undoubtedly be changed for the better, and many who left might want to return.

(t)   An acknowledgement of, and respect for, human rights and religious freedom are the key to the successful co-existence of Christians and Muslims.

On Emigration

(u)   For Syriac Christians, both in India and the Middle East, migration is not an entirely new phenomenon.

(v)   Regarding the migration of Syriac Christians from Kerala, it is important to note that they left their country for other states of India or abroad not because of persecution or political problems in India, but mainly for economic reasons. The impact of migration is being felt in every aspect of life in the State of Kerala. In particular, almost all families are affected by migration abroad in one way or another. Their integration into their new cultural environment is different according to the three main destinations: Gulf Region, United States of America or Europe. The relations of the migrants with their homeland and Syriac Indian culture remains generally very strong, and liturgical worship is still a central part of their social life. In the USA they are more easily assimilated and especially the youth are more oriented to Western culture.

(w)   Although the economic reasons for the emigration of Syriac

Christians from the Middle East are also very important, religious and cultural freedom, equal rights, the possibility to participate in the political life, fair educational opportunities are even more important (quite apart from the dire situation in Iraq).

(x) In general, Syriac Christians quickly integrate into the local communities of their host countries, taking advantage of educational opportunities. At the same time a change of consciousness in their relationship to the abandoned homeland is taking place.

(y) As for the situation of the migrants in their new environment and their relations to their homeland and traditional religious and cultural heritage the following are important points:

—For a harmonious integration of the migrant communities, the formation of the church leaders is of great importance, in the theological field as well as in openness to Western contemporary culture.

—For Syriac Christians who have emigrated the question remains, how can they preserve their religious and cultural identity and what influence can and should they exercise back in their homeland?

—It is necessary for the Western Churches to seize the opportunity of the presence of the Syriac Christian communities in their midst for a mutual enrichment. Those Churches should assist the Christians who have emigrated in every possible way to preserve their cultural and spiritual traditions (including their language) and welcome them in their guest society. This could be achieved for instance by making available church and educational facilities.

—A difficult problem is: What kind of engagements should Churches and persons or organisations develop with political society and civil authorities to help Syriac Christians to continue to live in their homeland, on the one hand, and to integrate harmoniously in their new environment, with a mutual enrichment for both hosts and guests?

—Lately, some countries or governments have encouraged Christians to leave the Middle East: what should be the reaction of our Churches? Another query is how can Christians in the West encourage and help Christians to remain in the Middle East since the fewer the Syriac Christians become in their homeland the more difficulties they face.

—Migration leads to the fact that many Syriac Christians are in danger of losing their religious and cultural roots. They are often absorbed into the larger Christian Churches of the West, or they may become completely secularized. This is a great loss, not only for themselves, but also for the whole of Christendom, the diversity of whose spiritual and cultural richness is thereby impoverished.

9. On the basis of the *Second Colloquium Syriacum* participants express their gratitude and their deep desire to pursue this initiative of PRO ORIENTE in the field of the common study of the Syriac tradition. It is to be hoped for that this enriching endeavour may help the Syriac Christians to better preserve and fructify their rich heritage and offer their unique contribution to the search for Christian unity. Participants therefore urge the *Forum Syriacum* to consider and decide upon the topic for the *Third Colloquium Syriacum*.

APPENDIX II

PRO ORIENTE
Ecumenical Study Seminar
'Special Assembly of the Synod of Bishops for the Middle East'
Sulaymaniyah (Iraq), May 26-27, 2010

In its endeavour of facilitating and supporting mutual understanding and exchange between the Oriental Churches (Catholic, Oriental Orthodox and Assyrian), PRO ORIENTE Foundation (Vienna/Austria) with its fifth *Forum Syriacum* organized a study seminar on the 'Special Assembly of the Synod of Bishops for the Middle East'. The study Seminar took place on 26-27 May 2010, at the invitation of Archbishop Louis Sako (Chaldean Archdiocese of Kirkuk) in Sulaymaniyah/Iraq.
Participating Archbishop-Metropolitans, Bishops, and Reverend Fathers named below came from the Assyrian Church of the East, the Ancient Church of the

East, the Syrian Orthodox Church, the Chaldean Church, the Maronite Church, the Syrian Catholic Church, and the Syro-Malabar Church. Likewise the Pontifical Council for Promoting Christian Unity, along with PRO ORIENTE expert scholars, were present. With a letter of May 17, 2010, signed by Archbishop Cyril Vasil SJ and Mons. Maurizio Malvestiti, the Congregation for the Eastern Churches apologized for not being able to send a participant, but expressed its lively interest in the results of the study seminar.

In the opening session, a letter of greeting of Cardinal Emmanuel III Delly, Patriarch of Babylon of the Chaldeans, was delivered, whereby he appreciates that this initiative of PRO ORIENTE could take place in Iraq.

Participants appreciated the reflections presented in the *Lineamenta,* and—after extensive discussion and exchange in plenary and workshops—would like to draw attention to the following points:

I. Relationship between Churches: Communion and Witness

1. The Special Assembly of the Synod of Bishops for the Middle East is characteristically different from similar Synods concerning different geographical areas. In the Middle East, we are faced with the unique ecclesiastical situation that the Catholic Oriental Churches, with the exception of the Maronites, have a long common spiritual and liturgical tradition with their Orthodox Sister-Churches.

2. For this reason we believe that the invited persons from the Orthodox Churches should be present at the Synod not only as fraternal delegates, but should be able to fully participate in the various activities during the Synod. In general we are concerned about the constant ecumenical dimension of the whole synodal process in its different stages. For instance we would have liked that the Orthodox Churches had been invited to take part at the preparatory stage and we hope that they will also be able to participate in the implementation of the decisions and recommendations of the Synod.

3. The challenges put to the Eastern Catholic and Orthodox Churches are common, a supplementary reason for close cooperation. This is particularly true of the burning issue of massive emigration from the Middle East.

4. For this reason one has to reconsider the division made in the *Lineamenta* (Ch. III Christian Witness), where a division is suggested between witnessing to the Gospel within the Church and witnessing together with local Orthodox Churches. Catechesis should not be considered an issue only for the Catholic Church, but should be elaborated in cooperation with

the other local Orthodox Churches.

5.   The concept of communion of Churches considered distinctively from jurisdictional communion launched some years ago, deserves ongoing and further study.

6.   One of the results of the Synod should be that the situation of the Christians in the Middle East come to be better known in the West. Now Middle East Christians are faced with ignorance and indifference. Initiatives should be taken to encourage Western Episcopal Synods, theological faculties, church members and youth organizations, etc. to undertake visits to the region. Serious analyses are to be offered to the West. There is a need to reach out also more to the media.

7.   In the field of witness: common witness is a form of communion. Possible new initiatives that can be taken (and which in some regions are already being taken) are: common schoolbooks, common school curricula, common pastoral work and diaconia, etc.

II. Witness to the Islamic World

1.   Christians and Muslims have a long history of coexistence. The present situation in the Middle East has to be studied and evaluated from this perspective, especially in the context of a growing political and extremist interpretation of Islam.

2.   In order to find an answer to political Islam, Christians and Muslims have to develop common strategies, e.g. in the field of study and research, by a common reading of Sacred Texts.

3.   Christians should also be encouraged and prepared to actively take part in the public life in the countries they are called to life in.

4.   It would be useful to develop a common program of promoting publications on different levels (academic and more popular) to present Christianity in a way that is understandable for the Muslim community. So far we have only isolated initiatives. A new apologetic endeavour in the good sense of the word is much needed.

5.   Educational institutions should impart a culture of coexistence, mutual respect and understanding. Joint educational programs are needed in this respect, where common religious, spiritual and cultural values are presented.

6.   Educators and religious leaders should have a good, reflective knowledge

of religion, not only of one's own community, but also of that of the other communities. They have to respect the religious sensitivities of all students. School authorities should take the necessary steps that textbooks used in educational institutions give proper information about the religions.

7. Periodical and occasional inter-religious meetings of religious leaders should be organized, not only in official, international encounters, but also on a more regional, local and intermediate level, since these kinds of gatherings are more effective for promoting better mutual understanding.

8. Media is a powerful instrument to promote a proper image of Christianity in the region. More coordinated efforts should be taken to ensure an objective presentation of Christian beliefs and values. It should be made clear that some evangelical movements of Western Christians give a distorted image of Christianity.

9. Both Christians and Muslims ought to be more open to the ideas of civil society, including the distinction between the religious and the political domains and the struggle against corruption and social injustice. Meetings intended for both decision and opinion makers (including future clergy and politicians) are to be organized. They also have to be informed on the historical developments of Christianity and Islam and their mutual relations (including some mutual misconceptions and negative experiences in the past).

10. True expertise has to be developed among Christians and Muslims concerning inter-religious dialogue (by university training, in seminaries and sharia schools, by special programs, etc.).

11. Another form of common witness is in the field of charity. Much needed housing projects, hospitals, care for handicapped persons, marginalized etc. However, all initiatives taken should not be limited to the Christian communities only, but should be for the benefit of all.

Final remarks

It would be useful to organize a follow up 'Synod' or meeting (preferably in the Middle East, e.g. convoked by the Council of Catholic Patriarchs of the East or another body) in order to evaluate the implementation of the decisions taken at the Synod.

Because of the urgency of the situation in the Middle East, we express the wish that the Apostolic Exhortation communicating the results of the Synod be published soon.

List of participants

Mar Joseph Powathil, Syro-Malabar Archbishop emeritus of Changanacherry, Kerala, India

Mar Gregorius Y. Ibrahim, Syrian Orthodox Metropolitan of Aleppo, Syria

Mar Mikhael Jules Al-Jamil, Archbishop and Apostolic Administrator, Rome, Italy

Mar Boulos Matar, Maronite Archbishop of Beirut, Lebanon

Mar Louis Sako, Chaldean Metropolitan of Kirkuk, Iraq

Mar Awa Royel, Assyrian Bishop of California, USA

Chorepiskopa George Khoshaba, Archdeacon of the Ancient Church of the East, London, Great Britain

Fr Frans Bouwen M.Afr., Editor-in-Chief of *Proche Orient Chrétien*, Jerusalem

Fr Philip Nelpuraparampil, Secretary of the Syro-Malabar Synodical Commission for Public Affairs

Fr Gabriel Quicke, Pontifical Council for Promoting Christian Unity, Rome, Italy

PRO ORIENTE experts:

Dr Johann Marte, President of PRO ORIENTE Foundation

Dr Aho Shemunkasho, University of Salzburg, Austria, secretary of the study seminar

Prof Herman Teule, Radboud University, Nijmegen, Holland; University of Louvain, Belgium

Prof Dietmar W Winkler, University of Salzburg, Austria; research director of the Study Seminar

EASTERN CATHOLICISM:
MODERN HISTORICAL, ECCLESIAL AND CONTEMPORARY CONTEXTS
A Background Study to the Synod for the Middle East

Constantin Simon SJ

INTRODUCTION

Jerusalem. The Holy Sepulchre. The Syrian-Orthodox Chapel. A tumbledown chapel which looks like an outhouse ... the walls and ceiling are black—the legacy of centuries of smoke ... At the south wall there is a hole through which by bending one's body backwards, one may enter the tomb of Nicodemus and Joseph of Arimathea. But suddenly, someone lays out a carpet, the altar and the sacred vessels are adorned with brocade of cloth of gold, they array the archbishop in striking scarlet vestments and they place in his hand the golden cross of benediction, from the foot of which hangs a long swath of purple cloth also ornamented with gold, while in the other hand they place a crosier topped by two bronze serpents and the cross, the symbols of salvation in both the Old and New Testaments. Two priest monks array themselves in their stoles, one of turquoise and the other of green. Three deacons begin their service, garbed likewise in stoles of motley colour: red, violet and green. Out comes the thurible and the ripidia with their little bells, they light the torches and candles, many candles for such a tiny area. The Holy Sacrifice is about to commence and behold—the chapel outhouse takes on an air of paradise ...[1]

No, it was not I who witnessed the liturgical epiphany with which I begin. It was a French Canadian pilgrim to the Churches of the East. Neither did he witness an Eastern Catholic but rather a Syrian, non-Chalcedonian, 'Jacobite' Syrian Orthodox service. But I too, on the few occasions when I was afforded

---

1   Lucien Coutu, *Pèlerinage aux Églises d'Orient*, Quebec, 1990, pp. 182-183.

the chance to visit the Holy City of Jerusalem, did manage to spend a few moments in the dismal Syrian Orthodox chapel at the rear of the *cubiculum* in which lay the body of the Lord, although when I was there no liturgy was in progress and the transfiguration from sordid to sublime which our author describes did not occur. But I think that the description above is exemplary in that it juxtaposes the dignity and spiritual wealth of the Eastern Churches of the Middle East with today's often sordid and grim reality.

Actually, I must confess to being much more familiar with the history and culture of the Slavic Orthodox Churches and in particular the Russian Orthodox Church; I know no Arabic and feel a bit unequal to the demands placed upon me in speaking about the Eastern Catholic Churches of the Middle East in preparation for the coming Synod of Bishops. But a few weeks ago, during one of my many visits to Moscow, I was taken to tour the monastery of Patriarch Nikon's New Jerusalem, located in the village of Istra in the Russian countryside to the north-west of Moscow. The Russian patriarch, a liturgical reformer, whose reforms had disastrous consequences for his own Church, as well as an ardent Hellenist, had built a sanctuary which in his own mind was to duplicate that of the Holy Sepulchre in Jerusalem, but on Russian soil.[2] Today, most of it is still sadly in ruins, in spite of promises for further renovation. But one can still recognise the duplicate of the holy *cubiculum*, of the stone on which Christ's body was anointed and which in Jerusalem is a focal point of local Arab Christian devotion, and of a replica Golgotha at the top of a treacherous staircase, a part of the complex which miraculously did not suffer damage from the German bombardment and ensuing blaze. But while being guided around the church, the monk, incongruously dressed in soldier's camouflage, pointed out a chapel to the rear of the huge edifice etched with the curious inscription: '*zde sluzhat armjane*— here officiate the Armenians'—although no 'Monophysite' Armenians had ever served or would have been allowed to celebrate a liturgy in the Russian monastery. Nikon, who received much of his information from his two Arab guests, Makarios, Patriarch of Antioch and his son, Deacon Paul of Aleppo, thought to duplicate the Church of the Sepulchre in every detail— yes, through the visor of the Russian imagination, but still in every facet—so significant was the Church of Jerusalem and the Christians of the eastern Patriarchates in the mind of the Russian hierarch. And Nikon had been told that even

---

2   For a more complete discussion of the importance of Jerusalem and the Holy Land in Russian religious culture compare Richard M Price, 'The Holy Land in Old Russian Culture', *Studies in Church History*, 36 (2000), pp. 250-262.

the, for him, heretical Armenians claimed their chapel in that most sacred sanctuary of the Christian Church. And so he determined that they should enjoy a symbolic place in his own replica.

How brightly loomed Jerusalem, the Holy City of Christ's passion and resurrection, in the consciousness of this seventeenth-century Russian patriarch and how aware he was of his bond of communion with the ancient Churches of Jerusalem, Constantinople, Alexandria and Antioch, all then as still now, drowning in a sea of Islam. What a pity that times have changed and the idea of the significance of the Churches of the Middle East has dimmed at least for the Western Christian. Our Canadian pilgrim went on to deplore the fact that Western visitors to the Holy Land often take little or no interest in the affairs of the local Churches, which remain for them a closed book or as though hidden by a veil. They content themselves with innumerable church services celebrated in their own Western tradition at the holy sites and with the minutiae of ecclesiastical architecture. How sad, our author notes, since the local Churches which hold no interest for the Western pilgrim are often of equal antiquity to the stones which inebriate his fantasy, so enthralled by ecclesiastical archaeology. Yet the stones are dead matter: the Churches are a living, if dwindling, reality.[3]

I do not propose to discuss the subject of the Eastern Churches and particularly the Eastern Catholic Churches in any great detail. Rather I will confine myself to briefly identifying the protagonists of our story, and then by looking at them from both the outside and from the inside. How do Rome and Orthodoxy view the Eastern Catholic Churches of the Middle East and how do they view themselves? Finally, what are their perspectives, if any, for the future?

DIVISION AND THE IDENTITY STRUGGLE

An oxymoron is appropriate here. If the Middle Eastern Christians are united by anything it is by their awareness of their division. Division is for them a vital issue since it determines their precious identity and justifies their *raison d'être* in the ecclesiastical as well as in the political world. We should remember that in the not so distant past, the Ottoman *millet* system grouped them into divisions which blurred the religious and political spheres.

Today, their division may be conceived as at least sevenfold: faith, the division of Chalcedonian or non-Chalcedonian, religious confession, ecclesial

3   Coutu, pp. 94-98.

identity or ritual tradition, to use the older term, ethnicity, language, patrimony. It is obvious that their Christianity sets them apart from their majority Muslim and Jewish neighbours. It is also evident that Catholicism and Orthodoxy are different religious confessions, despite their dogmatic similarity. Therefore, we must concentrate on the ritual, ethnic, and linguistic differences with a brief look at the state borders which divide them politically.

Eastern Catholics of the Middle East all derive from the ancient patriarchates of Alexandria, Antioch and Jerusalem as well as later from Constantinople and the Catholicates established outside the frontiers of the Roman Empire. They also, with one exception, all issue from the Orthodox Chalcedonian, non-Chalcedonian in the case of the Alexandrian Copts and Ethiopians or the Antiochian Syrians, or pre-Chalcedonian Churches in the case of the Chaldean Catholics and the Assyrian Church of the East.

The one exception is, of course, the Maronite Church, which claims to have always been Chalcedonian and in union with Rome, despite some earlier Roman Catholic scholarly literature which tried, at times rather successfully, to impute the obscure Monothelite heresy to the Maronites. Naturally, for the Catholics, the issue of Chalcedonian or non-Chalcedonian has less importance and is but a question of their origins, since all Catholics accept the dogmatic statements of the Roman Church including the Council of Chalcedon.

The Armenians represent another anomaly since in their case ritual or ecclesial identity, ethnicity and language are equivalent and exclusive although political borders had in the past divided them so greatly as to produce two variants in their language—an eastern and a western, each of which possesses its own method of pronouncing the fricative consonants. Fortunately, almost all Armenian Catholics speak the western dialect, although some did appear in Armenia after the fall of the Soviet Union, much to the distress of their Orthodox Gregorian counterparts. These newcomers speak the eastern variant, as do the Armenian Catholics of Iran. This leads us to conclude that the Armenians are also particular in that they have settlements not only in Arabic-speaking Lebanon and Syria but also in today's Armenia as well as in Farsi-speaking Iran, together with a dwindling presence in Turkey. This last fact is noteworthy since recently published Turkish guidebooks to the Christian monuments of Istanbul and Turkey include a number of still functioning Armenian Churches, Orthodox and Catholic, both within the city and without.[4] After an Ordinariate for Eastern Europe for Armenian Catholics

---

4   Hakan Alan, *Churches of Turkey*, Istanbul, 2007; Ali Kılıçkaya, *Churches of Istanbul*, Istanbul, 2008.

in Eastern Europe, or more precisely for Armenia, and based in Gyumri (Armenia), was created in 1991, the number of Armenian Catholics increased dramatically from 142,000 in 1990 to about 540,000 in 2008, although the conviction of these newly discovered Catholics is at times disputed.[5]

But in terms of size, it would seem that the Arabic-speaking Maronites and Melkites are dominant among the Eastern Catholics of the Middle East. The former, as we have already noted, are enormously proud of their continuous history of Catholicism and their pro-Western and especially pro-Gallic proclivities, although they ultimately descend from the ancient patriarchate of Antioch. They have long been conspicuously present in the Lebanon and the fate of the Maronite Church and people is inseparably bound to the cause of Lebanon. The Melkites, on the other hand, previously popularly known as Syrian Greek Catholics, are present in much of the Arabic-speaking Middle East, where there is a Christian minority, but particularly in Syria and Lebanon. Although they descend from Greek and later Arabic-speaking Orthodox Christians, they came about as the result of an eighteenth-century split within the Greek Orthodox Patriarchate of Antioch. But they have, in contrast to the Maronite fixation with the West, integrated themselves to a greater extent in the Arabic community. Many Greek Catholic Melkites have taken an active part in the battle for this cause. While the Melkites number about a million and a half, around half that number are found not in the Middle East but in their world-wide diaspora, especially, and rather oddly, in South America. In this respect, the Maronites present a similar situation. In 2008, they numbered over three million; almost two-thirds of which, however, lived in the diaspora.

Of the other groups, all of which are considerably smaller than the Maronites and Melkites, the Chaldeans are the largest and the oldest, originally dating from 1553 and issuing from the Church of the East, although the line of Catholic patriarchs cannot be traced uninterruptedly throughout this time, due to defections to 'Nestorianism'. They form a peculiar example of an Eastern Catholic Church which has a greater number of members than its non-Catholic counterpart. In 2008, they were about 450,000, mostly in Iraq and Lebanon, but also in Turkey and Iran, although the war and subsequent unrest, together with discrimination and the murder of Christians and their clergy, has significantly decreased their numbers in their homeland and once again forced emigration. Three other groups are much smaller than even the Chaldeans and all stem from partial unions of Christians belonging to

---

5   Statistics given here are compiled by Ronald G Roberson, *The Eastern Catholic Churches 2008. Source: Annunario Pontificio* (private publication).

Churches which were previously considered Monophysite and today non-Chalcedonian. Syrian Catholics stem from the Syriac Orthodox Church and in the Middle East are found mostly in Syria and in Lebanon. They number about 160,000. Their archeparchy of Hassaké-Nisibis in Syria in recent years showed remarkable growth—from about 4,000 in 1990 to around 35,000 in 2008. In eastern Turkey and Istanbul, they are a small and today dwindling presence. The tiny Coptic Catholic Church is rather recent and dates from a split from or union with, depending on one's point of view, the Coptic Orthodox Church at the end of the nineteenth century. They form a rather insignificant number of about 160,000 faithful when they are compared with the six million Orthodox Copts, although they have shown growth in recent years. Like their Orthodox brethren, Catholic Copts are found particularly in and around Alexandria, Cairo and several villages in Upper Egypt which are almost completely Catholic. An Ethiopian Catholic Church was likewise formed from its Orthodox counterpart during the Italian occupation of Eritrea and later of Ethiopia. Although never very large, it has shown some remarkable growth in the past twenty years almost doubling its membership form 100,000 in 1990 to around 200,000 in 2008. Its members are mostly concentrated in the more westernised Eritrea, which today is another country with its own Orthodox patriarchate.

All these Churches are recognised today by the Roman Catholic Church as Churches *sui juris* and all, except for the Ethiopians, who have a Metropolitan Archbishop in Addis Ababa, are ruled by a patriarch who is usually, but not always, admitted to the cardinalate and is resident in the Middle East: in Egypt (Copts), in Lebanon (Melkites, Maronites, Armenians, Syrians), or in Iraq (Chaldeans). All, while preserving the essentials of their original identity, have been progressively latinised through the course of their time as Catholics, although today it is agreed that this process must be reversed. It is to this and related issues that we now turn.

EASTERN CATHOLICS OF THE MIDDLE EAST AND ROME

The Dominican Father Vannutelli visited Alexandria in the last years of the nineteenth century. He briefly noted the Copts, whom he found rough and barbaric, but also pious and quite attached to their religion. He pointed out that they were Eutychian or Monophysite heretics. The same attribute was used for the Armenian Gregorians. He mentioned the fact that he had visited a church, clean and well ordered, but belonging to the Greek Photians, who had separated from the Roman Church, in Vannutelli's opinion, as early as the ninth century. In Alexandria, Vannutelli even found two Christians belonging to the Church of the East. But finally, the Dominican father visited the Catholic or Latin church, served by Franciscans. Here Vannutelli swells with pride. Let us listen to the voice of the pious Dominican:

> But the Catholic Church holds its post of honour amongst all these others, through the virtue of her antiquity by means of which she comes before all other Christian confessions and as well as by her eternal youth, by means of which she makes continual progress. All this proves the fact that she alone is the unique true work of the Divine Redeemer, that he calls her to life for the salvation of the world, and distinguishes her from all those withered branches, which have been detached from the source of life …[6]

Some months ago, I was presented by Orthodox friends from Kiev with just such a sketch of a tree with fresh branches and some torn and dry. But the green tree was labelled the Orthodox Church and the dry branches bore the names of the various Christian confessions of the West including that of the Roman 'Papist' Church. Another branch, torn and hanging for dear life off the trunk of the green tree represented the Uniate Churches. At the same time, I had before me a chapter of a book written by Jesuit father Francis McGarrigle on the Eastern Catholic Churches and published in 1936,[7] which he entitled precisely the Eastern Branches of the Tree of Life and describes the Roman Catholic Church as, I quote, the Divine Trunk. It would seem that the imagery defined and perfected by Roman Catholic authors of the past has simply been appropriated and given another name by their fundamentalist Orthodox counterparts of today.

But how in the past did Rome view the Eastern Catholic Churches of the Middle East? Of course any discussion must be weighed against the fact that Roman Catholic authors of yesteryear could not but write in a laudatory manner of Rome and the Vatican. For that matter, the renowned liturgist of the Roman rite and scholar of the Eastern Christian Churches, Adrian Fortescue, referred to Blessed Pope Pius IX, known for his humiliation of

---

6   V Vannutelli, *Primo sguardo all'Oriente. La Terra Santa. Appunti di un pellegrinaggio*, Rome, 1892, pp. 4-25.

7   *The Eastern Branches of the Catholic Church. Six Studies on the Oriental Rites Compiled by the Liturgical Arts Society*, New York, 1938, p. 1.

the Melkite Patriarch and his latinisation policies, as a pope who particularly favoured Uniates.[8] Of course Fortescue was referring principally to the documents of the Roman Pontiff and particularly to his Epiphany Encyclical of 1848. In theory, the Roman Pontiffs, even notorious latinisers such as Pius IX and Saint Pius X did praise the hoary venerability *(venerabili antiquitatae suae originis)* and the magnificence of the liturgical celebration *(splendido quodam ac magnifico apparatu celebrandos)* of what they termed the oriental rites.[9]

But in practice, the attitude of Rome and particularly of the Roman Curia towards the Eastern rites was quite different and much less positive. The presence of a Latin-rite Catholic Church in the Middle East was seen as necessary, with its myriad monasteries, convents and especially schools, including those of higher education. Numerous members of Latin-rite religious orders, among them Franciscans, Capuchins, Carmelites, Dominicans, Christian Brothers, Jesuits and White Fathers, were active in the Middle East. While their general headquarters were usually located in the West, several had opted for bi-ritualism and even tri-ritualism while working among the local Eastern-rite Christians. Usually favoured and well funded, this Latin rite presence was seen as necessary especially in the Holy Land to combat the Protestants, particularly the Anglicans and Lutherans who possessed their own properties and institutions and were adept at making conversions among the local populace. Then too, the Roman Church had its own diplomatic interests in the Middle East and especially in the Holy Land. It still possesses accredited representatives in several countries and intervenes whenever Roman Catholic interests are at stake—during the repeated crises in Lebanon, in determining the status of Jerusalem, or during the war in Iraq.

The clergy of the Eastern Catholic Churches, who often were not on the same intellectual level with their Latin counterparts, could not be trusted with such a delicate mission, although many had been trained in Roman pontifical colleges, which, in some cases for over four centuries, were devoted to training clergy of the Eastern rites—the Greek, Maronite, and Ethiopian colleges. But, in spite of this exposure to the Eternal City and at least in the not so far off past, their Catholicity or rather *Romanità* was somewhat suspect. In the Jesuit administered Greek College, for instance, for several centuries, the Greek rite was at times banned or at times permitted, but only in a private chapel behind closed doors. The liturgical rites themselves, until the middle of the twentieth century, were viewed by conservative

---

8   Adrian Fortescue, *The Uniate Eastern Churches*, London, 1923, p. 37.
9   *Ibid.*

members of the Roman curia as somehow impure and infected with the disease of the schism.

Jean-Pierre Valognes, the author of a monumental study[10] of the situation of Christians in the Middle East succinctly describes this attitude:

> The relations of the Holy See with Eastern rite Catholics has not ceased to be marked by a certain malaise. This is the result of a difference in conceiving the nature of the universal Church and has never been resolved. According to Rome, Catholicity is by its very nature Latin by full right and Eastern only by tolerance towards those minorities in virtue of the fact that historical circumstances have prevented them from becoming completely latinised. According to the Eastern rite Catholics, who, on the other hand, have a similar ecclesiology to that of the Orthodox, the universal Church is the communion of Churches of particular rites,[11] equal in dignity and rights. Here we can detect a lack of agreement regarding the nature of supreme authority and the degree of freedom possessed by each of the Eastern communities. This discordance in ecclesiology was not clear at the time when Rome allowed them the use of their rites and particular structures, with a patriarch at the head of each community who seemed to be the incarnate guarantee of the full autonomy of each of them. But time has revealed the extent of these misunderstandings ... [12]

Didier Rance, another historian of the eastern Churches remarks in a similar vein:

> ... the Eastern Christians were often seen more or less openly as second class Catholics, incapable or at least not yet capable of acceding to the plenitude of Latin Catholicism, which was considered the only really universal form. Their ritual, canonical, and ecclesiological peculiarities were seen as remnants of the past, condemned to more or less a long term survival and which constituted a sort of menace for doctrinal orthodoxy. The Roman Church was very wary of the theoretical sources of Eastern Christianity (the Greek and Syriac Fathers were as greatly suspect as they were as poorly known) and considered the Eastern

---

10   Jean-Pierre Valognes, *Vie et mort des Chrétiens d'orient. Des origines à nos jours*, Paris, 1994.
11   Today we would say particular Churches *sui juris*.
12   Valognes, p. 193.

traditions to be somewhere on the fringe of heresy. Because of this, it was thought best to substitute Latin ways of doing and understanding things, at the level of theology (sacramental dogma and in particular the conception of marriage as a contract,[13] at the level of ecclesiology and canon law (the introduction of the rules promulgated by the Council of Trent), at the level of clerical discipline (the accent was laid on the importance of clerical celibacy), and finally through the introduction of Latin forms of piety and devotion. This process only gained in efficiency since it was accompanied by most flattering papal discourses on the richness of the Eastern liturgies, as, for example, the encyclical of Pius IX of the 5th of January 1848 and especially the *Orientalium dignitas* of Leo XIII of the 30th of November 1894. But it did, at times, run into a bit of resistance, as, for instance, when Rome in 1867 promulgated the *Reversurus*, a papal bull which attacked the freedom of the Eastern Catholic Churches in choosing their own hierarchy ...[14]

Of course the Roman Church has progressed on that long road which took it from the time of Pius IX when it considered the Orthodox as separate groups of 'schismatic Photians' ready to be 'reduced' to the see of Peter and Holy Union, to that of *unianisme* when it viewed itself as the sun around which revolved the wayward schismatic and heretic planets to that finally of ecumenism when it began to attempt an earnest dialogue as an equal partner with the Orthodox East. So too, Rome's attitude toward the Eastern Catholic Churches has evolved. But here, it must be said, not always in a direction which is acceptable to the latter. Once viewed as the model and method of Church union, they were later conceived as bridges between Rome and Orthodoxy. Today, the bridge model is also not considered politically correct by an ecumenically aware Vatican. The Eastern Catholic Churches are sometimes criticised for their liturgical hybridisation and often represent for some more of an obstacle than an aid for an eventual and very hypothetical re-union with the Orthodox.

But even before the Second Vatican Council, the Eastern rites were accorded at least in theory and in papal pronouncement an equal dignity with that of the Latin Church as long as this did not contradict the teaching of

---

13   In the Eastern rites, on the contrary, the minister of matrimony is the priest and not the spouses.

14   Valognes, p. 193.

the Church. So the Encyclical *Orientalis ecclesiae decus* of Pius XII. The Holy See was to contribute to their preservation and latinisation was forbidden. Vatican II placed the Eastern Churches on an equal footing with the Latin Church and recognised in its fullness the juridical person of the patriarch. It is well known that several of the documents of the Vatican Council were inspired by teachings of the Eastern fathers and the Melkites played an especially active role in the deliberations of the Council. So great and forceful was the contribution of the Melkite Patriarch Maximos IV that Athenagoras of Constantinople publicly complimented him for his role in representing himself, the patriarch, and the whole of Orthodoxy at the Council. The comment of one of the Eastern participants in the Council became legend defining the Christology of the Latin Church as well evolved but claiming that its pneumatology was still in its adolescence and adding the caustic comment that 'today, we are living in the times of the Holy Spirit.'[15]

But this euphoria proved ephemeral, particularly in regard to the figure of the Eastern Catholic patriarch, whose authority and powers were often questioned and even disregarded by the Roman curia, especially as regarding his right of administering Eastern Catholic communities in the diaspora. Rome is open to the idea of liturgical pluralism and this is often demonstrated, it must be said, with an absence of good taste, when members of the Eastern rites at papal liturgies appear to show their colours, but in questions related to jurisdiction and especially in the instances of both universal and local jurisdiction it is loath to cede its ground to the Eastern local Churches. They, on the contrary, see the Church as a communion of autonomous Churches, equal in rights, in the affairs of which Rome should intervene only in the case of a direct appeal. Of course, this is the model preferred by the Orthodox who point to this as the role of Rome during the first millennium. The recent promulgation of a new code of canon law for the Eastern Catholic Churches, the work of the very devotedly papal Jesuit Ivan Žužek, among others, has been criticised precisely for these reasons as well as for the fact that it steadfastly attempts to legislate for all the Eastern Catholic Churches, ignoring the basic differences apparent between, for instance, the Ethiopians and the Maronites or even, to take a better example, the Indian Malabars and the Ruthenian Slavs. It has also been criticised for its insistence on papal prerogatives and its underlying Latin spirit in juridical matters.

---

15 Joseph Hajjar, *Le christianisme en Orient*, Beirut, 1971, p. 277.

EASTERN CATHOLICS OF THE MIDDLE EAST: A VIEW FROM THE INSIDE

In his fascinating study of the Catholics in the Ottoman Empire, Charles A Frazee comes to this rather negative assessment of Roman influence on the Eastern Christian communities of the Middle East:

> Catholic communities profited by receiving personnel to staff their parishes and funds for their schools. Catholic facilities offered the best educational opportunities in the Ottoman world. Moreover, the presence of French or Italian clergy in their midst gave them a broader horizon and links to Western Europe denied to the Orthodox and Eastern Christians.
>
> On the other hand, the Latin missionaries' role among Eastern Christians was a divisive one. For half a millennium, hundreds of missionaries laboured to convert Eastern Christians to the West European point of view on how the church was meant to be structured and serve as a means of salvation. In spite of long and arduous years spent at this task, in the end ... it was obvious that only limited success had been attained and that the cost far outweighed the results.
>
> The ultimate goal of the papacy and Catholic missionaries was a united Christian Church, one in doctrine and moral teaching, and looking to the bishop of Rome as head of all believers. The Council of Florence was always in the mind of the Latins: union had occurred once and it could happen again. Most missionaries believed that if the leaders of the Eastern Churches were convinced that they should sign a Catholic profession of faith it would only be a matter of time until the whole Church was brought into corporate union with Rome.
>
> Some Orthodox and Eastern Christian hierarchs were won over, but their communities did not follow them, the risks were too great, the advantages too intangible. Therefore the missionaries turned to making individual conversions. Every Eastern Church had its malcontents, and professing allegiance to Rome was one way of settling differences. People were willing to convert for a great many other reasons: social, economic, ... greater educational opportunities and, of course, the conviction that becoming a Catholic meant following the will of Christ.

Unfortunately, in pursuing individual conversions the higher goal of corporate reunion had to be abandoned. Splinter Churches were set up, joined to Rome, but their members were too few to influence the course of their original communities ... Eastern Catholics, in the view of the Turks, had become apostates to their communities—they had joined the Franks and were no longer to be trusted ...[16]

Of course, Frazee wrote describing the situation under the Ottomans, but the gist of what he wrote is still valid in the contemporary situation. He was astute enough to remark that most conversions from Orthodoxy to Catholicism and vice-versa were and are not the result of deep philosophical and theological ponderings, but rather arise from the nasty spats between the faithful and their parish priest or between the parish priest and his bishop.

Distrust towards the Catholic partner was also, naturally, the view of the Orthodox communities from which the Eastern Catholic communities had sprung. Part of the understanding of how the Eastern Catholics view themselves can be found in the way they view their relationship to the Orthodox or to the non-Chalcedonian Churches. Here we must discuss the ticklish issue of what I would call 'auto-latinisation'.

Many years ago, when I was just seventeen, I was delegated to be crosier bearer for the Melkite Patriarch when he visited New York City. After the liturgy, which was conducted in Arabic and Greek, I was asked to sit at the banquet honouring His Beatitude. Since I knew practically no one, I was placed at the side of a Melkite lady, who was effusive in her praise of the Patriarch. And so she asked me how I liked their little church. I responded with tact—it was quite latinised with numerous statues and no iconostasis—and said it must hold great significance for her, being the church where apparently she had been baptised and married. 'Oh no', she answered, 'baptised yes, but I was married in the Lady Chapel of Saint Patrick's Cathedral. It was so much nicer, even though we had to receive special permission to have the ceremony in a Latin church.' Why did the good lady choose to be married in a strange cathedral when she had such a nice little church of her own. But I was no fool. Of course, she did it because it was more prestigious—and this goes to the heart of the problem of auto-latinisation.

Cirille Korolevskij wrote his classic study of latinisation of the Eastern Catholic Churches calling it *Uniatisme; définition—causes—effets—étendue—*

---

16   Charles A Frazee, *Catholics and Sultans. The Church and the Ottoman Empire 1453-1923*, London, 1983, pp. 312-313.

dangers—remèdes.[17] Naturally, when it was published in the Belgian revue of the Monastery of the Exaltation of the Holy Cross, still at Amay-sur-Meuse, his article did cause many Latin and Eastern Catholic hairs to stand on end. But his findings cannot be dismissed as the fanatical ravings of a Western convert to Eastern Christianity. And then too, while no friend of the latinised rites of the 'Uniates', which he termed not only wrong but hideously ugly, he was no enemy of papal prerogatives and constantly defended the role of pope and curia. Perhaps, however, his assertions need to be studied taking into account of how Eastern Catholics actually and those of the Middle East in particular have viewed themselves in the light of their relationship to both the Roman and the Orthodox Churches. This leads us to propose at least three modes or reasons for the process of auto-latinisation: latinisation as a way of imitation, latinisation as a way of modernisation, and finally, and most unfortunately, latinisation as a way of distinction which most deliberately sets the Eastern Catholic apart from his Orthodox neighbours, both in theory and in practice.

The encounter which I had with the Melkite lady in New York might be seen as an example of the first—latinisation as imitation of a Church which was conceived as more erudite, elegant and prestigious than one's own. Probably this occurred more frequently in the diaspora than in the homeland.

Latinisation as a method of modernisation is perhaps still a problem, for it entails the attraction of Eastern Catholics for the *devotionalia* of the Latin rite: the incorporation of Latin rite feasts such as Corpus Christi and the Sacred Heart together with devotions such as the rosary, Lourdes and Our Lady of Fatima. I can recall visiting a Greek Catholic church, not in the Middle East, but in Bukovina, in what is today the Ukraine near the Romanian border. The church possessed a striking iconostasis—full and high. The icons were of course Western holy pictures crafted in Vienna during the eighteenth century—but what could one expect? But then I was taken up to the front of the church where a table had been decorated as a makeshift altar surrounded by candles and lights. And there they were—a number of familiar friends from my Roman Catholic boyhood—statues of the Infant of Prague, Saint John Bosco, the Little Flower, the Lourdes Grotto and Our Lady of Fatima, among others, together with myriad rosaries and scapulas. Was this a statement, that here was the real religion? I hope not, but regrettably it probably was. Neither could I contain my surprise when, after visiting the Coptic Lourdes

---

17 Cirille Korolevskij, 'Uniatisme; définition—causes—effets—étendue—dangers—remèdes', *Irénikon-Collection*, 5-6, Prieuré d'Amay-sur-Meuse, 1927, pp. 3-64.

at Zeytoun in Cairo, when I was taken by my Muslim guide to the religious shop adjoining the shrine, hoping to purchase a Coptic icon. How great was my surprise when I was confronted with Western holy pictures fashioned in the worst Italianate taste possible, hundreds of Catholic rosaries and even statues of Our Lady and this in the sanctum of a non-Chalcedonian church which often requires the rebaptism of Catholic converts.

Finally there is liturgical latinisation arising as a definite response to or rather denial of the Orthodox counterpart and which includes examples of what also may be conceived as a desire for modernisation and simplicity as well as those meant to be direct imitation. They would include the wearing of Latin liturgical vestments, a practice which was formerly common among the Maronites and Chaldeans, as well as the use of Latin hosts by the Maronites, Chaldeans, Armenians, Copts, and Ethiopians. Changes in church architecture which reflected Latin models—not only the lack of an iconostasis among the Byzantines, but also the lack of a sanctuary barrier or veils or for that matter a *bema*, among the Armenians, Chaldeans, Syrians, Copts, and Ethiopians were also common. Another issue concerned the words of institution, considered essential by Roman Catholic Scholastic theology, missing from the anaphora of Addai and Mari in use among the Christians of the Church of the East but which have been added to the Chaldean Catholic missals. Thankfully, most of this is in the past and the new trend is towards the restoration of more ancient usages as well as the desire to resemble rather than differentiate oneself from the Orthodox brethren.

But a certain mentality remains. When the Latin Church abolished the subdiaconate after the Vatican Council, the rather latinised Armenian Catholics quickly followed suit to be just like Big Brother, although the meaning of the subdiaconate and the liturgical function of the sub-deacon are not exactly identical in the two rites. Today, it has once again been restored by the Armenians, who are also attempting to strive towards liturgical purity. Another example is the differing reaction of many Orthodox and some Eastern Catholics to the *faux pas* of Pope John Paul II when in May 1999 he kissed a Qur'an, a book which contains teachings which cannot in any way be reconciled to those of the Christian Church, proffered to him by a Moroccan mufti. One wonders what the Pope and for that matter his suite were thinking. The incident caused sorrow, bewilderment and outrage among Orthodox Copts as well as among some conservative Roman Catholics. But the Chaldean Patriarch Raphael I of Baghdad was present and his reaction could not have been more different than that of the Copts. In fact, he justified the Pope's gesture:

The Pope bowed to the Muslim holy book and he kissed it as a sign of respect. The photo of that gesture has been shown repeatedly on Iraqi television and demonstrates that the Pope is not only aware of the suffering of the Iraqi people, he has also great respect for Islam ...

Similar misunderstandings were provoked by John Paul II's prayer on Jordan's banks asking Saint John the Baptist to protect Islam, as well as by Benedict XVI's respectful attitude in the Blue Mosque of Istanbul. But the rather subservient remarks of the patriarch, made by one who should have known better, underline a certain mentality of subservience towards Roman authority which persists among the Eastern Catholics and tends to justify even that which is not justifiable. Yes, diplomacy at times does have its limits ...

Of course, the question of de-latinisation or the return to Eastern forms of worship and theological thought may not be reduced to a puerile witch-hunt which merely unmasks latinisations and forbids them. Some of the latinisations have become part of the ethnic and religious identity of the Eastern Catholics and it would be imprudent and unjust to create resentment by simple interdict.

On the other hand, Eastern Catholics in the Middle East have not and do not react with the same degree of aggressive hostility towards Orthodoxy as do their brethren in Eastern Europe. The Melkites are among those who have most distanced themselves from this anti-Orthodox mentality and have worked the hardest at recapturing their Eastern identity. Some Eastern Catholic Churches, especially those in Eastern Europe did not react favourably to the Declaration of Balamand, a document which was signed by Catholic and Orthodox representatives in a monastery of the Antiochean Patriarchate in Lebanon, and which rejected proselytism and uniatism as both model and method. But the Melkite reaction was quite favourable. In fact, after the Declaration, a brochure entitled *Orthodoxe uni? Oui! Uniate? Non!* appeared by Élias Zoghby, the former archbishop of Baalbeck, in which he called for the reestablishment of communion between the Greek Catholic (Melkite) Church of Antioch and the Orthodox Patriarchate in a re-united Patriarchate. The ideas proposed by Zoghby were later developed in the form of a concrete profession of faith signed by the majority of the Greek Catholic bishops of the Melkite Patriarchate of Antioch assembled in synod in July 1995. The profession included a double clause: 1) I believe in all that is taught by eastern orthodoxy; 2) I am in communion with the Bishop of Rome, in the limits recognised by the Holy Fathers of the Eastern Church, of the first millennium and before the separation, and consider him as first among the bishops.[18] It was the Orthodox synod of Antioch in October 1996 which surprisingly urged prudence and tended to view the project in a more realistic, less theological and more canonical light. While it greeted the initiative of the Greek Catholics, it clearly argued that they tended to confuse an *Antiochian* local *level* with an *international level* signifying that the *double communion* requested by the Greek Catholics cannot be separated from the renewal of communion between the Roman See and all of Orthodoxy.

A similar reticence on the part of the Church of the East occurred in June 2008 when Assyrian Bishop Mar Bawai Soro entered the Roman Catholic communion taking himself and his flock into the Chaldean Catholic Church after he became convinced of the truth of the Roman primacy. Although the Church of the East had renounced its presumed Nestorianism and had even come to a form of Eucharistic agreement with the Roman Catholic Church, it suspended its dialogue with Rome and excommunicated Soro, a fact which caused an added schism in an already beleaguered ecclesial community.[19]

CONCLUSIONS

I shall be brief in stating a few conclusions. I hoped to provide a brief survey of the ecclesial structures and the problems which confront the Eastern Catholic Churches of the Middle East. I hope I have been at least partially successful.

But in all the foregoing I have omitted, perhaps intentionally, the all too obvious—the precarious state of the Churches in the Middle East in today's world due to reasons which are all too evident from even the most cursory news report. Their ecclesial communities are today in crisis—a crisis which stems from serious causes: the still very unsettled conditions in most of the Middle East, the unfavourable and changing political structures, the pressure from Islam and the Jewish State of Israel, the extremely difficult economic and political conditions, terrorism, everyday violence, and a very real danger to life and limb. All this has resulted in the mass emigration of Christians from the Middle East, and all its resulting problems. If Christians in the Arabic-speaking countries of the Middle East can at least proclaim their

18   Benoît Bourguine, 'La réception de la déclaration de Balamand', *Catholiques et orthodoxes: les enjeux de l'uniatisme. Dans le sillage de Balamand*, Paris, 2004, p. 254.
19   'Assyrian Bishop Enters Full Communion', *Catholic Online* (6.6.2008), Internet Source.

solidarity with the Arabic movement and with Arabic culture and civilisation as their patriarchs did in their pastoral letter of 1992,[20] this option does not exist for the Armenians, Syrians and Chaldeans of Turkey or Iran. But these problems first and foremost also entail finding something of a *modus vivendi* with Islam, which alternately shows both an accommodating, bordering on syncretism, and an aggressive face. There is also the question of how much a Church should identify itself with politics or the preservation of an ethnicity and not with more eternal, less transient questions. Finally, there is an internal identity crisis apparent in several of the Eastern Catholic Churches, particularly in the more exiguous of them. Valognes saw the future role of the Coptic Catholic Church, for instance, in its 'role as a thorn in the bosom of Egyptian Christianity', and asked whether it might not be better for it to continue its historical mission by contributing to the end of the Eastern schism by melting into the Coptic Orthodox Church.[21] Perhaps, others of these Eastern Catholic communities might ask themselves the same question. On the other hand, Orthodoxy is too divided in the Middle East and both Greek and Russian Orthodoxy have high stakes in the region. All this makes it very difficult to predict what will happen to these Christian communities during even the next decade.

We began with a tableau of squalor and splendour. But while there is much squalor on the streets of today's Middle East, there is also much splendour, and the Eastern Catholic ecclesial communities have an important role in preserving this cultural heritage. It remains to be seen how well they can achieve this purpose in the near future.

To end, we may recall how Patriarch Nikon, that Hellenophile hierarch of Old Muscovy, whom I mentioned at the beginning of this paper, held dear the image of the earthly Jerusalem as a reflection of the heavenly paradise, and although separated from it by forest, desert and sea sought to recreate it in his own Russia. We too, here in the West, should not forget our Christian brethren in the Middle East who are seeking to recreate their lives and culture both in their traditional homelands and abroad amidst the blows and trials of a shattered existence.

---

20 *La presenza Cristiana in Oriente. Lettera pastorale dei Patriarchi Cattolici d'Oriente—1992*, Milan, 1997, pp. 17-20.
21 Valognes, pp. 276-277.

UNITY AND CHRISTIAN PRESENCE
IN THE MIDDLE EAST

Frans Bouwen

When, on 19 September 2009, Pope Benedict announced the convocation of a Special Assembly of the Synods of Bishops for the Middle East, he clearly indicated, from the outset, in the general theme he proposed, the two main subjects of this initiative: communion and witness. In fact communion and witness are inseparable in the life of the Church, just as mission and unity have been absolutely inseparable throughout the history of the contemporary ecumenical movement.

Regarding the Middle East, the interdependence between communion and witness is forcefully affirmed in the common pastoral letters of the Catholic patriarchs of the Middle East. Christian unity for the Churches in this region is, in the first place, a question of being. In their second pastoral letter the Catholic patriarchs use this expressive formula: 'In the East, we Christians will be together or we will not be.'[1]

Christian unity is at the same time a fundamental condition for the true witness and service which the Churches are called to offer to the human communities in which they live, as the patriarchs emphasized in their fifth pastoral letter, dedicated to ecumenism, in 1999:

> We believe to be called to be a sign of hope for our societies, in a Middle East that for many long years is in search for stability and true peace, amidst contrasting internal tensions, and rival exterior interventions. The pluralism of the cultural and religious traditions of our communities is a reflection of

---

1   Council of Catholic Patriarchs of the Middle East, *The Christian Presence in the Middle East. Witness and Mission*. Collegial pastoral letter of the Catholic Patriarchs of the Middle East to their Faithful in their different countries of residence, Easter 1992, § 39. The patriarchs repeat this sentence in their tenth pastoral letter: *The Arab Christian Facing Contemporary Challenges:* 'The love of God has been poured out into our hearts by the Holy Spirit which has been given us' (Romans 5:5), 2009, § 12.

the human societies where our heavenly Father has placed us. To the extent that we will be able, with the grace of God, to accept one another with our diversity and to unite our words, our witness, and our service, we can contribute increased inspiration and fraternal understanding. The service we offer is a disinterested service for the salvation of all. But our words and witness will not have any profound echo unless we are capable to surmount divisions amongst us: if not, we will only increase the general disarray.[2]

In the light of all this, it is surprising to see that this inseparable link between communion and Christian presence or witness in the Middle East is not affirmed more explicitly in the *Instrumentum laboris* of the Special Synod.[3] It is likewise surprising that the ecumenical issue is dealt with under the heading 'Witness' and not under the heading 'Communion'. This seems to ignore the fact that all major ecumenical dialogues of today study the mystery of the Church and the search for unity within the vision of the ecclesiology of communion. Unity is conceived as the search of full communion in faith, in the celebration of the sacraments—in particular the Eucharist, and in the exercise of apostolic ministry. The non-Catholic Churches, especially the Orthodox Churches, are not totally foreign or external to the Catholic Church, because there already exists a real although still imperfect communion that allows Catholic and Orthodox Churches to recognize each other as Sister Churches.[4]

The fundamental link between communion and collaboration among the various Catholic Churches—Eastern and Western, on the one hand, and the search for unity and collaboration with the other Churches, on the other—should constantly be taken in consideration throughout the whole work of the synod. It would be an illusion to pretend to work for ecumenism with others, if we do not earnestly work for greater communion among Catholics

---

2   Council of Catholic Patriarchs of the Middle East, *The Ecumenical Movement.* 'May They All be One' (John 17:21). Fifth Pastoral Letter, Easter 1999, § 79.

3   Synod of Bishops, Special Assembly for the Middle East, *The Catholic Church in the Middle East: Communion and Witness.* 'Now the company of those who believed were of one heart and soul (Acts 4:32)',. *Instrumentum Laboris*, Vatican City, 2010.

4   John Paul II's Post-Synodal Apostolic Exhortation, *A New Hope for Lebanon*, published in 1997 as a conclusion of the Special Assembly of the Synods of Bishops for Lebanon, held in Rome from 25 November till 14 December 1995, did include the ecumenical dialogue in chapter IV: 'Communion', distinguishing: I. Communion within the Catholic Church in Lebanon; II. Dialogue with the Orthodox Churches; III. Relations with the Ecclesial Communities originating from the Reformation; IV. The Middle East Council of Churches (§§ 80-88).

first. Wanting to work for a stronger Catholic communion, strengthening ongoing collaboration, without associating to this effort the other Churches in one way or another, could be interpreted as an attempt to reinforce Catholic identity against the other Churches and could create new misunderstandings.

We will, therefore, firstly consider communion and collaboration among the Catholic Churches, then the search for unity and collaboration with the other Churches, before dealing with the call to common witness and service addressed to all Churches.

COMMUNION AND COLLABORATION AMONG THE CATHOLIC CHURCHES
On the Level of the Middle East

The close link between better collaboration among the Catholic Churches and ecumenical openness can be eloquently illustrated by a small concrete fact, without great visibility but not without significance. The first concrete steps towards a regular meeting and collaboration among the Catholic Patriarchs of the Middle East were taken in the framework of the fifth General Assembly of the Middle East Council of Churches (MECC), Nicosia, Cyprus, January 1990, the same Assembly that celebrated the entry of the Catholic Churches into the Council of the Middle East as full members.[5] One evening, the Catholic Patriarchs present at the Assembly met in a very informal way in the lobby of the hotel and agreed on the need to meet more regularly in the future. They confirmed this decision in Rome, in October of the same year, on the occasion of the promulgation of the new Code of Canon Law for the Eastern Catholic Churches. The first meeting of what would become later the Council of Catholic Patriarchs of the Middle East took place in Lebanon, in August 1991.[6]

Since then the Congress of the Catholic Patriarchs of the Middle East has been meeting every year, hosted in turn by one of the members in his respective country. Usually, each Congress has a central study theme, besides more practical issues that call for common reflection and decisions. Often, after the meeting, these themes are further deepened by one of the Patriarchs with the help of some experts, and the outcome is communicated to the

---

5   Frans Bouwen, '"L'unité de l'esprit par le lien de la paix." Vᵉ Assemblée générale du Conseil d'Églises du Moyen-Orient', *Proche-Orient Chrétien* 40, 1990, pp. 93-119, in particular pp. 94-97; Jean Corbon, 'L'engagement des catholiques dans le Conseil d'Églises du Moyen-Orient', *Proche-Orient Chrétien* 41, 1991, pp. 86-102.

6   Cf. *Proche-Orient Chrétien* 41, 1991, pp. 111-113.

faithful in the form a common pastoral letter. Today there are ten of these. The first six letters take on a special significance, and constitute a kind of charter for the life of the Church in the context of the Middle East.[7]

At the very beginning, the creation of this Council raised some questions in certain Orthodox Churches. Precisely at the time that they entered the Council of Churches of the Middle East, the Catholic Churches manifested their intention to close ranks, to strengthen collaboration among themselves. To what purpose? Do they want to be able to better defend themselves and to exercise a greater influence, at the expense of others? In order to dissipate any misunderstandings, the Catholic Patriarchs decided to dedicate one day of their Congresses every year to an ecumenical meeting with the leaders of the other local Churches. This initiative proved very timely and fruitful.

A privileged moment in these ecumenical encounters was the 1996 Congress, which took place in the Syrian Catholic Patriarchate, in Charfeh, Lebanon, and had precisely ecumenism as its main theme. Thanks to thorough preparation, the presence of H.B. Ignatius IV Hazim, Greek Orthodox Patriarch of Antioch, of H.H. Ignatius Zakka I Iwas, Syrian Orthodox patriarch, and of H.H. Aram I, Armenian Apostolic Catholicos of Cilicia, made it possible for a common pastoral agreement to be signed with regard to a number of concrete points that had at times caused friction in interchurch relations: mixed marriages, the practice of first communion in the Catholic schools, the preparation of a common catechism.[8] It directly concerned the traditional territory of the Patriarchate of Antioch, primarily Lebanon and Syria, but also gave strong encouragement for other countries.

A highlight of the activities of the Council of Catholic Patriarchs of the Middle East was the first Congress of Catholic Patriarchs and Bishops of the Middle East, held in Lebanon, in May 1999, in the perspective of the

---

7   These six letters are: *First Pastoral Letter* (without title) (1991); *The Christian Presence in the Middle East. Witness and Mission* (1992); *Together in the Presence of God for the Good of the Person and the Society. The Coexistence between Muslims and Christians in the Arab World* (1994); *The Mystery of the Church* (1996); *The Ecumenical Movement* (1999); *Together towards the Future* (1999). Rafiq Khoury, priest of the Latin Patriarchate of Jerusalem has republished these six letters, with introductions and notes, in one volume: *A Hexalogy for the New Times: the First Six Pastoral Letters of the Catholic Patriarchs of the Middle East* (in Arabic), Jerusalem-Beirut, 2008.

8   'Accord pastoral entre catholiques et orthodoxes, Charfeh, 14 octobre 1996', *Proche-Orient Chrétien* 46, 1996, pp. 396-401; Jean Corbon, 'Accord catholique-orthodoxe sur trois questions pastorales importantes (Charfeh, 14.10.96)', *Courrier œcuménique du Moyen-Orient* 29-30, 1996, pp. 8-17.

preparation of the Great Jubilee of the Year 2000.[9] All the Catholic Patriarchs and bishops of the region took part, together with the superiors of the main religious orders and institutions. A good number of representatives from Rome and from the Catholic Church around the world were invited, as well as a group of consultants and experts. The Sister Churches were also actively involved. For the Catholic Churches of the Middle East, it was an extraordinary ecclesial event, and shows many similarities with the Special Synod now in preparation. The interventions, discussions and resolutions were mostly of high quality, including those relating to ecumenism. However, one concrete remark deserves to be made on this last point: while the passages of the resolutions regarding ecumenism are truly pertinent, being the work of specialists, one regrets the almost total absence of ecumenical concern in the other topics and texts. This does not seem to be in conformity with a fundamental demand expressed many times by Pope John Paul II, in particular in his encyclical *Ut unum sint*:

> It is absolutely clear that ecumenism, the movement promoting Christian unity, *is not just some sort of 'appendix'* which is added to the Church's traditional activity. Rather, ecumenism is an organic part of her life and work, and consequently must pervade all that she is and does.[10]

This will be a clear challenge for the future synod for the Middle East: the search for full communion with the other Churches should be a constant dimension of every effort for renewal and an integral part of the search for a greater communion among the Catholic Churches. One would have wished to see this more clearly emphasized in the *Instrumentum laboris*.

On the Local Level

On the local level, this collaboration among Catholic Churches is realised through the Assemblies of Patriarchs and Bishops, the Assemblies of the Catholic Hierarchy, or the Assemblies of Catholic Ordinaries, various names are used, that were created in different places and at different times. Living conditions and the relationships between the Churches are very different from one country to another. Hence the operation and working methods of these

---

9   Conseil des Patriarches Catholiques d'Orient, *'Pour qu'ils aient la vie et qu'ils l'aient en abondance'* (Jean 10,10). *Actes du 1er Congrès des Patriarches et Évêques catholiques du Moyen-Orient, mai 1999*, Secrétariat général, Bkerké, Lebanon, 2000.
10   John Paul II, *Ut unum sint*, § 20.

local assemblies will also vary considerably, and, as a consequence, it is not possible to describe them in great detail here. In the first place it should be noted that it is on the local level that the authenticity of true collaboration is demonstrated. Usually, it is easier to come together and to speak about collaboration on the international level than to live it concretely in the local context, where people and communities constantly rub shoulders with one another, may more easily enter into conflict, and are confronted with the same problems. On the other hand, it is not enough that these local assemblies exist and meet more or less regularly. The heads of Churches concerned should from time to time ask themselves these questions: to what extent are we really committed to this local expression and means of Catholic communion? To what extent are we ready to share, not only our needs, but also our resources? What needs to be done in order to reach that situation? What instruments for common pastoral work have been created and are really operational? How does one build awareness among the faithful for this inter-ritual communion and solidarity? On the other hand, it must be said that lay people often experience these needs more profoundly than the clergy. Last but not least, in some countries these assemblies fall victim to routine and are in need of a new impetus.

A concrete preparation for true ecumenical relationship would be a mutual respect for and positive acceptance of the varied liturgical and spiritual traditions within the Catholic communion, with a readiness to allow each to safeguard its own identity and to offer its specific contribution to the enrichment of all. At times, stronger or better equipped communities risk not sufficiently taking into consideration the presence or the specificity of weaker ones. The latter may thus feel marginalised and even fear absorption by the others. Certain communities have at their disposal sufficient resources in means and personnel to organize their pastoral work, others do not. Where is the true spirit of sharing? Does it not reveal itself when sharing becomes costly? This is only one of the many ways in which communion and collaboration among Catholic Churches can become a concrete learning process for ecumenism in the Middle East.[11]

---

11   Cf. Frans Bouwen, 'L'œcuménisme au Moyen-Orient: questions posées aux catholiques', *Proche-Orient Chrétien* 46, 1996, pp. 373-395.

SEARCH FOR FULL COMMUNION AND ECUMENICAL COLLABORATION

As elsewhere in the Catholic Church, the second Vatican Council marked a new starting point for ecumenical life in the Middle East. In this part of the world, however, special mention should be made of Pope Paul VI's pilgrimage to the Holy Land in January 1964. His meetings, in Jerusalem, with the Ecumenical Patriarch, H.H. Athenagoras I, and with the Greek Orthodox Patriarch of Jerusalem, H.B. Benedictos I, inaugurated a new era in relations between the Churches in Jerusalem and also in the Middle East, especially between the Catholic and Orthodox Churches.

At the same time it should be noted that some sort of grassroots 'ecumenism' has been practised in day-to-day life for many centuries in the Middle East, accepting that the term 'ecumenism' is used here in a somewhat improper sense. It was, rather, a common life shared by Christian communities at the grassroots level, where mutual recognition was not a problem. Throughout the centuries, these minority communities, often living in a diaspora situation, shared the same difficult life, recognised each other's presence and tradition, venerated the same saints and martyrs. Many of them also belonged to the same spiritual traditions and the same culture. When there was only one priest available in far-off villages, the faithful had no problem in turning to him when in need, even when he did not belong to their own Church. This age-old living co-existence helps us to better understand the way in which the Greek Orthodox Patriarch of Antioch, H.B. Ignatius IV Hazim, described ecumenical life, when welcoming Pope John Paul II in Damascus, on 5 May 2001:

> In this country and in Lebanon, Christians have adopted a dialogue of daily conviviality that helps them to overcome the blocks of the past. For years we have been laying the foundations for a wider understanding and a real collaboration in the fields of catechesis and pastoral work. More than before, we are driven by fraternal love. In spite of legitimate diversities, linked to our different cultures, we believe that an identical reading of tradition remains possible. That is why we have the feeling that we constitute one and the same Christian presence to welcome Your Holiness today.

In order to get a better idea of the ecumenical progress made in the Middle East in recent years and of the major challenges that arise for the immediate future, we will first consider the theological dialogues and the role of the

Middle East Council of Churches, before giving two representative examples of the varied local contexts.[12]

Theological Dialogues

Regarding the theological dialogue between the Catholic Church and the Eastern Orthodox Church of the Byzantine tradition, announced in 1979 and begun in 1980, the most authoritative evaluation, at least of the first phase, can be found in the common declaration signed by Pope John Paul II and the Ecumenical Patriarch Bartholomew I, at the end of the latter's visit to Rome in June 1995:

> This dialogue—through the Joint International Commission— has proved fruitful and has made substantial progress. A common sacramental conception of the Church has emerged, sustained and passed on in time by the apostolic succession. In our Churches, the apostolic succession is fundamental to the sanctification and unity of the People of God. Considering that in every local Church the mystery of divine love is realized and that this is how the Church of Christ shows forth its active presence in each of them, the Joint Commission has been able to declare that our Churches recognize one another as Sister Churches, responsible together for safeguarding the one Church of God, in fidelity to the divine plan, and in an all together special way with regard to unity.[13]

Thanks to this rich common foundation, the Commission was able, in a second phase of the dialogue, to embark upon the study of the ecclesiological question that is at the heart of the relationship between Catholics and Orthodox: the role of the Church, and the Bishop of Rome in the communion of the Church on the universal level.

The theological dialogue between the Catholic Church and the Oriental Orthodox Churches—those churches that did not recognize the Council of Chalcedon (451)—is no less important for the Middle East, given that most of these Churches have a living presence in this region. The dialogue itself was preceded by several christological agreements, signed jointly by the Pope

---

12   Cf. Frans Bouwen, 'Les relations œcuméniques au Moyen-Orient : pour une évaluation théologique', *Proche-Orient Chrétien* 52, 2002, pp. 92-111.

13   The Council for Promoting Christian Unity, *Information Service* 90, 1995/IV, pp. 123-124.

of Rome and the heads of these Churches, often on the occasion of a visit to Rome: with the Syrian Orthodox Patriarch, H.H. Ignatius Yacoub III, in October 1971, and his successor, H.H. Ignatius Zakka I Iwas, in June 1984; with the Coptic Orthodox Patriarch, H.H. Pope Shenouda III, in May 1973; with the Catholicos of All Armenians, H.H. Karekin I, in December 1996, and the Armenian Apostolic Catholicos of Cilicia, H.H. Aram I, in January 1997. A christological agreement between the Catholic Church and the Malankara Syrian Orthodox Church was approved by the authorities of both Churches in 1990. These agreements put an end to the theological differences that for fifteen centuries were regarded as the very cause of division, and are now described as non-existent and as misunderstandings. Did our Churches duly realize the far-reaching significance of these agreements?

Pope John Paul II also signed, in 1984, together with the christological agreement, a significant pastoral agreement with the Syrian Orthodox Patriarch Zakka I Iwas. Its central provision is the possibility for the faithful of both Churches to turn to a priest of the other Church for the sacraments of penance, the eucharist and anointing of the sick, should a priest of their own Church not be available. This agreement is explicitly based on the unity of faith that is said to already exist between the two Churches, although not yet complete.[14] Even if this agreement applies in the first place to exceptional cases, it presupposes that all the required theological conditions are in fact fulfilled for a sacramental communion. What does this mean for mutual relations between these Churches? Should they just go on living alongside one another as before or should they explore how they can use this recognition as a basis for a wider pastoral collaboration?

The theological dialogue between the Catholic Church and all the Oriental Orthodox Churches started in 2004, after a preparatory meeting in 2003. At the outset, many experts and even some Catholic members of the Joint Commission were inclined to think that it would move at a slow pace and that dialogue would prove complex. However, in the course of the annual

---

14 'Our identity in faith, though not yet complete, entitles us to envisage collaboration between our churches in pastoral care [...]. It is not rare, in fact for our faithful to find access to a priest of their own church materially or morally impossible. Anxious to meet their needs and with spiritual benefit in mind, we authorize them in such cases to ask for the sacraments of penance, eucharist and anointing of the sick from lawful priests of either of our sister churches, when they need them' (Common Declaration between John Paul II and Mar Ignatius Zakka I Iwas, Vatican, 23 June 1984, in *Growth in Agreement II, Reports and Agreed Statements of Ecumenical Conversations on a World Level, 1982-1998*, eds J Gros, H Meyer and W G Rush, Geneva-Grand Rapids-Cambridge, 2000, pp. 691-693).

meetings it soon proved very fraternal, confident and promising. Indeed, in 2009, after five meetings, the Commission was able to adopt a first common document, entitled 'The Nature, Constitution and Mission of the Church'. Following an ecclesiology of communion, the text expresses a broad consensus on the mystery of the Church, on apostolic succession, on the principles of collegiality and its inseparable link with primacy, and even deals with the delicate issue of proselytism that had more than once poisoned the ecumenical atmosphere in the past. The Churches concerned are thus invited to become more vividly aware of all that already unites them and to carefully ponder on what, as a consequence, should change in their mutual relations.

The horizon of christological agreements was notably broadened by the common christological declaration signed, in November 1994, by Pope John Paul II and Patriarch Denkha IV of the Assyrian Church of the East, a Church that did not recognize the Council of Ephesus (431) and therefore used to be called 'Nestorian' in the past. The drafting of this document constantly took into consideration the agreements previously signed between the Catholic Church and the non-Chalcedonian Churches, not only in order not to jeopardize these agreements, but also with the hope of opening new possibilities of understanding between two traditions, pre-Chalcedonian and pre-Ephesian, so far removed from each other. Seven years later, in 2001, the official recognition, by the Congregation for the Doctrine of Faith, of the validity of the eucharistic anaphora of Addai and Mari, commonly used in the Assyrian Church, in spite of the fact that it does not contain an explicit institutional narrative, opened the way for a new pastoral agreement, allowing Chaldean and Assyrian faithful to receive communion in the other Church when no priest of their own Church is available. The questions raised regarding the pastoral agreement with the Syrian Orthodox Church thus apply here also, in a much wider pastoral perspective.

The promising results of these dialogues undertaken by the Catholic Church should not make us lose sight of another, for the Middle East, very important dialogue, namely that between the Eastern Orthodox Church, of Byzantine tradition, and the Oriental Orthodox, non-Chalcedonian, Churches. After a long unofficial preparation going back as far as 1964, an official dialogue was inaugurated in 1985. After three meetings, in 1985, 1989 and 1990, the Joint Commission in charge of the dialogue was able to produce an agreed statement on Christology, which was to be submitted for approval by the authorities of both traditions in order to take effect. In fact, this agreed statement went well beyond Christology, affirming: 'Our mutual agreement is not limited to Christology, but encompasses the whole faith of the one undivided church of the early centuries.'[15] Thus we are here in the presence of a theological agreement that is, in principle, complete. Neither theological tradition would any longer have any doctrinal reason to remain separated. Indeed, the Joint Commission even started preparing canonical and pastoral guidelines for an effective union. Unfortunately, for various reasons, only very few of the Churches involved officially approved this agreement, and the whole process seems halted at present. The future of this theological agreement is a formidable challenge to the Churches involved, and even to the whole ecumenical movement. If two Churches, which recognize that they have both always remained faithful to the apostolic tradition and that there is no theological reason for their being separated, are not capable of concluding effective union between them, the whole ecumenical enterprise is in fact called into question. Why continue praying and working for unity, if the Churches do not really have the will or the courage to take the final step? No-one has the right to pretend that these questions can be ignored.

In the meantime, the Greek Orthodox Patriarchate of Antioch and the Syrian Orthodox Church decided to start putting this agreement into practice in the life of their Churches. In 1991, the two Patriarchates concluded a pastoral agreement stipulating, among other points: 'when in a given place there is only one priest, belonging to one or the other Church, he will celebrate the holy mysteries as well as the liturgical and spiritual services, including the holy eucharist and the sacrament of marriage, for the faithful of both Churches.'[16] The only two exceptions made are the concelebration of the eucharist by clergy of both Churches and the ordination of priests, most likely because these liturgical acts are considered as sacramental signs of full and visible unity. So the horizon of pastoral agreements is already wide open: between the Catholic Church, on the one hand, and the Syrian Orthodox and Assyrian Churches, on the other hand; at the same time the Syrian Orthodox Church has a similar pastoral agreement with the Greek Orthodox Patriarchate of Antioch. What does this mean for the relations between the Catholic Church and the Orthodox Church? This deserves serious reflection. The answer is certainly not easy, but one is entitled to raise the question.

To conclude this brief survey of the theological dialogues, we can take stock of the importance of the work that has already been accomplished,

---

15   *Ibid.*, p. 193.
16   Cf. *Proche-Orient Chrétien* 31, 1991, pp. 424-426; *SOP* 163, December 1991; *L'Orient-Le Jour* 21.11.1991.

we can imagine the riches contained in them, which remain largely unknown and unexploited. We are justified, then, in profoundly regretting that the *Instrumentum laboris* hardly mentions the outcome of these dialogues, and only in a very general way.[17] Nevertheless the dialogues and their results should concern the whole Church. According to the words of John Paul II in his encyclical *Ut unum sint*, the results of the dialogues 'cannot remain the statements of bilateral commissions, but must become a common heritage.'

> For this to come about and for the bonds of communion to be thus strengthened, a serious examination needs to be made, which, by different ways and means and at various levels of responsibility, must involve the whole People of God. We are in fact dealing with issues which frequently are matters of faith, and these require universal consent, extending from the Bishops to the lay faithful, all of whom have received the anointing of the Holy Spirit. It is the same Spirit who assists the Magisterium and awakens the *sensus fidei*.[18]

Should the forthcoming synod not be a providential occasion for remembering this truth and sincerely reflecting on how it can be practised in the Middle East?

The Middle East Council of Churches

At the time of its creation, in 1974, the Middle East Council of Churches (MECC) was composed of three families of Churches: Oriental Orthodox, Eastern Orthodox and Episcopalian-Evangelical. Since the entry of the Catholic Churches of the Middle East, celebrated at the general Assembly of 1990, the Council now comprises four families, and almost all the historical Churches of the region are represented.

The MECC is in the first place a visible sign that the Churches of the Middle East are determined to journey together in the search for unity, common witness to the Gospel and common service to the human society among whom they are called to fulfil their mission. This sign was particularly visible during the first General Assemblies that followed the entry of the Catholic Churches as full members. Almost all the Patriarchs and Heads of Churches were present personally, surrounded their by bishops, priests and other ministers, as well as by an impressive and varied representation of

---

17 Cf. *Instrumentum Laboris*, § 78.
18 John Paul II, *Ut unum sint*, § 80.

lay people, men and women. These Assemblies were not merely meetings of delegates but of Churches. From this point of view, the MECC looked much richer in ecclesial significance than most councils of Churches around the world.

At the same time, the Council became a privileged instrument at the service of the Churches and the Christian presence in the Middle East. Fraternal links were created, new possibilities for collaboration opened and certain mentalities began to change. The Council also allowed the Churches to speak with one voice, the Christian voice, beyond the many differences of tradition and confession. Nevertheless it must be admitted that theological dialogue in the strict sense of the word, or common theological reflection, remained, for most of the time, rather limited, because of the great diversity of traditions present. For instance, it has still not been possible to convince the Churches to officially adopt the common Arabic translation of the Our Father and of the Nicene-Constantinopolitan Creed, which have been prepared with great competence and perseverance.

The many programmes of relief and development, made possible thanks to the substantial financial means contributed by Western Churches, gave the Churches in the Middle East the ability to bear an important common witness of charity and solidarity in their troubled surroundings. The most promising projects were regrouped under the common heading: 'Christian Presence in the Middle East'. In this field, the MECC was a truly unique place for the Churches to reflect and act together in facing the tensions, threats and instability of the political context in the region, as well as the possibilities for further collaboration in the areas of justice, peace and reconciliation. As minority groups, the Christian communities are often among the first to pay the price for a deteriorating situation and to become the target of religious and political extremism. Emigration and dialogue with Muslims were the two major priorities. The MECC also succeeded in calling three meetings of the Patriarchs and Heads of Churches in the Middle East, held in 1985 and 1998 in Nicosia, and in 2000 in Beirut. These meetings had, in the first place, a symbolic meaning, as visible expressions of their determination to intensify their efforts for visible unity. However, they were also a precious opportunity for starting a common reflection and action at the highest level with a view to consolidating the Christian presence in the Middle East. These summit meetings were possibly the forums where the inseparable link between unity and Christian presence were manifested in the most forceful way.

Unfortunately, during the last ten years or so, the MECC has been passing through a very difficult period. The causes are many and varied. After the initial enthusiasm, an increasing lack of interest on behalf of some Church leaders could be felt, because of the slow progress in decision-making and in the execution of decisions taken, as well as because of conflicting interests. At the same time, financial aid, coming mostly from Western Churches and covering more than two thirds of the budget, began to diminish, as a result of the global financial crisis. Consequently, the MECC was obliged to reduce the number of its employees and its activities, to the point of becoming, at times, almost paralysed and ineffective. For a number of years now, talk has continued about the need for a radical restructuring of the Council, reducing its size to something better adapted to the needs and capabilities of the Churches of the Middle East, so that these Churches may really own and support it. However, the difficult necessary decisions were not taken in time, and at this moment the situation of the Council is becoming truly critical. Will it be able to survive? Who will have the required clear-sightedness and commitment, and be able to show the much needed leadership required to mobilize Church leaders and competent lay persons? It might be necessary to invent a new council, but in no way should the present one be allowed to die, since it still remains the only place where the Churches of the Middle East can come together and take the necessary steps to face together the threats and challenges of a situation that continues to deteriorate, and raises serious questions about the future of Christian presence in the region. A group of Patriarchs and Heads of Churches, together with some committed and qualified lay people understand the gravity of what is at stake, and are determined to do everything possible to safeguard this unique instrument of encounter and collaboration. It is thus all the more incomprehensible that the *Instrumentum laboris* makes no reference to this issue and mentions the MECC only *en passant*, in the middle of a long list of other possibilities—of a very different kind—for promoting Christian unity.[19]

On the Local Level

This brief description of the ecumenical situation in the Middle East should be complemented with a survey of the different initiatives that were taken at the local level in the different countries of the Middle East. Given the variety of contexts, this is an almost impossible task, and this presentation will

---

19   *Instrumentum Laboris*, § 82.

therefore limit itself to two examples that can be considered representative of the inseparable link between ecumenism and Christian presence and witness.

In the Holy Land, the fraternal relations that exist at present between the Churches are the outcome of a long process that was inaugurated by Pope Paul VI's pilgrimage in January 1964 and the ecumenical meetings that happened on that occasion. However, it is very significant to note that it was in the midst of a situation of occupation, marked by injustice, violence and suffering, at the time of the first Palestinian Intifada, which erupted in December 1987, that this rapprochement received a decisive new impulse. The dramatic character of events pushed the Heads of Churches in Jerusalem to come together and to reflect jointly on what they could and should say and do, for the good of their communities but also that of wider society. They began publishing common statements, calling for an end to all violence and a just and peaceful solution to the Israeli-Palestinian conflict, for the benefit of all parties involved. They also took a common stand on some of the issues and problems they were facing at the time, including: freedom of access to Jerusalem and to the Holy Places, difficulty in obtaining a residence permit for clergy and religious, questions regarding the payment or non-payment of taxes. Twice, in 1994 and in 2006, these religious leaders published a common memorandum on the religious significance of Jerusalem for Christians and on the rights of the local Christian communities. If the urgency of the human, social and political situation sufficed to bring these Heads of Churches together, this proves that a profound desire for greater unity already existed, although in a hidden way, and that it only needed this external stimulus for it to surface and come to life. Indeed, too often it is political tensions that divide the Churches instead of bringing them closer together. Since that time the Heads of thirteen Churches in Jerusalem have met approximately every two months, or whenever there was a special emergency, in order to share their concerns, to publish a common declaration, and to coordinate their stands whenever needed and possible. In the face of the many threats that hover over the Christian presence, and in particular over the Palestinian Christians of the Holy Land—political and economic situation, emigration—a common vision and strategy on the part of the Churches proves of vital importance.

The *Kairos Palestine* document, published in December 2009,[20] is another vivid illustration of the fact that common commitment to justice, peace and reconciliation simultaneously strengthens Christian unity and Christian

---

20 *A Moment of Truth. A word of faith, hope and love from the heart of Palestinian suffering. Kairos Palestine,* 2009; the text can be found on www.kairospalestine.ps in various languages.

witness and service. This document was prepared and published by a group of Palestinian Christians belonging to different Churches in the Holy Land, clergy and lay people, men and women. Given the deadlock in the peace process, and the continuing deterioration of the living conditions of the Palestinian people, they call out to their religious and political leaders, to Palestinian and Israeli society, to the international community and to their Christian brothers and sisters around the world. 'It is a cry of hope in the absence of all hope, a cry full of prayer and faith in a God ever vigilant, in God's providence for all the inhabitants of this land.' On the one hand, the text is the fruit of a broad ecumenical reflection and sharing of concerns. On the other hand, it also has created new possibilities for ecumenical collaboration in the future.

In Iraq, on the other hand, the lack of a common vision and the absence of a leadership capable of addressing the Christians of the country as a whole or of speaking in their name, has been an important negative factor in the gradual deterioration of their situation and greatly contributed to the uncertainty of their future. Already many complaints inside the Catholic Church in Iraq, could be heard on this subject. The lack of co-ordination between the leaders of the different Churches also considerably weakens their influence with the civil authorities. Some Christian parties or communities are in favour of the creation of an autonomous Christian region, others reject this idea outright, and opt deliberately for a true integration in Iraqi society in virtue of their specific Christian vocation. Should the Churches encourage emigration or not? What can be done in order to offer Christians a real option to stay in the country or to encourage them to come back after they have left? The creation of a Council of Churches in Iraq, at the beginning of 2010, aiming at bringing together all the Church leaders of this country, is therefore, a reason to rejoice. Regrettably, at the inaugural meeting a considerable number of Church leaders were missing. This is not a very hopeful sign. Are they not convinced of the timeliness and the usefulness of this initiative, or do they prefer to lock themselves up in their confessional or tribal options?

Many other examples deserve to be considered. In every country of the Middle East one can find situations and initiatives that illustrate in a convincing way the interdependence between unity and collaboration between Christians, on the one hand, and their capacity to bear a common witness and to offer an effective service *(diakonia)* in their social and national societies, on the other.

COMMON WITNESS AND SERVICE

After all that has already been said about the facts and factors that influence and shape Christian presence of witness and service in the Middle East, we need not delay here much longer. We may, however, usefully draw attention to the latest pastoral letter of the Catholic Patriarchs of the Middle East, published in 2009, with the eloquent title: *The Arab Christian Facing Contemporary Challenges*.[21] A careful reading of this letter should be a priority for all those who feel concerned by the lot of Christians in the Middle East, and particularly for those who are invited to take part in the Special Synod.

The letter starts by describing the present situation in the Arab countries: an increasing poverty in contrast with scandalous riches, corruption, favouritism and tribalism, foreign interference, disarray and nervousness in the face of a modernity that is often experienced as a threat, the rise of an ever more politicised and at time extremist Islam. In the midst of all this, the Arab person suffers in his human, political and cultural aspirations, longing for more freedom and dignity. Arab Christians are equally affected by this situation, because they are part and parcel of their societies; not infrequently they suffer the consequences even more severely, being minority groups, and are sometimes confronted with particular problems and sufferings exactly because they are Christians. This is particularly true for the whole question of emigration, especially that of the younger generation.

The second chapter considers more directly Christian reality in the Arab and Muslim world: the creative and innovative spirit of Christians, but equally their contrasting reactions in the face of the many challenges, going from steadfastness to discouragement, passing through doubt, fear, withdrawal into oneself and emigration.

The third chapter is entitled 'What to do?' In the first place it presents the Christian vision, founded on the fact that Christians belong to their society. They nourish their vision with their Arab and Christian culture, and their faith is for them a source of spiritual energy. The starting point and guiding principle of all Christian action is the commandment of love, with its universal dimension embracing all human beings equally. The letter then analyses the specific responsibilities of the Heads of Churches, clergy, faithful, theologians and Christian intellectuals, as well as the necessity and modes of collaboration with Muslims and Jews.

---

21 See reference in note 1. Unfortunately, to my knowledge, the text is at present only available in Arabic and in French.

The conclusion, 'The future of Christians', is on the whole characterized by the same orientations and emphases as those of the *Instrumentum laboris* for the Special Synod.

At the heart of our reflection there is the inseparable link between Christian unity and Christian presence in the Middle East, both being conditioned by and oriented towards a common Christian witness and service within the larger human and national communities. The following passage of this latest letter is therefore particularly meaningful:

> The presence of Christians in the Middle East is deeply marked by their divisions and confessionalism, which have profound roots in history. To the divisions between the Churches, one has to add sometimes the divisions within the same Church. We dealt with this question in detail in one of our previous letters—the fifth one, on Ecumenism, in 1999. We stressed at that time the consequences of our divisions for our presence in society, besides its meaning for the very identity of the Church and of the Faith in Jesus Christ. It is time to know that we are first of all believers in Jesus Christ, and only afterwards divided. It is time to know that our faithful and our Arabic societies expect from us a contribution that is the fruit of our love for one another, because no one of us lives for himself, as Saint Paul says, but for Jesus Christ (cf. Rom 14:7-9; Gal 2:19-20) and for our societies, which are looking forward to our specific input, stemming from our faith and our love, in the midst of the difficulties we are experiencing all together.
>
> Already in our second letter we said: 'We will be Christians together or we will not be' (§ 39). This remains true today and tomorrow, if we do not hasten to take the way of love that was opened in front of us by Jesus Christ, even if it is the narrow way. If we do not love one another, the whole Church is weakened, our faithful will feel weak and be filled with fear, and we will deprive our societies of the fruits of our love. [...[22]]

---

22 Here the letter quotes the passages of the pastoral letter of ecumenism that we already quoted in the beginning of this article (cf. note 2).

All Christians, even if they are still only on the way towards unity, are called to bear witness together, and from now on, to the Gospel and the Gospel values.[23]

The Special Synod for the Middle East is a unique opportunity to start putting these orientations into practice. Full use should be made of this opportunity. All the Churches of this region have to be actively involved and the worldwide Church must feel itself concerned. The first responsibility is obviously incumbent upon the Churches of the Middle East and their heads. This synod should not confine itself to beautiful ceremonies and eloquent speeches. It will not be enough to send rich texts across the world. Certain mentalities need to be reformed, certain working methods and structures have to be changed, and that will only be possible thanks to the strong collaboration of all, and to concrete projects in which everyone has his or her place and responsibility. Not only should the ecumenical urgency not be lost sight of, but it should be a constant dimension of every analysis and resolution. Only then can this synod really become a source of new life and confident hope for the Christians of the Middle East, who occupy a unique place in the universal Church.

---

23   *The Arab Christian facing contemporary challenges*, § 12, translated from the French.

THE SYRIAC CHURCHES
OF THE MIDDLE EAST
AND DIALOGUE
WITH THE CATHOLIC CHURCH

Sebastian Brock

INTRODUCTION

The title of this paper[1] might at first seem surprising, seeing that Syriac Churches constitute only small minorities among the different Churches of non-Chalcedonian tradition, with whose dialogue with the Catholic Church this paper is in fact concerned. The prime reason for my choice of title lies in the fact that the Syriac ecclesial tradition is the only one which has preserved, right up to the present day, representatives of all the three different christological traditions which emerged in the course of the fifth and sixth centuries as a result of the controversies over how best to formulate the relationship between the divinity and the humanity in the incarnate Christ. These three christological traditions are thus today represented by:

(1) The Syrian Orthodox Church, which accepts the Council of Ephesus (431), but not that of Chalcedon (451); it also accepts the Second Council of Ephesus (449), whose decisions were reversed at the Council of Chalcedon.

(2) The Church of the East (today the Assyrian Church of the East, under Patriarch Mar Dinkha IV, and the Ancient Church of the East, under Patriarch Mar Addai II). The Church of the East does not accept either the Council of Ephesus or that of Chalcedon.

(3) The Eastern Catholic Churches of Syriac tradition, namely the Maronite, Syrian Catholic and Chaldean; and in India, the

---

1 The same topic is covered (in a different way) in my earlier 'The Syriac Churches and dialogue with the Catholic Church', *Heythrop Journal* 45 (2004), pp. 466-76, and more briefly in 'The Catholic Church and Dialogue with the Syriac Churches', *One in Christ* 40:4 (2005), pp. 34-8; also, from a wider perspective, see my 'The Syriac Churches in ecumenical dialogue on Christology', in A O'Mahony (ed.), *Eastern Christianity. Studies in Modern History, Religion and Politics,* London, 2004, pp. 44-65.

Malankara Catholic and the Malabar Catholic Churches. These of course, like the Roman Catholic Church, along with the Eastern Orthodox and Reformed Churches, accept both these disputed Councils.

My concern here is with the dialogue between the Roman Catholic Church and the first two of these Syriac Churches, the Syrian Orthodox and the Church of the East. In so far as the Syrian Orthodox Church is one of the Oriental Orthodox Churches, dialogue with the Oriental Orthodox in general will also be covered. My aim is simply to give a summary overview of what has taken place so far in these two sets of ecumenical dialogue.

The Background

Historically, both the Syrian Orthodox Church (along with the other Oriental Orthodox Churches) and the Church of the East have been regarded by both the Latin West and the Greek East as, at best schismatic, and at worst, heretical and so provided with the highly misleading labels 'Eutychian' or 'Monophysite', and 'Nestorian'. These terms, given in the heat of the controversies, unfortunately came to be, as it were, fossilized when, in the seventh century, the Arab invasions effectively cut off most of the Christian communities of the Middle East from the Byzantine and European world.[2] The polemical attitudes engendered by this three-way split within the Eastern Christian tradition have, with a few noble but short-lived exceptions,[3] continued unchanged right up to modern times, and it was only with the Second Vatican Council, that a complete change of attitude started to emerge. Of prime significance here was the Decree on Ecumenism promulgated by Pope Paul VI (21 November, 1964), stating that 'The restoration of unity among all Christians is one of the principle concerns of the Second Vatican Council'. It was this new attitude which gave rise to ecumenical dialogue, not

---

2   The exception being the Chalcedonian (Rum) Orthodox Patriarchates of Antioch, Jerusalem and Alexandria, which remained in contact with Constantinople.

3   Thus two Syrian Orthodox writers, 'Ali ibn Da'ud al-Arfadi in the eleventh century, and the polymath Gregory Abu'l-Faraj (Barhebraeus) in the thirteenth. For the former, see G Troupeau, *Études sur le christianisme arabe au Moyen Age*, Aldershot, 1995, chap. 13; and for the latter, W Hage, 'Ecumenical aspects of Barhebraeus' christology', *The Harp* 4 (1991), Kottayam, pp. 103-9 (a translation of the relevant passage is given in my 'The Syriac Churches in ecumenical dialogue', pp. 65-6).

only with the Eastern Orthodox Churches, but in due course also with the Oriental Orthodox (from 1971), and later on (from 1984) with the Church of the East.[4] These dialogues have been on two separate levels, Non-Official, and Official; in some cases they have been bilateral, while in others multilateral.

THE CATHOLIC CHURCH AND THE ORIENTAL ORTHODOX CHURCHES

A particularly important role in Non-Official dialogue has been played by the PRO ORIENTE Foundation in Vienna, founded in 1964 by the late Cardinal König (+2004) with the specific aim of promoting East-West dialogue. At first PRO ORIENTE's activities were confined to dialogue with the Eastern Orthodox, but this changed in 1971 when a series of meetings with theologians from the Oriental Orthodox was inaugurated. Here it might be noted in passing that dialogue between the Eastern Orthodox and the Oriental Orthodox Churches had started already in 1964, and by the end of 1971 four rather successful meetings had taken place.

In the sixth century Christology had been the locus of division, and so obviously this needed to form the basis for discussion in all ecumenical dialogue. In the course of the fifth and sixth centuries various different, sometimes verbally conflicting, formulations on Christology were put forward, among which that of the Council of Chalcedon proved to be the most controversial and divisive as far as the Eastern Christianity was concerned. Returning to these issues in the late twentieth century and removed from the heat of polemical argument, it soon became clear at all these modern dialogues with the Oriental Orthodox that, lying beneath the surface of verbal conflict in formulations, there existed a common understanding of what was really meant by the mystery of the incarnate Christ. In the course of dialogue it came to be realized that the underlying causes of misunderstanding and conflict lay in two key terms of the Chalcedonian Definition of Faith in particular, namely *physis*/'nature' and *hypostasis*, both of which were understood in different ways by the different sides. For the Chalcedonian Churches (and the Church of the East), the sense of *physis* is closer to *ousia* than to *hypostasis*, whereas for the Oriental Orthodox it is closer to (and implies) *hypostasis*; this meant that, on their understanding, the Chalcedonian Definition was not only illogical,

---

4   In general, see A Olmi, *Il consenso cristologico tra le chiese calcedonesi e non-calcedonesi (1964-1996)*, Analecta Gregoriana 290, 2003, chapters 9 and 10.

but it also implies that there were two subjects, the divine and the human, in the incarnate Christ—a position that the Chalcedonian Churches equally hold to be heretical. In the case of the Church of the East, it was the term *hypostasis* that was objectionable, since it was translated into Syriac as *qnoma*, a term that had different sense in the East Syriac theological tradition; for them too, the Chalcedonian Definition was illogical, though for different reasons.

Early on in both the Orthodox-Oriental Orthodox and the Catholic-Oriental Orthodox dialogues, it was realized that in the sixth century each side had understood its opponent's position only from the standpoint of their own understanding of the technical terms involved, and not as their opponents in fact understood them. This meant that each side had a misconception, often just a caricature, of what the other side really held. What is necessary today is that each side should make the intellectual effort to understand how the other side was using the ambiguous technical terms, and what the other side really intended. What is required is a new openness, and the willingness to accept that there can be more than one legitimate way of formulating the relationship between the divinity and the humanity in the incarnate Christ. No longer is to be seen as a question of 'either/or', but one of 'both/and'; not of course that there was any question of any Church having to change its preferred Christological formulation, but only that each should accept that another formulation can also be possible and legitimate. Thus already at the end of the First PRO ORIENTE meeting in 1971 with the Oriental Orthodox it proved possible to issue an agreed statement on Christology:[5]

> We believe that our Lord and Saviour, Jesus Christ, is God the Son incarnate; perfect in His divinity and perfect in His humanity. His divinity was not separated from His humanity for a single moment, not for the twinkling of an eye; His humanity is one with His divinity without commixtion, without confusion, without division, without separation. We in our common faith in the one Lord Jesus Christ regard His mystery as inexhaustible and ineffable and for the human mind never fully comprehensible or expressible.
>
> We see that there are still differences in the theological interpretation of the mystery of Christ, because of our different ecclesiastical and theological traditions; we are convinced,

---

5 The full text can be found (e.g.) in PRO ORIENTE, *Syriac Dialogue* 1, Vienna, 1994, pp. 27-8.

however, that these different formulations on both sides can be understood along the lines of the faith of Nicaea and Ephesus.

This agreed formulation in due course came to be known as the 'Vienna Christological formula', and elements from it were picked up in the subsequent Official Dialogue and in some of the agreed statements between the Pope and individual Oriental Orthodox Patriarchs.[6]

Following on from the first Non-Official meeting of 1971 with the Oriental Orthodox, PRO ORIENTE arranged four further Non-Official meetings, in 1973, 1976, 1978, and 1988;[7] these were followed by seminars devoted to specific topics in 1991 (Primacy), 1992 (Councils and Conciliarity), 1994 (Ecclesiology), and 1996 (Authority in the Church).

Eventually it proved possible to inaugurate an Official Dialogue with the Oriental Orthodox Churches,[8] with an initial meeting in Cairo in January 2004. This has continued annually, and at the fourth meeting (2007) a sub-committee was set up to draw up a text on 'The Nature, Constitution, and the Mission of the Church'. A draft of this was discussed at the fifth meeting (2008), and then at the sixth meeting (2009) final text was agreed upon.[9]

Following the introduction, this important document consists of four parts: I, The mystery of the Church (sections 5-25); II, The apostolic succession of bishops (sections 28-33, on the episcopacy; 34-38 on the apostolic succession); III, Synodality/conciliarity, and forms of primacy (sections 39-52); and IV, The mission of the Church (sections 56-66). At the end of Parts I and III points for further study and discussion are listed. These include, under Part I, the need for clarification of certain terms used by one side that are obscure, or raise problems for, the other: thus for the Oriental Orthodox the terms 'real but imperfect communion' and 'degrees of communion' remain unclear, while for the Catholic side, the

---

6   For example, between Pope Paul VI and Pope Shenouda III in 1973, and between Pope John Paul II and Patriarch Ignatius Zaka I 'Iwas in 1984; the most important passages of the latter text are quoted in my 'The Syriac Churches in ecumenical dialogue on Christology', in A O'Mahony (ed.), *Eastern Christianity. Studies in Modern History, Religion and Politics,* London, 2004, pp. 51-52.

7   For these, see PRO ORIENTE, *Five Vienna Consultations between Theologians of the Oriental Orthodox Churches and the Roman Catholic Church,* Vienna, 1993.

8   The official title being 'The Mixed International Commission for Theological Dialogue between the Catholic Church and the Oriental Orthodox Churches'. A valuable reflection on this dialogue is provided by F Bouwen, 'The goal of our ecumenical dialogue: the unity we seek', *Proche-Orient Chrétien* 58 (2008), pp. 292-308.

9   A French translation is published in *Proche-Orient Chrétien* 59 (2009), pp. 77-100.

phrase 'family of Churches' raises difficulties. For Part III, quite a number of points are raised, notably the question of primacy at the universal level, the number and the authority of Councils after that of Ephesus, and how to resolve points of open discord concerning these, and the modalities for the reception of Councils. Significantly, no points for further discussion were raised for Parts II and IV, since there was basic agreement on these; here it is significant that section 63 in Part IV specifically rejects proselytism, and exhorts that this practice, that has caused so much ill-feeling in ecumenical relations, should cease.[10]

The document, which was to be submitted to the authorities of the respective Churches 'for consideration and action', concludes that, while a common celebration of the Eucharist is not yet possible (section 24), convergence in faith does allow for theological and pastoral accords, especially in response to pressing needs where the two sides are living together (section 27).[11] Among the recommendations in the final section (66) are the encouragement of common prayer and education, and cooperation in pastoral and humanitarian activities. Furthermore, the document urges that there should be frequent and regular contacts, especially between bishops, on either side.

THE CATHOLIC CHURCH AND THE ASSYRIAN CHURCH OF THE EAST[12]

The third Christological tradition, that of the Church of the East, had effectively been by-passed in the ecumenical dialogue of the 1960s and 1970s, and it was only after a meeting in 1984 between Pope John Paul II and the Patriarch of the Assyrian Church of the East, Mar Dinkha IV, that dialogue finally got under way. The fruits of this were seen ten years later in the Common Declaration of Faith between Pope John Paul II and Patriarch Mar Dinkha IV on 11 November, 1994. This was a momentous event from the point of view of the Church of the East, for it represented the first time it had been officially recognized by another Church as a legitimate partner

---

10 It is interesting to note in passing that the wording reflects that of the Common Declaration made in 1973 by Pope Paul VI and Pope Shenouda III.

11 The need for a mutual recognition of baptism and mixed marriages is singled out.

12 An account from the perspective of the Assyrian Church of the East can be found in Mar Aprem, *The Assyrian Church of the East in the Twentieth Century*, Kottayam, 2003, chapter 6.

in ecumenical dialogue. The following year, in 1995, Official Dialogue between the Roman Catholic Church and the Assyrian Church of the East was initiated. This continued until the tenth meeting, in 2004, after which the Dialogue was suspended owing to the complications that had arisen as a result of a disagreement between one of the bishops of the Assyrian Church of the East and his Patriarch. In June 2007, however, Patriarch Mar Dinkha IV met with Pope Benedict XVI, and plans were made for the resumption of Official Dialogue. The following year (June 2008) a Non-Official Consultation took place in the Chicago area and it was agreed that, while both sides were eager to keep up relations, it was not yet the time to resume the Official Dialogue

Just over a decade earlier, in summer 1997, quite independently of the Official Dialogue, the Synod of the Assyrian Church of the East had taken two extremely important initiatives. Firstly, it had declared that all anathemas and condemnations of individuals should be removed from its liturgical books; and secondly, it had agreed with the Synod of the Chaldean Catholic Church 'to inaugurate a bilateral programme to bring about the full ecclesial union of the two Churches'. Both these can be seen as developments of great ecumenical significance: by removing the condemnations of individuals from their liturgical books the Assyrian Church of the East set an admirable example for other Churches to follow; and by initiating the programme with the Chaldean Catholic Church, the Assyrian Church of the East was setting in motion what might one day provide a model for action in resolving thorny issues concerning 'Uniatism'. As yet, however, little progress has been made, and matters have been considerably complicated by the case of Bishop Baway Soro, alluded to above.

One extremely important outcome of the Official Dialogue with the Assyrian Church of the East remains to be mentioned: this was the publication, on 26 October 2001, of the Vatican 'Guidelines for admission to Eucharist between the Chaldean Church and the Assyrian Church of the East'. What made these 'Guidelines' so significant was a paragraph concerning the Anaphora of the Apostles Addai and Mari: this, the oldest of Christian Eucharistic Prayers still in use, is noteworthy for the absence from it of an 'Institution Narrative'; in the past, this had been considered by Rome as rendering it invalid, and so an Institution Narrative was inserted into it for use in the Chaldean Catholic and Malabar Catholic Churches. In the light of modern liturgical scholarship, however, with its more holistic understanding of the Eucharistic Rite, a different attitude

113

has become possible, and the 'Guidelines' are now able to state that the Anaphora of Addai and Mari in its original form, without the Institution Narrative, 'can be considered valid'.[13]

PRO ORIENTE'S 'SYRIAC DIALOGUE'

Besides inaugurating in 1971 the Non-Official Dialogue with the Oriental Orthodox Churches, PRO ORIENTE took on another important initiative in 1994, entitled 'Syriac Dialogue'. What made this a unique development in ecumenical dialogue was the fact that it brought together, for the very first time, theologians from all the Churches of Syriac tradition, thus covering the entire Christological spectrum, ranging from the Syrian Orthodox Church and Malankara Orthodox Church, through the various Chalcedonian Catholic Churches of Syriac liturgical tradition, to the Church of the East (represented by the Ancient Church of the East as well as the Assyrian Church of the East). It was not surprising that at the first meeting one could feel a sense of distrust inherited from the past, and it sometimes seemed as if the Church of the East, whose Christology was the main topic, was being put on trial. At the second meeting, held in February 1996, significant advances were made and it was possible to issue an important communiqué; this not only provided clarification concerning the ambiguous and controversial terms 'nature' and *hypostasis*, but it also stated that 'the theological thought and formulations of the Church of the East are considered to be in line with the Ecumenical Councils of Nicaea and Constantinople, and compatible with those of Ephesus.' Important too was the realization that, while the aim of dialogue was unity, this does not mean uniformity: what was needed on each side was a genuine understanding of the Christological teaching of the other, leading to an acceptance of its validity; also, that there was never any question of one Church having to *change* its traditional Christological teaching.

A further sense of rapprochement between the different Syriac Churches was achieved the following year, at the third meeting of Syriac Dialogue in the Chicago area (July 1997). It was at this meeting that the removal of anathemas from liturgical books by the Assyrian Church of the East and its bilateral programme with the Chaldean Catholic Church were announced.

---

13 See the comments by the leading liturgical scholar, R F Taft, 'Mass without the consecration? The historic agreement on the Eucharist between the Catholic Church and the Assyrian Church of the East. Promulgated 26 October 2001', *Worship* 77 (2003), pp. 482-509.

The remarkable advances achieved during the first three meetings of the Syriac Dialogue were, however, met with an adverse reaction in some quarters, especially from the Coptic Orthodox Church. Although in January 1995 theologians of the Coptic Orthodox Church and of the Assyrian Church of the East had produced a remarkable agreed statement,[14] subsequent hostility on the part of the Coptic Orthodox Church towards the Church of the East meant that this document never came before the Synod of the Coptic Orthodox Church. This negative attitude towards the Church of the East has resulted in two unfortunate effects, in particular. In the first place, it has successfully blocked the application by the Assyrian Church of the East (first considered in 1994) to become a member of the Middle East Council of Churches (MECC); as a result of this, there is now the highly anomalous situation that Protestant Churches, of European origin, are members of the MECC while the indigenous and venerable Church of the East is not. The second unfortunate effect was brought about at a meeting of the Oriental Orthodox Patriarchs, convened by Pope Shenouda in March 1998, at which it was decided that any future ecumenical dialogue with other Churches should involve *all* the Oriental Orthodox Churches together. This effectively put an end, not only to PRO ORIENTE's 'Syriac Dialogue' in its original form, but also to the planned Dialogue between the Syrian Orthodox Church and the Assyrian Church of the East. In the case of 'Syriac Dialogue', the ensuing meetings of Syriac Dialogue (fourth to seventh, held in 2000, 2002, 2003 and 2004) were simply styled 'Study Sessions' (on the Sacraments). Subsequently, in 2005, after the commencement of the Official Dialogue in 2004 (see above), it was renamed as 'Forum Syriacum'; so far two helpful study sessions have taken place.

BY WAY OF CONCLUSION

Undoubtedly much has been achieved over the course of the last four decades in the dialogue between the Catholic Church and both the Syrian Orthodox Church and the Assyrian Church of the East. It is perhaps with the latter that some of the most significant developments have taken place.

The course of dialogue with the different Syriac Churches has also brought to light a hazard that needs to be avoided. In the communiqués of some of the

---

14 The main part of the text is given in my 'The Syriac Churches in ecumenical dialogue on Christology', pp. 56-58.

earlier dialogues with the Oriental Orthodox Churches statements had been made, or wording used, which were in due course to prove regrettable once dialogue with the Church of the East had commenced. This could be observed in the early meetings of 'Syriac Dialogue', where some features incorporated into the 'Vienna Christological Formulation' were to cause difficulties when dialogue was with a very different Christological tradition. Likewise, advances in one set of relationships could have a negative impact on another set: thus the Common Declaration of Faith between Pope John Paul II and Patriarch Dinkha IV (1994) unfortunately led to a deterioration of relationships between the Vatican and the Coptic Orthodox Church.

While it is obviously extremely important to maintain dialogue on both Non-Official and Official levels, the reception of the findings reached on these two levels is also a matter of great weight and importance. Here one can applaud and admire some of the developments in the Middle East, such as the regular meetings and co-operation between the bishops of the different Churches in Aleppo, and the various ecumenical and inter-faith initiatives by Archbishop Louis Sako in Kirkuk. While it would be impertinent to suggest what more could be done in the various countries of the Middle East, as far as Europe, America, and Australia are concerned, there are a number of obvious ways which can be suggested by which a greater wider awareness of the findings of modern dialogue might be achieved. There is, above all, an urgent need for well-informed instruction in seminaries about the different Churches of the Middle East and their teaching; this also means that the stereotyped and misleading pictures of the non-Chalcedonian Churches provided in the older textbooks of Church History and the History of Doctrine need to be replaced, and a much better balanced presentation of them provided instead. But education in such matters should not just be confined to the clergy, for it is equally important that the laity should become aware of developments in ecumenical dialogue. While schools and catechesis should play an obvious role in the dissemination of knowledge about the different Churches, radio, television and the internet offer a huge potential that still awaits to be better exploited.[15] To take a single example involving just the first of these media, one might take as a helpful example 'The Voice of Orthodoxy', which broadcasts above all to Russia; having started out well before the collapse of the Soviet Union, it still continues to provide well-balanced teaching on Orthodox tradition that reaches a very wide public.

---

15 This is indeed pointed out in the *Lineamenta*, § 50.

On an everyday level, too, there are many things that can be done. One of the most obvious is the avoidance of the use of the old polemical terminology in referring to the non-Chalcedonian Churches. Thus 'Eutychian' should never be applied to the Oriental Orthodox Churches, which from the first have specifically rejected that position, according to which Christ is consubstantial with the Father, but not with us, his humanity being somehow swallowed up in his divinity. Likewise to be avoided is the term 'Monophysite', which is understood by many people as being co-terminous with 'Eutychian', with the result that its use is definitely misleading. A much more neutral term, which has now come to be employed in modern ecumenical dialogue, is 'Miaphysite', since this aptly describes the teaching of the Oriental Orthodox Churches, namely that the incarnate Christ is 'one nature out of two', in contrast to the dyophysite formulation 'in two natures' of the Council of Chalcedon.[16]

Likewise, in the case of the Church of the East, it is of great importance to avoid the term 'Nestorian'. Although this Church has regularly been designated throughout the centuries by this name, it is a term that likewise originated in the polemic of the fifth and sixth centuries; furthermore, it is a highly misleading term, and has given rise to all sorts of misunderstandings.[17] Essentially, this is because the name Nestorius, along with the term 'Nestorian', means three completely different things:

> —to the Church of the East, Nestorius, the Patriarch of Constantinople who was deposed at the Council of Ephesus, is simply regarded as someone who unjustly suffered for his dyophysite teaching, and so is commemorated in the liturgy. His actual writings were little known, and far more influential on the theological teaching of the Church of the East were those of Theodore of Mopsuestia.

> —to the Oriental Orthodox Churches in particular, but also to the Chalcedonian Churches, 'Nestorius' was an arch-heretic who taught that there were two *prosopa* in Christ, and that the Son of God and the son of Mary were distinct—neither of which positions has ever been held by the Church of the East.

---

16 For this term, see D Winkler, 'Miaphysitism: a new term for use in the history of dogma and in ecumenical theology', *The Harp* 10 (1997), Kottayam, pp. 33-40.

17 See further my 'The "Nestorian" Church: a lamentable misnomer', in J F Coakley and K Parry (eds), *The Church of the East: Life and Thought*, Manchester, 1996, pp. 22-35, reprinted in *Fire from Heaven. Studies in Syriac Theology and Liturgy*, Variorum Reprints, 2006, chapter 1 (chapters 2-4 are also of relevance).

—to modern scholars the true nature of Nestorius' teaching on christology remains a matter of uncertainty and dispute.

Quite apart from their misleading character, avoidance of these old and offensive polemical terms in connection with the non-Chalcedonian Churches should also be seen simply as a matter of courtesy and politeness.

These various considerations are all the more important in the contemporary context when the large-scale emigration from the Middle East of recent years, above all of Christians, has led to the establishment in Europe and elsewhere of sizeable communities belonging to the indigenous Middle Eastern Churches with their own clergy and, in several cases, bishops with dioceses that have been newly established in the diaspora. In all the places where these communities are present there are certainly going to be many practical opportunities for local co-operation, and in most cases it will be necessary for the host community to take the initiative.

EASTERN CATHOLIC ECCLESIAL AND LITURGICAL IDENTITY: A MELKITE PERSPECTIVE

Robin Gibbons

MELKITE PRESENCE IN ENGLAND: SIGN AND STUMBLING BLOCK

There is an intrinsic dissonance in being a Melkite priest in Great Britain and also not being of Arab stock, especially as our present Patriarch Gregorios III keeps on reminding the Melkite faithful that we are an 'Arab' Church, with historical roots in all our *(sic)* eastern homelands. The Church is, as he states, attached to its Christian origins and its Arab heritage. In his address to Pope Benedict XVI during Vespers on his visit to Jordan in May 2008 he stated:

> We are a Church in daily vital dialogue, Church of meeting, of perfect solidarity with our Arab peoples, with our different Christian communities in their diversity and richness and also with all Muslim communities.[1]

The Patriarch has coined a particular phrase, '*A Church with Islam*', which he often uses to stress the unique and relational connectivity this Arab Church has in the Middle East, one that Western Christianity needs to hear and understand, but nevertheless it is also important to remember that our Church is now very much present in differing circumstances throughout what is often a called the Diaspora. It is well established in Canada, the USA, Argentina, Brazil, Mexico, Australia and Europe. In this sense the Diaspora Church outside the Middle East reflects the historical development of Christianity itself, the going out in mission of the apostolic community to proclaim the Kingdom of God (Mt 28:19-20).[2] This in turn will change the structure and ethnicity of the

---

1   Address of His Beatitude Patriarch Gregorios III to His Holiness Pope Benedict XVI, Melkite Greek Catholic Cathedral, Amman, Jordan. Vespers, 9 May 2008, § 3. The text can be found at Melkite Greek Catholic Patriarchate, Patriarchal Letters, www.pgc-lb.org.

2   Cf. John Paul II *Redemptoris Missio,* § 23.

Melkite community, but we who are part of this development understand it as an enrichment and natural development, for in the end ethnicity cannot be the measure or route of belonging. St Paul speaks to this image of oneness when he says in Galatians: So in Christ Jesus you are all children of God through faith, for all of you who were baptised have clothed yourselves with Christ. There is neither Jew nor Gentile, neither slave nor free, neither male nor female, for you are all one in Christ Jesus.(Gal 3:26-28) The Patriarch also recognises this point of development, in the same address he points out: 'We are and will remain the Church of mankind, created in the image and likeness of God.'[3] It is important even in discussions and debates about the Church in the Middle East, that we need to recognise in ecclesial terms the theological and pastoral realities in that any Melkite presence in Britain and Europe must be seen as a natural evolution and a legitimate and important opportunity for a particular church *sui iuris*, to root itself in another culture, one hungry for the *lumen orientalium*.[4] This will, one hopes, re animate Christians and make those in the West aware not only of the problems of our brothers and sisters abroad but also provide, as the *Instrumentum laboris* for the synod suggests, a positive approach which sees emigration and its integrative factors as a transformation into 'a new opportunity'.[5] It is as Pope John Paul II pointed out in *Orientale Lumen,* when speaking of the example of Saints Cyril and Methodius concerning their evangelisation of the Slav peoples, another opportunity for 'incarnating the gospel in native cultures of the people'.[6]

This personal dissonance I mentioned earlier is not necessarily a negative experience, in fact it commits me and those Melkites born here in Great Britain to a working out of new developments. I firmly believe that this ancient Church of Antioch has a place here now and in the future and that far from simply being an immigrant community, in which I work as a chaplain to help the faithful retain custom, identity and language, there is also a deeper purpose and reality. For me (and I know for our Melkite native English and British people) belonging to the Melkite church was the result of the promptings of the Holy Spirit and not an easy journey. I joined them and remain one of them in response to the growing need of that particular Eastern Catholic

---

3   Address 9 May 2008, § 7.
4   See Apostolic Letter, *Orientale Lumen*, John Paul II, 11 May 1995, Vatican City, § 1, 2, 5, 26.
5   *Instrumentum Laboris:* Synod of Bishops Special Assembly for the Middle East: *The Catholic Church in the Middle East; Communion and Witness,* Vatican City, 2010. I. *The Catholic Church in The Middle East*, B, 4. Emigration, 3, 47.
6   *OL* § 8.

community here in England. I moved over, so to speak, from the Latin Church in order to help root this Antiochian Church here. Now any gesture of willingness on the part of those non-Arab Christians to integrate and root themselves in such a community, in itself makes several presuppositions. The first is that there will *not* be vast numbers of (at least second generation) Arab Christians returning to their 'homeland'. Secondly, that this Catholic and Eastern church has a future here and will have to adapt pastorally, for example, in time make English the primary language of rite and Church.[7] Thirdly, that it is essential that their identity and spiritual heritage needs to be preserved but also carefully integrated into the ecclesial life of this country so that they remain true to their own origins. Fourthly, it will need to develop, not seeking to rely on clergy or religious from the Middle East but encourage vocations from within; and fifthly, it must also be theologically literate, representing a valid and authentic theological and spiritual voice that is ancient, eastern, Orthodox and Catholic, able to speak up for itself and open to ecumenism especially working towards reunion with the Orthodox as well as being part of a consistent and continual reminder of the eastern roots of Christianity.[8] A visible witness that the mother church and place of origin for all Christians lies not in Rome or Constantinople or Antioch but Jerusalem. As Saint John Damascene wrote: 'Rejoice, O Jerusalem, mother of Churches, dwelling place of God, because you have received the first remission of sins, through the resurrection.' In these ways the Melkite presence in Europe and Britain is an expansion, not attrition of the Church in the Middle East.[9]

In one sense this is precisely what the Special Assembly for the Middle East is about, as the *Instrumentum laboris* says, the aims of the synod are, 'firstly to confirm and strengthen the members of the Catholic Church in their identity, through the word of God and sacraments' and secondly 'to foster ecclesial communion among the *sui iuris* churches, so that they can bear witness to Christian life in an authentic, joyous and attractive way.'[10] But how can this special synod work for us here in this Diaspora situation? My

---

7 Whilst it respects its catholicity, perhaps it ought to show a distinctive link with its Orthodox roots, not only through its rites but also such issues such as sharing their date for Great Lent and Holy Pascha!

8 This was at the heart of Archbishop Elias Zogbhy's work to insist that the place, theology and tradition of the Melkite Church is firmly within its Orthodox roots and not in any subsequent Latin development. See Archbishop Elias Zoghby, 1981. *Tous Schismatiques?*, Heidelberg Press-Lebanon, Beirut.

9 See *Instrumentum Laboris*, I a. The Situation of Christians in the Middle East, 13, 14, 18.

10 *Instrumentum Laboris*, A. The Goal of the Synod, 3.

own contention, based upon the theological insights of several key Melkite theologians amongst them, Frs Jean Corbon, Ignace Dick, Néophytos Edelby and of course Elias Zoghby, is that one cannot keep returning to issues from the past in order to start dialogue afresh. The wonderful title of Zoghby's work, *Tous schismatiques?* (with a question mark) still leaves me with a sense that the Spirit is trying to make us look again at our origins, not to see things as a fragmentation from some original universal Church with echoes still present in the Catholic Church and certain others, but to acknowledge that history teaches another a more complex lesson.[11] The existence of the various Eastern Church families, Orthodox and Catholic, is a constant reminder that unity in diversity existed from the inception of the community called Christian. Their ecclesiology and in particular the deep spirituality of liturgical action bear witness to the often misunderstood and more painful hidden histories of our Church of Christ.[12]

The small, but growing presence of the Melkite Greek-Catholic Church in this country is very much a stumbling block for Catholics, Orthodox and Anglicans alike. It leads to misunderstanding about ecclesial identity—'are you Orthodox or Roman Catholic?', or as one unpleasant priest put it 'playing at orthodoxy'. It leads to pastoral problems with the Latins over schooling, church attendance, marriage arrangements and a theological suspicion that we really must be heretics for not doing things in the same way and yet this stumbling block is also a sign. As I frequently tell my parish in sermons, we are the light of the East, bridging the gap between our Orthodox sisters and brothers and our Western Christian communities. Patriarch Maximos IV Sayegh proclaimed it like this in a Conference entitled: *Orient catholique et unité chretienne* (Düsseldorf 9 August 1960) 'Our vocation is to be "uniters".'[13] Joseph Kallas puts it in another way: 'That which restores the unity of the Churches, is the (vocation to) service which goes on until martyrdom not discussions and accusations without end. By devoting ourselves to service without any "conditions", perhaps we can receive this gift of unity and place it at the feet of one another.'[14] I certainly believe that we Melkites in the Diaspora sense that our task is to be different for the sake of the kingdom and to make part of ourselves the vocation to the martyrdom of ecumenism

---

11   Zoghby, *Tous Schismatiques?*, pp. 39, 51.

12   See Fr Robin Gibbons, *The Eastern Church*, CTS, London, 2006.

13   'L'oecumenisme au service de la presence chrétienne au Moyen-Orient', *Actes du colloque international en memoire du P. Jean Corbon*, 16 Mars 2002, Kaslik, p. 63.

14   Archbishop Joseph Kallas, 'Homilié au cours de la sainte liturgie clôturant le colloque', *Actes du colloque*, p. 139.

in an age where ecumenism seems to be less of a priority than before. That is a gift we can share with our sisters and brothers in the Middle East. It is as Father James Graham of the Melkite eparchy of Newton so aptly put it, to 'be like Zaccheus, willing to climb up a tree-perhaps even go out on a limb to overcome our limitations. The Lord will recognise us, reward our efforts and bring salvation to our house.'[15]

ECCLESIOLOGY AND ECCLESIAL REALITY

Benedict XVI, in one of his general audiences, talked about Saint Paul's teaching on the Church. In his address he noted firstly that the word *ekkelsia* makes its first appearance; 'in the incipit of the first letter to the Thessalonians' but he then went on to look at the various ways in which this word is used, many times in reference to local communities and at others the new community in Christ as a whole:[16]

> And thus we see that 'the Church of God' is not only a collection of various local Churches but that these various local Churches in turn make up one Church of God. All together they are 'the Church of God' which precedes the individual local Churches and is expressed or brought into being in them.[17]

This pre-existence of the Church as a whole before the particular has been the matter of debate and was certainly criticised by other 'ecclesial' communities when it was equated with a certain take on primacy in the document *Dominus Jesus* formulated partly by the then Cardinal Joseph Ratzinger.[18] It must be noted *en passant* that the eastern Churches response was far from positive. Gaby Hachem in a paper given at the colloquium in honour of Father Jean Corbon pointed out the flaws in the document, 'She recalls contrary to the assertion of *LG* 8 which evoked the term "plura elementa", that the Church of Christ does not subsist in the non-catholic Churches and ecclesial communities'[19] but urged that 'We may find it greatly beneficial to specify these concepts in order to avoid any ambiguity or

15 Fr James Graham, Archbishop Elias Zoghby's 'Vision of Christian Unity', article in *Sophia*, Melkite Eparchy of Newton, Winter 2008.
16 Benedict XVI General Audience, St Peter's Square, Wednesday, 15 October 2008.
17 Benedict XVI General Audience.
18 Declaration *Dominus Jesus*, 16 March 2000, Vatican City.
19 Gaby Hachem, 'Pluralisme écclesiologique et communion', *Actes du colloque*, p. 84.

confusion between the Universal Church and our Churches. And it is in the same context that the use of the term "sister-churches" must be defined,'[20] in fact the CDF *Letter to the Bishops of the Catholic Church on some aspects of the Church understood as Communion, Communionis notio*[21] went further, placing the ecclesiology of a universal Church at the centre of any ecclesiological model in particular Roman (Latin) Church thought, making the empirically bold statement that 'it is a reality ontologically and temporally prior to every individual particular church' and whilst acknowledging the potential in a more Orthodox liturgical/Eucharistic model criticised it.[22] 'The rediscovery of a Eucharistic ecclesiology, though being of undoubted value, has however sometimes placed unilateral emphasis on the principle of the local Church.'[23] In other words the more organic principle of universality seems incompatible with that of local Eucharistic gatherings—even one presumes with Ignatius of Antioch's model of bishop! Even with these 'single' model statements, there is room for manoeuvre, in the same audience, Benedict XVI went on to speak about the additional qualification of God in the Church: 'she is not a human association, born from ideas or common interests, but a convocation of God. He has convoked her, thus, in all her manifestations she is one.'[24]

Peter de Mey in an article investigating the potential for development of an Eucharistic ecclesiology,[25] writes about the insights of those twentieth century theologians of the eastern tradition, Afanassieff, Bulgakov, Schmemann and Zizoulas, who point to the primacy of the *lex orandi* especially in a developed ecclesial and liturgical theology of Church as Eucharistic celebration in contrast to the universalist model found in *Dominus Jesus*. Mey points out that in a famous article *Una sancta*, Afanassiev himself contrasted these two types of ecclesiology and criticised both the Orthodox and Catholic tendency for subscribing to the universal ecclesiology of St Cyprian of Carthage, according to which only one true and universal Church can exist.[26] The local Church, according to this ecclesiological model, is only part of the universal Church. In this way the four marks, One, Holy, Catholic and Apostolic

---

20 Hachem, pp. 86, 87.
21 *Communionis Notio*, 28 May 1992, Vatican City.
22 *Communionis Notio*, §. 7, 8, 9, 14.
23 *Communionis Notio*, § 11.
24 Benedict XVI General Audience.
25 Peter de Mey, 'Eucharistic ecclesiology in Roman Catholic Magisterial Teaching', *Journal for Theology in Europe*, Vol. 19, 2008, Issue 2, p. 79ff.
26 N Afannasieff, 'Una Sancta', *Irenikon* 36, 1963, pp. 436-475; see also J Zizioulas, *Being as Communion*, St Vladimir's Seminary Press, Crestwood, NY, 1985.

found in the Nicene Creed have been ascribed to the universal Church and not to the local community of faith, but as Afanasieff points out according to the eastern theology of Eucharistic ecclesiology, 'the Church is where the Eucharistic assembly is.'[27] Looking at the issue of rupture and lost communion, Afanassieff also pointed out that in a universal model where one Church claims to be the 'true' Church, there can only be the inevitable separation from other Churches by excommunication, but in a Eucharistic ecclesiology where the stress is on the Eucharistic assembly of the local Churches, there can only be an interruption of communion with one another.[28]

This links to Zoghby's 'partial or double communion' between Churches especially in light of the Melkite-Orthodox initiatives:

> The Antiochian Orthodox, in the event of a resumption of communion with the Melkite Catholics would be indirectly in communion with Rome and Melkite Catholics indirectly in communion with Orthodoxy. The case of Antioch (Melkite Orthodox and Catholic) would be a stimulant for the resumption of full, total communion between Rome and Orthodoxy and a foretaste of recovered unity. It is worthwhile testing and reflecting on this proposal.[29]

There are of course difficulties which emerge in the contemporary understandings of both models, for the East the notion of 'bishop-church-liturgy' is unrealistic in practice, whilst Zizoulas criticises Afanassiev's notion that a parish can be in itself a complete and catholic Church.[30] I am not so sure that I agree with Zizoulas, there is mileage in examining the wider notion of parish and church, especially in terms of other developments such the recent phenomenon of grouping clusters of parishes together and more especially in the deeper histories of our communities (such as the Anglo-Saxon model of minster and church) and in light of that wonderful theology of *economia*! Our own experience is as a diaspora community, separated from the Mother Church by space, time and lacking an authentically Melkite hierarch (the Latin oversight of Westminster is generous but one hopes is but a temporary provision). It may be ecclesiologically traditional to have one bishop, one Church, but in practice this has proved to be far from the case and certainly in pastoral

27 Mey, p. 80.
28 Mey, p. 80.
29 Ignace Dick, *Chretiens en Syrie: Heritiers De L'Eglise au Cour de L'Islam et a La Pointe de L'Oecumenisme.* Aleppo, 1999, p. 106.
30 J Zizioulas, *Being as Communion*, p. 251.

and ecumenical terms it needs further examination. For the Catholic West, the problems of universality versus local, papal primacy and the Orthodox/ Eastern Catholics and the delicate theological balance between council and pope needs more working out, especially in the light of the teaching of the Second Vatican Council such as *Lumen Gentium*. In the section on Ecclesial communion in the *Instrumentum laboris* this debate finds expression in two models, communion through baptism and eucharist and then with the Pope of Rome. It is to be hoped that the situation of the Churches in the Middle East and the discourse engendered will renew this avenue of exploration.[31]

A MELKITE EXPLORATION

This is precisely where the Melkite and Antiochian orthodox theological insights such as that quoted above concerning double communion, need to balance out what can be one-sided arguments about apostolicity, authenticity and the inevitable truth claims of one or other of the ancient Churches, Rome included. Elias Zoghby's question 'are we all schismatics?' is an important one, for it suggests that the whole story is more complex than portrayed in academic intellectual arguments and a simplistic view of theological history. It also bears upon the actual relationship the Eastern Catholic Churches have with Rome itself, she is certainly NOT their mother church, as P de Halleux wrote:

> With respect to the Orthodox Church, the (Roman) Catholic Church is not in a maternal relationship nor their source (origin). Their relationship is one of fraternal communion, the Church of Rome is not the ecclesial origin of other (Orthodox and Eastern Catholic) Churches, she only recognises and regularises this when she admits them to full communion (with herself).[32]

How does our experience in Europe connect and link with the deep concerns of Christianity in the Middle East? In the first place by being a Melkite presence here, we are a constant reminder of that Christian Middle

---

31   *Instrumentum Laboris*, § 54, 55.
32   A de Halleux, quoted in 'L'oecuménisme au service de la présence chrétienne au Moyen Orient', *Actes du colloque*, p. 87. See also Robin Gibbons, 'Pride or Prejudice; The Vocation of Eastern Catholic Churches', *One in Christ*, Volume 32, Number 2, Winter 2009, pp. 35-53.

East, a small but important presence of the origins and source of our resurrection faith. Secondly by being rooted in the Antiochian tradition we connect through our sources to the great Syriac, Aramaic and Greek traditions of the Church—to what Gregorios I I calls a 'plural culture', where things have been done differently to the Latin tradition, yet are authentic and ancient.[33] Once again we bridge the divide between Byzantine Orthodoxy, which is essentially European and the Oriental traditions of the ancient Church, what I would call the 'deep tradition'.[34] This is a witness to the diversity of tradition, and the continual inculturation of the Church in the local community. Thirdly, there is no doubt that being part of an Arab Christian Church, and one that goes beyond Arab to deeper roots is a difficult one at this period in time especially in the European Union. Whilst we are very much a Church where the traditions and customs of the community can be kept alive for those who have emigrated, we cannot remain, nor should we become, a ghettoised Church, linguistically and culturally cut off from the host society. In this respect the diaspora Melkite Church should feed back to the Church in the Middle East some of the theological, pastoral and ecclesial insights (and concerns) of new developments, especially where they are deemed to be positive. Fourthly, in maintaining our liturgical and ecclesiological connections with our tradition we can challenge not only attitudes but also false history. As Patriarch Gregorios III often says we are also (in the Middle East in particular), a Church for the Arabs and a Church in connection and dialogue with Islam.

With Islam

In our muddled approach to Islam here in Europe, the inspiration and historical engagement (whatever that might have been) of our Church over several centuries in Islamic territories should provide examples and focal points for rapprochement both for Christian and Muslim alike, but it will also require a brave and clear voice so that the emotive voices of radicalism and fundamentalism receive courteous but truthful response.[35] The Melkite Church has something to say to Islam, we hear a lot about the Islamic contributor to civilisation but forget their indebtedness to the Eastern

---

33 Patriarch Gregorios III Laham, *Introduction to the Liturgy, Services and other Symbols of the Eastern Church*, Eastern Christian Publications, Fairfax, 2009, p. 11.
34 Gibbons, 'Pride or Prejudice', p. 39, 40.
35 I Dick, *Chretiens en Syrie*, 1999; see 'Contexte socio-politique', pp. 5-35.

Christian tradition, not only in prayer but in language. This reciprocity is important for truthful dialogue, for though Islam gives much to civilisation it has also received much from the Judaeo-Christian tradition and especially the Eastern Church. A short aside may give a powerful example of why this is so necessary. I was present at a lunch and speech given by the Deputy Prime Minister of Indonesia in Oxford recently. At the lunch I had been discussing the case of Islamic fundamentalists objecting to the use of Allah by the Christians claiming it was an Islamic name for God, together we both agreed that the name came before Islam and was rooted in Arabic, a language associated with, but not coterminous with Islam, especially as I represented a Church which uses Arabic a great deal. Yet in the afternoon speech the Deputy Prime Minister claimed that the word was NOT suitable for a Christian understanding of God, a claim without foundation in the Arabic-speaking world, for it is also a word I hear on the lips of our Melkites at prayer and in greeting here and abroad! It is in the *acta* of history that our Melkite story may be able to unlock the door of half truth to reveal a better, truer version including the different types of existence the Christian community experienced after the Arab conquest.

> Melkites were the first to arabise Christian culture. They harnessed the translations into Arabic of the Bible, the Liturgy and the Church Fathers. They also worked out an 'Arab' theology to try and introduce the Christian faith to Moslems ... Arab Christians of all confessions contributed to Arab culture and civilisation ... their survival is a miracle and their presence is a grace, because they are a leaven of openness and progress for the Arab countries.[36]

For All

Bishop John Eliya, Eparch emeritus in the USA for the Melkite Church summed up part of the many concerns that one hopes will be touched on in the Synod when he commented on the great Zoghby initiative and the process already established by our Holy Synod for re-union with our sister Church of Antioch. It is a statement of humility and bravery, and I summarise some of his main comments. The situation of the Eastern Catholic Churches and Rome especially in administrative matters is not ideal as it remains; for example, the

---

36   Dick, p. 33.

Code of Canon law for the Eastern Catholic Churches is inadequate and too Latin in tone, style and content; the application of Latin norms (especially in Diaspora countries) has often been unfortunate![37]

The true tradition of the East presupposes communion with Rome, so that the Orthodox cannot claim total legitimacy of apostolic succession—but then neither can Rome without the East, for the Spirit breathes through both lungs of the Church,

> the complete eastern tradition requires absolutely the communion with Rome, although in a special way as it was in the first millennium. On the other hand the Greek Catholics, by keeping their union with Rome, have kept a fundamental principle of Eastern tradition, especially the Antiochian tradition. However, this principle has been exposed in its application to different things which deformed it so that communion became almost absorption.[38]

For the Catholic West the problems of universality versus local, papal primacy and the Orthodox/Eastern Catholics and the delicate theological balance between council and pope and of course Benedict's own rejection of a patriarchal title (important especially in the vexed issue of cardinals in the Eastern Catholic Churches!). The Melkite understanding sees the patriarch as higher and ecclesially different to the Roman concept of cardinals. All this needs more working out, especially in the light of *Lumen Gentium, Orientale Lumen, Balammand* and other pertinent documentation. The *Instrumentum laboris* makes great play of this 'At the level of the patriarchal church, communion is expressed by a Synod which gathers the bishops of an entire community around the Patriarch,'[39] but there are other ways, a liturgical ecclesiology is one of the great gifts of the East and could if expressed and opened out give new ventures and new approaches.

One cannot go backwards, only forwards in trust and hope. Issues such as the conversion of Muslims to Christianity in the Diaspora for valid reasons often go unremarked, but they happen in practice, as does a direct concern for justice and peace. Many of my parish for instance are connected to the continuing events between Israeli and Palestinian communities, and as too

---

37 Robin Gibbons, 'Pride or Prejudice; the Vocation of Eastern Catholic Churches', *One in Christ*, Volume 32 Number 2, Winter 2009, pp. 48-52.

38 Bishop John Elyia, *Newton Eparchy Melkite Perspectives*, 1997.

39 *IL*, pp. 55ff., see also Archbishop Elias Zoghby, *Projet de Ré-unification du Patriarchat Byzantin D'Antioche*, Usek, Syria, 1999.

often happens are witnesses to a martyrdom that claims lives, land, hope and joy. But for these *pierres vivantes,* the living stones of the Holy land, our task is to keep that connection in faith and love alive in hope. We stand together with them. Not only are we, the Melkite Church, charged to maintain a spiritual relationship and a distinctive fraternal dialogue with our sister Orthodox churches especially the Antiochian one, we are called to dialogue beyond that to the Arab heritage, both Christian and Islamic of the Middle East. As Pope John Paul II wrote in *Orientale Lumen*:

> … the experience of the Christian East is offered to us as an authoritative example of successful inculturation. From this model we learn that if we wish to avoid the recurrence of particularism as well as of exaggerated nationalism, we must realise that the proclamation of the Gospel should be deeply rooted in what is distinctive to each culture and open to convergence in a universality, which involves an exchange for the sake of mutual enrichment.[40]

May we work for the Lord and the Kingdom and may the indwelling Trinity be the continual presence of love between and with us.

---

40   *OL,* p. 7.

LITURGICAL THEOLOGY
AND CHRISTIAN IDENTITY:
A REFLECTION

Petrus Yousif

Our title indicates that a plurality of liturgies supposes or gives rise to a plurality of liturgical theology and Christian identities. This means that in a particular liturgy there are different elements constituting a specific Christian identity. So, from the plurality of liturgies (rite, spirituality, etc.) we arrive at a plurality of Churches, each with its own identity, and vice versa, at least in the formative period of liturgies.

Our short study is analytico-synthetical and presumes the existence of different elements: rites and sacraments, dogma, history, Canon Law.

We may proceed from this hypothesis: the plurality of Churches is, to some extent, concomitant with the plurality of liturgies. To each Church corresponds its proper liturgical heritage, theology, and so on, and this forms the Christian identity proper to each rite or Church.

PENTECOST, THE FOUNDATIONAL EVENT

Pentecost was the feast of renewal of the assembly of the Covenant sealed with God in Sinai and forming a new and united people: one people as the repository of God's Law, and disciples of the Lord. The unity of the people and the Law which formed it were the basis for sending them to share the *mirabilia Dei* with the peoples. Now it was time, having formed this people, that communication of the *mirabilia Dei* which it had received should begin for all people, as prophesied by Joel: the new era of a new generation of prophets filled with the Spirit, announced by the prophets and proclaimed by Peter.[1]

With this new Pentecost a new era begins: One Spirit, but with everyone understanding in his own language what was destined for all peoples. Here

---

1   Acts 2:14-24; Joel 2:24-32a.

131

we are confronted by a new event: while at Sinai the dispersed people were united through one language and law to form a national and religious entity with its own identity, now the one people is sent out to all peoples to evangelise them in their own language. One Spirit speaks through Peter and the other 'Galileans' and each hears them speaking their own language.[2] The Covenant has now become cosmic and universal.[3]

MISSION AND PLURALITY OF RITES

From that time the Church began to spread the Gospel message and to worship in different countries, cultures and languages, glorifying the Lord in these different idioms, incarnating the divine worship and celebrating the mysteries in each region, progressively forming a local way of realising the one true manner of worship 'everywhere in God and in the Spirit'.[4] The same worship required by the Lord, 'do this in memory of me', was celebrated in the language and expressed in the practice of the local community or *ecclesia* of a particular people. All Christians have a sense of sharing the same worship, the essence of which was commended by the Lord, and the same faith, but also celebrate and express them according to local practice and language. So it is that the plurality of these 'primitive' rites preceded the relative unification into a smaller number, as celebrated in influential missionary centres, especially in the major cities. The unification of the local hierarchies of local churches unified worship in their region. So the historical formation of rites did not arise from the spread of a common rite to different regions, but it was from different local rites that Christian communities formed local or regional, and then national Churches and rites. The unification of the local hierarchy led to the unification of rite in the territory of that hierarchy. As A Baumstark has established,[5] this seems to correspond better to a logical way for the Church to develop. It does not mean that in these united rites covering a large area it was not possible to have liturgical particularities. Indeed, this is what happened following the unification of rites in a major area, in, for example, the Byzantine or Antiochene rite. In all these variations, the unity of the Church and the

---

2   Acts 2:7-12.
3   See Robert Murray, *The Cosmic Covenant,* Heythrop Monographs, London, 1992.
4   Jn 4:23-24.
5   *Vom geschichtlichen Werden der Liturgie,* Freiburg in Breisgaw, 1923.

fundamental unity of Christian worship (Eucharist, sacraments, prayer) was presumed.

RELATION BETWEEN CHRISTIAN IDENTITY AND SACRAMENTS

There is no *Christianus vagus* or generic Christian. Although there are sacraments common to all Christians, forming their fundamental unity and so their belonging to the Christian Church as a whole, the process of becoming Christian shows that there are concrete elements which distinguish different categories of Christian according to the elements associated with baptism and specific to different Churches. The difference in liturgies establishes the difference in identity between the Eastern Catholic Churches,[6] indeed a Christian is baptised into a particular Church, rite, or liturgical tradition. In the Code of Canons of the Eastern Churches, Canon 28, §2, mentions six rites originating from six eastern traditions, listed in alphabetical order: Alexandrian, Antiochene, Armenian, Chaldean and Constantinopolitan. Using Aristotelian terms, we may say that 'Christian' is a genus, to belong to one *sancta catholica* tradition is the 'species', to be a concrete member of a Church is the 'individual'.

INDIVIDUAL CHRISTIAN AND INDIVIDUAL CHURCH

The individual Christian belongs to a particular Church, the Church and rite in which he is or should be baptized. Even if *de facto*, for incidental reasons, he is baptised in the rite of a Church which is not that of his parents, he will be a member of his parents' Church.[7] Unless he is more than 14 years of age, and is not yet baptised, then he can choose the rite of the Church in which he is prepared for baptism and is indeed baptised.[8] So the faithful belong to the Church in which they should be baptised. In the diaspora it is not infrequent to have cases occur where, for example, a Chaldean child is baptised in the Latin rite because of the lack of a Chaldean minister. The family later presents the child in a Chaldean baptismal ceremony so as to be confirmed.

---

6   See Congregation for the Eastern Churches, *Instruction for applying the Liturgical Prescriptions of the Code of Canons of the Eastern Churches*, Rome, 1996, § 16.
7   *CCEO*, 677 § 1 and 678 § 1.
8   *CCEO*, 30.

Church Human and Divine: 'Theandric'

Being his body the nature of the Church of Christ is, like him, a theandric reality: earthly and celestial The faithful belong to a geographical area incarnated in a territorial Church, although by baptism each is a member of the *una, sancta, catholica et apostolica ecclesia*. Liturgy is also theandric. Incarnated in the space, the particular Church is a community of faith in a special area or geographical region. Theandric, the Church is not only incarnated in a particular region, but also in what is proper to this region on the human level: culture, language, even ethnic belonging. This is the principle of incarnation in which the Word assumed human nature as a whole and in the particular: Jesus was perfect man, but perfectly incarnated in a particular milieu and race: Son of God and son of David, Universal Man and an individual living in a country, speaking a language, having an ethnic identity.

Particular Liturgy and Particular Church

A particular Church is the community of faithful living in a determined area, and so in a delineated geographical space. It is the incarnation of the Universal-Catholic Church in a particular territory. Territoriality is basic to the Church; this same Church is also a community of faithful, sharing faith and expressions of it such as worship, in a specific culture, language, etc., in which this faith is expressed on the level of meaning and practice. This is what is expressed by such terms as 'inculturation', 'acculturation', etc. The faith and worship of the Catholic, that is universal, Church, fundamentally identical in this same Church, are expressed in the idiom and behaviour of a 'local' Catholic Church: worship is expressed in her liturgy, and faith in her theology. So the particular Church is the incarnation, in different rites and cultures, of the One Catholic Church with its own rite or liturgy.

The Status of a Member of the Faithful in the (his) Church

Returning to the notion that there is no *Christianus vagus* we may define a specific member of the faithful as follows: 'a baptized individual or person in a particular individual and territorial Church, with its proper hierarchy and rite or liturgy.' Since this Church is the Catholic Church in a local territory, the baptised person belongs to the Catholic Church not despite but because of baptism in a particular Church. Indeed, the Catholic Church is a communion of particular Churches. Catholicity supposes unity and universality, and through baptism those who receive it are members of the Catholic Church, founded by Christ, as it subsists in a particular Church. Needless to say, the hierarchical unity of the Catholic Church does not weaken the 'particular' Churches, rather it strengthens them. *Confirma fratres tuos!*[9] should be the attitude of the Catholic faithful. Paradoxical as it may seem, then, a member of the Catholic faithful belongs wholly to the Catholic Church and wholly to their particular Catholic Church.

The Lesson of History

In speaking of Pentecost, we alluded that this Event was the starting point for constituting the Universal Church, destined for the whole world and every language. We then made reference to the spread of Christian worship and faith in different areas in the world. In apostolic times the formation of rites was preceded by the common elements of liturgy, for example, baptising in the name of the persons of the Trinity; in each region there was special care to perform the sacraments, especially baptism and the Eucharist, in a reverent way, the pastors being influenced by more important missionary centres and influential Churches, particularly in important cities with an apostolic heritage. So by the beginning of the third century, important centres emerged: Rome, Edessa, Byzantium, Antioch, with canonico-liturgical texts regulating worship. Thus there was progress from a large number of 'local traditions' to a lesser number of more important traditions.

---

9   Lk. 22:32.

PARTICULAR CHURCH AND RITE

The formation of different rites was concomitant with the constitution of different Churches in different territories, with their local liturgy. So particular Churches were—and are—communities with a hierarchical structure and their own liturgy and law. Mystical, sociological, cultural and territorial hierarchical elements are constitutive of a concrete Church or community in this world. In the beginning, each Church had its own territory; but then, because of human mobility and for other historical reasons there came to be two different Churches in same territory. It is not usual, therefore, for members of a Church *sui juris* to be submitted to another Church *sui iuris,* without a serious reason and spiritual benefit. This affirmation does not deny the necessity of collaboration between the different Churches. But territoriality should not mean the exclusion of Catholic hierarchy when there is a significant number of faithful in that territory. An example is the restriction of the territory of India regarding the Syro-Malabar Church, although an important number of local missionaries were Malabar.

PLURALITY OF RITES AND CHURCHES

This is a fact admitted as 'natural' by each of the Eastern Churches for their members and for those of the other Eastern Churches. The variety of rites is concomitant with the plurality of Churches. The fundamental unity and universality of the Christian Church includes and requires an astonishing variety, which means a plurality of Churches. Each Church has its own history; each Church has its own liturgy and rite. It seems that the most important constitutive element of a particular Church is her liturgy, even when it is shared by a counterpart Church[10] not united to the Catholic Church. Both Churches, united to Rome or autocephalous, consider liturgy as their most important heritage and constitutive of their identity. The liturgical identity is so strong that *Ritus* and *Ecclesia* are considered by some as being equivalent.[11] At the Second Vatican Council this identity was clearly asserted.[12] Besides, each Church originally had its own geographical area, at least until the eighteenth century, although this is

---

10   Except the Maronite Church.
11   E Hermann, 'De Ritu in Jure Canonico', *Oriens Christianus*, 32, 1933, pp. 96-158.
12   The second section of the *Decretum de Ecclesiis Orientalibus Catholicis* § 2 is entitled: 'de Ecclesiis particularibus seu ritus'—'On the particular Churches or Rites'.

no longer the case because of the emigration of Churches. As their distribution changes, territoriality should not be restricted to ancient geographical limits. Each Catholic Church now has the whole world as its territory, and territorial divisions from the time of the Ottoman Empire are now obsolete. Besides, each particular Church has not only its liturgy but also a liturgical theology and spirituality, and a proper theology *tout court*, within the unity of the Catholic faith. This is clearer in fields such as ecclesiology and Christology, and the recent agreements between non-catholic Churches with the Catholic Church, especially on Christology, has affirmed the Christological unity among the Churches.

THE PRESENT SITUATION IN THE MIDDLE EAST

For a member of the Eastern Catholic Churches in the Middle East, with which the coming Synod is concerned, the plurality of rites, each with its proper shape and tradition, is completely natural. It is not only tolerated but we willingly accept the variety of rites in the unity and universality of the One Church of Christ. We are one Church in the Catholic Church and many Churches in the same. We consider our identity as a bridge between the Catholic Church to which we belong and our counterpart Churches not in union with Rome, with whom we are proud to share the same liturgico-cultural heritage and with whom we are obligated to foster fraternal relations, in view of the unity desired by Our Lord. The politico-cultural situation is different now from that of the epoch during which our rites were developed. We live in an era and a milieu in which the Greek and Syriac cultures in which our heritage was transmitted are no longer dominant. In these countries Islam is the common religion. Arabic is the language of culture and communication in the majority of them: with the exception of Iran, Turkey and Cyprus. Our Churches are invited to be faithful to the golden age of their own culture, and at the same time to be present to the current culture of the countries in which we are present, in order to dialogue with it, to use it as a means to serve our countries and to achieve our mission of peace and fraternity. We have our role in the Middle East, we maintain our ecclesial communion, we continue our Christian witness in relationship with the other religions, and remain in contact with other Christians, despite the fact that we are a 'little flock',[13] but not so little in the eyes of Our Lord!

---

13   See *Instrumentum Laboris*, Special Assembly for the Middle East of the Synod of Bishops, Rome, 6 June 2010.

THE RENEWAL OF THE
COPTIC CATHOLIC CHURCH:
GRAPPLING WITH IDENTITY AND ALTERITY
A Theologian's Perspective

Fadel Sidarouss SJ

Two events, both giving it a particular focus, inspire this presentation: on the one hand, reflection on the renewal of the Coptic Catholic Church, launched in October 2008 by its Patriarch, His Beatitude Antonios Naguib, following an earlier initiative by His Most Eminent Beatitude, the late Patriarch Cardinal Stephanos II Ghattas, in 2000; and on the other hand by preparations for the Synod for the Catholic Middle East, to be held in Rome in October 2010. I offer, then, some elements of personal reflection, at once contextual, pastoral, spiritual and theological.[1]

I will approach the topic from two complementary angles: a diagnosis of the present situation of the Coptic Catholic Church and its challenges, and the principal elements for renewal.[2] By way of introduction, a brief description of the Egyptian Church is required for an understanding of the subject in hand.

---

1   Drawing on four of my previous publications:
    'Eglise Copte et Monde Moderne', Thèse de Théologie Pastorale, présentée à la Faculté des Sciences Religieuses de l'Université Saint Joseph, Beirut, 1978. Cf. a résumé in *Proche-Orient Chrétien* 30, Jerusalem, 1980, pp. 211-265.
    'Les nouveaux courants dans la communauté copte orthodoxe' (en collaboration avec P M Martin et C Van Nispen), *Proche-Orient Chrétien* 40, 1990, pp. 245-257.
    'L'Egypte Chrétienne—Traditions, Défis et Espérances', in *Eglises au Moyen-Orient: défis et espérances (ouvrage collectif), Cahiers de l'Orient chrétien* N° 3, CEDRAC, Beirut, 2005, pp. 15-31.
    'Pour une Théologie Contextuelle dans l'Orient Arabe Contemporain', *in Quo Vadis, Theologia Orientalis?*, Actes du Colloque 'Théologie Orientale: contenu et importance' (TOTT), Ain Traz, April 2005, Textes et Etudes sur l'Orient Chrétien N° 6, CEDRAC, Université Saint Joseph, Beirut, 2008, pp. 215-237.
2   Towards the middle of the nineteenth century, the Coptic Orthodox Church experienced a movement of 'reform' *(iṣlāḥ)* initiated by Patriarch Kyrillos IV, and of 'renewal' *(nahda)* inaugurated by Patriarch Kyrillos VI in the 60s of the twentieth century, continued (from the 70s) by his successor, the current Shenouda III.

A Brief Description of the Egyptian Church

The religious situation in Egypt consists of a Sunni Muslim majority (94-95 percent of the 80 million inhabitants). The country is governed by Islamic Law *(Sharī'a islāmiyya)*, which is *the* main source of the Constitution; religious guidance comes from *Al-Azhar*—the *ulema*, mosque, university, and schools of this prestigious thousand-year-old pan-Islamic institution; although this does not prevent the existence of numerous Sufi confraternities, somewhat removed from formal Islamic orthodoxy, and animating popular religion.

According to the tradition of the early centuries, Christianity in Egypt dates from St Mark the Evangelist. The whole of Egypt was Christian before the Islamic conquest of the seventh century. Following this, Egyptian Christians were called Copts *(Qibt or Aqbāt)*, from the Greek *Aiguptos*, probably originating in turn from a Pharaonic word, *Het-Ka-Ptah*, meaning 'house of the spirit of (the god) Ptah'.[3] The passage from Christianity to Islam and the Arabic language occurred progressively through the centuries.

Today, Egyptian Christianity consists of a Coptic Orthodox majority, the largest Christian community in the Middle and Near East. After them come the Coptic Catholics, with some 200-250,000 believers, and close to 50,000 other Catholic denominations (including 35,000 Sudanese of the Latin rite, together with Syro-Lebanese of various Eastern rites). Finally, there are Protestants of different denominations, mostly having arrived from the US in the nineteenth century, together with the Anglicans, representing some 150,000 believers.[4]

Article 18 of the United Nations Charter regarding liberty of worship and of conscience has been signed in principle by Egypt, but is not, in fact, respected. If Christian worship is tolerated, Muslim conversion to Christianity, by contrast, is not; marriage between Muslims and Christians is forbidden; the building of churches is authorised only by decree of the President of the Republic, in accordance with an Ottoman law of the nineteenth century—the *Khatt-i Humāyūn*—dating from the time of

---

3   According to official figures, Copts make up some 4 million people (5-6 percent of the population), probably an accurate figure, since as long as there have been statistics in Egypt, from the time of the French and the English, the proportion of Christians has scarcely altered. According to the Copts themselves, they number 8-10 million, a less likely figure.

4   All the figures proposed are subject to caution, as no credible official statistics are available. The number of Jews is currently less than one hundred, following massive immigration after the Suez War against Israel, England and France, although their community, of ancient origin, was particularly active in the commercial life of modern Egypt.

Ottoman rule and regulating relations between the State and the different Egyptian Churches.

A DIAGNOSIS OF THE SITUATION OF THE COPTIC CATHOLIC CHURCH AND ITS CHALLENGES

It appears to me that three traits characterise the diagnosis of the present situation of the Coptic Catholic Church, and represent, in fact, three major challenges: the identity and alterity which for me lie at the heart of the problem, and which govern two other aspects, one concerning its ecclesial mission, the other its minority relationship to Islam.

The Interaction of Identity and Alterity

The interaction of identity and alterity governs the entire issue of the diagnosis and consequent challenges with respect to a renewal of the Coptic Catholic Church.

Must the current international phenomenon of a return to specific identities be understood, in general terms, as a normal and natural reaction to the phenomenon of globalisation (economic, political, cultural, mass media, internet, fashion, etc.), in order to safeguard the inviolable uniqueness of every society, religion, community or person, or may the insistence on identity be due to a phenomenon other than globalisation, such as the invasive ideological fanaticism of a religion or community which imposes itself on an 'other', seen as different, menacing its existence or identity? Probably both at once. A too literal insistence on identity is always a dangerous phenomenon, since it cultivates, wittingly or unwittingly, dangerous social reactions: a withdrawal and closing in on oneself, a decline in relation to the other, the different, even suspicion or rejection of them; violence against others considered to be a threat and so on. It is at this moment, according to the suggestive title of the Lebanese writer Amine Maalouf, that 'murderous identities' arise.

The Coptic Catholic Church does not escape this diagnosis: confronted by foreign globalisation (modernity) on the one hand, and by two majority national identities on the other, it is in fact tempted, just like all the other religious communities in the country, to take refuge in its own identity in order to preserve it from what is outside of it, different and menacing. However, the remedy for this, which it bears within it, calls it back to its true identity,

141

an identity linked to its alterity: it is fully Coptic, such is the aspect of its identity; it is also fully Catholic, such is the aspect of its alterity, becoming an inseparable constitutive element of its identity. We are confronted here, in effect, with the well-known phenomenon of plural identities, thanks precisely to openness to the other, openness, in the final analysis, to the universal. The catholicity of the Coptic Catholic Church is a primordial agent of openness; an opportunity for the Coptic Catholic Church, if, however, it knows how to make good use of it and to work with it. By contrast, a unilateral insistence on its Coptic identity runs a strong risk of imprisoning it in an identity closed in on itself, even 'murderous', clearly not in killing the other—that is not the spirit of the Gospel—but in seriously compromising its own existence through a relational rupture, which would, in the long term, bring about its disappearance.[5] A unilateral insistence on its Catholic identity, on the other hand, would cause it to lose contact with the context of Egyptian reality, national and ecclesial. Today, it is particularly the insistence on its Coptic identity which represents a real danger. A balanced view, the only true one, consists in living out the particular (Coptic) and universal (Catholic).

This double identity of the Coptic Catholic Church is today severely threatened by feelings of doubt regarding its own identity, due, on the one hand, to its non-recognition by the Coptic Orthodox Church, which considers it dissident;[6] and on the other hand the bringing into question of its vocation as a 'bridge' between the Catholic and Orthodox Churches, insofar as the Roman Church takes the initiative to enter into direct contact with the Coptic Orthodox Church and to dialogue with it, without crossing the bridge represented by the Coptic Catholic Church. In the face of this threat, it is necessary to carefully redefine its double identity.

The Coptic part which constitutes the identity of the Coptic Catholic Church signifies that it adopts the Coptic tradition and integrates it into its basic personality in order to exist: history, tradition, patrimony, liturgy, and rites. It also signifies that the Coptic Catholic Church is an entirely 'national' Church, wholly integrated into Egypt and profoundly linked to its destiny.

---

5   Aided by the double phenomenon of emigration and conversion to Islam and to Orthodoxy.

6   It is difficult to trace the precise origin of the Coptic Catholic Church: the prolongation of an Egyptian Christianity faithful to Chalcedon in 451, not having shared in the separation of the Church of Alexandria after that Council (and described as anti-Chalcedonian), but following the other (Chalcedonian) Churches, resulting in the creation of a Coptic Catholic patriarchate in 1899, according to the understanding of the Coptic Catholic Church itself? a creation of Catholic missionaries in the nineteenth century, as held by the Coptic Orthodox? or both?

As a result, it is called to enter into a dialogue of life with the local Coptic Orthodox Church, in a community of feelings and of projects, desiring its renewal also, accepting it as it is, even if reciprocity is never actually granted.

In effect, the Second Vatican Council encouraged 'ecumenical relations' and prohibited what appeared to the Orthodox Churches as 'proselytism' (*indimām*, a term signifying adhesion, integration; *khatf*, a pejorative term signifying 'theft, abduction').[7] This approach, excellent in itself, was not without problems as regards the identity of the Coptic Catholic Church, particularly its vocation as 'bridge' between Orthodoxy and Catholicism, which the Catholic Church had always sought for it. How should it conceive of its presence in the midst of a Christian Coptic Orthodox majority, which does not recognise it, or even its right to exist, considering that members of the Coptic Catholic Church (and also Protestants) are all of Orthodox origin, and must therefore return to their mother-Church? How then can it live out the ecumenical dimension, confronted by a Coptic Orthodox Church which rejects it? The situation is delicate and serious. It is a source of real suffering for the Coptic Catholic Church, of grave doubt regarding its identity, of rancour and resentment both towards the Orthodox Church which rejects it, and the Catholic Church which sought its creation but does not sufficiently support it.

It is easy to understand to what extent 'ecumenical dialogue' remains a pious dream, at the level of desire, if indeed it still exists, since the reality does not correspond with intercommunal tensions having been strong for more than thirty years. At present, the 'ecumenical winter' experienced by the West in its relations with the various Orthodox Churches is experienced here as a breakdown of dialogue.[8] In effect, Coptic Orthodox culture is presently, just like Arab Muslim culture, strongly threatened by closure to the other in order to preserve the purity of its identity.[9] However, it is precisely this situation which represents an opportunity for the Coptic Catholic Church to bring a breath of change, inspired by its Catholic connection to Egyptian Orthodoxy.

---

7   See the conciliar decrees: *Unitatis Redintegratio* and *Orientalium Ecclesiarum*.

8   Without doubt, the forceful personality of Pope Shenouda III has much to do with this, without forgetting the context of the entire country, characterised by reciprocal defiance, not solely religious but also political, rather than an openness to the other, tolerance, a sincere desire for dialogue, and collaboration.

9   On the subject of Arab Muslim culture, see *infra*. On Coptic Orthodox culture, it is noteworthy that, after Chalcedon, having broken of relations with the other Churches, with the exception of the Syriac and Armenian Churches (all three anti-Chalcedonian), it has merely referred back to its glorious theological past before the fifth century, with no innovation since, and with the Islamic conquest serving only to reinforce its ecclesial isolation and favouring its theological conservatism.

Is it convinced of this? Perhaps not entirely; some degree of conscientisation is required. In any case, it remains a real challenge for the Coptic Catholic Church not to lose hope in a happier future.

In effect, the Catholic part of its plural identity serves precisely to indicate its alterity, through its openness to the different other, which expresses its catholicity in a specific way. In principle, it is called to have concern for it, as Paul bore the concerns of all the Churches of Christ (2 Col 11:28). However, what frequently characterises its attitude to the other is, on the contrary, one of fear and a closing in on itself, with regards, for instance, to foreign religious Orders, which it regards with suspicion; foreign ecclesial movements, which it strongly distrusts; modernity, which it fears spontaneously, not forgetting the two threatening majorities which encircle it, Islam and Orthodoxy.

In this context, it should see alterity as a source of enrichment and renewal of its identity, rather than as a threat. In effect, there is no true human identity without a real and constant contribution from what is different. Did Paul Ricoeur not state 'Oneself is an Other'? The alternative is to fall back on what is the same—what is equal, a sign of poverty and anaemia, at the opposite pole to any renewal.

How should we live in a Christian way in this critical situation of double belonging? Participation in the suffering of Christ, who was always misunderstood and rejected in his concern of opening himself up and of opening others to himself? Requesting forgiveness for the errors of the past? Purification of memory in the present? Ecumenical dialogue in the future, when intercommunal relations allow it? So many trajectories for reflection, and challenges to face.

In conclusion, the interaction of identity and alterity we have described requires analysis at two levels, one regarding the mission of the Coptic Catholic Church at the heart of Egyptian society, the other addressing its relations with Islam, in the majority in Egypt.

Sacred and Secular Mission

Taken together, the Christian communities of Egypt are characterised by a certain 'spiritualisation' which does not sufficiently value human mediation and does not seriously take into account the secular, the temporal, and the earthly. From this a real danger arises for Christians of a certain dichotomy between the spiritual and the temporal, the heavenly and the things of this world, the sense of ecclesial and civil belonging: in a word, between the sacred and the secular. In fact, a certain wind of enlightened secularisation is required, knowing how to distinguish human realities, recognising the specificity, particularity and autonomy of each.

The Coptic Catholic Church does not escape this, all the more so since its ecclesial mission is in fact, through its parishes, ordered to the spiritual and the pastoral. Secular activities do not yet impose on its ecclesial life, as its engagement with the social, educational and medical fields is still in its infancy. The domain of foreign Catholic missionaries since the nineteenth century, such engagement has reached only timidly into the bosom of the Coptic Catholic Church.[10]

Interest in cultural and intellectual affairs is practically non-existent,[11] although Syro-Lebanese Christians *(shawām)*, fleeing Ottoman massacre in the second half of the nineteenth century, settled in Egypt, land of openness and liberty, as well as in America, another land of freedom, and initiated a cultural renaissance *(Nahda)* for the entire Arab world.[12] Participation of members of the Coptic Catholic Church in the political life of the country, and in taking up political positions, is also non-existent, although its sister Orthodox Coptic community experienced a century (mid-nineteenth to mid-twentieth) of decisive political engagement, and played an effective role in the social life of Egypt and in all the Arab countries. How, under these conditions, is it possible to promote a culture within the Coptic Catholic Church open to the entirety of the human?

---

10   The Catholic Church has currently 165 schools, founded and run in the majority by members of religious Orders (few by the dioceses); a number of social, charitable and developmental institutions (such as Caritas, The Upper-Egypt Association, the St Vincent de Paul Conference, Faith and Light, Orphans), and medical institutions (hospitals, particularly dispensaries, and homes for the elderly) run by Religious. Two Coptic Catholic Church centres, the initiatives of two priests, have recently seen the light of day: an orphanage and a residential school for the mentally handicapped. Interest in the latter has arisen in the dioceses, and prison visiting has begun to spread in a number of dioceses, at the initiative of priests.

11   Today, the Catholic Church in Egypt has a Centre for Cinema and a Centre for Eastern Patristics, both supported by the Franciscans; a Centre for Islamic Studies run by the Dominicans, various Cultural Centres run by the Jesuits, a Centre for teaching Arabic to foreigners run by the Combonians, and a Centre for intellectual and socio-political reflection (Justice and Peace). Three great libraries belonging to the Franciscans (Eastern Patristics), Dominicans (Islamic Studies), and the Jesuits (Theology and modern and contemporary Egypt), are intellectually recognised throughout the country. The absence of the Coptic Catholic Church in all these fields is evident.

12   Syro-Lebanese Christians also clearly expressed their conviction that it is possible to be entirely Arab, notably Christian Arab, without necessarily being a Muslim.

145

In further emphasising its ecclesial mission through its parishes, we are led to recognise that the Coptic Catholic Church cannot envisage the incorporation of followers who are not Coptic Catholics into those parishes: the reception of Orthodox would be perceived as 'prosyletism' *(khatf)*; the reception of Muslims as 'evangelisation' *(tabshīr)*. Consequently, for good or ill, it is restricted to exclusive concern for its own followers. This cannot but reduce the evangelical spirit of openness and universality of all Christian mission. How to escape this dilemma?

It is precisely in its secular mission that the Coptic Catholic Church will find a motivating *raison d'être* for its evangelical life and its Catholic nature. In fact, the various secular activities, not directly religious and spiritual, enable it to serve non-Christians and non-Catholics without attracting the suspicion of those already suspicious and threatening.[13]

There is another means to corroborate this secular mission of the Coptic Catholic Church: the role within it of lay-people. In fact, to the extent to which their role has been clearly defined by the Second Vatican Council and strongly advocated by Pope John Paul II, they are authorised in principle to take up their responsibilities at the centre of their community, in parishes, movements and activities.[14]

However, the reality in the Coptic Catholic Church is very different, since co-operation between clergy and laity is not always easy, and is often governed by conflicting interests. Lay formation is not always much in evidence, even if institutes for catechesis and theology are being established in various dioceses. Central responsibility for the parish rests entirely with the parish priest, without always leaving a place of trust for lay people. International lay movements[15] struggle for a presence in Upper Egypt, where the predominance of the clergy is almost total, and they exist only in large cities such as Cairo and Alexandria, although still not without difficulty in terms of their recognition.[16]

---

13 By way of example, the Catholic schools have 55-50 percent Muslim students, and a Coptic Orthodox Christian majority. Such is the case in all the Catholic 'secular' institutions and projects, without any religious or confessional discrimination. Something universally recognised and appreciated.

14 Cf. Vatican II: *Apostolatum Actuositatem, Gaudium et Spes, Inter Mirifica* ...; cf. the Apostolic Exhortation of John Paul II *Christifideles Laici* (1988) and his numerous interventions and initiatives on their behalf on the occasion of the Third Millennium.

15 Focolare, Neo-Catechumenate, Charismatics, Community of Christian Life, Eucharistic Youth Movement, with the exception of the Legion of Mary, fully accepted and well represented in every parish.

16 It is significant that the renewal advocated by the Coptic Catholic hierarchy has been inaugurated by them and members of the diocesan clergy, and that the Commission

Relations between a Christian Minority and a Muslim Majority

To the difficulties above is added another, no less real and trying for the Coptic Catholic Church: the minority status *(dhimmīs)* of Egyptian Churches in an Islamic country, where they do not enjoy full civil rights: in employment, in senior positions; the building of churches, marriage, conversions etc.

Furthermore, the Egyptian Churches are influenced by the ambient Arab-Muslim culture, the strong or even exclusive sense of identity, allowing no space for alterity. While the Golden Age of the 'Abbasids (750-1258) was enriched both intellectually and practically by encounter with the different other—the philosophy and science of the ancient Greeks, thanks notably to those Christians who translated them into Arabic—a reaction closing in exclusively on Arab culture was not long in coming. To speak only of philosophy, *Mu'tazilism* (recognising the place of reason) was finally vanquished by *Ashā'irism* (belief based essentially in religion); similarly, the bold intellectual advances with regards to rationality of Averroes (1126-1198) and Ibn Khaldūn (1332-1406) were carefully avoided; the openness of the Arab renaissance of the nineteenth and twentieth centuries has been usurped by the Salafī-Wahhābī movement (coming from Saudi Arabia in 1902 through the house of Ibn Saud) and the ideology of the 'Muslim Brotherhood' (from Egypt, by Hassan el-Banna, 1906-1949), promoting a return to the Ancients in reaction to modernity, and the islamisation of society in response to its liberalisation. From a political perspective, all the regimes of the region are totalitarian and hereditary, allowing no opposition whatsoever, or any differing ideology. The evident consequence of these disputes is that Arab-Muslim culture is not currently disposed towards a true meeting with the other, nor to an integration of difference as part of its own identity. It is precisely in this closed context that the Coptic Catholic Church, having begun to open its own identity to alterity, may have a beneficial effect on the ambient culture of the country, and this through its secular activity, as indicated above.

Moreover, the minority situation of the Christian Churches permits their official recognition only through their religious leaders. In other words, clericalisation of the Christian communities is imposed, to the detriment of the role of the laity in civil society. Although, at the end of the nineteenth century and the first half of the twentieth, the laity of the Coptic Orthodox

---

selected to initiate reflection is composed of them exclusively. An alternative way of envisaging reflection on renewal would have consisted in the inclusion from the outset of lay people, a lively force within the Coptic Catholic Church; of men and women Religious active within the Coptic Catholic Church; of representatives of other Catholic communities; and of experts.

Church had an effective role and dominant activity in the cultural, civil and political life of the country, there occurred, with the Egyptian Revolution of 1952, a very pronounced clericalisation of the various religious communities of the country, including the Muslim community, since, under the dictatorship of Gamal Abdel-Nasser (1954-1970), political life was no longer a rallying-point, its role replaced by religious affiliation, Muslim or Christian. Before that time, political life had been a factor of national and civil integration for all the religious communities. With the dictatorship, only the mosques and churches, not the unions or a coming together for the *res publica*, enjoyed the freedom of gathering citizens together, hence becoming, in the long term, a source of division between the two sections of the populace. Furthermore, the rise of religious fanaticism, fuelled and exacerbated by Saudi Arabia and Libya, could only serve to deepen their division. From that time began, for the Egyptian Churches, firstly the Syro-Lebanese and then the local Coptic Churches, the phenomenon of mass migration of their lay people, representing the intelligentsia of the country. The precarious economic situation, caused by a poorly integrated Soviet socialism, could only further encourage this emigration.[17] The clergy, more educated than previously, now replaced the lay emigrants, and it was the clergy who now officially represented the Church, with charismatic personalities such as the Coptic Orthodox Pope Kyrillos VI (1959-1972) gathering his entire community around him in the face of threatening political and religious power, as well as the personality, at once both political and charismatic, of the present Pope, Shenouda III (1972-). This has favoured, ecclesially and not just politically, the emergence of a clerical class at the expense of the laity. Things are no different in the Coptic Catholic Church, which is officially represented by its religious leaders and not lay people.

However, the double 'belonging' of the Coptic Catholic Church, Coptic and Catholic, expresses its vocation to be faithful to the national and ecclesial context in which it is called to live and witness. It must witness, above all, to the values of the Gospel, distancing itself from surrounding values. It is 'salt for the earth' and 'leaven in the dough', often having to disappear, as well as 'light for the world', having sometimes to shine out. In the hostile context surrounding it, welcome, giving, forgiveness, love for enemies, grace, and hope remain as much challenges to be accepted as an opportunity to take on and transcend its difficulties, both internal and external. Its witness is also

---

17   Some 20,000 members of the Coptic Catholic Church emigrated, and several hundred thousand belonging to the Coptic Orthodox Church.

expressed through all the secular domains in which it finds itself, as we have previously noted. At the heart of its secular engagement, it is called to witness to its hope to all who ask it (1 Pet 3:15).

Constitutive Elements of Renewal

In considering the different elements of the analysis and challenges given above, two fundamental anthropological elements constitute, in my opinion, the content of the renewal of the Coptic Catholic Church, one concerning its connection with human time, the other its connection with human space.

Connection to Human Time

This connection concerns the three moments of human time: past, present, and future. I wish to indicate, from the beginning, that authentic identity is not located solely in the past, but also includes insertion into the present and openness to the future.

As regards the past, renewal requires a renewed vision: not simply a fixation on the past—the myth of a 'golden age' relegated to the past, but a clear distinction between 'Tradition'—essential to Christianity—and 'traditions' which are purely accidental. If the Coptic Catholic Church, like the Coptic Orthodox Church, is essentially a 'traditional' Church, in the positive sense of the word, the weight of tradition can, nevertheless, be hard to bear, especially for the increasing number of young people, who are a sign and agent of 'modernity'. In comparing the Coptic Catholic Church to its neighbours, the young African Churches, one cannot but notice their rapid development, free of a past characterised by circumstances, vicissitudes and bondage not essential for Christian life. A mature discernment between the essential and the accidental is required, to be undertaken in a spirit both wise and critical, courageous and respectful, creative and faithful, prophetic and wise.

In the present, realism remains the normative virtue for discerning the divine will; in fact, the present is the place *par excellence* where God reveals His plan of salvation through human mediation, representing the events and circumstances of the present time. Nothing is fortuitous, the fruit of chance or of mere luck, as the surrounding culture would have it, rather, everything signifies God's constant salvific action, which works for the good of all who love Him. (Rom 8:28)

As to the future, the Coptic Catholic Church is called to true development, forgetting, like the Apostle Paul, what is behind it in order to pursue the future, the glorious Second Coming, and the transfiguration and freedom of the children of God (Rom 8:19-21). Gregory of Nyssa called this disposition of mankind towards God *epectasis* (Phil 3:13), constituting an essential element of Christian anthropology, beyond our earthly life, the promise of future happiness.

Connection to Human Space

The renewal of the Coptic Catholic Church will operate through people, and at different levels. It is, in the first place, the whole of the human person which is affected by the renewal of the Coptic Catholic Church: their spiritual life (the basis of any renewal) clearly, but also the three forces of their soul (their affectivity, their will, and especially their rationality, which is not given the place it deserves in the surrounding cultural climate), their secular life (family and professional, social and civil, the stuff of their existence), and their sense of service as far as the total gift of themselves (Jn 13) in the image of Christ who came to serve and not to be served (Mk 10:45). Finally, what is fundamentally at stake in the renewal of the Coptic Catholic Church is, according to the fine expression of Jacques Maritain, *l'homme intégral*, 'the entire man'.

It is, also, all of humanity which is called, since Isaiah invited his people, crying, 'Enlarge the place of your tent' (Is 54:2, cf. 60), to welcome all who come. And Jesus universalised and radicalised this call: not simply to welcome those who come, but to go out to others: 'Go out into the whole world' (Mk 16:15); 'teach all nations' (Mt 28:19-20), particularly *ad intra* to non-Christians and non-Catholics, and *ad extra* towards Africa, as did the early Egyptian Church. Within the space of the Coptic Catholic Church, renewal is an opening to all without distinction, in a *koinonia* powerfully lived out in the early Church, with one spirit, one heart, one body, one prayer (Acts 4:32ff.): clergy, religious, lay-people, the young: adherents and others. In order not to remain simply an idealised life which is finally unreal, the points of tension in these different relationships must be expressed in a frank and open dialogue in order to integrate and overcome them: relations between regular and secular clergy, between priests and laity, between the young and their elders, between spirituals, charismatics, prophets, leaders, etc; all within the unity of the Body of Christ brought about by the one Spirit (1 Cor 12:12-13).

I would like to make particular mention of the importance of theological renewal, as there can be no renewal without a serious theological basis. The

Egyptian Church of Clement and Origen, of Athanasius and Cyril, of the Councils inspired by the extraordinary personalities of the Alexandrian School of theology, no longer has the universal impact of old. The Coptic Catholic Church of today could offer, at least, a locus of sound theology, open to East and West, united incontestably with that of Lebanon. This anticipated theology would not be limited solely to the religious and spiritual, dogmatic and liturgical, historical and traditional sectors, but also to a theology of the 'secular', such as that mentioned throughout this presentation, including the questionings of modernity and post-modernity by which the Coptic Catholic Church is constantly confronted.

CONCLUSION

It would appear that the renewal of the Coptic Catholic Church is fundamentally a grappling with its identity and alterity, the union of which gives birth to a multi-faceted plural identity which constantly integrates difference, something which cannot but enrich it through, on the one hand contextual insertion (its Coptic aspect), and through universality (its Catholic aspect) on the other, the double condition for a true renewal.

If I have inserted the expression 'grappling with', into the title of my presentation it is because the interaction of identity and alterity is emblematic of the Coptic Catholic Church, and can represent for its renewal a problem, a challenge, or an opportunity.

I would like to end with two signs of hope. The Coptic Catholic Church, like all Egyptian Christianity, is two thousand years old, bearing within it the charism of fidelity to its Christian faith throughout its long history, having survived Roman and Islamic persecution, in a way that, for example, the Church in North Africa has not. Furthermore, it co-exists alongside Orthodox and Protestant Churches, which is not the case for the Churches of Ethiopia, Greece or Russia, for example. On these two signs of hope the Coptic Catholic Church can found its renewal.

THE ARMENIAN CATHOLIC CHURCH
IN THE MIDDLE EAST

John Whooley

The Armenian Apostolic Orthodox Church, or, as even a number of Armenian Catholics often now refer to it out of respect, the 'Mother Church', has at the present time four jurisdictions, those of Etchmiadzin, Cilicia, Jerusalem and Istanbul. For many centuries the Cilician catholicosate had been at Sis (now Kozan in modern-day Turkey), but was forced to leave there shortly after the First World War and finally able to resettle in Antelias, a suburb of Beirut.

Though the catholicoses themselves had their seat at Sis, nevertheless they were often inclined to reside in Aleppo where there was a substantial Armenian community. It was here that a tendency to be sympathetic to Rome's claims was manifested from time to time, and the missionary activities, especially of the Jesuits, were the cause of a number of conversions in that direction, and the two Armenian groups, Catholic and Orthodox, in their rivalry, could cause some commotion in the city. We should also bear in mind the interdiction by the Holy See in 1729 of the practice of *communicatio in sacris*. In addition there was the long-held custom of lay involvement in the election of prelates in the Armenian Church. These factors had no small bearing on a developing crisis. In 1740 such matters did indeed reach breaking point when the openly pro-Catholic Abraham Ardzivian (1674-1749) was elected catholicos. Ardzivian went to Rome in 1742 to request recognition by the pope, Benedict XIV, who did indeed grant his wish, with Ardzivian being confirmed as Catholicos-Patriarch of Cilicia of the Catholic Armenians. This was the beginning of a formal Armenian Catholic hierarchy and seen very much as a rival to its long-established Orthodox counterpart.

However, due to another Orthodox catholicos of Sis having been elected in the meantime, Ardzivian was unable to return to Aleppo and was eventually obliged to settle in the Lebanon where he had already found the Maronites sympathetic to his situation. The monastery of Kreim was to be his seat, but shortly thereafter his successors were to install themselves in the newly-

153

constructed monastery of Bzommar. They were to reside there until 1866, when the then Armenian Catholic Archbishop of Constantinople, Andon Hassoun, was elected patriarch. He, however, being also 'Patrik'[1] at that time, was obliged to remain in the capital; hence, the removal of the patriarchal seat to Constantinople where it remained until 1928. The devastation that befell the Armenian people within the Ottoman Empire during the First World War—and which affected all three denominations: Orthodox, Catholic and Protestant—had necessitated a complete reorganization of the Armenian Catholic Church. It was decided to return the patriarchate to Lebanon where it still remains today.

The matters to which I have just referred do not by any means tell the full narrative of the contacts between the Church of Rome and the Armenian Church and people over the centuries. It is not possible here to enter further into that narrative, even though not to do so might offend a number of Armenian Catholics and others who would contend, for example, that there have always been Armenian Chalcedonians, albeit a minority, or that at various times there had been contacts and indeed forms of union, official or otherwise, with the Roman See, and that the present line of Armenian Catholic patriarchs based in the Lebanon should be understood as being the most recent evidence of that phenomenon.[2]

After these preliminaries, let us now turn to the present situation of the Armenian Catholic Church in the Middle East. In doing so, we recall that

---

1   The 'patriks' were the civil representatives to the Sublime Porte and directly responsible for the management and good behaviour of their Christian constituencies. The 'Katolik milleti' that had come into existence in 1830 extended emancipation to Armenian Catholics, liberating them from the harsh jurisdiction sometimes exercised over them by a number of Armenian Orthodox Patriarchs. The new arrangement covered not only Armenians in union with Rome, but also most of the various other Eastern Catholic Churches to be found in the Ottoman Empire at that time.

2   Cf., for example, Paul Chirikdjian, *L'Église Arménienne et le Saint-Siège de Rome. Aperçu historique, dogmatique et politique sur le 'Schisme Arménien' ses origines, ses causes et ses conséquences*, Alexandria, 1949. Regarding Armenian Chalcedonians, cf. Sidney H Griffith, *The Church in the Shadow of the Mosque*, Princeton University Press, Princeton and Oxford, 2008, p. 137. We may note that the accusation that Armenian Catholics and Protestants are no longer truly Armenian as they have quitted the 'Mother Church' is still heard today. It is curious that the following statements, though applied more than implicitly to Islam, may describe something of the Armenian case: 'Generally speaking, religion in the Middle East is a social and even a national choice, and not an individual one. To change religion is perceived as betraying a society, culture and nation, founded largely on a religious tradition.' *Lineamenta* (Preliminary document for the Synod of Bishops Special Assembly for the Middle East), § 22, Vatican City, 2009.

it is one of the 'twenty-two autonomous churches *(ecclesiae sui iuris)* which enjoy a status of relative independent self-governance vis-à-vis the Roman Pontiff with whom they are in full communion and in whose person universal communion is realized.'[3] It therefore functions in a somewhat different manner, and legitimately so, from the much larger Roman Church of the Latin rite. It bears, however, a particular burden in that its *raison d'être* is seemingly under duress, along with others of those autonomous Churches, due to recent ecumenical developments. Furthermore, its proximity to the catholicosate at Antelias can be an inhibitory factor.

In addition, that its centre and leadership find themselves in one of the world's most politically disturbed regions, due in large measure to the ever constant conflict between Israel and adjacent Arab states, and which has been the cause of a considerable migration of its constituents, along with those of other Churches of the area, is cause for many concerns. That this drama is staged in a largely Islamic theatre is of considerable consequence; the fate of Jerusalem, a city of significance for all three Abrahamic faiths, and also even to Jews of a secular disposition, is a focus that enflames passions on all sides. The Armenian Catholic Church, though small numerically and of its nature 'alien' to the cultures in which it finds itself in the Middle East, whether Jewish or Muslim, or even Christian, participates in those attempts to assuage such passions and eventually bring peace and justice for all protagonists.

Bearing in mind the forthcoming Synod in Rome that will be considering the state of affairs of the various Christian communities in the Middle East and how it might be possible to ameliorate their critical situation, this paper touches on a number of matters, social, religious, political, that are perhaps pertinent, not only to Armenian Catholics, but to other Christians as well. Many of the concerns of the Armenian Catholic Church would be similar, we may imagine, to those of other Christian Churches in the region, whether in union with Rome or not.

---

3   John D Faris, *Eastern Catholic Churches: Constitution and Governance*, Saint Maron Publications, New York, 1992, p. 46. He continues, 'Only one of these churches observes the Latin rite; the other twenty-one autonomous churches observe a specific rite derived from one of the five major Eastern traditions: the Alexandrian, Antiochene, Constantinopolitan, Chaldean and Armenian […] All churches and rites are equal.'

STATISTICS

To begin with, however, some statistics for the Middle East might prove of interest. Though the following are taken from the 2008 *Annuario Pontificio*,[4] we bear in mind how difficult it is to get accurate figures for these matters. For the Archeparchy of Beirut, the seat of the Armenian Catholic Patriarch, 12,000 faithful (1990: 15,000); the Archeparchy of Baghdad: 2,000; the Archeparchy of Aleppo: 17,500; the Archeparchy of Istanbul: 3,650; the Eparchy of Ispahan, Iran: 10,000 (1990: 2,200); the Eparchy of Iskanderiya (Alexandria), Egypt: 1,500 (1990), (2007: 6,000); the Eparchy of Kamichlié, Syria: 4,000; the Patriarchal Exarchate of Damascus, Syria: 4,500; the Patriarchal Exarchate of Amman and Jerusalem: 800 (2000: 280; 2005: 740). Altogether, there are thus almost 56,000 faithful in this region.[5]

Outside the region, once again according to the same *Annuario*, there are almost another 500,000 faithful, the great majority being found in the Ordinariate for Eastern Europe, based in Gyumri, Armenia, numbering 390,000. We could say, therefore, that, according to these figures, perhaps only 11 percent of the Armenian Catholic faithful reside in the Middle East itself where the Church has its roots and central organization. The remaining faithful may be said to be concentrated in France and the Americas, with numbers in Australia as well as in Greece and Romania.[6]

We may contrast these figures with those given for the Maronites: within the Middle East: 1,503,567; beyond: 1,603,767. Thus approximately 48 percent of the faithful are within our region of immediate concern. For Chaldeans: within the Middle East: 246,682; beyond: 112,000. Thus approximately rather more than two thirds are to be found within our area. Finally, for Melkites: within the Middle East: 777,390; beyond: 564,624. Thus roughly 65 percent are within our area.

4   Cf. Ronald G Roberson, 'The Eastern Catholic Churches 2008'. Catholic Near East Welfare Association. http://www.cnewa.org/source-images/Roberson-eastcath-statistics/eastcatholic-stat08.pdf.
5   Armenian Orthodox statistics for the Middle East (taken from a number of sources): in Jordan 4,500; Turkey 65,000; Egypt 5,500; Lebanon 138,000; Syria 74,000; Iran 100,000; Iraq 13,000; Cyprus 3,500; Israel and the Palestinian National Authority 4,000. Thus approximately 400,000 Orthodox Armenians are to be found in the Middle East.
6   The total number of world faithful for 2008 is given as 539,806, an extraordinary increase from the 1990 figure of 142,853. However, according to the *New Catholic Encyclopedia*, Vol. 1, p. 836, 1967 edition, the figure for Armenian Catholics outside the Patriarchal territory is approximately 45,000, with 52,100 within the patriarchal territory (i.e. the Middle East). Thus the total is not quite 100,000. No mention is made here of the Republics of Armenia and Georgia, states that now appear to contain the bulk of the faithful.

JURISDICTIONS

In contrast to the Armenian Catholic Patriarchate that presents a unified jurisdiction in the Middle East as a whole, the Armenian Orthodox Church presents a fragmented picture. Turkey and Crete are under the Patriarchate of Istanbul; the Jerusalem Patriarchate has responsibility for Israel, Jordan and territories under the control of the Palestinian National Authority. The catholicosate of Etchmiadzin has responsibility for Egypt, has Archbishops in Damascus and Baghdad with a Primate and Pontifical Legate to the Armenians in Greece. It also has a Diocesan Council for Iran.

The Catholicosate of Cilicia at Antelias controls the dioceses of Cyprus and Lebanon, as well as the diocese of Greece. It has three dioceses in Iran: those of Tehran, of Isfahan (New Julfa) and of Azarbaijan (Tabriz); in Syria, the dioceses of Aleppo and Jezireh, the latter having its seat in Kamishlié. A Catholicosal Vicar is appointed to Damascus; in the Persian Gulf, the diocese of Kuwait and the United Arab Emirates, its seat being in Kuwait.

The two patriarchates are aligned with Etchmiadzin and have their bishops consecrated by its Catholicos, as well as receiving their Holy Myron from there; Antelias consecrates its own bishops and blesses its own Myron. Though there are these differences, and sometimes difficulties, between Antelias and Etchmiadzin, nevertheless they profess the same faith, the same doctrines.

MEMBERSHIP OF CATHOLIC ORGANISATIONS IN THE MIDDLE EAST

The Armenian Catholic Church is a member of the Catholic episcopal conferences in the Middle East, all of which were established after the Second Vatican Council (1962-1965): the Assembly of Catholic Ordinaries of the Holy Land (1992), the Assembly of the Catholic Hierarchy of Egypt (1969), the Iranian Episcopal Conference (1980), the Assembly of the Catholic Bishops of Iraq (1976), the Assembly of the Catholic Patriarchs and Bishops of Lebanon (1970) and the Assembly of the Catholic Ordinaries in Syria (1969). Mention must also be made of the Conference of Bishops of the Catholic Church in Turkey (1979). The Armenian Catholic Patriarch is a member of the Council of Catholic Patriarchs of the East (1991). Thus though the Armenian Catholics are small in number they are given strength and influence by their participation in these representative bodies of the Catholic Church in the region as a whole; their involvement is therefore of no small importance and quite in contrast to the situation prevailing beforehand.[7]

PAST ISOLATION

In the not too distant past, and perhaps not so surprisingly, the Armenian Catholic Church, being not too dissimilar from the Armenian Orthodox Church in the region in this respect, had been somewhat in isolation, particularly as its adherents were not ethnically Semitic and its culture not fundamentally Arab. Thus they were in a sense separate not only from their Muslim neighbours, but also from most of their fellow Christians, including those who were also in union with Rome. This might often result in a greater need for community support in their new environment. It is nevertheless uncertain as to whether the Armenian political parties were as influential among Armenian Catholics as they were among the majority Orthodox. These parties, especially the Tashnags, now played an important role in the life of Armenians in the Levant and elsewhere, superseding in many respects the role thitherto played by the Church, though the latter had and still has importance.

There was also, it appears, some tension between the new arrivals, refugees from Anatolia and Cilicia, in particular, and those Armenians already long established in such centres, or 'colonies', as Alexandria and Baghdad. Nor was Arabic usually the first language of its constituents; even as late as 1978, we find the following statement: 'Armenian Christians differ from the rest of the population in speaking a language other than Arabic, a fact which has helped to make them unpopular with the local population.'[8] However, it would appear that many if not most Armenians in the region who are descended

---

7   We may note that the Conference of the Latin Bishops in the Arab Regions was established in 1965. 'In inter-ecclesial relations among Catholics … communion is manifested in each country by the various assemblies of patriarchs and bishops so that Christian witness might be more sincere, credible and fruitful.' *Instrumentum Laboris*, Working Paper for the Synod of Bishops Special Assembly for the Middle East, § 55, Vatican City, 2010.

8   Peter Beaumont, Gerald H J Blake, Malcolm Wagstaff, *The Middle East. A Geographical Study*, John Wiley & Sons, Chichester, New York, Brisbane, Toronto, 1976, reprinted 1985, p. 371.

from the refugee generation are now fluent in Arabic.[9] Church publications are found both in Arabic and Armenian.

It would seem that other Eastern Catholic Churches had the same tendency to isolation, thus usually not acting in co-ordination, when it might have been for the general benefit of the Catholic Church so to do, if not indeed for all the Christians of the area. Any co-operation with the Orthodox was out of consideration till a greater ecumenical sense was to be developed within the Catholic Church, and this was not to take place effectively till the Second Vatican Council, and only becoming efficacious some years after that.

TENSIONS BETWEEN EASTERN CATHOLIC CHURCHES

There had also been tensions, it appears, or at least rivalries of sorts between the various Eastern Catholic Churches themselves. It is thought that this originally stemmed from the time of the Ottoman 'millet' system that kept religious groups apart. Though, as mentioned earlier, with the formation of the 'Katolik milleti' in 1830, most Catholics found themselves under the Armenian Catholic 'patrik', this still proved unsatisfactory, each Catholic group eventually gaining its 'autonomy' and therefore becoming responsible for its own rights and duties vis-à-vis the Sublime Porte.[10] This, too, though, could create rivalry by the fact of often having to win the favours of persons of influence at both the local level or at the Ottoman court itself, so that, if

---

9   In Aleppo, the 'Arevig' centre for Armenian handicapped children had to be established as the children concerned knew only Armenian and were therefore at a disadvantage in similar centres run by the Lebanese state where Arabic alone was spoken. We may note that Armenians 'have never adopted Arabic as a church language although they have lived in all parts of the Islamic world since the very beginnings of Islam and have long been fluent in Arabic for purposes of everyday life.' Griffith, *The Church*, p. 137.

10 'When it was at first reported that the Sultan intended to appoint a common head of the three sects of popish converts, viz. the Armenians, Greeks and Syrians, and that this head was for the present an Armenian, the Greeks expressed their determination sooner to return to their mother church than to yield obedience to a chief from their Armenian brethren, and so they still remain, as it appears, nominally unknown at Constantinople.'(Smith and Dwight, *Missionary Researches in Armenia. Including a Journey through Asia Minor, and into Georgia and Persia*, George Wightman, London, 1834, p. 62, n. †) According to Pierre Rondot, *Les Chrétiens d'Orient*, J Peyronnet & Cie., Paris, 1955, pp. 81-82, the Ottoman government was to recognise the various Catholic Patriarchs as 'patriks' or 'civil' leaders of their respective communities as follows: Greek-Catholic in 1848; Chaldean in 1861; Syrian-Catholic in 1866; Coptic-Catholic in 1898.

possible, one's own community might have certain inconveniences removed or be able to gain certain privileges for its own members.

There was also some tension between the Latin Catholic parishes and those of the various other Catholic rites, the latter sometimes losing members to the former, as the Latin rite was then often understood as being superior to the others, in the sense that it was taken to be the pre-eminent rite of the Catholic Church; being thus the *ritus praestantior*, it was thought to contain the fullness of Catholicity, as did those Catholic clergy, eastern and western, who had been trained in Rome and were thereby indelibly marked with a true and enviable 'Romanitas'. In addition, European Catholics working or living in the Turkish Empire, perhaps over several generations, and who enjoyed the benefits of the 'Capitulations', were usually Latin in their rite. This was a further incentive to change one's birth-rite whenever it was possible to do so, not simply for the sake of fashion, but for gaining a greater security for oneself and one's family when facing the hazards of Ottoman administration.[11] Thus the re-establishment of the Latin Patriarchate of Jerusalem by Pius IX in 1847 had not necessarily been greeted with universal delight at the time, as there was a likelihood that not only Orthodox might be tempted in that direction, but also Catholics of the non-Latin rites, thereby weakening their communities of origin, especially if the families concerned were of note.[12]

---

11 Regarding, for example, Armenian Catholics in the Holy Land, Fr Hoade remarks, almost in surprise, how many of them actually belonged to the Latin rite rather than the Armenian: *Guide to the Holy Land*, Franciscan Printing Press, Jerusalem, 1978, p. 71. The Latin Catholic cemetery in Şişli, Istanbul, also contains the remains of Armenian Catholics, even though not far away is the actual Armenian Catholic cemetery itself. A number of the members of various Latin religious orders in the Middle East were and are Armenian, one of the most noteworthy being a Capuchin, Guregh Zohrabian (1881-1972), at one time Eparch of Kamishlié.

12 Evidence that there may still be some problems between the various Catholic Churches in the Middle East may be gathered when it is stated that one of the two goals of the future Special Assembly of the Synod of Bishops is 'to deepen ecclesial communion among particular Churches, so that they can bear witness to the Christian life in an authentic, joyful and winsome manner.' *Lineamenta*, § 2. More forthrightly: '... the attitude of the two apostles, James and John, who asked Jesus to grant them the first places at his right and his left, can still be detected, posing difficulties among the brethren. Instead of coming together to face difficulties in common, we sometimes argue among ourselves, counting the number of faithful in our Churches to ascertain who is the greatest. This spirit of rivalry destroys us.' *Ibid.*, § 43. Cf. also *Instrumentum*, § 55.

The Patriarchate was itself under pressure to increase its faithful, and Muslims could not be evangelized.

RECENT LATIN SENSITIVITY TO EASTERN CATHOLIC CHURCHES

Perhaps some of this tension has now been dissipated, since the present Latin Patriarch of Jerusalem, Fouad Twal, is Palestinian, as was his immediate predecessor, Michel Sabbah. Under the direction of these two prelates, and perhaps with their deeper appreciation of the nuances of circumstance of their fellow Christian Arabs of whatever denomination, the patriarchate appears to have been showing a greater care for the sensitivities, not only of their companion rites of the region, but for the sensitivities of the Orthodox as well. In addition, during his time of office Michel Sabbah proved himself a very active leader in many joint efforts to defend the Christian community in the region whenever it felt threatened or needed to make statements about common concerns.[13]

PALESTINIAN CHURCH LEADERS—A RECENT PHENOMENON

The appointment of Palestinians to the Latin See is part of a notable phenomenon of how the Churches in the Holy Land are now reacting to the political situation that has arisen due to the Arab-Israeli conflict. Both the Anglican and Lutheran bishops in Jerusalem are, since recent times, also Palestinians. The continuation of control by bishops and other clergy from Greece and Cyprus of the Greek patriarchate, whose constituency is overwhelmingly Palestinian, is in today's climate difficult to comprehend, though the consecration in 2005 of Theodosios Atallah Hanna as Archbishop of Sebastia seems to provide evidence of a change of policy; he is only the second Palestinian in the history of the patriarchate to be consecrated as an archbishop.

It does appear that Israel is content to support the position of those in control of the synod, rather than encourage the creation of a more thoroughly Palestinian base that would oppose more vehemently matters concerning

---

13   As Patriarch Emeritus, he was the leading signatory of the Kairos Palestine document published in December, 2009. As it is a purely Palestinian initiative, inspired by the Kairos South Africa document of 1985, Armenians were not involved in its preparation or dissemination.

patriarchal land and property being rented or sold to the Israelis. It would seem that something of this nature had also been the case in the past with the Armenian Orthodox patriarchate and its property holdings, though, naturally, for this institution there could never be any attempt to elect a Palestinian to its leadership. However, this has not prevented the two patriarchs, Armenian and Greek, from being involved when necessary in voicing criticism of the government or stating their views on the status of Jerusalem, together with the Latin patriarch and the other Christian leaders. These have usually been voiced in their joint Pastoral Letters, the tenth of which was published in 2009.

In these matters concerning Israel and the Palestinians, as well as the Christian presence in the Holy Land, of necessity the Armenian Catholic Church plays only a minor role due to its paucity of faithful in that territory. Nevertheless, it is part of the general Christian wish for and contribution towards the final goal of establishing justice and peace in the region and for the preservation of those 'living stones' that form the indigenous Christian communities. It could be said that there is further *kudos* gained when the patriarchal exarch, at present Fr Raphael Minassian, adds his signature, on behalf of Nerses Bedros XIX Tarmouni, to joint statements largely initiated by the grander Church leaders on matters concerning the social and political problems that beleaguer not only their flocks, but also the majority Jewish and Muslim populations.[14]

In contrast to the Armenian Catholic Church in the Holy Land, the Armenian Orthodox Patriarchate has substantial importance, this being acknowledged when we take into consideration its monastic institution in the Armenian Quarter in the Old City and its long and consequential involvement in the major Holy Places.[15] It would have had, for example, a decisive role, along with the Greek and Latin Patriarchates, in the closing of the Holy Sepulchre for 24 hours in protest at the Israeli settlers' occupation of St John's Hospice in

---

14 'The pressure of the Palestinian *Intifada*, coupled with the change in Israeli priorities and policy making, led the Patriarchate to a major break with its tradition of co-operating closely with state policy in exchange for internal autonomy. In April 1987, Patriarch Diodoros joined other Church heads in signing a statement demonstrating their concern and anxiety over the state of affairs in the Occupied Territories and actually condemning Israeli policy in the matter.' Sotiris Roussos, 'The Patriarchate of Jerusalem in the Greek-Palestinian-Israeli Triangle: Is there a place for it?', 2003, p. 4. hcc.haifa.ac.il/Departments/greece/events/greek_orthodox_church/pdf/sotiris.pdf, The Easter Message for 2010 issued by the Heads of Churches of Jerusalem included the name of the Armenian Catholic Patriarchal Exarch.

15 The Armenian Catholics have the church and exarchate that are associated with the Third and Fourth Stations on the Via Dolorosa in the Old City.

1990, the first such closure in 800 years and one which is understood as marking a turning point in the relations between the Churches and the Israeli State.[16]

END OF ISOLATION BETWEEN EASTERN CATHOLIC CHURCHES

Even before the initiatives, direct or indirect, of the Vatican to encourage the Eastern Catholic Churches, including the Armenian Catholic Church, to work more consciously together in order to face the various pressing problems that have arisen since the Second World War, there had been some successful examples of what has been termed 'interritual cooperation'. This development probably had its roots in the stimulation Pius IX gave for greater Catholic lay participation in matters social and educational.[17] Much of this activity seems to have been a phenomenon of the post-Mandatory period.

Raymond Etteldorf reports as follows on such collaborations: 'The Catechetical Society of Aleppo is a striking example of lay action on the basis of interritual cooperation. The bishops of the various rites take turns in heading the organization: the priests who are connected with it act only as supervisors or counselors; teaching the catechism is carried on by lay men and women.'[18] He continues, 'Also of special significance are the Interritual Catholic Youth Clubs of Aleppo, directed by a Jesuit with the assistance of the diocesan clergy, and the Interritual Union of Catholic Workers of Syria, directed by diocesan priests of the Syrian rite.'[19] Further on: 'La Flamme, started in 1946 in Syria, has become there and in Lebanon one of the most energetic and efficacious lay organizations of the Church in the Middle East. Its 250 members, all well educated women,

---

16 Michael Dumper writes of 'the covert support that the Likud government gave to the activities of Israeli settlers in the Old City and their attempts to penetrate the Christian quarters. This culminated with their occupation of St. John' Hospice, belonging to the Greek Orthodox Patriarchate by Israeli settlers in April 1990 and can be seen as the defining moment in the relations between the Israeli government and the established Churches of Jerusalem with ramifications that are still being played out today. What the St. John's Hospice Incident revealed is the degree of support the settler movement in the Old City was receiving from official government sources.' ('The Christian Churches of Jerusalem in the Post-Oslo Period', *Journal of Palestine Studies*, Vol. 31, no. 2 [Winter 2002]) Ariel Sharon and other Israeli politicians spoke openly in support of the occupation.

17 Cf. Encyclical *Ubi Arcano Dei Consilio*: Dec. 1922, particularly sections 53-58.

18 *The Catholic Church in the Middle East*, Macmillan, New York, 1959, p. 82. We may bear in mind, at this point, that there are six Catholic communities to be found in Aleppo, each with its own bishop: Latin, Chaldean, Syriac, Armenian, Maronite, and Melkite.

19 *Ibid.*

are of different rites and work among the people without distinction of rite. They give religious instruction and help to organize missions and retreats. They are active especially in villages that are without priests or in areas where it has been difficult for the Church to penetrate. They work in conjunction with priests and sisters of different rites. La Flamme has conclusively demonstrated that a successful lay apostolate can be carried out through interritual co-operation.'[20] This form of co-operation, though, does not seem to have been much in evidence in other places in the Middle East at that time.

The following point made by Faris is of no small interest in this context: 'In the past, issues touching on the relations between the autonomous churches were designated as *interritual matters*. In light of the *CCEO* (*Codex Canonum Ecclesiarum Orientalium*, 1990), a more precise term would be *Catholic interecclesial matters*.'[21] This is clear evidence of a honing of terminology in order to be more exacting in describing the status of Eastern Catholic Churches, and indeed to ensure that they are given proper recognition in the Catholic Church. This recognition was often lacking in the past, Latin Catholics, both laity and clergy, having little or no knowledge of the existence or customs of their Eastern Catholic brethren, an oversight for which there is still evidence today.

A Recent Example of Interecclesial Collaboration

Though in Etteldorf's discussion of 'interritual cooperation' from half a century ago the Armenian Catholic Church is not specifically mentioned, nor, indeed, apart from one, are there particular references to the other Catholic bodies, we may note the involvement of the Armenian community in more recent times in the founding of the Séminaire Éparchial Interrituel International Missionnaire 'Redemptoris Mater'. This was begun in Cairo in 1995 and was under the auspices of the Maronites, the Catholic Copts and the Catholic Armenians. Mgr Boutros Taza, then Armenian Bishop of Alexandria, acted for the latter; he himself was to be elected Armenian Catholic Patriarch

---

20   *Ibid.*, pp. 98-99. Referring in particular to Lebanon, he continues, 'In recent years … there are indications of a trend toward interritual cooperation. [...] Catholic Action is organized on an interritual basis, so that the laity of the various rites can work together for the universal objectives of the Church. In this way not only do they present a unified front, but the members themselves become conscious of their role as members of the great body of the Church rather than only as adherents to this or that rite.' (p. 98)

21   Faris, *Eastern Catholic Churches*, p. 108.

in 1999 and is still in that position. In that same year, the seminary was moved to the Lebanon, probably to facilitate its operation.

As its title suggests, it has a particular concern for the Eastern Catholic Churches in the Middle East, but also concern for those of the Maghrib and the Sudan. It is now the responsibility of the same Armenian Patriarch, as well as the Maronite Archbishop of Beirut and the Greek Melkite Archbishop of Tyre. It is not known if there are any Armenian seminarians there at present. Normally, Armenian Catholic candidates for the priesthood whose origins are in the Middle East would pursue the early years of their training at the minor seminaries in Aleppo or Bzommar and thence to the major Bzommar seminary (founded in 1747) and perhaps pursue higher studies at the Armenian College in Rome founded in 1885 by Pope Leo XIII. Those who might be influenced by the Mekhitarists might be sent to the seminaries in Bikfaya, Lebanon, and thence to the monasteries in Venice or Vienna.[22]

However, there is at present, as in many other places, a vocation crisis in the Middle East. This is largely due to '… families emigrating, a declining birth rate; and a youth culture which is increasingly becoming devoid of Gospel values. The lack of unity among members of the clergy is both an obstacle and counter-witness, hindering a man from choosing the priestly life. At times, the human and spiritual formation of priests as well as men and women religious is inadequate.'[23] We may also note the recent restoration of the custom of having married clergy in the Armenian Catholic Church, the practice of clerical celibacy through Latin influence having become the norm by the end of the nineteenth century.[24]

THE NEO-CATECHUMENATE

Of interest is that the 'Redemptoris Mater' seminary in Beirut follows the Neo-Catechumenal Way.[25] It would appear that both the Armenian Catholic

---

22   Mekhitar of Sebaste (Sivas) (1676-1749) was the founder of the monastic order that was later named after him and which was to prove by the many scholars it produced and by the assiduity with which its members pursued the retrieval of Armenian manuscripts probably the most widely acclaimed achievement of Armenian Catholicism.

23   *Instrumentum laboris*, § 22. The section concludes regretfully: 'The contemplative life … is noticeably absent in a majority of congregations of men and women in the Eastern Catholic Churches *sui iuris* in the Middle East.'

24   By 2004, there were at least seven priests and five permanent deacons who were married.

25   The Way's communities in the Middle East are as follows: Egypt 30; Iraq 9; Israel 15; Jordan 1; Kuwait 3; Lebanon 52; Palestine 15.

Patriarch and his successor in Egypt, Mgr Augustine Coussan, are supporters of this movement which they feel is capable of contending with the forces of secularism and indifferentism coming from the West as well as an answer to the proselytism of various sects that are troubling the traditional Christian Churches in the region, and as a creditable means of strengthening Christian resolve in face of the growing influence of Islamic fundamentalism. It is uncertain whether it meets the same sort of opposition from the local Catholic Churches as it does occasionally in the West, for the situation in the Middle East is obviously more critical.[26]

BISHOP TAZA AND THE AFRICAN SYNOD

Mention of Bishop Taza earlier may bring to mind his intervention at the African Synod of 1994 when he made the following points that seem to be of relevance. On the positive side, he saw that there was now a commitment of a greater number of lay people in the life of the Church, especially after the formation of a Pastoral Council in 1980. Furthermore, the charismatic movement as well as that of the Neo-catechumenate had encouraged, he believes, both personal and community conversion. In recent years, the faithful were being faced with serious challenges from the spirit of Western scepticism,[27] and as the understanding of the faith for many had often not much progressed beyond that of the First Holy Communion stage, thus remaining very superficial, there was a real danger of being easily seduced by purely materialist values. Divorce or separation was becoming more acceptable as was the practice of abortion. In addition there is the question of apostasy, sometimes used as an instrument to solve matrimonial conflict. Though in Egypt this is a phenomenon that largely affects the Copts, nevertheless the Catholic Church has not been untouched by this. Presumably, this may also be problematic for Christian communities in the Middle East in general.

---

26 The great interest and investment that the Movement takes in the region may be seen in the impressive 'Domus Galilaeae' recently constructed by them on the Mount of Beatitudes in Israel. The plan by the Melkite Archbishop of Acre, Haifa, Nazareth, and All Galilee, Mgr Elias Chacour, to open another 'Redemptoris Mater' in the 'Domus Galilaeae' now seems to have been accomplished. It is, though, for the Melkite rite alone; the Armenian Catholics do not appear to have been involved in the scheme due doubtless to their lack of numbers.

27 The positive and negative aspects of 'Modernity' are discussed in the *Instrumentum*, §§ 103-105. Though the bishop does not use this term, its meaning and implications are dealt with by him in other terms.

The bishop also mentions how the missionary spirit was very weak among both laity and clergy, but, then, taking the situation in Egypt into consideration where Islam is very much in the dominant position as elsewhere in the region, and where violence against the Copts is not infrequent, this should not be too surprising. It is difficult to be open about one's Christian beliefs even on a personal level in such an environment. This, again, might be described as not untypical for the Middle East. The problem must be compounded for Armenians by the very fact that, whether Orthodox, Catholic or Protestant, they are seen as specifically attached to a particular ethnic identity as their very name indicates, an identity that is judged as definitively 'alien'. It is understood that by the quality of their lives they might hope to express their Christian faith, but the very fact of their 'Armenianness' could be seen as a handicap even here.

The bishop also refers to the well-known 'counter-testimony' that is created and sustained by Christians themselves, for they usually celebrate the major feasts of Easter and Christmas on different dates. Orthodox Armenians, for example, though celebrating Easter at the same time as the Latin Church, within the Jerusalem Patriarchate, still following the Julian calendar, Easter is celebrated thirteen days prior to that. This compounds the fact that Christianity presents so many faces in the Muslim Middle East that it constantly loses credibility in the region, credibility already low historically due to the *dhimmi* status accorded Christians in the past. However, there have been some changes in this matter: in Syria, the Melkites and the Syrian Catholics have decided to celebrate Easter on the same day as the Orthodox. What of the Armenians, Orthodox and Catholic? It is doubtful that the Armenian Catholics in Syria would re-adopt the Julian calendar and then celebrate Easter at a different time from their Armenian Orthodox counterparts, even though their own community is substantial. Thus the lack of co-ordination continues in this respect.

ECUMENISM: THE MIDDLE EAST COUNCIL OF CHURCHES

The Middle East Council of Churches (MECC) was founded in 1974 and has representatives from the Oriental Orthodox Churches, the Eastern Orthodox (Chalcedonian) Churches, the Catholic Churches, and the Evangelical Churches, including the Union of the Armenian Evangelical Churches in the Near East. One important activity of the MECC is performed by its Christian-Muslim Dialogue Committee.

The Catholic Churches joined as a group in 1990 and among them may be found the Armenian Catholic Church, whilst among the Oriental Orthodox may be found the Armenian Apostolic Church represented by the Catholicosate of Cilicia. As referred to earlier, and not unnaturally, there have been some difficulties in the past between these two Armenian allegiances, the leaders of which, since the 1930s, have found themselves cheek by jowl in Beirut, both having left Turkey and finding refuge in the city or its environs almost at the same time. The MECC can provide a setting for the possibility of reconciliation, bearing in mind how the intensity of such tensions wax and wane over the years. However, the proximity of Antelias to the Armenian Catholic Patriarchate could be intimidating, or at least there could be a sense of not being totally at liberty to act as a *sui iuris* Church might like. This is compounded by Rome's watchfulness that relations with the Orthodox be as harmonious as possible.

A Particular Example of Tension: Armenian Catholic and Armenian Orthodox

It is perhaps worth mentioning one particular example of such tensions, one that arose a few years ago and is indicative of a larger problem. It concerned the non-liturgical dress code of the present Catholic Patriarch. This is in some contrast to that of his predecessor, Hovhannes Bedros Kasparian XVIII, who is now in retirement. The latter had, on most occasions, been generally Latin in dress, but the present holder of the See has chosen black robes with a headdress of the same colour and material, with a diamond cross affixed to it; he also carries a staff. In other words, he is much more 'Armenian' than some of those who preceded him. These accoutrements may appear to most of us to be of no great consequence. However, they have been of some import for the neighbouring Orthodox, to such an extent that accusations were made in the local Armenian press that such an appearance on the part of the Catholic patriarch caused confusion among the faithful, and was, moreover, a wilful encroachment on the prerogatives of the Antelias catholicosate in particular.[28]

---

28 Cf. the *Instruction* issued by the Congregation for the Oriental Churches in 1996: 'Pour l'Application des Prescriptions Liturgiques du Code des Canons des Églises Orientales'. Yet it is Rome that has indirectly encouraged this development—in principle to foster closer relations, though not dictating the details to be pursued. As regards the vestments used by the Armenian Catholic Church in liturgical celebrations, they have always retained much of the usage of the 'Mother Church'

For Armenians in general, it is said, the Latin costume had been, and still is, a clear signal of 'who was who, and what was what'. It is claimed that that distinction has now been blurred. If we were to study, for example, the formal photographs of Armenian Catholic bishops that are to be found in Mgr Naslian's *Mémoires*,[29] photographs taken approximately one hundred years ago, we would sometimes find it difficult to distinguish them from their Latin colleagues, despite the full, untrimmed beards—such a style would not be an unusual feature for Latin bishops in the Middle East at that time. There is not much blurring here. The trend to return to some form of Armenian ecclesiastical dress code seems to have created a mixture of styles that in some sense reflects something of the position of the Armenian Catholic Church itself at the present time, a sense of uncertainty as to its role on the ecumenical stage. Along with other Eastern Catholic Churches, its role of being a 'bridge' or a model for eventual union with its 'Mother Church' is no longer so assured. Indeed, even in the full flush of Rome's aspirations in this respect, the Orthodox Churches as Churches were never tempted to be impressed or to follow suit. Rather did it arouse suspicion, if not further animosity, at what they would have regarded as an impertinent assumption. As with other pejoratively termed 'Uniate' bodies, the Armenian Catholic Church was seen as a 'Trojan horse' operating within the greater Armenian community and causing disruption to its well-being. However, numbers of individuals have made that transition and it would seem that a portion of Armenian Catholic clergy were at one time members of the Armenian Orthodox Church which is cause for irritation.[30]

---

in colour and material, though the great splendour of senior Armenian Orthodox prelates in celebrating the 'Badarak' on major feasts would be difficult to surpass.

29   *Les Mémoires de Mgr Jean Naslian, Évêque de Trébizonde. Sur les Événements Politico-Religieux en Proche-Orient de 1914 à 1928*, two vols, Imprimerie Méchithariste, Vienna, 1955.

30   There have been cases illustrating an opposite flow, most famously the Revd Malachia Ormanian who was later elected Patriarch of Constantinople in 1896.

SOME OTHER CONCERNS FOR THE ARMENIAN CATHOLIC CHURCH

The storm unleashed by this matter of dress-code has now diminished, yet it could be seen as indicative of other difficulties being faced by the Armenian Catholic Church as regards, for example, the use of Latin devotions, such as the recitation of the Rosary, novenas, processions of the Blessed Sacrament, or the use of Stations of the Cross, of statues and confessionals in the churches. The question then arises should the Armenian Catholic Church try to persuade its faithful to abandon these devotions and to have statues, some would say 'alien objects', removed? This is also a question that may perplex other Eastern Churches in union with Rome. To disturb, though, intimate congregational or even family associations with these buildings and their contents can cause anger and distress. Aidan Nichols has remarked in caution '… not every onslaught against "Latinisation" can be justified. One important aspect of inclusion within Catholic communion is precisely openness to what other traditions within the Church can offer. If Westerners can learn from the riches of the East, should Orientals reject everything that originates in the treasury of the Christian West?'[31]

There is also the need to meet the requirements of very different communities throughout the diaspora and how to prevent their faithful from losing their particular ethnic, linguistic, and religious inheritance in societies where the temptation to become completely assimilated can be strong. The visits of the Patriarch, as 'Father and Head' of his Church, including one in 2009 to the faithful in Armenia and Georgia, contribute to some sense of cohesion, as do the pastoral gatherings held in recent years in Bzommar, including not only clergy, but lay men and women from all over the Armenian Catholic diaspora. This demonstrates a greater willingness than in the past to be open to the contributions that the laity of the Church may be able to offer in information and advice to the patriarch and his synod.

The use of Classical Armenian in the liturgy can be a cause of difficulty, as few of the laity understand it, either in the Middle East or beyond. Despite occasional calls for the liturgy to be celebrated in modern Armenian, either in its Eastern or Western variants, or for translations into local languages, there is a reluctance to abandon a sacral language that has so much significance for both Orthodox and Catholic Armenians. It has been one of the markers of Armenian identity through the centuries and was invaluable

---

31 *Rome and the Eastern Churches. A Study in Schism*, T&T Clark, Edinburgh, 1992, pp. 100-101.

for the very survival of the people, often surrounded by military hostility or cultural antagonism. For the Armenian Catholics of the Middle East, though Arabic is often used by some worshippers, the central matters, the *Anamnesis* and the *Epiclesis*, remain in Krapar. There is also the near example of the dominant Orthodox whose leadership refuses to countenance any alteration or compromise as regards this particular matter.[32]

REASONS FOR ECUMENICAL CO-OPERATION IN THE MIDDLE EAST

The most recent example of ecumenical co-operation in the Middle East has been the establishment in Baghdad of the Council of Christian Church Leaders of Iraq. This occurred in February 2010. The Council consists of the fourteen Christian communities that were registered in the official Gazette *al-Waqa'e' al-Iraqiyeh* in January 1982, and which include both the Armenian Catholic and Orthodox Churches. This particular detail is evidence of the desire of the traditional Christian Churches to exclude other so-called Christian bodies that are seen by them to be, as elsewhere in the Middle East, a threat to their own flocks.

The following statements from the press release given by the Council succinctly present what we would probably understand to be the common agenda of all such attempts at co-operation between the Churches in the Middle East: 'The aim of the new Council is "to unite the opinion, position and decision of the Churches in Iraq on issues," related to the Churches and the State, for 'upholding and strengthening the Christian presence, promoting co-operation and joint action without interfering in private matters of the churches or their related entities. [...] The Council will be involved in activating dialogue and ecumenical initiatives among member churches, as well as with churches and heads of churches around the world. It will activate dialogue and relations with our Muslim brothers and sisters and promote the acceptance of the other. It will attend to the issue of Christian education, and the renewing of religious curriculum in public schools in co-ordination with concerned governmental institutions. It will work toward making a civil status law for Christians in Iraq, and will promote the participation of Christians in public

---

32   However, far beyond the bounds of the Middle East and possibly to the knowledge of the Catholic Patriarch and the Synod in the Lebanon, the *badarak* seems to be able to be celebrated entirely in Arabic or English, the former for those originating from the area under consideration.

life based on the rights of citizenship and partnership in building the nation, as a tent and a house for all." '[33]

Ecumenical cooperation may help remove problems between the Churches. As an example, we may mention here the question of marriage. At one time the various communities, whether Muslim, Christian or Jewish, would have kept the celebrations of marriage largely within the confines of their own communities, and this would still be largely the case. Such a custom would apply also to the various constituencies within the wider Christian community. Thus, marriage between Chaldeans would have been the *desideratum*, or between Orthodox Armenians, and this would still be the expectation. However, due both to the greater level of education among all such groups and often to the very places of their education, as well as the porousness of new residential areas in the cities, there is certainly now much greater interaction among different Christians. In addition, the almost overwhelming Muslim cultural influence,[34] and perhaps its more strident expression in recent years, has thrown Christians of whichever denomination more closely together; they are ever more keenly aware of being minorities.

Marriage between the Christian denominations might have been frowned on in the past, especially between Orthodox and Catholic, where, for example, the bride in question could be seen as lost to her own family and community, perhaps signified, it has been said, by the tolling of her local church bell on the day of her marriage elsewhere. However, such marriages have now become more acceptable; indeed, have had to become more acceptable. They would usually be more desirable than marriages between Christians and Muslims, unions that can produce difficult situations, often for the Christian spouse. In recent years, though, difficulties affecting mixed Christian marriages seem to have been largely resolved. The Catholic-Orthodox Accord reached in Lebanon on 14 October 1996, is an attempt to ameliorate those situations. Six Oriental Catholic Patriarchs and the representative of the Coptic Catholic Patriarch put their signatures to the agreement, along with those of the Syrian and Greek Orthodox Patriarchs of Antioch and that of Aram I Keshishian, Catholicos of Cilicia. The Armenian Catholic Patriarch at that time was Hovhannes Bedros XVIII.

It was resolved that the bride could remain faithful to her own beliefs without having to convert to the groom's faith, that though the marriage

---

33   Cf. WCC and *Ekklesia*.
34   '… Islamisation also penetrates families through the media and school, leading to an unconscious change in attitudes which is Islamic in character.' *Instrumentum*, § 34.

would be celebrated in the groom's church, the bride's own priest could be invited by the presiding priest to participate in the ceremony, and, finally, that children of the union would be baptised in the Church of their father.

The same Accord also dealt with the question of First Holy Communions. It was agreed that in future such celebrations would be held not in the schools, but in the parishes of the children in question. This was to prevent Orthodox children from being puzzled, if not upset, by their Catholic peers undergoing an elaborate and popular ceremony, whilst they themselves were being deliberately excluded from the joys of such an occasion.[35]

Another matter, the third agreed upon by the Patriarchs, was for the production of a communal catechism and this is now in progress.[36] However, the fourth item that concerned them, the communal dating of Christmas and Easter, 'is facing insurmountable difficulties (of discipline, of tradition, etc.). The great desire of the faithful in all Middle Eastern countries ... is to be able eventually to celebrate these two feasts together.'[37] As we have already seen, this weakness in the Christian witness to their faith in the Middle East was described by Bishop Taza at the African Synod as 'counter-testimony.'

MONUMENT OF GRATITUDE

Though in some cases Armenian refugees at the time of their expulsion or flight from Anatolia did meet hostility from certain local Arab tribes, nevertheless most were received with sympathy, as both peoples had suffered from Ottoman misgovernment. Matters changed somewhat later when it was perceived that many of the newcomers were not only succeeding in business, but were judged, rightly or wrongly, to have been in favour of the Mandate regimes at a time when Arab nationalism was urging the latter's

---

35   We may mention in passing that there have been calls made by some of the Catholic Fathers of the Synod of Lebanon to return to the custom prevalent before Latin alterations were accepted in this respect, that is to say, the administration of the three sacraments of initiation together, as is the continuing Orthodox practice. It is uncertain as to whether the Armenian Catholic Patriarch included himself in this expressed wish.

36   'Book 6 of this ... catechism has been issued for Grade 6 in elementary schools.' Cf. *Lineamenta*, § 58. On the question of publishing in general, the *Instrumentum* insists that 'Of primary concern is to ensure that religious education expressly treats the subject of ecumenism so that everyone will agree on not publishing anything which might offend or upset other confessions.' (§ 77)

37   *Lineamenta*, § 58.

departure.[38] In addition, there is still the general impression that Christians, who form an ever-decreasing minority throughout most of the Middle East, feel themselves being treated as second-class citizens, despised, secretly or otherwise, by the majority Muslim population.[39] In contrast to this, a number of Muslims do regard the minorities among them as a valued presence, contributing to the advancement of society; they would be loath to witness their disappearance.

Perhaps to counter the negative aspect of this historical legacy, as well as to ameliorate present matters in the region, a 'Monument of Gratitude' is being constructed in Yerevan, Armenia, to mark the debt Armenians owe to the Arab peoples as a whole during the former's most critical period of their history. Particular debt is being expressed to the people of Syria, the project having among its sponsors Bishop Armash Nalbandian (Primate of the Armenian Orthodox Diocese of Damascus), Archbishop Boutros Marayati (Primate of the Armenian Catholic Diocese of Aleppo), and Revd Mgrdich Karagozian (President of the Union of the Armenian Evangelical Church of the Near East). This appears to be yet another example of the long-standing co-operation, particularly in Syria, of the three Armenian denominations, being somewhat removed from what appears to be the sometimes tense relations in Beirut.

EVANGELICAL SECTS

The question of sects and 'underground/house churches'—which seem to have proliferated in the region in recent years—had led the 'Council of Church Leaders' in Jordan to request the expulsion of a number of persons

---

38 Concerning Arab Christians: 'Their contribution in the past, in the areas of education and culture and works to benefit society, has been outstanding. They have played an essential role in the cultural, economic and political life of their countries and have been pioneers in the rebirth of the Arab nation.' (*Instrumentum*, § 107) Armenian Christians would not have been so involved in the Arab nationalist movement; they had enough concerns with their own political parties. However, they made significant contributions in the other fields mentioned –their role in Egyptian society, at least before 1952, was not inconsiderable. They also began to take an early interest in the Lebanese political scene, due in large part to the existing numerical strength of the Maronite community.

39 The close identity between religion and politics in the Islamic world can have consequences for minorities within that world, often being seen thereby as deliberately casting themselves adrift from being true or reliable participants in the Arab, Iranian or Turkish socio-political milieux.

from the Hashemite Kingdom, which request has seemed in fact to have been implemented. The Council consists of four bishops: the Melkite Bishop of Petra and Philadelphia, the Latin Bishop of Amman, as well as the Greek Orthodox and the Armenian Orthodox bishops of the city. Although there is an Armenian Catholic parish in Amman, it is cared for by the patriarchal exarch in Jerusalem where he resides; to be members of the said Council, residency in the Kingdom is obligatory.

This matter of the sects demonstrates the serious concern that the local Churches have regarding the influence that this development has been exercising. This concern appears to be the case throughout the region, for numbers of their own youth, whether Catholic or Orthodox, are attracted to these new 'Christian' assemblies where the old family and tribal connections to certain rites no longer seem to carry weight; rather, there is an emphasis on being 'Christian' pure and simple. There is also a less complicated pattern of worship, probably better facilities available, and the possibility, especially for those who are poor or unemployed, for education and eventual employment.

In the case of Jordan, part of the government action was initiated by what was judged to be indirect attempts by these groups to influence numbers of the kingdom's Muslim subjects by their educational and philanthropic activities. Both the government and the traditional Churches of the land did not wish anything or anyone to disturb the usually tranquil balance being maintained there between Muslims and Christians.[40] There is, however, a possible embarrassment for the traditional Churches as regards the activities of their rivals: the sectaries and evangelicals are less inhibited in communicating their message to those around them, whilst those Christians long-established in the region are very circumspect, the latter thus appearing to those influenced by the sects as less enthusiastic, less inspired by the Spirit, and this to the advantage of the newcomers.

What poses a particular threat to the more traditional Churches is the belief held by a number of the evangelical groups that the reappearance of Christ, the Second Coming, depends on the return of all the Jewish people to the land of Israel. If this be the case, then, for the evangelicals, it is essential to encourage Jewish settlements whatever expense this involves in human terms for the local Palestinians, and this, in the long run, for 'the greater good of all'. The policy of support by certain Christians for the

---

40   Cf. article: 'Are Evangelicals triggering Islamic Radicalization in Jordan?' (http://www.buzzle.com/articles/are-evangelicals-triggering-islamic- …)There have also been recent expulsions of 'clandestine' evangelicals from Morocco. (*The Tablet*, 29 May 2010)

Israeli judaization of Jerusalem, for example, can arouse anger in the general Muslim population against the whole Christian community, the distinction involved in this case being left unclear, sometimes conveniently. Thus Christians, including Armenians—Orthodox, Catholic, and Protestant—who would now be more sympathetic to the Palestinian situation, can find themselves misjudged.

They may also be the victims of hostility shown by Jewish extremism, abuse in recent years being not unknown, especially in Jerusalem itself. Armenian processions to and from the Monastery of St James to the Holy Sepulchre have been subjected to some harassment, as have individual clergy and seminarians, often at the hands of Jewish theological students. Once again, due to the fairly low profile they maintain in the city, this does not seem to affect Armenian Catholics to the same extent. Nevertheless, such incidents cause further unease.

DIMINISHMENT OF THE CHRISTIAN POPULATION AND ITS CONSEQUENCES

A major reason for the establishment and growth in membership of the MECC and other ecumenical endeavours in the past few years, such as the new Iraqi Council mentioned earlier, has been the departure of great numbers of Christians from the region due to the unstable and often dangerous conditions to be met there.[41] The question of the general political situation in the Middle East, most especially the presence of Israel and its continuing confrontation with the Arab world, as well as specific internal problems in Iraq and in Lebanon, are important factors contributing to that instability.[42] This instability necessarily affects the economic situation, the sometimes parlous state of which urges emigration.

---

41 A new phenomenon that the Churches of the Middle East are now faced with is the emigration of thousands of Christians into the area, many of whom are women from Africa and Asia. 'Oftentimes, these people are subject to social injustice by the State which receives them and exploitation and sexual abuse by either the agencies which provide passage for them or their employers. [...] oftentimes international laws and conventions are not respected ...' *Instrumentum*, § 49. There is therefore 'the pastoral responsibility to assist them in both religious and social matters' and 'At the same time, to overcome any temptation to look down at or scorn these people, the faithful need to be instructed in the Church's social teaching and the concept of social justice.' *Ibid.*, § 50.

42 'In Lebanon, Christians are deeply divided at the political and confessional level and are lacking a commonly acceptable plan of action.' (*Instrumentum*, § 34)

There is also the simplistic equation being made that Christians in the Middle East are natural allies of Western 'Christian' governments, whose policies are usually seen as anti-Arab or anti-Muslim, or both. In particular, until fairly recently, there was in the West almost unquestioned support for Israel, whose presence for many Muslims seriously challenges the now long-established *Dar al-Islam* in the Middle East. Are not the Christians, including Palestinian Christians, despite denials, the fifth columnists of those governments? The growth of Islamic fundamentalism that often and conveniently judges the local Christians to be in collusion with the West, sees these communities as legitimate targets for their anger. That influence of Russia and of Communism in the Middle East, which so preoccupied Eddeldorf in the 1950s, has virtually disappeared since the collapse of the Soviet Union and the end of the Cold War, being replaced by these new concerns.

Apart from the Lebanese Civil War (1975-2000) and the Arab-Israeli struggle, the following also have contributed to the diminishment of the Christian populations in the region and have also affected the Armenian Catholic Church: the 1952 revolution in Egypt and its aftermath, the 'socialist' policies pursued by the Syrian government of the 1960s; the establishment of the Islamic Republic in Iran and the ensuing and lengthy conflicts between Iran and Iraq; the two Gulf Wars; the two *intifadas* (1987-1993, 2000-2005). However, the Armenian population in Lebanon and Syria seems still to be fairly numerous, and the exodus from Lebanon, it would appear, has somewhat abated in the past decade. However, the situation in Iraq continues to have a devastating effect on its Christian population.

With the diminishment of the Armenian presence in the Middle East, and exacerbating it, comes the threat of closure of businesses, schools and cultural associations, the disappearance of local Armenian newspapers and magazines. This leads naturally to a loss of confidence and a greater awareness of being a vulnerable minority.

The case of education can be a particularly fraught one. It is understood that the community schools are completely financed by the communities themselves. Furthermore, in some localities there can be schools of all three denominations, Orthodox, Catholic, and Protestant, and so competition might be high between them in order to keep their particular institutions open. In addition to schools run by the Mekhitarists and the Armenian Sisters of the Immaculate Conception, there are others maintained in the region by Latin religious orders, such as the Jesuits and Salesians, whose presence can also create competition. These, too, would attract Armenian students. There would also be non-denominational schools and colleges where a good portion of the curriculum might be conducted in English, a much-desired commodity.

Collaboration, however, is not unknown. Care of the elderly of whatever denomination in communal homes for the aged or for the handicapped may be undertaken by the three communities together. This is certainly the case in Aleppo and Beirut where there are homes for the elderly. The 'Arevig' day centre in Aleppo mentioned earlier and which is for mentally handicapped Armenian children is also run jointly by the three denominations, as is the Jinishian Memorial Enterprise.[43]

The temptation to leave for the West is powerful, especially for the educated young who seek not only freedom from doubtful regimes, and the sense of being regarded as incomplete citizens, but perhaps also from their own communities which they might consider as too close-knit and restrictive. Western values often challenge those of the more conservative environment of the Middle East, whether Christian or Muslim. The loss of such youth for their communities is inestimable.

CONCLUSION

The Armenian Catholic Church in the Middle East is small in numbers, but under one jurisdiction. In contrast, the Armenian Orthodox presence is still substantial, but divided jurisdictionally, reflecting the uneasy relationship between Etchmiadzin and Antelias. Armenian Catholics were isolated at first, not only from the Muslim world around them, but also from their fellow Christians, even those in union with Rome, due largely to differences in ethnicity and language. Like most other Armenians in the region, they were refugees and, though welcomed by some, others opposed them. The Armenians already *in situ* before the massacres and deportations were sometimes more than concerned about cultural differences and how Muslim neighbours might gradually feel hostility to all Armenians as a consequence. In addition, many newcomers had made good headway economically, a fact that could upset local Arab feeling.

---

43 There is also a sanatorium in Azounieh, Lebanon. It belongs equally to the Armenian Catholicosate of Cilicia and the Union of Near East Armenian Evangelical Churches.

In recent times, and certainly after the conclusion of the French and British Mandates, circumstances became more complicated. The newly independent states proved not so stable, more nationalist or socialist in aspiration and governance; they were either pressurizing 'foreigners' to leave, or, perhaps unwittingly, making it more difficult for them to stay. An exodus began, most dramatically in Egypt with the 1952 Revolution and its aftermath. There was also the 'repatriation' invitation issued by the Soviet Republic of Armenia in 1946 and to which many thousands of Armenians in the Middle East responded. Even though the Armenian Catholic Patriarch of the day, Cardinal Agagianian, expressed opposition to it, still many Armenian Catholics left the region for the Republic.

The continuing struggle between Israel on the one hand and the Palestinians and their allies on the other, being the most obvious threat to peace and stability in the region, is a major contributory factor to the decline of the Christian population. It is not simply the times of open warfare, or the fairly recent phenomenon of suicide bombings, but within Israel itself the spread of Jewish settlements and the attempts to infiltrate the Christian quarters of the Old City of Jerusalem are seen as highly provocative. There is also the desire by a number of Israeli fundamentalists gradually to remove any Christian presence from Biblical territory, apart, perhaps, from the guardianship of sites held sacred by many in the Christian world, thus leading inevitably to a simple curatorial pre-occupation. In response, this has necessitated in recent years the close co-operation of the Christian Churches. Ecumenism has indeed become an urgent matter and has been effective to some degree. Dialogue with Islam is also a matter of urgency, as a heightened sense of Islamic identity can be threatening to non-Muslim minorities and others. Self-criticism, however, is not so easily found among antagonists in the forum of the Middle East, for it would appear that too much is at stake and involvement in dialogue may be interpreted as weakness.

Relations between Rome and the Armenian Catholic Church, and, indeed, between Rome and other Eastern Catholic Churches, have perhaps been under some strain in recent years; the latter may be considered, by some, as now being 'neither fish nor fowl'. From what was regarded as an ideal arrangement to illustrate to the Orthodox that they need not feel anxiety in 'returning to the one true fold', there is, instead, a sense of embarrassment on the part of Rome for past missionary policies and their resulting ecclesiological structures that seemed legitimate at the time. The ultimate failure of the Council of Florence

(1438-1445) and the suspicions aroused by the practice of *communicatio in sacris* had led to the 'uniatist' model being seen as the only way forward for the restoration of that unity in the Church that had marked its earlier centuries. It was pursued with vigour.[44]

As regards the Armenians, however, Mekhitar and his followers had hoped and worked for a different, more nuanced approach whereby the Armenian liturgy and other factors of importance within Armenian tradition would be preserved intact and that no imposition of matters alien to that tradition would be allowed to intervene to exacerbate and entrench differences. They were inspired by such Armenian theologians as Nerses Shnorhali and Nerses Lambronatsi, both of the twelfth century and both of whom distinguished themselves 'as two solitary peaks amid all Medieval Christianity for their ecumenicity *avant-lettre*.'[45]

However, though allowing concessions, particularly in terms of liturgical practice, the mood of the Latin Church was becoming more ultramontane in mind and heart, wishing to exert greater control and watchfulness over its flocks, both of East and West, but particularly those, for one reason or another, that had come into being in the East, Churches which might have concealed, albeit unconsciously, heretical material that might cause invalidity in sacramental practice.

The process that now forms the 'atmosphere' prevalent today, where what has been called the 'Dialogue of Charity', seeking to understand the standpoints of the Orthodox Churches as they themselves understand them, and which itself has led to the present 'Dialogue of Doctrine',[46] may affect the Eastern Catholic Churches adversely. It seems to have created a sense of discomfort or numbness, or, to the contrary, may tighten them to seek and cultivate their own legitimacy: being complemental to the Latin Church; being critical yet remaining in union with it. Evidence of this may be found, for

---

44 For strong ripostes to Orthodox complaints concerning 'Uniates', cf. Robert F Taft, 'Reflections on "Uniatism" in the Light of Some Recent Books', *Orientalia Christiana Periodica*, Volumen 65, fasciculus I, 1999, pp.153-185; 'Anamnesis, not Amnesia: The "Healing of Memories" and the Problem of "Uniatism"', 21st Kelly Lecture, University of St Michael's College, Toronto, Canada, 1 December, 2000, published in *Logos*, vol. 41-42 (2000-2001), pp. 155-196.

45 Boghos Levon Zekiyan, 'The Religious Quarrels of the 14th Century Preluding to the Subsequent Divisions and Ecclesiological Status of the Armenian Church', *Studi sull'Oriente Cristiano* 1 (1997), fasc. 1-2, pp. 174-180. (p. 178).

46 Cf. Aidan Nichols: *Rome and the Eastern Churches*, second edition, Ignatius Press, San Francisco, 2010, pp. 356-375.

example, within the Melkite Church,[47] its greatest exponent being Patriarch Maximos IV Sayegh (1878-1967).[48]

Whether the Armenian Catholic Church can muster such energies remains to be seen, faced as it is with a number of problems, some of which we have touched upon. The exhausting and embarrassing schisms and defections that blighted its life, especially in Constantinople during the 1860s and 1870s, the trauma of the Genocide, the reliance on Rome for its recovery after the First World War, and its consequent subdued contribution during the proceedings of the Second Vatican Council, have somewhat weakened its ability or desire to act autonomously. There is also the continuing sense of being more deeply separate from the Arab Islamic world than their fellow local Christians, most of whom are deeply rooted within that same world. In addition, its ambiguous relationship with the 'Mother Church' which itself is recovering from its own traumas and with its continuing need to effect a more complete reconciliation between Antelias and Etchmiadzin, makes its present situation still more sensitive.

As an example of pressure on the Armenian Patriarchate to maintain or at least express what is meant to be its autonomy, especially in the eyes of such a critical neighbour as Antelias, there is the delicate question of the Patriarch's influence over his flock outside traditional patriarchal territory, so that he may be seen as exercising more stewardship and so be more truly the 'Father and Head' of his Church.[49] This means that the Holy See needs to relinquish its own immediate influence over certain areas where there are numbers of Armenian Catholic faithful who find themselves outside patriarchal territory,

---

47 Cf. Fran Colie, 'Roman or Melkite—What's the Difference?' (http://www.melkite. org/OES-RomanMelkite.htm): 'We have our own identity! We have a distinct, separate theology, tradition, spirituality, liturgy, and canon law—that is not opposed to Roman Catholicism, but complimentary *[sic]* to it.'

48 It was also evident with the Chaldean Patriarch Joseph Audo (1790-1878) who protested strongly against the latinizing directives of Pius IX's Bull *Reversurus* (12 July 1867) whereas the Armenian Catholic Patriarch Hassoun was keen to implement them.

49 This question concerns all the Eastern Catholic Patriarchs and Major Archbishops and was raised at the Pope's meeting with them in September 2009. 'Pope Benedict in response stressed the importance of maintaining the relationship of the people with the Church of their original territory to which they belong, even when they are in the Latin West. After all, Latin Christians are to be found in the territories of the Eastern Churches while remaining attached to the Roman Catholic Church. Pope Benedict's constructive development for solving the problem of jurisdiction when primacies and hierarchies overlap was warmly welcomed by the ... patriarchs and archbishops.' (Mark Woodruff, 'Ordinariates—Unprecedented and Unknown?' *Chrysostom*, New Series Vol. Ten, Pascha, 2010, pp. 31-46, p. 42)

if we take that territory to correspond roughly as being within the bounds of the former Ottoman Empire.

At the establishment of an Ordinariate for Armenia, Georgia and Eastern Europe in 1991, where it seems the majority of Armenian Catholic faithful are now to be found, Pope John Paul II appointed a Mekhitarist to the post, seemingly ignoring Kasparian, patriarch at the time. The latter had then angered the Orthodox authorities by his authorship of a Circular Letter (7 June 1992) that looked forward to when Armenian Catholic priests from Bzommar would be able to return to Armenia now that the Soviet Union had met its demise. This was taken to mean a campaign of proselytism in the newly liberated Republic, though that was not the intention of the patriarch's enthusiasm; he was concerned first and foremost with his own flock and any idea of tampering with the Orthodox faithful in Armenia would have been an invitation to disaster.

In 2005, a member of the Patriarchal Clergy of Bzommar was then appointed to the Ordinariate, which implied greater influence for the Patriarch.[50] However, on the resignation of the former in early 2010, an Apostolic Administrator, another Mekhitarist, replaced him, an appointment that again seems to lessen the authority of the Patriarch. The Mekhitarists, especially those of Venice, were not entirely supportive of there being a separate hierarchy for the Armenian Catholics, a development that for them would divide Armenians too sharply. This and their scholarly pursuits made them for the Orthodox the more acceptable face of Armenian Catholicism. Such matters only add to the concerns of the Patriarch whose possible vulnerability in this direction may weaken his moral presence and influence in the Middle East itself.

Taking all this into consideration, there is the possible self-questioning: 'Should the Patriarchate be in the Middle East at all? Should not our 'Father and Head' be in the Caucasus instead?'[51] The Patriarchate, however, would then be cheek by jowl with Etchmiadzin, an even more daunting proposition. This multi-faceted dilemma may explain something of the longing, often

---

50 Later that same year, 2005, the newly-elected Pope Benedict XVI raised the Apostolic Exarchate of the United States and Canada, then based in New York City, to that of an Eparchy in 2005, thus strengthening the authority of the Patriarch.

51 'What does the Word of God say to us here and now, to each Church, in each of our countries? How does God's loving Providence reveal itself to us in both the favourable and challenging situations of our daily life? What is God asking of us at this time: to remain so as to commit ourselves to these events which are under the care of Providence and divine grace? Or are we to leave?' *Lineamenta*, § 6.

privately expressed, of Armenian Catholics being finally reconciled to the 'Mother Church' with its lengthy and often embattled history. This could come to be if the Holy See adopted a different mode of being, somewhat akin to its role in the early centuries of the Church.

Finally, we may note how Pope John Paul II, to mark the 1700th anniversary of the official conversion of Armenia to Christianity, sent relics of the man instrumental in that conversion process, St Gregory the Illuminator, to Karekin II, Catholicos of Etchmiadzin, to Aram I, Catholicos of Cilicia, and to Nerses Bedros XIX, Armenian Catholic Patriarch of Cilicia. In doing so, the Pope quoted from his homily delivered at a celebration of the Divine Liturgy in the Armenian rite (18 February 2001): 'the relics of the same Saint are the symbol of a close unity in faith and a strong encouragement to unity in Christ. I am sure that, venerated by the Armenian people without distinction, they will increase the communion that Christ desires for his disciples. Thus brotherhood will be strengthened in charity. We are not dividing the relics; we are working and praying that those who receive them will be united. The same roots and a continuous history of saints and martyrs can prepare a future for your people of full participation and a visible sharing of faith in the same Lord'

IRAQI CHRISTIANS:
THE PRESENT SITUATION

Suha Rassam

INTRODUCTION

Since the invasion of Iraq in March 2003 by American and coalition forces, the civilian Iraqi population has been subjected to horrific levels of violence, with murders, car bombs, kidnapping, and extortion occurring mainly in the cities of Baghdad, Basra and Mosul. Violence, together with the breakdown of basic services, led to a situation in which living became a daily struggle, while caring for the sick and burying the dead was sometimes impossible. By the summer of 2008, security in Baghdad and Basra had improved while a fresh wave of violence against the Christians occurred in the city of Mosul. Some of the murders were driven by revenge and settlement of old scores, while others could be traced to inter-religious and sectarian tensions between Shi'ites and Sunnis, and between religious extremists from both sects against minorities.

However, political motivation, with resistance to the occupation and to the plan of dividing Iraq, was evident from the summer of 2003. After the invasion, the country was divided into three regional governments; the south for the majority Shi'ites (55 percent), the north for the Kurds (21 percent), and the Sunni Arabs (18.5 percent) were squeezed into a small area west of the country. The plan also included the formation of a special province for the Christians in the Nineveh plain of Mosul. Although the aim was to establish a federal state, the fact that it had a sectarian and ethnic basis, resulted in emphasis on tribal, ethnic and religious identity. Consequently, there was the re-emergence of deep sectarian tensions between Shi'ite and Sunni Muslims, and between Arabs and Kurds, which accelerated in scope and manifested itself gradually as an insurgency. It started with Ba'ath party members, who were still excluded outlaws and who were able to provide direct funds.[1] It

---

1   See Ali A Alawi, *The Occupation of Iraq: winning the war, losing the peace*, Yale University Press, New Haven, Conn., 2007, p. 173-176.

then gradually involved the Sunni Arabs who refused to accept the change in the political structure of the country. Having been, since 1920, the main political force in the creation of modern Iraq, they could not adjust to the new situation in which they found themselves a clear minority. The fear of marginalisation and impotence in the face of rising Shi'ite militancy and a powerful occupying force led some Sunnis to associate themselves with al-Qaeda and radical Islamist affiliates who instigated religious persecution of both Muslims and non-Muslims in an attempt to convert everyone to their own version of Islam. Although resistance to the plan of dividing Iraq came primarily from the Sunnis, there was also resistance to it from some Shi'ites and from minorities, who asserted their national identity within a unified Iraq.

The infighting between the Shi'ites and the Sunnis, as well as between different factions within each sect, led in some areas to a policy of religious 'cleansing' in an attempt to create purely Shi'ite or Sunni areas. Displacement of large numbers of Iraqis of all persuasions followed, fleeing to neighbouring countries or other parts of Iraq and creating a significant humanitarian problem. Kurdistan which is now officially in control of Dhok, Sulaimanya and Arbil, has *de facto* control of Kirkuk, Dyala and some parts of Mosul and possibly seeks to dominate these areas. This is being fiercely resisted by Sunnis, Turkomans and many Iraqis from among Shi'ites and minorities who have insisted upon a unified Iraqi state.

The influence of neighbouring countries further threatened the unity and sovereignty of Iraq. The alliance of some Shi'ite parties with Iran resulted in evidence of Iranian presence in Basra and other parts of the Shi'ite south, while the alliance of the Sunnis with al-Qaeda and radical Islamists demonstrated the influence of the extremist Wahhabi and Salafiyyah movements. Turkey, alarmed by the growing influence of the Kurds, had already militarily attacked the northern villages of Iraq and, according to some observers, threatens to claim Mosul if Kirkuk is to be taken by Kurdistan and Iraq dismantled into smaller sub-states. Jordan has remained neutral and accepted Iraqi refugees, while Syria, although sympathetic to the refugees and opposed to the plan of dismantling Iraq, has pursued its own policy orientation, sometimes in collaboration with Iran.

The re-ordering of Iraq's political framework together with the infighting between various factions not only destabilised the country as a whole but had a profound impact upon the country's minority groups. These include the Christians, Mandaeans, Yezidis, Shabak, Turkomans, Feli Kurds and Palestinians. The division of Iraq not only destabilized the country as a whole, but also disadvantaged all minorities, who became vulnerable in the absence of a unifying Iraqi political identity.

There is definitive evidence that minorities suffered more than the majority Muslim and Kurdish population. The United Nation Refugee Agency (UNHCR) in its report on the situation of minorities in October 2005 stated: 'Iraq's minorities have become direct targets of political, economic and religious-based violence. Since the fall of Saddam Hussein, violations inflicted on these groups have been noticeably aggravated.'[2] Taneja from Minority Group International reported 'While all Iraqis live under threat of violence, evidence supports the belief that in addition attacks are targeted against people because of difference in faith, creating a culture of distrust and fear between peoples of different communities.'[3] Mukhtar Lamani from The Centre of International Governance and Innovation in his report on the minorities of Iraq stated 'Iraqi minorities are facing a disproportionate level of violence and instability, which threatens to drive them out permanently.'[4]

This paper deals only with the Christian community. Their crisis is especially acute and their existence in their ancient homeland is now threatened for reasons that I will attempt to elaborate.

THE SITUATION OF THE CHRISTIAN COMMUNITY

The Christian community is by far the most important minority group, not only in view of its size, but also in view of the fact that it predated Islam by six hundred years and had played a vital role in the establishment of the Islamic 'Abbasid civilization as well as in the emergence of modern Iraq. Before the second Gulf War, Christians made about 4-5 percent of the population, at roughly one million individuals. Of these 70 percent are Chaldeans, the rest being Syrian Catholic, Syrian Orthodox, Assyrian Church of the East, Ancient Church of the East, as well as small numbers of Armenians, Protestants, Greek Orthodox and Greek Catholics, Copts, Latins and Anglicans. The majority lived in the cities of Baghdad, Mosul and Basrah and the rest in

---

2   UNHCR, Background Information on the Situation of non-Muslim Religious
      Minorities in Iraq. October 2005. http://www.unhcr.org/cgibin/texis/vtx/rsd/.
3   Preti Taneja, *Assimilation, Exodus, Eradication: Iraq's minority communities since 2003*,
      Minority Rights International, London, 2007, p. 11.
4   Mokhtar Lamani, 'Minorities in Iraq: The Other Victims', Report by 'The Centre
      of International Governance and Innovation' 2009, http://christiansofiraq.com/
      minoritiesiraq.pdf; see p. 6.

the towns and villages of the plain of Mosul and Kurdistan. Since 2003, a significantly high number of these Christians has been displaced, and about half have left the country.

The present plight of the Iraqi Christians has to be understood within the context of the political, economical and religious situation, not only of Iraq, but also of the wider Middle East. In addition, it must be linked to historical realities of co-existence as well as rivalries between Christians and Muslims over the centuries. While political and economic factors were most important in leading to the invasion of Iraq in March 2003, the religious element and its consequences are more difficult to assess and require a nuanced disentanglement from the other factors already mentioned.

At the local political level, apart from the fact that Christians are caught between the different groups in conflict, the division of Iraq into three federal regions on a sectarian and ethnic basis led to an undermining of the common national Iraqi political identity, which had been a unifying factor at times of difficulty. At the wider political level, Iraqi Christians found themselves caught up in the so called 'clash of civilizations' between the Islamists and the West. They are wrongly associated with the West because of the perceived similarity of religion, and have been called 'Crusaders' and supporters of the occupying forces.

When assessing historical factors, we are called to account by remembering what happened to previous generations of Iraqi Christians, of whose experience we are custodians. Throughout their history they have suffered massacres, genocide and displacement. Under Islamic rule these tragedies have been recurrent themes of Middle Eastern Christianity.[5]

With the rising current of worldwide Islamic radicalism, are we seeing previous patterns being repeated? Are we seeing the end of a presence that has spanned almost two millennia? Are the Christians of Iraq to be left to their own fate?

A short historical preamble may help answer these questions.

---

5   Sébastien de Courtois (tr. Vincent Aurora), *The forgotten Genocide: eastern Christians, the last Aramaeans*, Gorgias Press, Piscataway, NJ, 2004.

HISTORY

Christianity took root in Mesopotamia during the first Christian century and became a well-structured community by the end of the second.[6] Initially, its propagation was facilitated by the religious tolerance of the ruling Parthians. However, by the end of the third century (AD 286), the Sasanid dynasty adopted Zoroastrianism as the official religion of the state, which resulted in sporadic persecution. Soon after, the emperor Constantine converted to Christianity (312) and started to favour the Christians under his rule. The religious polarization that ensued within the two warring empires, together with political factors, resulted in extensive persecution of the Christians of Mesopotamia between the years 339-379. During these forty years, thousands of Christians were martyred under the rule of Shapur II, often with the accusation of being Roman collaborators. Following reconciliation with the Romans, Yazdigird I announced religious freedom within the Persian Empire in 410 and recognised the Christians as an independent community. However, the recurrence of persecution accompanied by the same accusations caused the Church of the East to announce its autonomy. This led, over time, to a distancing in its relations with the Western and Byzantine Churches. The bishop of the capital became a patriarch and strong missionary activity followed eastwards to Iran, Central Asia, India and China and southwards to the Arabian Peninsula.[7]

By the time of the arrival of the Muslim Arabs in the seventh century, the Church of the East rivalled the other major Churches in membership and learning, and its Aramaic-speaking Christians made up the majority of the settled population of Iraq.[8]

Under Muslim rule the Christians continued to work within the restrictions of *dhimmi* status and served their country in various professions, often in high office such as ministers. They conducted dialogues with Muslim caliphs and philosophers, and gained their temporary trust and protection without losing their identity.[9] They had near monopoly in the fields of medicine and the translation of Greek philosophical works to Arabic. The translation

---

6   Wilhelm Baum and Dietmar W Winkler, *The Church of the East*, Routledge Curzon, London, 2000, pp. 8-9.
7   J M Fiey, 'L'expansion de L'Eglise de Persia', *Istina*, Vol. 40, 1995, pp. 146-156.
8   D Gutas, *Greek thought, Arabic Culture: the Graeco-Arabic translation movement in Baghdad and early Abbasid society*, Routledge, London, 1998, p.18.
9   Sidney H Griffith, *The Church in the Shadow of the Mosque, Christians and Muslims in the World of Islam. Princeton*, Princeton University Press, Princeton, 2008 (2nd ed. 2010).

movement was of crucial importance since Greek works were the basis for the emergence of Muslim civilization.

However, Muslim tolerance diminished as their number increased and as the number of Christians in high office who could plead for their communities decreased. During the reign of al-Mutawakkil (847-861) churches were destroyed and a large number were dismissed from their office for no other reason than being Christian. Al-Jahiz wrote *Al-radd 'ala al-Nasara* ('Refutation of the Christians') and al-Tabari wrote *Al-Din wa 'l-Dawla* ('The State and Religion') reminding Christians that they were only *dhimmis*.[10] With increasing violence, due to the weakness of central governance and prejudice of local rulers, the Christians gradually moved to the north of Mesopotamia and the mountains became their safe haven and bastion.

After a short respite under Mongol rule, there were severe reprisals following the conversion of the Mongol Ghazan Khan to Islam in 1295.[11] Two massacres occurred in Arbil and Amida in 1310 and 1317 respectively, and massive destruction occurred under the rule of Timur Lang.[12]

Under the Ottomans, the Christians were treated as second class citizens under what was called the *millet* system.[13] The *jizya* was collected and the *dhimmi* rules were strictly applied in the cities, while the mountains were usually out of the reach of tax collectors, and the Christians lived next to Kurdish tribes where a balanced co-existence was reached. During five hundred years of Ottoman rule there was a continued decline of Eastern Christianity.[14]

With the disintegration of the Ottoman Empire there was a rise in internal tensions between different communities, and the carefully wrought balance between Christians and Muslims was disturbed. During the nineteenth century and until World War I, the claim of Christians for equality was interpreted as breaking the *dhimmi* contract of submission to their Muslim rulers. They

---

10   J M Fiey, *The situation of the Christians during the Abbasid Caliphate* (trans. into Arabic by H Zena), Dar al-Mashriq, Beirut, 1990.

11   Suha Rassam, *Christianity in Iraq—Its Origin and Development to the Present Day,* Gracewing, Leominster, 2005, p. 91.

12   J M Fiey, *Chrétiens Syriaques sous les Mongols (Il-Khanat de Perse XIIIe-XIVe s.),* Corpus Scriptorum Christianorum Orientalium, 362 (CSCO Subsidia 44), Peeters, Louvain, 1975, pp. x-110.

13   S Gero, 'Only a change of master? The Christians of Iran and the Muslim Conquest', *Cahiers de Studia Iranica,* Vol. 5, 1987, pp. 47-57.

14   Bat Yeor (tr. Miriam Kochan and David Littman), *The Decline of Eastern Christianity under Islam: From Jihad to Dhimmitude; Seventh to Twentieth Century,* Fairleigh Dickinson University Press, Madison, NJ, 1996. *Eadem* (trans. Miriam Kochan and David Littman), *Islam and Dhimmitude: where civilizations collide,* Fairleigh Dickinson University Press, Madison, NJ, 2002.

were treated ruthlessly, with evictions, forced conversions, rape and murder, and several massacres ensued from the middle of the nineteenth century and continued under the rule of the secular party 'The Committee for Union and Progress'.[15] Over a million and a half Christians, mainly Armenian but also large numbers from members of the Church of the East, Chaldeans, Syrian Orthodox and Syrian Catholics were massacred during the late period of the Ottoman Empire and the newly formed Turkish state.[16]

The modern state of Iraq was created after the war in 1932, with a constitution that stressed equality for all citizens irrespective of religion and race. The majority of Iraqi Christian welcomed the monarchy and integrated into the general population. However, the continued demand of some of the Assyrians for self-rule created a context for the unfortunate massacre at Simmel in 1933.[17] Despite several setbacks, the Churches flourished and there was no direct persecution of Christians until the end of Saddam's regime, when his co-operation with some Islamist groups resulted in isolated incidents of attacks on Christians.[18]

THE CONTEMPORARY PERIOD 2003-2010

Apart from the general violence that affected all sections of society after 2003, the Christian community suffered specific targeting from both Sunni and Shi'ite radicals and intimidation by the Kurds. Further evidence suggests that there are those who want to see the end of Christian presence in Iraq in order to create a pure Islamic state. Father Basil Yaldo, who was kidnapped in September 2006, in speaking after his escape to the Catholic News Service, stated that he has not been kidnapped for money, but that his abductors had some conditions, one of which was to tell Patriarch Delly that all Christians should leave Iraq.

The concentration of the Christians in troubled areas, namely Baghdad, Mosul and Basrah, made them more liable to acts of violence. Seen as soft

---

15   D Gaunt, *Massacres, Resistance, Protectors- Muslim Christian Relations in Eastern Anatolia during World War I*, Gorgias Press, Piscataway NJ, 2006.

16   *Ibid.*, also J Nai'm, *Will this nation die?* (translation from English to Arabic by Basil Qouzi), Nasira Publications, Baghdad, Iraq, 2006.

17   S Rassam, *Christianity in Iraq*, p. 145-147.

18   For example, the nun Cecile Moshi Hanna, a member of the Order of the Sacred Heart of Jesus, was murdered in her convent by being stabbed and beheaded on 15.8.2002.

targets they suffered more from kidnapping, extortion and humiliation than the general population. While the two factions of Islam as well as the Kurds are vying for power and have militias to protect them, Christians and other minorities, are unable to exercise power nationally and do not have militias to protect them. All they ask for is to be allowed to live in peace with equal rights, in what they feel is their own country, where they have lived before the arrival of Islam, and to which they have contributed at various stages of its development.

Specific anti-Christian activities include:

1 Attacks on individuals with specific professions and practices that are considered un-Islamic

Soon after the invasion, alcohol dealers, hairdressers, cinema owners, musicians and dealers in musical instruments, videos and CDs were targeted. These professions are considered un-Islamic and mostly practised by Christians. A large number of people with these professions have seen their businesses attacked and destroyed, thus robbing them of their livelihood. 'Human Rights Without Frontiers' reported that in May 2003, the Shi'ite Sheikh Muhammad al-Fartoosi, issued a *fatwa,* banning alcohol, commanding women to wear the *hijab* and cinemas to close, stressing that his *fatwa* is not just for Muslims but for all people, threatening that he has up to a thousand armed men under his control.[19]

2 Attacks on women

Christian women were forced to wear the *hijab* even though it is not part of their culture and religion. Many of those who did not comply were raped and killed.[20]

3 Intimidation, extortion and the language of hate

Messages were sent in different ways: graffiti on walls, on mobile phones or on pieces of paper thrust under the doors of Christian houses calling them dirty infidels, 'crusaders' and collaborators with Western powers, or *dhimmis* who have to pay the *jizya* or leave. Some mullahs spoke from their mosques saying: the properties of the Christians are

19   Human Rights Without Frontiers (HRWF), 'Shiite leader in Baghdad warns women, alcohol sellers, cinemas', 21 May 2000. Reported by *Associated Press,* 16 May 2003. Rory McCarthy 'Iron hand cleric issues a *fatwa* amid Baghdad chaos', *The Guardian,* 21 May 2003.
20   *Ibid.*

halal (lawful) for you, do not buy them as they will be leaving and all will be automatically yours. Such messages create an atmosphere of fear and render the community unsustainable. In addition, citizens in Mosul were approached directly by knocking on their doors and the *jizya* collected from them. Andrew Kramer reported that Archbishop Rahho was forced to pay the weekly *dhimmi* tax to the insurgents, and when this stopped he was killed.[21]

4 Threats to religious leaders

A threat to a church leader came as early as June 2003, to be followed by many others. Fifteen clerics have been abducted, some tortured, others released after large sums were paid.[22] Four priests, a Protestant pastor, six deacons and one bishop have been murdered, some after being kidnapped, others shot dead on the doorsteps of their church.[23]

5 Attacks on churches

More than fifty churches and places of worship have been attacked, and many more closed. The first concerted attack, on six churches, occurred on 1 August 2004, to be followed by many others. Crosses were removed from churches, convents emptied and occupied by militias and the seminary and Babylon theological college relocated to Arbil in the Kurdistan region in the north of Iraq.[24]

---

21 Andrew E Kramer, 'For Iraqi Christians, money bought survival', *New York Times*, June 26 2008.

22 1. Georgis Kasmousa, Syrian Catholic Bishop 18.1.05, 2. Ra'ad Washan, Chaldean priest, 17.7.06, 3. Sa'ad Sirop, Chaldean priest, 15.7.06, 4. Basil Yaldo, Chaldean priest 16.7.06, 5. Douglas al-Baz, Chaldean priest 19.11.06, 6. Sami Abdul Ahad al-Rais, Chaldean priest 5.12.06, 7. Gibrael Shammami, Chaldean priest 2.4.07, 8. Nawzat Putrus, Chaldean priest 19.5.07, 9. Hani Abdul Ahad, Chaldean priest 6.6.07, 9. Pios Affas, Syrian Catholic priest 13. 10. 07, 10. Mazin mattoka, Syrian Catholic priest 13.10.07, 11. Sharbil Gabriel, Chaldean priest, 12. Faraj Rahho1, Chaldean Bishop.

23 1. Poulis Iskander 11.10.06 Mosul (Syriac Orthodox) beheaded and dismembered after kidnap), 2. Mundhir al-Dibir 26.11.06 Mosul (Protestant pastor, killed after kidnap), 3. Raghid Ganni with three deacons, Mosul (Chaldean priests and deacons, 3.6.07 shot at the door of their church), 4. Faraj Rahho and three companions, 29.2.08 Mosul (Chaldean Bishop was kidnapped while his three companions shot dead on 29.2.08, the bishop's body was left in a shallow grave on 13.3.08), 5. Yousif Abboudi (Syriac Orthodox) shot dead at the door of his church in Baghdad on 4.4.08.

24 For the full list see Rassam, *Christianity in Iraq,* new edition 2010.

6 Religious Cleansing

During the summer of 2007 came a direct threat to individuals in their own homes: 'Convert to Islam, leave or face the consequences.' This is how the al-Dora district of Baghdad was practically emptied of its Christians. Al-Dora used to be called 'the Vatican of Iraq' in view of its predominantly Christian population, the presence of two cathedrals as well as several churches, the Chaldean seminary and Babylon theological college. Its population comprises middle and lower income families and some are very poor. They left with nothing but the clothes on their backs and are now dependent on the charity of relatives living abroad or the Churches. Some could not afford to leave the country and moved to other areas of Baghdad. One parish with which the charity 'Iraqi Christians in Need' was involved received over 1,000 families.

Between 2 September and mid-October 2008, another wave of ethnic cleansing occurred in Mosul. Fifteen individuals were killed and three houses blown up after their residents were evacuated and loudspeakers were heard commanding the Christians to leave their homes. As a result 15,000 individuals fled to the northern villages of Iraq. There is doubt as to who instigated these attacks. All previous attacks were attributed to Muslim radicals, while there is suspicion of Kurdish involvement in this incident, although they fiercely deny it. The British MP Edward Leigh, together with five other MPs, has recently proposed a motion to the British Parliament asking Her Majesty's government to investigate the issue.

While the security situation in Baghdad and Basra improved, that in Mosul continues to be perilous for Christians. During 2009 there were sporadic killings of Christians, escalating from December 2009 to February 2010, and reaching a total of twenty-three. On the 3 March 2010 car bombs targeted a convoy of buses transporting university students from the villages of the Nineveh plain to the city of Mosul, killing three students and injuring over seventy, many seriously.

7 Marginalisation and assimilation

Marginalisation of minorities in elections and the political process has been widely reported.[25] In Mosul, ballot papers were not delivered in a large number of villages, affecting Christian voters.[26] When the government was

---

25   *Catholic Herald,* January 6, 2006. 'Iraqi bishop questions the validity of national election'. J Pontifex, 'Election Catastrophe', *CAN News*, 4 January 2006.
26   Allawi, *The Occupation of Iraq*, p. 391.

formed in April 2005, minorities and women were under-represented.[27]

The long-awaited constitution contains ambiguities regarding the role of religion and the rights of minorities. It was drafted in haste, and minorities were under-represented in the drafting process.[28] Apart from enshrining Islam as the official religion of the state, there was fear of future misinterpretation of article 2. Section (a) of the article states that 'no law may be enacted that contradicts the established provisions of Islam,' while section (b) states that 'no law may be enacted that contradicts the provisions of democracy.' Interpretation of article 2 depends on Iraq's Supreme Federal Court whose composition is laid down in article 92 of the Constitution. It is feared by the minorities that lack of access to the judiciary will, in due course, make it difficult to find appropriate representation.[29]

In Kurdistan, the situation is characterised by an attempt at assimilation of minorities into a Kurdish nation. Iraqi citizens are forced to register with a Kurdish party before being allowed to live and work in Kurdish areas, and Arabs are not welcome. Christians have been welcomed but have had to register as Chaldo-Assyrians-Syriac and not as Arab Christians, which some of them consider themselves to be. Iraq's Minority Council spokesman stated: 'The Kurds are causing rifts between minority groups for their own purposes ... they are buying people ...'[30]

8 Displacement

Christians have been leaving the country in large numbers since 2003. Displacement is not new to Iraqi Christians. Immigration started at beginning of the nineteenth century, and well into and after World War I, following massacres in Turkey. With the economic attraction of the New World, many headed for North America. They subsequently attracted friends and relatives and formed large communities, especially in Detroit, Chicago and San Diego.

---

27 Rassam, *Christianity in Iraq*, p. 25; on 10 April 2005 Prime Minister Ibrahim al-Ja'fari formed the Cabinet in which there were 17 Shi'ite members (one of whom was a woman), eight Kurdish members (three of whom were women), five Sunni Arabs (one of whom was a woman), and one Christian woman.
28 F A Jabar, *The Constitution of Iraq: Religious and Ethnic Relations*. Minority Reports Group December 2005, available at http://www.minorityrights.org/957/micro-studies/the-constitution-of-iraq-religious-and-ethnic-relations.html.
29 Taneja, *Assimilation, Exodus, Eradication*.
30 *Ibid.*, p. 17.

Later political events and internal conflict following the formation of the modern state of Iraq led to further emigration, starting with the massacre of 1933 and up until the conflict between the government and the Kurds in the 1960s. During the Iraq-Iran war, people left because they did not want to fight a war they did not believe in. After the first Gulf war and during the long years of sanctions, immigration involved all sections of society. By then, people had lost hope of anything good happening to their country, and felt that there was no future for their children. The destination was no longer the USA, but Canada, Australia, and New Zealand. These countries accepted people with specific criteria, draining the qualified and those with financial resources from Iraq.

However, the displacement that occurred following the invasion of Iraq in 2003 is quite different. People have been fleeing for their lives. They are usually the impoverished, who could not afford to leave earlier, or those who previously would not leave for specific reasons. It is estimated that, since then, more than half of the Christian population have fled their homes to relatively safer areas of Iraq or to neighbouring countries. Initially they left for Jordan, while since 2007, as Jordan closed its borders to Iraqis, the main destination became Syria, but also Lebanon, Egypt, and Turkey, the Gulf States and other countries.

Amongst the estimated two million Iraqi refugees in neighbouring countries, Christians predominate. Mowafaq Abdul al Raoof, spokesman for the Ministry of Migration and Displacement in Iraq, told UN news agency IRIN: 'According to our estimates, nearly half of the minority communities have already fled to other countries.'[31] In Syria, 44 percent of Iraqi asylum seekers were recorded as Christians since UNHCR began registrations in December 2003, even though Christians constitute less than 5 percent of the population.[32]

In another report, an official from the UNHCR, speaking on condition of anonymity, told UN News Agency IRIN that the minorities of Iraq make up about 30 percent of Iraqi refugees, whose total number is thought to be 1.8 million.[33]

The Iraqi refugees living in neighbouring countries are not given official refugee status, although they are registered by the UNHCR as such. In some

---

31   Iraq: minorities living tormented days under sectarian violence. 4 January 2007, *IRIN*, http://www.irinnews.org/report.aspx?reportid=62981.

32   M Latimer, 'Mass exodus', *Guardian Weekly*, 26 October 2006.

33   *IRIN*, article cited above, n. 31.

countries, they have to pay fines when their visas expire, which can amount to large sums of money annually. This was especially so in Lebanon where hundreds ended up in prison because they could not pay the exorbitant price requested of them. The main help for these refugees comes from their relatives who had earlier left for Western countries. Those who have no relatives abroad are destitute, and are only helped by the Churches and some charitable institutions. Some are resorting to desperate measures, selling their kidneys or pursuing illegal activities, and the psychological problems are enormous. It is estimated that there were about 70,000-100,000 Christians in Syria, 100,000 in Jordan and probably another 100,000 in other neighbouring countries.

At the end of 2007 there were reports of improvement in the general security situation in Baghdad and immigrants were encouraged to go back to their homes. Buses in front of the Iraqi embassy in Damascus gave free transport, and families were given the equivalent of $800 in order to re-start their lives. Only a few Christians returned, as they needed more assurance of long-term safety. Their fears were substantiated when yet another series of co-ordinated attacks were launched on their churches. On 6 January 2008, six churches and an orphanage were attacked in Mosul and Baghdad, and three days later two churches were attacked in Kirkuk. These attacks were followed by the murder of the Bishop of the Chaldeans of Mosul, Raho, in February, and that of the Syrian Orthodox priest Yousif Abboudi who was shot in front of his house in Baghdad in August of the same year.

KURDISTAN AND THE SAFE HAVEN FOR THE CHRISTIANS

The Kurds have been especially welcoming to Christians and have several Christians in the KRG government.[34] With the help of the Minister of Finance, many Christian villages were rebuilt and ancient churches and monasteries reconstructed. Christians, who had inhabited villages in Kurdistan in the previous century were resettled in their original habitats, and new villages were built to accommodate others. This policy, together with the relative safety of Kurdistan, attracted many displaced Christian families from Baghdad, Mosul and Basra to settle there. Ankawa, previously a district of Arbil, has grown in

---

34 There are two ministers and three Members of Parliament: Sarkis Aghajan Memno, Minister of Finance in the KRG 1996-2008; Nimrud Baito, Minister of Tourism in KRG 2004—present: Andrawis Youkhana MP; Galawis Shaba MP; Romeo Hakkari MP.

size to become more like a city, and accommodated many displaced Christians as well as becoming home to the Chaldean seminary and theological college. Their website 'ankawa.com' is one of the best developed websites, giving news of and interviews with prominent political and religious Iraqi Christian figures, as well as general news. The Ishtar TV channel also operates in Ankawa with global outreach. Christians also flourished in other cities within the Kurdistan region, such as Zakho and Duhok.

However, the general situation for Christians in Kurdistan is problematic, in view of an attempt to assimilate minorities into a Kurdish nation and its plan of expansion. The Kurds are presently trying to establish and assert their Kurdish identity within a federal Iraq, but it is considered that the ultimate aim is an independent Kurdistan. The official language is Kurdish and those who want to live in Kurdistan have to register with local Kurdish authorities and belong to one of the official parties before getting a job, however menial it is. The Syriac language is taught in schools where Syriac Christians predominate, Arabic is prohibited. In Kurdistan the Iraqi flag is seldom seen, while the regional flag is everywhere, and checkpoints between Kurdistan and neighbouring governorates, resemble border controls between two different countries.

The Kurds are giving the Christians protection, but they expect them to be, for all practical purposes, Kurds. This is not acceptable to many Christians, especially those whose only language is Arabic and those, whether Arab- or Syriac-speaking who believe that their country is a unified state of Iraq.

More dangerous than assimilation is the plan of forcing all the Christians of Iraq to live in an autonomous province in the Nineveh plain. Such a plan seems to have been agreed upon between the Kurds, the Shi'ites, some Christian parties and the occupying authorities. However, disagreement exists among the planners as to whether such a province would be under Kurdish leadership or whether it would operate as an autonomous area within Iraq's federal state or under the control of the central government in Baghdad. Argument continues and a referendum has been suggested.

Christian politicians in the Kurdistan Regional Government (Sarkis Aghajan Memenu and Romeo Hakari) have requested that a clause should be included in the Constitution, to include the plain of Mosul under KRG control, since they argue that this area lies within the expanded boundaries of Kurdistan. In an interview with Mark Lattimer, Aghajan stated 'As Christians we regard Nineveh as our region. Throughout history our people have been obliged to leave and live elsewhere. This includes those who fled Saddam

Hussein's campaign to Arabise Kurdish and Christian areas in the north, where land was distributed by force to Arab settlers. Now about 3,500 Christian families had come from Mosul and Baghdad to settle in the Nineveh plain.'[35]

The plan of creating a Christian province is fiercely resisted by the Sunnis of Iraq in general, and those of Mosul in particular, as well as by many Christians. In addition, Turkey has long claimed Mosul as part of its territory since the Allies occupied it during World War I and after the Armistice.[36] It was given to Iraq by a special decision of the League of Nations after the war. That decision was influenced by the vote of the Christians of Mosul during a referendum organized for the purpose. It would not be long before Turkey moved to foil Kurdish plans. It has already attacked the villages at its border with Iraq in order to check the progress of the Kurds' political aspirations. The Christians would certainly be totally trampled underfoot in this political conflict, and will suffer greatly if they ally themselves with the Kurds. History tells us that both Kurds and Turks were ruthless in their treatment of the Christians, for example, before and after the First World War. Although the Turkish government opposed Kurdish claims to independence and fought the Kurds, they allied themselves with them and used them in order to get rid of the Christians from Turkey during the nineteenth and twentieth centuries.[37]

The majority of Iraqi Christians do not belong to a political party, and do not want to live in an exclusive area. These include members of the mainline Churches namely: Chaldeans, Syrian Catholics, Syrian Orthodox, the Ancient Church of the East, as well as smaller denominations. It is only the Assyrians and a small number of politically motivated Christians from other denominations who have been lobbying for an independent province for the Christians. Those who oppose the plan argue that for such a province to be viable, it needs the protection of Western powers as well as that of the Kurds. Such a relationship will alienate them from the Sunni Arabs and link them more with the West, confirming the false accusation of radical Muslims, that the Christians are Western collaborators.

Amongst Christian religious leaders opinions vary, but the majority have not been supportive of the idea of an exclusive safe haven for the Christians. Although the Patriarch of the Chaldeans, Mar Emmanuel III Delly, has honoured the finance Minister Sarkis Aghajan for his help to Christians

---

35   M Latimer, article cited above, n. 32.

36   See *ibid.*

37   See Rassam, *Christianity in Iraq*, p. 133. Cf. also Peter Balakian, *The Burning Tigris: a history of the Armenian genocide*, Harper Collins, New York, 2003; Courtois, *The forgotten Genocide*.

during the period of crisis,[38] he has recently made an appeal, together with other Catholic bishops of Iraq, rejecting the idea of an independent province for Christians. Leaders of the Ancient Church of the East and the Syrian Catholic and Orthodox Churches have also voiced similar reservations. However, the Assyrian Church of the East and their patriarch Mar Dinkha IV, are more supportive of Kurdistan and the formation of an independent presence under its control.

Religious leaders of all denominations (except the Assyrians) expressed their concern as early as 12 December 2004: 'we would like to express our sadness at what has been happening in our country. We would like to stress that we support an independent and united Iraq which guarantees equality and justice to all regardless of religion and race … we would like to encourage dialogue between religions so as to ensure peace, reconciliation and cooperation … we would like to remind everybody that the Churches should be listened to through their official leaders … the teaching of our Church and its directions in politics, sociology, and morals takes its inspiration from the words of Our Lord, expressed by peace based on justice and fraternity and the general good …'[39]

The Chaldean Archbishop of Kirkuk, Louis Sako, has described such an enclave as a Christian ghetto, which would engender endless violence, as in Palestine and Israel. He has reiterated that the only way to achieve a lasting and peaceful existence for the Christians of Iraq is to live in peace with their Muslim brethren, working together towards a strong democratic government, demanding that all Iraq should become a safe haven, not only for Christians but also for all its citizens.[40] In an interview with *Asia News* on 16 January 2007 he expressed his concern: 'there is a danger that they may end up in a ghetto. The division of Iraq will have serious consequences for neighbouring countries like Turkey, Iran and Syria where the local Kurdish population are demanding autonomy or independence to which their governments are opposed … for this idea to be viable, they have to be protected. Presently the Kurds and the Americans view this idea favourably, but it remains a dangerous plan. In my opinion it is better to work at the constitutional level and to ensure that each area is guaranteed religious freedom and equal rights for all

---

38 He was awarded the honour of Knight Commander of the Order of Saint Gregory the Great by the Pope Benedict XVI.

39 *Najm al-Mashriq*, no. 41, 2005, pp. 129-130 (translation from Arabic by the author).

40 Christopher Howse, 'On the plains of Nineveh', *Telegraph*, 7 July 2007, available at http://www.ankawa.com/english/?p=166.

believers of all faiths throughout the land including Christians who can be found anywhere.'[41]

Antoine Audo, Chaldean Bishop of Aleppo has also made similar statements: 'The Sunnis in Mosul will take this so-called "Safe Haven" as a pretext to attack the Christians. They will say: "look, the Christians are asking for independence from us. We must stop them." The Christians have to live with everybody else. That is the way it should be.'[42]

A statement was made regarding this issue in a special meeting in the village of Ain Sifni convened by the Chaldean bishops of the northern provinces of Iraq, Zako, Arbil, Kirkuk, and Amadyya, on 2 July 2007: '... We refuse the idea of creating a special Safe Haven for the Christians in the Nineveh plain because all Iraq is our country and we would like to be able to live in any part of it in safety and peace with all our Iraqi brothers and sisters.'[43]

The Latin Archbishop of Baghdad, Jean Sulaiman, made the following statement regarding this issue during his visit to London in September 2008:

> Regarding an autonomous Christian province in Nineveh plain: In our assembly of Catholic Bishops and the heads of all Christian churches in Iraq, this solution has been rejected. It seems like a ghetto. It will isolate the Christians as a social and cultural group. Instead, it is important to help Christians face the turmoil of Iraq not as minorities but as full Iraqi citizens with rights and duties rooted in the country and always prepared to make a difference with their ideals, proposals and services. Even if Christians are enjoying peace now in Kurdistan, it does not mean that they are achieving their aspirations. It damages their relation with the Sunni Arabs. We also think that the province is not big enough for all the Christians and does not provide or guarantee for their security and their social and economic life. The displaced population that reached there is finding it difficult to live. There are not enough houses, factories, jobs, schools, hospitals and so on. Many of those who went there have now left and are now refugees waiting to emigrate.

Christian religious leaders have also spoken about the fragmentation of the Christian community in politics. They have said that the division of the

---

41 http://christiansofiraq.com/movingtowarddivision.html.
42 J Pontifex, 'Flight from Fear', *The Tablet*, 25 November, 2006.
43 Report signed by Bishop Petrus Harbouli Bishop of Zako, Bishop Louis Sako of Kirkuk, Bishop Rabban al-Kass of Amadyya, Bishop Andrawis Sana (retired).

Christian community into small factions and political parties, does not aid a unified voice, and urged them to be united in order to set an example for others and helping the reconstruction of the country in a spirit of unity and respect. Unfortunately, however, there does not seem to be a strong leadership to unite all Christian denominations in order to achieve such an aim.

THE CHALLENGE

The challenge that now presents itself to Iraq is how to deal with the complicated religious-political situation that has its roots deep in our history. This is not to forget the difficulty in dealing with the economic factor, oil, and the wider political factors, the Palestinian-Israeli problem and the interest of neighbouring countries in Iraq.

The question that poses itself is, will there ever be a stable situation in which the Christians of Iraq are treated as equal citizens in the near future? With the Islamist orientation of the majority political parties that are ruling the country at the present time, the Christians do not feel secure.

As for the safety of the Kurdistan area for Christians, it is clear that this safety is only relative and temporary. The conflict with Turkey has already erupted and there are reports of Kurdish Islamicists. Moreover, one cannot forget that the Kurds were party with the Turks to the massacre of Christians during Ottoman times. The Kurds are presently trying to absorb the Christians into Kurdistan in order to increase their regional demographic presence, in an effort to strengthen their claim for an independent state. The plan of including the Christian villages of the Nineveh plain within Kurdistan is being fiercely resisted by the Sunnis of Mosul in particular.

As for the solution of providing an independent province or safe haven for Christians, I think that it is even more contentious. Apart from questions as to whether such a project is viable at all, in view of the relatively small number of the Christians in question, such an enclave can only survive with external Western support. Apart from the fact that it cannot ensure such support in the future, its consideration would only fortify the claim of the Muslims that Christians are Western agents. Squeezed between Iran, Turkey and Syria, can it ever survive? I think it will merely be an easy dumping place for Christians and a recipe for disaster. It is some of the Assyrian Christians who are asking for the creation of a safe haven. Leaders from other denominations have spoken strongly against it. Bishop Sako of Kirkuk has been outspoken in this respect, and has reiterated that the only acceptable way for Christians to live in Iraq is within a united democratic state, where Christians and Muslims are treated with equality and justice.[44]

SUMMARY AND CONCLUSION[45]

1 Are we seeing previous patterns being repeated?
When viewed through the lens of history, events now seems to be a repetition of what happened in previous centuries, and a continuation of what happened in late Ottoman times. Under Muslim rule there seems to be a pattern repeating itself: tolerance of non-Muslims with discrimination as *dhimmis*, pressure to convert by different means such as marriage or financial gains, violence by extremists, displacement and massacres, then back to 'dhimmitude' again. The short periods of secular rule in between gave the community a chance to recover and re-build itself, only to be stifled by a backlash from Muslim radicals. Mixing religion with politics, their retaliation against the defenceless Christians, their brothers and sisters who have co-existed with them over the centuries, has been the cause of the progressive diminution of Christians in the area

2 Are we seeing the end of a presence that has spanned almost two millennia?
It is obvious that the impact of the 2003 war on Iraqi Christians has been devastating, and that this community is now under threat of extinction. The Bishop of the Chaldeans of Syria, Antoine Audo, stated in November 2007: 'What a loss it is for Islam, the Western world, and for Israel, if the Christians of Iraq suddenly disappear. Should the minorities of the Middle East pay the price for what one Harvard professor, Samuel Huntington, called "the clash of civilizations" or should not their continuing presence through all the misadventures of history be a sign of hope, respect and justice for the whole world? Do the Christians of Iraq pose a challenge to the world beyond themselves?'[46]

---

44   Interview with *Asia News*, 16 January, 2007.
45   For further detail, see my earlier study: 'The Plight of Iraqi Christians', *One in Christ: a Catholic Ecumenical Review*, Vol. 142 no. 2 (2008), pp. 286-301.
46   Lecture, 'Christianity in Iraq', Heythrop College, University of London, November 2007.

3 Are the Christians of Iraq to be left to their fate?

Iraqi Christian leaders of various denominations have spoken on different occasions, asking the government for full representation in the political process, and stated that the only acceptable way for Christians to live in Iraq is within a united democratic state where Christians and Muslims are treated with equality and justice.[47] Within a federal Iraq, Christians should be able to choose to live in any of the three regions, and if there is need for a province in which Christians predominate, its safety should be guaranteed by the central government in Baghdad.

The Holy Father Pope Benedict XVI has expressed his concern over Iraqi Christians on a number of occasions, and expressed his spiritual closeness to Iraq's Christians during the elevation of the Patriarch of the Chaldeans, Emmanuel III Delly, to the College of Cardinals on 24 November 2007.[48] He has met with President Bush, with the Iraqi president Talabani and, most recently, with Iraqi Prime Minister Nouri al-Maliki in Rome, and specifically asked that the rights of Christians be safeguarded.

In June 2008, the international Catholic organisation Pax Christi hosted a Christian delegation from Northern Iraq at its international office in Brussels, where they met with representatives of the European Union and the European Commission. The aim was to make the voice of Iraqi Christians heard in Europe by decision makers. Iraqi representatives portrayed the dangers their communities are facing and asked for help from the international community to ensure that 'policies are not simply words but are being put into practice ... it is not aid so much as the right climate that was needed so that all communities benefit from reconstruction.'

The Canadian Catholic Bishops' Conference wrote a letter to their Prime Minister on 25 January 2008, portraying the special plight of the Christians of Iraq as victims of injustice and irrational retaliation, and asked the government to give special consideration to Christians applying for visas at Canadian Consulates.[49]

In November 2006, the Chaldean Patriarch, Mar Emanuel Delly, attended the Council of Catholic Patriarchs of the East in Beirut entitled 'The Church

---

47   Interview with *Asia News,* 16 January, 2007.
48   'Pope elevates Patriarch to show closeness to Iraq', *The Catholic Herald,* 30 November, 2007.
49   Canadian Conference of Catholic Bishops: www.cccb.ca/site/content/view/2560/1217/lang.eng/.

and the Homeland'. The bishops discussed emigration, its causes and problems, and confirmed their solidarity with Iraqi Christians.

Another conference was convened in Beirut on the 19 February 2009 concerning the Christian presence in Iraq, with the topic 'Christian Existence in Iraq: on the Rise or the Demise'. This conference was attended by religious leaders from both the Christian and Muslim communities, by delegates from various local and foreign Churches, together with members of the public, as well as representatives of many secular, cultural, educational, military, diplomatic and political organizations. It was covered by a considerable number of local, Arab and foreign media television and radio stations. A documentary film was shown, together with live testimonies from Iraqi Christians, who spoke about their anguish, despair and pain, as well as their deep faith, which gave them peace and strength during these difficult times, and the hope they have of someday returning to their beloved homes.

The situation of Christians in the whole of the Middle East was also addressed, and the role of Muslims regarding the protection of Christians. Recommendations were issued to neighbouring countries, asking them to provide adequate social care for Iraqi refugees, to the Iraqi authorities to guarantee the representation of the Christians in the government, to the international community, the UN, and the Arab League, as well as the Conference of Islamic States, to issue statements that will protect the Christian presence in Iraq and the rest of the Middle East.[50]

The refugee problem has been partially addressed by various international organisations, as well as by the local Churches. They have been distributing food parcels, blankets and other necessities. Our newly formed charity, 'Iraqi Christians in need' is helping by providing school fees for some children who have lagged behind, sustenance for widows who have no relatives in Western countries to support them, as well as funding projects to provide young adults with skills that help them get on in life, such as a course for teaching English and computer skills. Unfortunately, although such efforts are of great help, the problem is that they are fragmented and intermittent. More concerted effort is badly needed, and the international community should make sure that these refugees, who have lost their homes and livelihood, are properly compensated.

In as much as further emigration is not in the interest of the Christian community of Iraq, as it will ultimately lead to emptying the country of its Christian population, I think that Western countries should accept some of

---

50   *Najm al-Mashriq*, no. 57, 2009, pp. 104-105.

the refugees, especially those traumatised by the kidnapping or killing of their relatives. Sweden, France and Germany have accepted some.[51] However, the plea of Germany to the European Union to accept Christian refugees was refused.[52] During 2009, large number of refugees stranded in Syria and Jordan have been accepted by the USA and Canada, especially those who have relatives to support them.

As for the specific Christian-Muslim conflicts, it is clear that confrontation only causes further problems. The only possible way forward is that of dialogue. We should seek irenic Muslim voices, and support those countries that have a positive attitude towards Christians. There are numerous Muslim voices that abhor what is happening. Christians are understood to have been at the forefront of intellectual and cultural revival in the Middle East, as well as leaders in nationalist movements in the Arab world, and their departure would be a great loss for the Muslim world.

The increasing influx of Eastern Christians to Western countries raises the issue of the importance of supporting them in preserving their cultural identity in the diaspora. The Churches are obvious places where this can be done, but Western religious institutions should all be involved in supporting them, not only for their own sake, but also in order to address the ignorance amongst Western Christians of the importance of Eastern Christianity in general and the Church of Iraq in particular.

In addition, academic institutions should make an effort to include the study of Eastern Christianity in their curriculum. An academic Institute for Eastern Christianity will not only support Eastern Christians but also give prominence to their rich culture and importance within the Islamic world where they lived for centuries. Their survival against all odds, and their remarkable spiritual development within the dominant Islamic culture, hold the seeds of hope for all who seek understanding between the two religions.

It will also help to promote understanding between Eastern and Western Christianity, and to promote ecumenical relations, which will be a key marker in future European religious and political identity. In this respect I would like to end by quoting Sidney Griffith:

> Now is the time to take steps to remedy the situation, first of all because the intellectual heritage of the Eastern Christians belongs to the whole church and we are the poorer without any knowledge of it, but it is also the case in the multicultural

---

51   *Le Figaro*, 10 December, 2007, *Le Monde*, 23 March 2008.
52   www.azzaman.com/index.asp?fname=2008/04/04-18995.htmandstorytitle.

world of the twentieth century, when Muslim-Christian relations
are becoming daily more important worldwide, the experience
of the Christians of the Orient who have lived with Muslims
for centuries and who have immigrated to the West together
with the Muslims, is immediately relevant for those in the West
who could be in dialogue with Muslims today and who would
welcome some deeper knowledge of the history of our shared
religious and intellectual heritage. The time is long overdue for
the Christians of the West to extend their modern ecumenical
concerns to their co-religionists in the Islamic World.[53]

53 Sidney H Griffith, *The Church in the Shadow of the Mosque, Christians and Muslims in the World of Islam*, Princeton University Press, Princeton, NJ, 2008 (2nd ed. 2010).

A PERSPECTIVE ON THE SYNOD FOR THE MIDDLE EAST WITH REGARDS TO THE CONTRIBUTION CHRISTIANITY MAKES TO THE MIDDLE EAST, SOCIETY, CULTURE AND RELIGION, FROM OUR EXPERIENCE IN LEBANON

Najla Chahda

The immigration of Christians into the Middle East from across the world is an important theme of the *Instrumentum laboris*, and in 5.49-50 we find two significant paragraphs which serve as a necessary preamble to this paper:

> 49. A new and important phenomenon taking place in Middle Eastern countries is the arrival of hundreds of thousands of immigrant workers from Africa and Asia. Generally speaking, these immigrants are women engaged in work as domestic servants so they can give their children an education and a better life. Oftentimes, these people are subject to social injustice by the State which receives them and exploitation and sexual abuse by either the agencies which provide passage for them or their employers. In addition, many responses point out that oftentimes international laws and conventions are not respected in this area.

> 50. According to the responses, this immigration calls for the attention of our Churches which have the pastoral responsibility to assist them in both religious and social matters. Oftentimes, these immigrants find themselves in tragic situations in which the Church does what she can within the limits of her power and resources. At the same time, to overcome any temptation to look down at or scorn these people, the faithful urgently need to be instructed in the Church's social teaching and the concept of social justice

From our perspective, the synodal assembly is primarily pastoral in character, dealing only indirectly or secondarily with socio-political problems. With this in mind, whilst the *Instrumentum laboris* deals *in extenso* with the question of the emigration of Christians from the region (4.43-48), some attention needs to be focussed on the subject of immigration into the region.

An important aspect of the *Instrumentum laboris*, and of our own concerns, is the raising of the awareness of all Christians in the Middle East, beginning with their pastors, to the essential character and challenges of this immigrant presence in our society. I would like to urge that the Christian Churches of the region need to become more aware of this presence and to be able to respond to their needs in a more active way. Each Christian, of no matter what country, is the bearer of the message of Christ to society, which must be announced even amidst trials and persecution.

The challenges presented by immigration should be seen as a transforming opportunity to support their religious needs and acknowledge their presence. In 1994, following a history of humanitarian work aimed at Lebanese citizens by Caritas Lebanon, the Caritas Lebanon Migrant Centre was created, and begun to work among the immigrant population. In 1972, Caritas South Lebanon was founded to help the population of this area. Following the outbreak of civil war in 1975, the organization expanded to become Caritas Lebanon. In 1981, the Assembly of Catholic Patriarchs and Bishops of Lebanon approved Caritas' status and designated it the socio-pastoral arm of the Church. Slowly, Caritas expanded and established branch offices throughout Lebanon to meet increasing social needs. Following this decentralisation, Caritas Lebanon created specialised sectors in order to respond to the specific needs of each area. Caritas Lebanon respects the decentralisation and the local autonomy of its sector offices, while encouraging the co-ordination and exchange of information with its Head Office in Beirut. Caritas Lebanon is one of the largest charitable non-governmental organizations in Lebanon, offering a broad range of social services on a national basis without regard to race, creed, ethnicity or political beliefs.

In the mid-1990s, Caritas Lebanon first began to be approached by several migrant groups requesting assistance: Sudanese refugees and then Iraqi asylum-seekers. The number of new migrants in Lebanon from different nationalities in need of social, legal, and humanitarian assistance grew to include refugees, asylum seekers and migrant workers at risk. In response to the growing needs on the ground, Caritas Lebanon established the Caritas Lebanon Migrant Centre (CLMC) in 1994 to provide specialised assistance to meet their needs.

The Caritas Lebanon Migrant Centre is a specialised centre of Caritas Lebanon. Combining both individualised legal and social support, as well as advocacy efforts with the public and relevant government agencies, CLMC carries out a range activities in support of respect for the human rights of migrants. It also conducts training and offers technical support to other NGOs in the Middle East serving similar groups of people. In 2000, CLMC initiated efforts to expand its range of activities, and to reach out to more vulnerable destitute groups, a process requiring a more comprehensive vision and mission statement for the organization.

The vision of CLMC may now be expressed as: 'All refugees, asylum-seekers and migrants in Lebanon have their rights recognised, protected and respected,' and its mission as: 'To strengthen and protect the human rights of migrants, refugees and asylum-seekers in Lebanon.'

THE LEBANESE CONTEXT: AN OVERVIEW

An important phenomenon took place in Middle Eastern countries especially in Lebanon with the arrival of hundreds of thousands of immigrant workers from Africa and Asia. Generally speaking, these immigrants are women who take on work as domestic servants in order to give their children an education and a better life. These people are frequently subject to social injustice by elements of the state authority which receives them, and to exploitation and sexual abuse, either by the agencies which provide passage for them or by their employers. There are also clear indications that the relevant international laws and conventions are not sufficiently respected.

The last census in Lebanon was carried out in 1933. We have no formal statistics since then, but we do know informally that the number of Christians, formerly 50 percent of the Lebanese population, has decreased to 35 percent, if not less. Approximately 4 million Lebanese citizens live in the country, along with 1 million foreigners: 450,000 Palestinian refugees, 200,000 migrant workers, 50,000 Iraqi refugees, and others nationalities. The 2009 statistics of the Ministry of Labour show that 145,679 work permits were issued: of these, 45,619 were for newcomers and 100,060 were renewals. Domestic workers accounted for 111,945, of whom 40,665 were starting new contracts and 71,280 renewing contracts. Officially, women accounted for 77 percent of the migrant population. The statistics did not include migrant workers whose status was irregular. It is estimated that the number of irregular migrants is equal to 15-20 percent of the official figure. It is important to note here that 77 percent of the migrant workers referred to above are Christians.

In view of these statistics, immigration demands the attention of our Churches, which have a pastoral responsibility to assist them in both religious and social contexts. As the *Instrumentum laboris* notes, these immigrants frequently find themselves in tragic situations, in which the Church does what she can within the limits of its power and resources. At the same time, in order overcome any temptation to look down on or treat these people with scorn, there is an urgent need for the faithful to be instructed in the Church's social teaching and the concept of social justice.

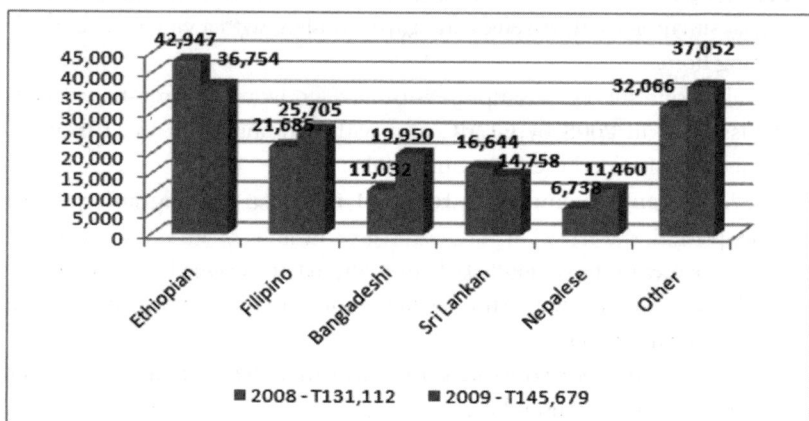

Statistics of work permits given to all nationalities. (Source: Lebanese Ministry of Labor)

THE SITUATION OF DOMESTIC MIGRANT WORKERS

In Lebanon, the demand for migrant women for those low-skilled or unskilled jobs shunned by local workers has gradually increased since the 1980s. Foreign employees on temporary contracts are the preferred category, because there are no expectations of permanent settlement or citizenship rights. Migrant workers are willing to work in Lebanon and other Middle Eastern countries which seem to have circumvented the global economic crisis.

However, the situation in Lebanon does not always offer them the best conditions, as many will fall victim to violence, violation of their human rights, and exploitation. In addition to the fact that the Lebanese government has not ratified the international convention on protection for human rights of migrant workers and their families, a combination of inadequate laws, bureaucratic procedures, cultural norms and official indifference exposes many migrant workers, especially women, to abuse and exploitation.

Many of the migrants are illiterate, some do not have a language in common with their employer, and some have never travelled outside their own country. The only point of contact they have when they arrive in Lebanon is their employment agency. Women migrant workers in this situation are extremely vulnerable to violations of their rights, and the most extreme forms of violence against women migrant workers are cases of beatings and sexual abuse. Working for low wages in oppressive conditions, migrant workers endure their situation in order to send remittances home and to improve the financial situation of themselves and their families, with a view to eventually returning home.

A telephone survey of employers of foreign women domestic workers, commissioned in 2008 by CLMC and with funding from the European Commission, provided the following results:

—92 percent of employers reported retaining the migrant worker's passport;

—83 percent reported generally limiting her freedom of movement;

—73 percent reported restricting her communications with other people, including her family;

—26 percent reported locking the maid into the apartment when the family goes out without her;

—25 percent reported hitting/punishing the maid;

—22 percent reported retaining all or part of her salary to guarantee her completing her contract or preventing her from absconding.

Common Problems Faced by Migrant Workers

Lack of privacy: a large number of domestic workers have no privacy. They do not have their own room, and have to sleep in the kitchen or living room. This means that they cannot rest until everyone in the house goes to bed, and that they can never have a moment on their own.

Deprivation: migrant workers do not have the freedom to cook their own meals. There have been cases where a lock was put on the refrigerator.

Absence of freedom of movement or communication: some domestic workers do not have the right to communicate with their own families by letter or phone. Some have seen their letters (received or to be sent) discarded as rubbish. They are not even allowed to meet friends working in the same country, because employers worry about 'the ideas they can get', such as demanding higher salaries or better living conditions. They effectively live like prisoners.

Harsh working conditions: Domestic workers do not have holidays. They work seven days a week and often up to 14 hours a day, and at the end of the month most of them do not receive their salaries. Migrant workers cannot defend their rights, because there are no laws supporting them, and the employment agencies simply abandon them to their fate.

Lack of medical care: employers are bound by the contract they sign to provide domestic workers with medical insurance and proper healthcare. Instead, in case of illness, employers simply 'return' the maid to the employment agency, and sometimes demand that she pays them back the recruitment fee. Although the Lebanese government requires proof of medical insurance to register a person as a domestic worker, these proofs are mostly forgeries, and merely provide an appearance of legality. In some cases, when the employers are honest and pay the costs of a ticket and the expenses for a sick worker to return home, the agency responsible for her 'repatriation' will simply take the money, and, instead of sending her home, place her with another family, obliging her to continue working.

Physical and psychological violence: violence is always part of the picture. It can take several forms. Domestic workers are daily subjected to insulting terms such as 'idiot' or 'donkey', as well as threats of beatings or even death. Physical violence forms part of everyday life for some migrant workers. They are beaten harshly for any reason, serious or not, and are generally struck around the head.

LEGAL ISSUES

Problems with documentation: when they arrive in the country, domestic workers have to give their passports to their employers, who then hold their papers. This is done in order to prevent the workers from absconding and looking for another job. Although holding the identity papers of another person is considered a crime in most countries, it is General Security officers themselves who give the passports of migrant workers to their employers.

Absence of legal protection: In a context where there are no laws whatsoever covering women migrant workers, they are bound to be abused as they have no recourse to the authorities. Although violence and sexual abuse are considered crimes, domestic workers are required to provide medical proof. It is practically impossible to obtain such medical reports, because this would require the employer's consent for the employee to leave the house with her identity papers and contact a doctor. Conversely, no one is able to contact the workers or convince them to testify about their situation.

Discrimination is also part of the picture. When women migrant workers arrive in their destination country with a work visa and permit, they are not allowed to enter freely, but have to wait for their employer to come and take them from the airport. Sometimes the employers are late, and workers are forced to wait for hours at the airport, without food or facilities, deprived of their identity papers.

When a migrant worker is arrested for any reason, the security forces adopt a dismissive and superior attitude. They speak mostly in Arabic, while many migrant workers hardly speak the language. Consequently, enquiries can be protracted, especially if the migrant's employer is unwilling to help.

HEALTH AND PSYCHOLOGICAL PROBLEMS

Some women migrant workers have physical injuries, such as wounds, broken legs or arms, head injuries, and the like. Many also suffer from skin rashes as they are not given gloves to wear when they use detergents and because they are not allowed to use warm water, from arthritis due to the change in climate, and from chest infections and various pulmonary problems.

Often, alone in a society whose culture is very different from their own, women migrant workers are ill-prepared for the unexpected and harsh reality that they experience in their host countries. They are shocked by the situation in which they find themselves, leading to high levels of anxiety, exacerbated by living under constant threat and worrying about themselves and their families.

REASONS FOR THEIR VULNERABILITY

A number of characteristics make women domestic workers particularly vulnerable to serious abuse. By the very nature of their jobs, being forced to live with their employers, they are vulnerable to all sorts of abuse and exploitation. The lack of official control, and the ignorance in which women migrant workers are kept, work together to 'legalise' their abuse. Their exploitation appears legally sanctioned.

They are not protected or recognised under legal or regulatory frameworks, as Lebanon did not sign up to or ratify the 1990 UN Convention related to the Protection of the Rights of All Migrant Workers and their Families, nor has it implemented in its legal system the main labour Conventions relating to migration and migrant workers. Hence they are not covered under local labour laws. They receive little or no legal or social protection. They are also unable to enforce contracts or have rights to security of property. They are excluded from or have limited access to the public infrastructure and to benefits, and are highly dependent on the attitude of the authorities. They stand in clear need of daily and urgent intervention and assistance from both civic and religious organizations.

WHAT ARE THE CHURCHES DOING TO HELP MIGRANTS IN LEBANON?

The migrants in Lebanon present pastoral challenges for all the Churches in the country. Exchanges, and the co-ordination and enlargement of these activities started after the ending of the war in Lebanon, and with the preparations for the Special Assembly for the Synod of Bishops for Lebanon in 1996. Since then, the friendship group formed by the Latin priests engaged with the Afro-Asiatic immigrants, has been integrated into the Episcopal Committee for Cooperation between the missionary Churches, with the status of a subcommittee of the Pastoral Committee for Afro-Asiatic Migrants (the PIA or PCAAM).

THE PASTORAL MINISTRY

PCAAM has a significant and important role to undertake with the migrants, especially on the level of religion and morality. Being away from their countries, their families, and their loved ones they risk losing contact with them and forgetting their religion and often becoming the target of proselytising sects. For this reason, the members of the Commision do their best to provide migrants with measures which allow them to remain loyal to their own Church and to make their stay in Lebanon a time of spiritual growth and to remain faithful to their family. These include:

Masses celebrated in a variety of languages:

- For those migrants who speak English: Mass in English is celebrated in six churches: Achrafieh, Antelias, Badaro, Hamra, Jounieh and Nabaa, occasionally at Taanayel.
- For the Filipinos: a Filipino priest celebrates Mass in Tagalog at Mansourieh and Ashrafieh every Wednesday afternoon, on Saturday evening and Sunday morning.
- For French-speaking migrants: these have the opportunity of participating in all the masses celebrated in French in all the Latin Churches of Lebanon.
- Those Sudanese who speak only Arabic can attend the Maronite or Melkite liturgies which are celebrated all over Lebanon. A Sudanese priest has been given responsibility for the Sudanese Christians in Lebanon; he celebrates Mass and holds prayers meetings in a street in the Nabaa region.

Additionally:

- Many members of PCAAM, priests and religious assisted by lay people, facilitate a weekly or monthly group for prayer and reflection.
- The Filipino community organises visits to the sick once a month at the government hospital in Roumieh.
- PCAAM organises days of pilgrimage, picnic and recollection on up to six Sundays of the year.
- Use of the media: the Voice of Charity has a programme for migrants each Sunday evening and a quarterly newsletter.

This is not an exhaustive listing of the pastoral activities provided but it does make clear that that it is a small group formed basically of non-Lebanese nationals which is organising activities. The pastoral care of Christian migants is not well-integrated into local perspectives and concerns. PCAAM must raise awareness among these local Churches about the religious, moral and other problems faced by migrants, especially those who came at the request of Lebanese employers.

The Social Services provided by the Churches

1. The Laksetha Centre, created by Father Selim Rizkallah, Sr Angela, and Father Albert Pleber, is a reception centre for Sri Lankans

and Ethiopians who have been mistreated and abused or are sick. Since 2004, Laksetha has operated under the supervision of the Caritas Lebanon Migrant Centre.

2. With the assistance of the Lazarists and Daughters of Charity, an Afro-Asian Centre was opened in 1997 at Ashrafieh in order to help Filipinos and Africans. In 2003, this Centre was moved to the premises of the Jesuits. Here the members of PCAAM meet monthly and organise religious and cultural meetings or simply to celebrate anniversaries and national holidays.

3. A prison chaplaincy has been created for prison visits. All the members of reception centres and PCAAM work collaboratively in order to make those visits to men and women in virtually all Lebanese prisons. These visits often involve a religious element, and the distribution of food, clothing and toiletries.

4. PCAAM works with the extensive and qualified staff of Caritas Lebanon Migrants Centre: social workers, lawyers and all those needed to accomplish this mission including raising awareness among Lebanese citizens about the problems and the rights of migrant workers and refugees.

In the last 25 years, the problem of migrant workers and refugees has been taken account of by Church bodies, but the response remains insufficient. The problems of immigrants, especially Christians from Africa and Asia, are not mentioned in the Post-Synodal Apostolic Exhortation of May 1997: 'New Hope for Lebanon'. Nor are these problems the object of the pastoral letter of the Eastern Catholic Patriarchs, and remain unmentioned in their letters for Lent, Easter, and Christmas. Consequently, the difficulties and mistreatments of migrant workers who come to work in Lebanon are never mentioned.

Services provided by CLMC to Migrant Workers

CLMC maintains a wide range of comprehensive and inter-related services aimed at securing equal rights and opportunities for women migrant workers in Lebanon. All services are based on a foundation of direct assistance through social work methodology, a methodology which is tailored to the individual, but also allows CLMC to be aware of trends in other countries.

CLMC provides direct legal, social, medical, and psycho-social assistance to migrant workers in need. This personalised service, whether for detainees or non-detainees, whether for those in need of preventative measures or those in crisis situations, allows CLMC to build a strong base of support whilst also keeping abreast of developing trends.

The detention centre, The Administrative Detention Centre for Foreign Persons (RCFP), run by the General Security service (GS), the governmental agency responsible for all matters related to foreigners, is the terminus for all detained migrants. All formerly convicted migrants who have served their sentences, and those detained for irregular status, are channeled to this facility, where the required administrative procedures are carried out before repatriation to their respective homelands, or release in Lebanon.

Since 2000, the Detention Centre has been located two floors below ground level, under a car park, with no access to daylight or fresh air. It consists of 12 overcrowded, gender-segregated cells, each holding up to 45-50 individuals. At any given time, there are usually round 500 women and men from 30 different nationalities. The average duration of detention in the facility varies between 6 and 12 months. Caritas Lebanon Migrant Centre is the sole NGO allowed by the Lebanese authorities to operate inside the Detention Centre, where its multi-disciplinary team maintains a protective presence twenty-four hours a day, seven days a week, throughout the year.

Through awareness campaigns the CLMC works to educate Lebanese citizens on human rights, and to dispel the myths and cultural practices which allow the abuse of women migrant workers to occur. It also works to provide migrants with the relevant information and skills to uphold their own rights and protect themselves from abuse.

As the pre-eminent service provider to women migrant workers, and through its direct assistance, other UN personnel, international agencies, and the Lebanese authorities are all well-aware of the work of CLMC and consider them to speak authoritatively on the issue of women migrant workers. The CLMC uses this position to advocate policies and public interventions aimed at improving the situation of such women in Lebanon.

The CLMC is an active participant in several networks which work to promote improvement in the human rights of women migrant workers throughout the Middle East and beyond. In some cases, these connections lead to concrete action and to projects such as those to create referral mechanisms between countries. In other cases, these networks provide the opportunity to develop institutional relationships, the ability to share best practice, and to learn more about trends in the various countries of origin.

Due to its significant capacity to support vulnerable populations, the CLMC has developed a role in regional leadership, and has recently begun acting in a training and capacity-building role for other NGOs in the Middle East who serve migrant workers and refugees. The CLMC has, for instance, recently provided training sessions and job mentoring for NGOs in Jordan and Syria.

The CLMC is regularly called upon to speak and make presentations at major conferences, as well as to take part in multi-country initiatives. It recently collaborated with Human Rights Watch on a press conference to launch a national campaign aimed at Lebanese women employers, with the aim of upholding the rights of domestic migrant workers, and using the catchphrase 'if you were in her shoes.'

PALESTINIAN REFUGEES IN LEBANON

According to the United Nations Relief and Works Agency for Palestinian Refugees (UNRWA), Lebanon currently hosts 450,000 Palestinian refugees who lost their homeland and means of livelihood as a result of the Arab-Israeli conflict of 1946-48. Of this number, 56 percent live in 12 refugee camps with poor social, physical and economic conditions. Sixty-two years after their eviction, Palestinian refugees in Lebanon are still granted status with only limited civil and social rights. The most critical issues for Palestinian refugees in Lebanon today are inadequate medical services and unemployment. We will talk in this paper about one of the most critical and vulnerable camps, Dbayeh.

THE STATUS OF DBAYEH CAMP

Dbayeh camp, one of twelve UNRWA registered camps in Lebanon, is situated 12 km east of Beirut, on a hill overlooking the Beirut-Tripoli highway. It was established in 1949 for refugees who originated from al-Bass village in Galilee in northern Palestine. Dbayeh camp is situated on land owned by a Lebanese monastery which struck a deal with UNRWA, allowing Palestinian refugees to live in the camp on condition that no new compounds or extensions to the existing houses should be built. Duly provided with their refugee cards, they settled into small houses with corrugated iron roofs, in the hope of soon returning to their homeland. Some fifty-six years later, they and their descendants are still there in the only remaining Palestinian refugee camp in the eastern suburbs of Beirut.

Dbayeh camp, where all the residents are Christians, is a neglected area; even UNRWA itself seems to have forgotten its existence. Housing conditions are bad. Linked by narrow alleys, the corrugated iron roofed houses are humid and unsanitary. Overcrowding is apparent, and at times numerous large families share a two-room residence. There is no drinking water system installed and the sewage system is damaged.

Currently, 4,211 registered Palestinian refugees live in the camp, of whom 67 families totalling 162 persons are officially registered as cases of special hardship. The residents of Dbayeh camp are confronted by more issues than the general Palestinian population in Lebanon, and their main concern is daily survival. Many of them being unemployed, they live in severe economic hardship, although a few men are able to find work as casual labourers, and some young women work in shops in the area or as cleaners.

Children are the main victims of this situation, as they are frequently forced to leave school in order to work and support the needs of their families. As a consequence, the illiteracy rate is increasing among youngsters. Access to free or low-cost education (other than in UNRWA schools) is limited. The CLMC social workers present in the camp have repeatedly been approached by the parents of children attending non-UNRWA schools. These, unlike those of UNRWA, follow the French system instead of the English one. Having had an English education, the parents have little or no knowledge of French, and face difficulties in supporting their children in their studies. Moreover, they lack the resources to pay for the services of a special French-language teacher. Currently, students are increasingly expected to conduct research projects on their own. This is a daunting requirement for low-income students and those with little or no support outside the classroom.

Services provided by CLMC in Dbayeh Camp

CLMC provides education at a number of levels for Palestinian children living in Dbayeh camp: teaching a group of illiterate children so that they become able to read and write in Arabic, English and French, providing French courses to groups of school pupils attending schools using the French system, and providing internet access and research training for young people. CLMC wishes to extend its services in the camp to further involve children.

Already, for over five years, it has been implementing projects for Palestinian refugees in Dbayeh camp, and a social club has been opened to receive elderly Palestinians who have been abandoned and marginalised.

A Community Health Education programme has been implemented, with workshops for the elderly, parents, young people and children. Topics covered have included: dental care, prevention and treatment of infant and child diarrhoea, upper respiratory problems, infection prevention and treatment, preventing misuse of medicines, domestic accidents, and back strain.

Since 2002, special care has been provided on three levels for the elderly: direct services through home-care visits from nurses and physiotherapists or in the CLMC centre at the camp, the introduction of a medical card system specifically to avoid the misuse of medicines among the elderly, and an awareness campaign to stimulate the community. Social opportunities for the elderly are provided, especially around ongoing engagement in the community. In support of this, there is also the provision of education for families and the community on the issue of age and ageing, intended to help families cope better with the challenges that might be posed by an elderly member, and to help the community at large to appreciate and welcome the contribution made by elderly people.

IRAQI REFUGEES
STATUS ANALYSIS

Lebanon is home to approximately 50,000 Iraqi refugees. Most now enter legally and overstay their tourist visas, and initially live with friends or relatives until they can rent a house. Although this number is low in comparison with neighbouring countries, they have the potential to overwhelm social services in a country currently experiencing an economic downturn and a severe political crisis which often results in periods of instability. It should be noted that more Iraqi Christians are now arriving, since they are increasingly becoming the targets of violence.

These families come mainly from Baghdad, northern Iraq, Mosul, and small villages such as Teleskouf, Batnaya, Talkef, Bakoch.

All of them are currently in the country legally. Despite this, they arrive with little by way of financial reserves and are extremely vulnerable. In order

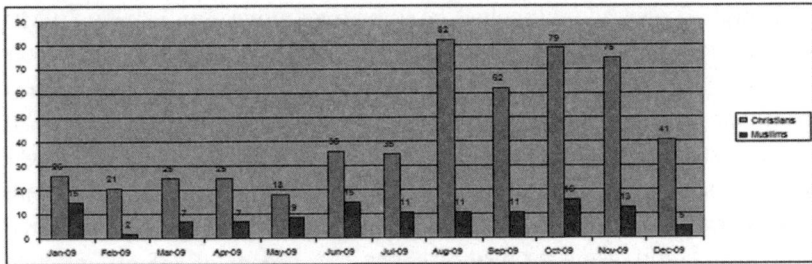

Total = 525 Christian families Total = 122 Muslim families

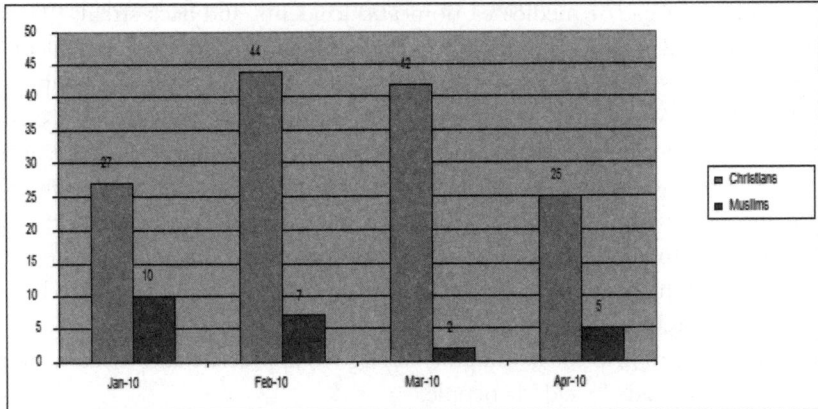

Total = 138 Christian families Total = 24 Muslim families

to get to Lebanon they have paid around 500 US dollars per person for an airline ticket, and a visa, provided by agencies in Iraq. On arrival in Lebanon, they must prove at the airport that they have 2,000 US dollars in cash and a hotel reservation.

The arrival of women who have been widowed or are the head of the family, accompanied by their children, following the assassination or kidnap of their husband, has become a noticeable feature.

Nearly every member of Iraqi families arriving in Lebanon requires psychosocial support due to violence experienced in Iraq. The trauma that began for them in Iraq is further compounded by the difficult conditions for their survival in Lebanon, where they live in cramped, unhealthy conditions, with the daily worry of finding low-paying jobs to provide food, shelter, education and healthcare costs. The increased price of housing is also obliging some families share accommodation. Despite their difficulties, however, it is interesting to note that the majority voted during the last election.

The challenges and difficulties faced by Iraqi refugees in Lebanon might be characterised as follows: the question of illegal entry, which in fact affects very few; visa expiry and non-renewal; abuse and exploitation in the workplace; inadequate payment; unsafe working conditions; an ongoing risk of detention and deportation; health problems; discrimination, domestic violence towards women and children; an increase in drug use; difficulties in school enrolment or absence from school in order to care for younger siblings; and exclusion from national provision for medical expenses.

As the only service provider of its kind with a presence throughout Lebanon, CLMC has attempted to respond to these needs. Newly arriving families, single women with children, women released from prison, and the victims of sexual and gender-based violence towards women and children have access to a CLMC shelter. Further assistance is provided through activities in the fields of health care, humanitarian aid, education, pyschological follow-up, legal assistance, cultural organisation, and a wide range of community services.

THE CATHOLIC CHURCH'S THOUGHT ON JUDAISM, ZIONISM AND THE STATE OF ISRAEL: MID-NINETEENTH CENTURY-1965

Dominique Trimbur

The topic of the present paper serves as a continuation of my former texts. In the past I have focused on the Catholic attitude to early Zionism, in the time of Theodor Herzl,[1] on the attitude of French Catholics up to the beginning of the British mandate in Palestine,[2] or on the attitude of a specific French congregation, the Assumptionists, those based in Jerusalem at Notre-Dame de France, dealing with Judaism/the Jews and Zionism from the very beginning of Zionism up until Vatican Council II.[3] All the papers reflect my approach, a political rather than theological stance, although I have previously had the opportunity to work on theological topics such as Jewish and Christian theologies after Auschwitz.[4] This said, the present paper will mention only *en passant* the Catholic attitude (what is 'the' Catholic attitude?) to Judaism, otherwise leaving it to those with greater expertise. It will be

---

1   'L'Église catholique et le sionisme au temps de Theodor Herzl, 1897-1904', *Mélanges de Science Religieuse*, Université catholique de Lille, tome 61, n° 4, October-December 2004, pp. 19-34.

2   'Des catholiques français et les débuts du sionisme', in (eds) Sobhi Boustani, Françoise Saquer-Sabin, *Nationalisme juif et environnement arabe*, Université de Lille 3 (Collection UL3—travaux et recherches), 2005, pp. 109-133.

3   'Les Assomptionistes de Jérusalem, les Juifs et le sionisme', *Tsafon-Revue d'études juives du Nord*, n° 38, winter 1999-spring 2000, pp. 71-111. See also my article: 'Entre rejet et respect—Les communautés catholiques françaises de Palestine, les Juifs et le sionisme, 1880-1939', in (eds) Ilana Y Zinguer/Sam W Bloom, *L'antisémitisme éclairé—Inclusion et exclusion depuis l'Époque des Lumières jusqu'à l'affaire Dreyfus/Inclusion and Exclusion: Perspectives of Jews from the Enlightenment to the Dreyfus Affair* (Jewish Studies 34) Brill, Leiden, 2003, pp. 369-396.

4   'La Shoah dans la mémoire religieuse juive', in (eds) Bruno Béthouart, François Ars, *Christianisme et lieux de mémoire* (XVème université d'été du carrefour d'histoire religieuse contemporaine), Les Cahiers du Littoral—2—n° 6, 2008, pp. 195-205; 'Faire de la théologie après Auschwitz (?)', in (eds) Dominique Avon, Michel Fourcade, *Un nouvel âge de la théologie? Théologiens et théologies dans le monde francophone, 1965-1980*, Karthala, Paris, 2009, pp. 317-334.

considered here in parallel to the attitude towards Zionism/the State of Israel from 1948, since the two are intertwined.

This presentation seeks to elaborate on the main points of a topic which has already received considerable scholarly attention, even if due only to its sensitivity, complexity and actuality. To examine the Catholic Church's perception of Zionism/the State of Israel requires us to focus on relations between two very specific entities: on the one hand a young political movement that, arising from almost nothing, becomes a state, and on the other hand, a Church with a universal vocation; both entities having a specific interest in the Holy Land/Palestine (*Eretz Israel* for the Zionists). I will present here only the main points and stages of development, since, as I have noted, we already have at our disposal many profound, and still relevant studies on the topic by historians dealing with one or other perspective. For the sake of brevity, I will mention here only Henry Laurens,[5] Sergio Minerbi,[6] Uri Bialer,[7] Ulrike Koltermann,[8] Father Jean Dujardin,[9] and a paper by Anthony O'Mahony.[10] In chronological sequence I will first present the perception of the Holy Land by the Holy See and Catholicism at the time of the appearance of Zionist ideas, then return to the attitude to Zionism, and end with the Catholic attitude to the State of Israel up until 1965.

THE HOLY SEE/CATHOLICISM AND THE HOLY LAND

The perception of the Holy Land in Catholic mentality and by the Holy See represents part of the 'rediscovery of Palestine',[11] the 'invention of the Holy

---

5   Henry Laurens, 'Le Vatican et la question de la Palestine', in (eds) Hélène Carrère d'Encausse, Philippe Levillain, *Nations et Saint-Siège au XXe siècle*, Fayard, Paris, 2003, pp. 303-342.

6   Sergio I Minerbi, *The Vatican and Zionism—Conflict in the Holy Land 1895-1925*, Oxford University Press, New York/Oxford, 1990.

7   Uri Bialer, *Cross on the Star of David*, Bloomington-Indianapolis, Indiana University Press, 2005.

8   Ulrike Koltermann, *Päpste und Palästina: Die Nahostpolitik des Vatikans von 1947 bis 1997*, Aschendorff, Münster, 2001.

9   Jean Dujardin, *L'Église catholique et le peuple juif—Un autre regard*, Calmann-Lévy, Paris, 2003.

10   Anthony O'Mahony, 'The Vatican, Jerusalem and the Palestinian Christians: Faith, diplomacy and politics in the Holy Land', in (eds) Anthony O'Mahony, Michael Kirwan, *World Christianity—Politics, Theology, Dialogue*, Melisende, London, 2004, pp. 416-448.

11   Yeoshuah Ben Arieh, *The Rediscovery of the Holy Land in the Nineteenth Century*, Magnes

Land'[12] that took place in the mid-nineteenth century, with mixed political/ colonial and religious dimensions. From the very beginning, the Holy See participated in the global European movement of the time, towards an appropriation, or a new appropriation, of a place where European culture was deeply rooted. For the Holy See and Catholic understanding of the time, this meant a logical continuation of history, of the Catholic history of the area. So it is that, for instance, the Crusades were still a concrete memory, with a real political and religious dimension in the mind of the Holy See.[13] This remained valid even if, for a long period of time, the Franciscan Custody had been the only official Catholic body there. Concretely, however, the Holy See was limited in its action towards the Ottoman Empire and Palestine, due to the prevalence of the French protectorate, stemming from the sixteenth century. The pre-eminence of French consuls throughout the area with respect to the representation and the defence of Latin Catholics imposed indirect relations with the Ottoman authorities up until the end of Turkish domination of the whole region.[14] The Holy See renewed its practical interest in Palestine during the 1830s-1840s, reacting to international and religious competition. With the creation of an Anglo-Prussian bishopric in Jerusalem in 1841, and with intense Greek but above all Russian Orthodox initiatives in the area, the Holy See decided to re-establish the Latin patriarchate in 1847.[15] The high-point of this renewed interest in the affairs of Holy Land was the 1852 Status Quo regarding the Christians. The settlement of rival Christian interests in the Holy Places included the Latin Catholic side, to the benefit of the Vatican, which (apart from the Franciscan Custody) had been absent from the area for almost eight centuries.[16] The Status Quo also meant the affirmation of Catholic interest and positions. This led to the establishment of many Catholic institutions in Palestine in the second half of the nineteenth century, illustrating the renewed interest of the Holy See in the area, even if, once again, this was done in connection with the European

---

Press-St Martin's Press, Jerusalem-Detroit, 1979.

12   Henry Laurens, *La question de Palestine, Tome Premier 1799-1922, L'invention de la Terre Sainte*, Fayard, Paris, 1999.

13   Regarding the use of the motive of the Crusades in the Catholic discourse of the time, see my article: 'Les Croisades dans la perception catholique française du Levant, 1880-1940: entre mémoire et actualité', *Cristianesimo nella storia*, 27 (2006), pp. 909-934.

14   For details: Bernardin Collin, OFM, *Le problème juridique des lieux-saints*, Centre d'études orientales, Cairo-Sirey, Paris, 1956.

15   Paolo Pieraccini, *Il restibilimento del Patriarcato Latino di Gerusalemme e la Custodia di Terra Santa*, Franciscan Center of Christian Oriental Studies, Cairo-Jerusalem, 2006.

16   Bernardin Collin, *op. cit.*, pp. 157-159 of the documentation section.

powers of the time, especially France.[17] In parallel, the Holy See developed a growing interest in the Eastern Churches, particularly those united to Rome, in contemplation of a growing role in an area where Eastern Christianity still prevailed.[18] The Western Catholic institutions symbolised and incarnated power; for the Holy See they also meant frustration, with the Vatican being largely dependent on French goodwill, even, we may note, during the time of France's most aggressive anticlericalism,[19] even though, at the beginning of the twentieth century, Germany and Italy, the rival powers to France in the field of Catholicism, conquered some Catholic positions, modifying the traditional French protectorate to the benefit of the Vatican.[20]

This was the situation when Zionism first appeared in the political and geographical spectrum of the Holy Land.

THE HOLY SEE/CATHOLICISM AND ZIONISM

The Holy See and the Catholic world quickly became aware of the existence of the new movement founded and launched by Theodor Herzl, and of its potential implications for the fate of the Holy Land. The Holy Father and the Vatican were, like other, mainly political, leaders of the time, soon contacted by the founding father of the Zionist movement, eager to explain its aims and ambitions, and to create a new and favourable climate of opinion throughout Europe and the Ottoman Empire. Herzl was indeed keen to gain support, or at least approval from the Holy See. In early 1904, a meeting took place between Pius X and Herzl (and between Herzl and Secretary of State Rampolla) at the Vatican. The only response received at the time by Herzl is famous through the Latin expression which summarises it: *non possumus*. As

---

17   Claude Langlois, 'Les congrégations féminines françaises à l'oeuvre en Orient', and Christian Sorrel, 'Les congrégations religieuses masculines françaises en Orient', in (eds) Hervé Legrand, Giuseppe M Croce, *L'Œuvre d'Orient. Solidarités anciennes et nouveaux défis*, Ed. du Cerf, Paris, 2010, pp. 89-111, and pp. 223-253.

18   Etienne Fouilloux, *Les Catholiques et l'unité chrétienne: du XIXè au XXè siècle, itinéraires européens d'expression française*, Le Centurion, Paris, 1982; Claude Soetens, *Le Congrès eucharistique international de Jérusalem (1893) dans le cadre de la politique orientale du pape Léon XIII*, Nauwelaerts, Louvain, 1977.

19   Jean-Dominique Durand, Patrick Cabanel (eds), *Le grand exil des congrégations françaises 1901-1914*, Ed. du Cerf, Paris, 2005.

20   For the case of Italy: Daniel J Grange, *L'Italie et la Méditerranée (1896-1911): les fondements d'une politique étrangère*, Rome, Ecole française de Rome, 1994; for that of Germany: Haim Goren, *'Echt katholisch und gut deutsch': die deutschen Katholiken und Palästina 1838-1910*, Wallstein, Göttingen, 2009.

a matter of fact, The Holy See saw no way to support, or even to encourage Zionism, as long as Jews did not recognize the divine character of Jesus Christ. This theological argument, going back to the very origins of Christianity, and its negative appraisal of the Jews, also precisely reflected Vatican fears regarding the Holy Places, and Catholic possessions in the Holy Land, even if, as Herzl told the Holy Father, he would like to guarantee their protected status. Nevertheless, the Vatican completely rejected any Jewish sovereignty of the Holy Land.

How is this rejection to be explained? Is it an expression of anti-Judaism? We may reply in the positive, since in the mind of Pius X, like most the Catholics of the time, the Jews had been and remained those who had killed Jesus. Is it also the rejection of a political agenda? The answer here too is positive, since, according to the Holy See, the Jews no longer had any right to the Holy Land, since they had broken their alliance with God. Christians, or more precisely Catholics, were the new, the true Israel *(verus Israel)*, they were the heirs of ancient Israel. The negative attitude of the Vatican also expressed a misunderstanding, since, according to Father Jean Dujardin, the Catholic Church of the time had difficulty in understanding and accepting a very concrete dimension of Zionism, emanating from a decidedly religious aspiration: its relation to the soil of Palestine.[21] All in all, with few exceptions, the Catholic position reflected a poor knowledge of the true nature of Judaism and Zionism.

The position established in 1904 would be long-lasting, informing Catholic attitudes for the following decades. There was new contact between the Holy See and the Zionist movement, with an audience between Benedict XV and Nahum Sokolov in 1917, a meeting which took place in the context of the Pope's peace initiatives during the First World War. However, Sokolov was not a character of great significance for the fate of Zionism, and the true attitude of the Holy See is shown by the demands and thinking of the Holy See regarding the Holy Land. The internationalisation of Jerusalem was already being contemplated at the time, in order to exclude the Holy City from every kind of monopolistic—that is to say non-Christian or non-Catholic—domination of it. This rejection and fear were strengthened by the evolution of Palestine in 1917-1918, with a Protestant power, Great-Britain, now in charge of the country, having promised the Jews a national political framework, the 'Jewish national home' mentioned in the Balfour Declaration of 2 November 1917. The position of the Holy See was officially announced

---

21   Dujardin, *op. cit.*, p. 214.

in a declaration by Benedict XV to the Sacred College on 10 March 1919, in which he refused to have Jerusalem and the Holy Places in the hands of non-believers—the Protestant United Kingdom—and non-Christians—London's Jewish allies. Following the establishment of peace, the Vatican was willing to have its position represented at the international conferences then taking place to decide the fate of those areas no longer dependent on the great empires. Excluded from direct participation in the meetings,[22] the Holy See was represented through petitions sent to the various delegations, petitions emanating from the Franciscan Custody or from so called 'Muslim-Christian committees', all of them rejecting Palestine's fate as then agreed.

After the First World War, the Holy See was prepared to see the ending of the French protectorate. According to the Vatican, the earlier arrangement was no longer valid, due to the collapse of Ottoman, i.e. Muslim, domination of the area. Western Catholics no longer had to be protected, since the context was no longer hostile, or at least not as difficult as before. To put an end to the French protectorate was seen as the best way of gaining autonomy for shaping Catholic positions in the new context.[23] On its side, French officialdom did its best to avoid what it saw as the Anglo-Jewish solution regarding the Holy Land, promoting instead the idea of making Palestine part of Greater Syria, under French auspices of course. French Catholics thought and acted in the same way, as shown by the texts, speeches and actions of famous representatives of French Catholicism of the time, including Monsignor Baudrillart, head of the Catholic Institute in Paris,[24] or Father Lagrange, head of the French Biblical School in Jerusalem, among others.[25] We have here a combined political and religious rejection of Zionism, linked to the desire to preserve former rights. Furthermore, in 1919-1920, this combination was expressed through visits to Palestine by high-ranking Catholic prelates, insisting on Catholic interests and aspirations there. These included the British Cardinal Bourne, the Italian Cardinal

---

22 During the First World War Italy had managed to avoid any direct involvement of the Holy See in future political arrangements: Sergio I Minerbi, *L'Italie et la Palestine, 1914-1920*, Presses Universitaires de France, Paris, 1970.

23 France had to accept the move, and from 1926 restricted her specific prerogative to the reception of 'liturgical honours' by French representatives entering Catholic churches in the Orient, retaining only the appearance of the former prevalent position of the French consuls, still valid today.

24 See my paper: 'L'Orient de Monseigneur Baudrillart', in (ed.)Paul Christophe, *Cardinal Alfred Baudrillart*, Éd. du Cerf, Paris, 2006, pp. 235-272.

25 Marie-Joseph Lagrange, 'Le nationalisme juif et la Palestine—Autrefois et aujourd'hui', *Le Correspondant* , CCLXXI (Nouvelle Série CCXXXV), 10 April 1918, pp. 1-30.

Giustini, and above all the French Cardinal Dubois, illustrating Catholic pretensions regarding the fate of the area.[26]

After a short while, Catholic (and French-Catholic) ambitions were proved vain: France was forced to make concessions during the conference of San Remo (1920), establishing the fate of the former Ottoman Empire, and recognised the end of the protectorate; while the Arab—Muslim as well as Christian—populations in Palestine progressively came to support a specifically *Palestinian* nationalism, disregarding their belonging to a greater Arab entity. From its side, the Holy See promoted a more active policy, opposing the threats to Palestinian Arabs caused by privileges granted to the Jews by the British mandate authorities. The acceleration of history, as shown by the future aspect of the Holy Land, was interpreted in Rome as the entry of Palestine into modernity, into history. This was refused by the Catholics, on the basis of a logical continuation of former considerations. On the contrary, the Vatican and those Catholics who expressed a position, promoted the restoration of a kind of Latin Kingdom, a return to a kind of 'golden age' as reconstructed in Catholic memories of the time. For some of them, to oppose the evolution meant to refuse any move that would 'let Christ lie'.[27] In this context, we note the reception at the Vatican of an Arab delegation on 28 July 1921, with a precise declaration against the idea of a Jewish national home. By contrast, Haim Weizmann, while in Rome in 1922, was unable to meet the new Pope, Pius XI. During a discussion with Secretary of State Gasparri, he was again told the official position: Jews may come back and settle in Palestine, and then enjoy the same rights as others, but this may not go beyond, and especially not against, the interests of other groups in the population. This position was summed up in the pontifical declaration *Vehementer Gratum*, dated 11 December 1922, with an anti-Zionist stance that would last during the whole mandate period. In Palestine itself, the central point of view was strongly shared and supported by the Catholic clergy and religious of the period. Not only do we have a refusal of any growing Jewish presence in and ambitions for the Holy Land, these people went so far as to regard Jews and Zionists as the main source of troubles within the British mandate. This was the case in 1920, and became worse later: according to

---

26 My paper 'Une appropriation française du Levant : la mission en Orient du cardinal Dubois, 1919-1920', in (ed.) Patrick Cabanel, *Une France en Méditerranée—Écoles, langue et culture française, XIXe-XXe siècles*, Créaphis, Paris, 2006, pp. 109-128.

27 The establishment of Zionism as the restoration of Jewish power in contradiction to the Gospel revelation is for instance condemned by the French Assumptionists (see my paper: 'Les Assomptionistes de Jérusalem, les Juifs et le sionisme', *op. cit.*)

them the critical situation in 1929, and then in 1936-39, was nothing but a confirmation of the opinion that Arab violence is a result of Zionist ambition and boldness.

A negative attitude still prevailed at the Holy See, even while some tendencies appeared indicating a new perception of Judaism, as shown by the *Amici Israel* committee, by Pius XI's speech to Belgian pilgrims in 1937—speaking of Christians being 'spiritually' Semites, or by the famous—and never published—encyclical devoted to and rejecting anti-Semitism, in 1938.[28] In fact, a new, and somewhat positive, appraisal of Judaism did not lead to an acceptance of Zionism: the Holy See rejected the notion of a partition of Palestine, first contemplated in 1937 (the Peel report), which would lead to the creation of a Jewish State there alongside an Arab one; and the Vatican approved the White Paper published by the British authorities in 1939, intended to limit Jewish immigration to Palestine, which was interpreted as the cause of continuing violence there.

The same attitude remained during the Second World War, even though individual Catholics or Catholic institutions did rescue Jews from Nazi persecution—throughout Europe, and, very symbolically, in papal Rome.[29] For the very same reasons as in the past, such a benevolent attitude can in no way be seen as promoting the creation of a Jewish State which might host persecuted Jews. In a way, the Finaly affair, in the direct aftermath of the conflict, illustrates the chasm, distrust and continuing prejudice: the protection and rescue of two young Jewish boys followed by a refusal to return them to their relatives based in Palestine/Israel.[30]

THE HOLY SEE/CATHOLICISM AND THE STATE OF ISRAEL

After the end of the Second World War, confronted with a new acceleration of history, the Holy See was willing to revive an idea that had first appeared during the First World War: special status for Jerusalem and its vicinity. The idea of a *corpus separatum* clearly illustrates a refusal to promote one side or

---

28 Georges Passelecq, Bernard Suchecky, *L'encyclique cachée de Pie XI: une occasion manquée de l'Eglise face à l'antisémitisme*, La Découverte, Paris, 1995.

29 Michael Phayer, *The Catholic Church and the Holocaust, 1930-1965*, Indiana University Press, Bloomington, 2000; Saul Friedländer, *Pie XII et le IIIe Reich*, Ed. du Seuil, Paris, 1963 (new edition: 2009).

30 See also Virginie Sansico, 'L'affaire Finaly: une controverse religieuse ?', *Revue d'histoire de la Shoah*, 192, January-June 2010, pp. 291-316.

the other, and, further, can be perceived as a way of renewing the idea of a kind of a Latin Kingdom, under the auspices of the Holy See. In this period the Vatican was worried about the evolution of the area: it condemned the prospect of desecration of the Holy Land by, on the one hand, the very probable creation of a Jewish State, and, on the other, a parallel Arab State, feared to become a Muslim majority. In the critical period December 1947-May 1948,[31] the Holy See protested against massacres perpetrated, in an increasingly violent context, by both sides in the Holy Land. On 1 May 1948, with the declaration *Auspicia quaedam*, Pius XII demanded the restoration of peace in Palestine. The Vatican, however, could remain merely an observer, confronting the heavy damage endured by some Catholic institutions, mostly perpetrated, in its view, by Zionists, and, after mid-May 1948, by Israelis. Hoping to avoid events during massive Arab-Israeli conflicts leading to a situation in which it would have no control whatever, the Holy See supported Count Bernadotte's efforts towards a truce and the ending of the conflict. In the encyclical *In multiplicibus curis*, dated 24 October 1948, Pius XII demanded once again the internationalisation of Jerusalem, seen as the rejection of any (Jewish or Arab) monopoly on the Holy City. The Vatican also rejected the *fait accompli* of the situation, settled by the February 1949 armistice. Its demands regarding a special status for Jerusalem and the Holy Places is confirmed by the encyclical *Redemptoris nostri* of 15 April 1949, and subsequent declarations in 1949-1950. The texts emanating at this time from the Holy See illustrate a continuing rejection of the very Zionist idea that had led to the creation of a Jewish State. If most of the Holy Places were, at the time, under Jordanian control, the different considerations regarding the former territory of Palestine principally demonstrate a problem with the existence of Israel. For instance, *Redemptoris nostri* and its eight requests constitute, from an Israeli perspective, eight challenges to the very existence of the new State of Israel, considered as responsible for the dangerous situation in the Middle East and the tragic fate of Palestinian refugees.[32]

In the following years, having not opposed the creation of the State of Israel, the Holy See refused to recognise the new body and continued to question its justification. Its demands regarding the internationalisation and/or demilitarisation of Jerusalem and vicinity are the *leitmotivs* of Vatican declarations of the time, as well as those dealing with the question of the

---

31   Authors speak of a genuine civil war in Palestine at the time (Benny Morris, *1948: a History of the first Arab-Israeli War*, Yale University Press, New Haven, 2008).

32   Bialer, *op. cit.*

Palestinian refugees. As may be expected, these aspects were perceived by Israel as illustrations of hostility, and during the following years. The Holy See was perceived by the young Jewish State as a harmful power that should be brushed aside, at least as long as the risk of internationalisation remain.[33] Unsurprisingly, we may note Israeli mistrust of the attitude of the Catholic Church embodied by the Cardinals of the Curia, with the exception of Cardinal Tisserant, Secretary of the Congregation for the Eastern Churches, who was known for his benevolent attitude towards the Jews, for his distrust of the Muslim world, and for his difficult relations with Pope Pius XII.[34]

Nevertheless, despite the lack of official relations, some contacts and dialogue were possible. Israel was prepared to show good will, being eager to gain support, or at least to lessen hostility, in the international arena of the time. The Vatican and Israel were able to reach some agreement regarding the consequences of the first Arab-Israeli war, with regard, for instance, to guarantees for Catholic institutions which had been damaged during the conflict. In a similar way, Israel accepted the continuation of the special status enjoyed by Catholic institutions on her territory, following Ottoman and British regulations, and granting them tax exemptions.[35]

Up until 1965, despite a continuing lack of official relations between the Vatican and Israel, some moves regarding the status of local Christians were possible. By the end of the 1950s, in a first moment of rapprochement under the auspices of the newly-appointed Pope John XXIII and the leading Israeli diplomat Maurice Fisher, both of whom had been in contact immediately following the Second World War, it was agreed to send an apostolic vicar to care for Catholics in Israel. This decision, however, is not to be interpreted as a first step towards official relations, since the newly designated prelate had his seat in Nazareth, and enjoyed no connection to the Israeli Foreign Office, but only to the Ministry for Religious Affairs. At the beginning of the 1960s, after the difficulties of the preceding decades, the atmosphere between the Holy See and Israel became less tense. During the polemic of 1963 linked to the play *The Representative*, which questioned and harshly denounced the 'silence' of

---

33 In the second half of the 1950s the topic seems to vanish, together with the dangerous character of the policy followed by the Vatican.
34 My paper: 'Eugène Tisserant et le Quai d'Orsay', in *Le Cardinal Eugène Tisserant (1884-1972)*, Unité de Recherche Histoire et Théologie de l'Institut Catholique de Toulouse/Groupe de Recherche en Histoire Immédiate, Université Toulouse-Le Mirail (Sources et travaux d'Histoire immédiate, n° 14), 2003, pp. 215-252.
35 The 'Sauvel-Fisher correspondence', 1949, with a recognition by Israel of the privileges granted in 1901 and 1913 by the Turks to the Catholic institutions in the Ottoman Empire.

Pius XII during the Holocaust, Israeli leaders were eager not to worsen links with the Vatican. The Hebrew version of Rolf Hochhuth's play was shown neither before nor during the January 1964 pilgrimage to the Holy Land of Paul VI. However, the Pope's journey, even if of fundamental significance from many perspectives, did not mean any progress in the perception of Israel by the Vatican and the Catholic Church. Although there were meetings between senior officials on both sides, with symbolic pictures showing Pope Paul VI and president Salman Shazar standing together, political issues were not discussed.

The maintenance of political distance did not preclude the possibility of theological encounter, with renewed reflection on the Catholic side regarding Judaism. In a continuation of isolated efforts in the 1920s-1930s, the 1940s-1950s are known for meetings and reflections aimed at concretising the possibility of thinking in a new way about the Jewish roots of Christianity,[36] and for developments strengthened by the tragedy of the Holocaust.[37] In Israel itself, this is illustrated by the founding of a Hebrew-speaking Catholic community in Israel,[38] and by the opening, in connection with Paul VI's pilgrimage, of the Christian Centre for Jewish Studies in Jerusalem. Above all, there was new Catholic thinking on Judaism at the Holy See, as part of the preparation and achievements of the Second Vatican Council. During the preliminary work which led to the Council declaration *Nostra Aetate*, a common interest appeared through meetings and collaboration, particularly between Jules Isaac and Cardinal Augustin Bea. Even if, in October 1965, Judaism was only finally integrated into a text generally dealing with non-Christian religions, we are theologically, nevertheless, some distance from Pius X and his *non possumus*.[39]

---

36 François Laplanche, *La crise de l'origine: la science catholique des Évangiles et l'histoire au XXè siècle*, Albin-Michel, Paris, 2006; François Delpech, 'Notre-Dame de Sion et les Juifs, Réflexions sur le Père Théodore Ratisbonne et sur l'évolution de la congrégation de Notre-Dame de Sion depuis les origines', in *Sur les Juifs. Études d'histoire contemporaine*, Presses Universitaires de Lyon, Lyon, 1983, pp. 321-371.

37 Among others, see the summaries by Bernard Dupuy OP, 'La théologie chrétienne après la Shoa', in *Istina*, 36 (1991), pp. 291-307; 'Théologie chrétienne après Auschwitz—Méditations du Père Michel de Goedt', *Sens—Juifs et chrétiens dans le monde aujourd'hui*, 3-2005.

38 See the presentation by David Neuhaus SJ in the present volume. See also Danielle Delmaire, 'La communauté catholique d'expression hébraïque en Israël. Shoah, judaïsme et christianisme', *Revue d'histoire de la Shoah*, 192, January-June 2010, pp. 237-287.

39 On the preparation, writing and voting of *Nostra Aetate*, see Giuseppe Alberigo, *Pour la jeunesse du christianisme: Le Concile Vatican II*, Ed. du Cerf, Paris, 2005, in particular

CONCLUSION

The attitude and policy of the Holy See towards Zionism and Israel from the end of the nineteenth century up until 1965 was one of rejection and refusal; a political stance based on territorial as well as theological motivations. Judaism/ Zionism, as ancient Israel, had no specific right to return to its homeland, Christianity, more specifically Catholicism as *verus Israel*, was in charge, and had inherited the duties and rights of the earlier alliance. However, general political developments contradicted this policy and led to the Holy See's policy failing. Zionism won, and the State of Israel was founded 50 years after the gathering of the first Zionist Congress, and progressively universally recognised. 1948 did not mean the end of the Holy See's political animosity towards Israel, and after 1967 things became even worse. The final step would be accomplished only in 1993, with the establishment of diplomatic relations between the two states.

The political constellation is not specifically linked to a continued religious rejection of Judaism. If, in the first decades a classical, traditional Catholic anti-Judaism prevailed in the appraisal of Judaism, one notes, from the 1930s, a progressive theological recognition, if only on the part of a few people. This trend developed in the 1950s, to be finally crowned in *Nostra Aetate*.

---

pp. 95, 97, 102, 115, 118, 142 and 163-164.

CATHOLIC-JEWISH RELATIONS IN THE STATE OF ISRAEL: THEOLOGICAL PERSPECTIVES

David Neuhaus

We gather here in London to discuss the upcoming Synod for the Catholic Church in the Middle East just a few days after the Holy Father handed the *Instrumentum laboris* to the heads of the Catholic Churches in the Middle East during his most recent visit to Cyprus. I have been asked to address the particular subject of theological perspectives regarding Catholic-Jewish relations in the State of Israel, however, I will do so from within the context of the Synod with particular reference to the *Instrumentum laboris*.

I must say at the very outset that this subject is not absolutely central to the proceedings of the Synod for reasons that should be obvious. In fact, it is only the Church in Israel, out of all the Churches of the Middle East, which has an important and living relationship with Jews. Whereas there are small Jewish minorities in Turkey and in Iran, the Jewish communities of Iraq, Syria, Lebanon and Egypt have all but vanished over the past sixty years. Jewish-Catholic relations are certainly central to the life of the universal Catholic Church in the past half century. However, the particular circumstances of the Middle East create certain obstacles to relations between Jews and Catholics that need to be considered when we are talking about a Synod within the concrete reality of the contemporary Middle East. The *Instrumentum laboris* makes direct reference to these obstacles.

I will deal with three issues:

—Who are the Jews and who are the Catholics in the Israel/ Palestine context?

—What is the particular context that defines relations between Jews and Catholics in Israel/Palestine?

—What perspectives might the Synod contribute to Jewish-Catholic relations in Israel/Palestine in particular and within the Catholic Church in the Middle East in general?

WHO ARE THE JEWS AND
WHO ARE THE CATHOLICS IN ISRAEL/PALESTINE TODAY?

Before we plunge into our subject, I would like to briefly define who we are talking about when we say Jews and Christians in the State of Israel. The State of Israel is a political reality, established in 1948 within recognized borders. For the first time since the beginning of Christianity, Jews became a sovereign majority in a particular territory in which there was a Christian minority (Christians are just over 2 percent of the population of the State of Israel today). After 1967, Israeli territorial control expanded when Israel occupied territories that had been administered previously by Jordan, Egypt and Syria. This problematic situation has still not been resolved and Christians live in these territories as well (Christians are around 2 percent of the population in the Palestinian Territories). That being said, we can turn our attention briefly to who are the Jews and who are the Catholics that we are talking about.

Jews in Israel are very heterogeneous. There are believing, practising Jews and non-believing, non-practising Jews and many varieties in between. Well-known is the division of religious Jews among ultra-Orthodox, modern Orthodox, traditional, Conservative, Reform and Reconstructionist Jews. As important for understanding Jewish life in Israel are the diverse cultural backgrounds of the Jewish communities that originate in Western and Eastern Europe, North America, Latin America, the Middle East etc. A helpful distinction with regard to our subject is the distinction between Jews that come from the countries of Christendom and those that come from the Islamic world. However, each community has its own history that moulds attitudes towards Christians and Christianity. Jewish Israeli society is still in formation and this does not always facilitate relations with those defined as outsiders. It is also difficult to define what unites the Jews; however, it would seem that religion divides them today more than ever. What seems to provide for the unity of the Jewish people today are two historical factors: the experience of anti-Semitism culminating in the Shoah and the modern sense of solidarity with the State of Israel, both central themes in relations between Jews and Catholics.

Catholics in both Israel and Palestine are a small statistical minority. They form part of a very heterogeneous Christian population made up of Orthodox, Catholic (Eastern and Roman Catholics), Eastern non-Chalcedonians (Armenians, Syrians, Copts), Protestants and Evangelicals, as well as Messianic Jews. The largest group of Catholics is the Greek (Byzantine) rite Catholics, followed by the Latins (known elsewhere as Roman Catholics), followed by the Maronites, with small groups of Syrian and Armenian Catholics too. Today, confessional divisions are less important in understanding Christian identity than socio-political and cultural factors that define attitudes and behaviours and here I would distinguish five groups:

a) Christian Arabs make up the overwhelming majority of the Christians in Israel/Palestine. Between two-thirds and three-quarters of these Christian Arabs are citizens of Israel.

b) A relatively large number of expatriates, (including many priests and religious) who live and work in the area.

c) Christians who have immigrated to Israel and have become citizens due to family or other links with Jews, particularly from the countries of the former Communist bloc. The vast majority are Orthodox but among them are also Catholics.

d) Tens of thousands of Christian foreign workers and refugees. Many are Catholics, including Filipinos (close to 40,000 in Israel today), south Sudanese, Eastern rite Indians and Maronite Lebanese.

e) A small number of indigenous Israeli Jewish converts to faith in Jesus, Christianity. The biggest number would be Messianic Jews (about 10,000) but there are Catholics among them too, including your present speaker.

Theological perspectives on the dialogue with the Jews would vary greatly depending on which particular group of Catholics we are talking about. The Synod will focus particularly on the first group—Arab Catholics—and so will I in this paper.

THE CONTEXT FOR JEWISH-CATHOLIC RELATIONS IN ISRAEL/PALESTINE

Jewish-Catholic relations in Israel/Palestine are sharply distinguished from the type of relations that exist in Western Europe and North America, where Jews and Catholic have been in a fruitful and passionate dialogue for the past six decades. This dialogue has been powered by two strong motors. One is the awakened sense of contrition that Catholics have sensed for the tragic fate of the Jews during periods when anti-Judaism and anti-Semitism dominated, culminating in the catastrophe of the Shoah. The other is the embrace of the Biblical and Jewish heritage of the Church and at its centre the fact that Jesus, his disciples and the early Church were part of a Jewish world that has bequeathed to us a rich shared heritage. Whereas both these factors do affect Catholic-Jewish relations in Israel/Palestine, the overwhelming contemporary reality of the political conflict between Palestinians and Israelis has a preponderant role in relations between Catholics and Jews.

Most of the official Jewish-Catholic dialogue that does go on in Israel is between expatriate Christians and foreign-born Jews. This dialogue tends to be conducted along the same lines as dialogue elsewhere in the Western world, often only minimally taking into account the particular context in Israel. Three significant exceptions are noted in the *Instrumentum laboris*:

> a) The Latin Patriarchate, under the leadership of Patriarch Michel Sabbah, initiated a special commission for relations with the Jewish people, which has been meeting for the past eight years, focused particularly on Jewish-Catholic dialogue within the particular context of the Holy Land. This was a direct result of the Synod of the Catholic Churches in the Holy Land, which ended in 2000, and called for this kind of contextual dialogue.

> b) Jewish, Christian and Muslim religious leaders have been meeting and dialoguing within a framework that was initiated at Alexandria in Egypt and that is focused on the conflict and the search for a religious response that would contribute to justice and peace.

> c) The dialogue between the Chief Rabbinate of Israel and the Holy See which has needed to address at certain times the lived reality of a small Christian minority face to face with a dominant Jewish majority.

Local Catholics and Jews do collaborate in different organizations promoting justice, human rights, peace and dialogue—and this collaboration is often less theological or even religious and more social activist and even politically oriented.

I do believe it is significant too that the *Instrumentum laboris* makes direct reference to the Latin Vicariate for Hebrew-Speaking Catholics, that has as one of its objectives the development of communities that are Israeli and Hebrew-speaking, facilitating Christian life and witness at the heart of Jewish society and thus engaging constantly in a certain type of dialogue with Jews in Israel.

I would like to underline seven characteristics of the particular context for Jewish-Catholic relations in Israel/Palestine.

1 The Conflict as Definitive: Justice and Peace as Fundamental

The fact that the majority of Catholics in Israel/Palestine are Arabs means that the ongoing conflict in the Middle East makes Catholic-Jewish dialogue difficult. Local Catholics who are Palestinian Arabs, whether living under Israeli occupation and/or under siege, or being citizens of the State of Israel, tend to focus on justice and peace as an essential element of any dialogue. Jewish Israelis who are interested in dialogue with Christians are sometimes unwilling to engage in a dialogue in which these political issues are centre stage. The result is that there are few forums of inter-religious dialogue where local Christian Arabs participate. The *Instrumentum laboris* (§ 89) does stress the importance of justice and peace for relations, making reference in particular to Pope Benedict's 2009 visit to Israel/Palestine where the theme of justice played a central role.

2 The Reversal of Power Relations

When Israeli Jews and indigenous Catholics do meet, a unique reality moulds the dialogue. Unlike anywhere else where Jews and Catholics are talking, here Jews are the dominant and empowered majority within the society in which dialogue is happening. This fundamentally changes the dynamic in the dialogue. Thus the local Church does not reflect on this dialogue from the same starting point as its European and North American counterparts, strongly influenced by the history of anti-Judaism and anti-Semitism. Christians in Israel/Palestine live as a minority face to face with a Jewish majority. This is an absolutely unique historical situation. Nowhere else in the world do Christians experience directly the sovereignty and power of a Jewish polity and never in history have Christians experienced Jewish sovereignty and power (these only having been established in 1948 with the creation of the State of Israel). For many of the Holy Land faithful, the Jew is often first and foremost a policeman, a soldier or a settler. This unique situation must inform dialogue that takes place between Jews and Catholics in Israel/Palestine.

3 The Place of the Bible

The shared Biblical heritage is a fundamental principle in the decades of Jewish-Catholic dialogue. One of the richest experiences in many places in Europe and North America has been joint study of the texts that Jews and Catholics share. The *Instrumentum laboris* points out that the experience of the shared Biblical heritage in the context of Israel/Palestine is not simple. The Bible has been used as a foundational text when it comes to establishing a contemporary Jewish claim to the land that Palestinians see as theirs. Zionism, the ideology of Jewish nationalism, often reads the Bible as a legal, historical or even divinely revealed deed to the land. For many indigenous Catholics, the problem is the use of the Bible to dispossess Palestinians and legitimate injustice.

4 The Presence of Islam

One aspect of Jewish-Catholic relations in Israel/Palestine that is essential is that neither Jews nor Catholics can ignore the presence of Muslims and Islam in their reality. Islam is the dominant religion in the Middle East and Muslims are the majority in all countries in the Middle East except for Israel. The Christian Arab and the Muslim Arab, whatever their religious differences might be, live in one society, speak one language, share one culture and experience one socio-political reality. Thus, dialogue with Muslims is a priority for the local Church in a way that is not self-evident in the European and North American context where the most developed form of inter-religious relations is often that between Christians and Jews. The 2000 Catholic Synod of the Holy Land document on inter-religious dialogue places the dialogue with the Jews within a framework of a larger dialogue that puts first and foremost the relations with Muslims. 'Relationship cannot be divided up; relationship in our countries being tripartite, among Muslims, Jews and Christians'[1]. It can be pointed out that a large number of Israeli Jews also have their origins in Muslim countries (e.g. Morocco, Iraq, Yemen, etc) but there is almost no explicitly inter-religious dialogue that takes as its starting point the shared cultural heritage of the Muslim world.

---

1   Assembly of the Catholic Ordinaries in the Holy Land, *The General Pastoral Plan*, Jerusalem, 2001, 157.

5 A New Openness to Christianity

Relations between Jews and Catholics are moulded by the centuries of history in which Jews lived as a marginal and sometimes persecuted minority in various parts of Europe. The rise of the Jewish national movement at the end of the nineteenth century strengthened the tendency to read the long and complex history of Jewish-Christian relations as monochromatic and uniquely as a tale of woe; simplistically presented: Christians persecuted Jews always and everywhere. This was one essential argument to persuade Jews to immigrate to Palestine/Israel. Understandings of history, religious ideology and nationalism leave their mark on how many modern Israeli Jews talk about Christians and Christianity and undoubtedly this impacts very strongly on how Christians and Christianity are presented in the education system. On the one hand, Christians in Israel are so marginal that they are almost invisible: many Jewish Israelis have never consciously met a Christian Israeli or a Christian Palestinian and many would not even know of their existence. Palestinians, and Arabs in general, are almost by definition Muslim. Furthermore, the ongoing conflict between Israelis and Palestinians has impacted the perception that today the Muslim is the enemy rather than the Christian and the Christian (assumed to be a Westerner) is in some cases even an ardent friend.

6 The Indigenization of the Dialogue

All the above implies that relations between Jews and Catholics in Israel/Palestine need to be coherently formulated in the light of the newness of the context as defined by Israel/Palestine today. This coherent formulation might then serve as an important bridge between the Church in Europe and North America, where relations between Catholics and Jews are paradigmatic not only in the theology of the inter-religious encounter but also in Biblical and theological research as well as in the formulation of Christian spirituality, and the Church in the wider Arab Middle East, which has tended to ignore the question of Jewish-Catholic relations because of the political context. Whereas Jewish-Catholic dialogue in Israel/Palestine still follows in the footsteps of the incredible progress made in Europe and North America, there is an increasing need to indigenize the dialogue so that it emerges from the contemporary local reality, so different from what might be experienced elsewhere.

7 A Shared Culture

In addition to taking into account the conflict, the reversal of status, Islam, and so on, I do want to mention a particular concern and interest of mine. Catholics and Jews in the Middle East could benefit enormously from the retrieval of a culture shared through the centuries in the wider Middle East. The Holy Land Synod of 2000 concluded that 'in our countries, Muslims, Christians and Jews have lived together in fruitful social and cultural interaction, this being evident in the clear traces we find of this interaction in Arab civilization.'[2] These traces include the contribution of prominent Jewish figures within Arab culture whether in the medieval period (e.g.. Saad bin Yusuf al-Fayoumi known as Saadia Gaon, great Biblical commentator and translator into Arabic, or Maimonides) or in modern times (e.g., the accomplished Jewish Egyptian singer Leyla Mourad, the Jewish Moroccan fighter for democracy Abraham Serfaty, etc). This common cultural and historical heritage is evident in the works of literature, music and cinema that are still being produced by Jews and Christians who are Arabs culturally and historically. Jewish-Catholic dialogue would certainly be enriched by a dialogue rooted in the world of Arab Islam alongside the dialogue rooted in the world of Judeo-Christian Europe.

THE SYNOD AND JEWISH-CATHOLIC RELATIONS IN ISRAEL/PALESTINE

It is striking that the *Instrumentum laboris* consecrates ten paragraphs to relations with Judaism. I would like now to mention five points of impact that the Synod might have on Jewish-Catholic relations in Israel/Palestine and throughout the Church in the Middle East with regard to Jewish-Catholic relations.

Inter-religious Relations in the Church in the Middle East

First the *Lineamenta* and now the *Instrumentum laboris* clearly lay out the inter-religious context in which the Catholic Churches of the Middle East live and move and have their being. Whereas relations with Muslims are fundamental to all the Churches throughout the Middle East, actual, lived relations with Jews are not a significant element in the lives of these Churches except in Israel/Palestine (and to a lesser degree in Turkey and Iran). This was not

---

2 Assembly of the Catholic Ordinaries in the Holy Land, *The General Pastoral Plan*, Jerusalem, 2001, 153.

always true as before 1948 there were important Jewish communities in Iraq, Egypt, Lebanon and Syria, and Jews and Christians interacted in a variety of different domains, often collaborating in politics and culture. It may be hoped that the Synod might reawaken an awareness of the Jewish presence in the Middle East that precedes the conflict, of a time before the opening of an abyss between Jew and Arab, of a time when some Jews were Arabs.

However, a much more central question is that of relations with Muslims and with Islam. This impacts strongly on the vision of relations with Jews and Judaism. Our faithful are often bewildered and anxious in the face of the rise of forms of political and radical Islam that are seen as threatening. This is a central question in the Synod. The *Instrumentum laboris* is careful to enunciate the theological principles that found the dialogue with Islam rather than simply stating that Christians are fated to share a world with Muslims.

The presence of Islam and Muslims within the context of relations between Catholics and Jews is too often negatively perceived within much of the present discourse on Jewish-Catholic relations. Middle Eastern Catholics are often perceived as not free to develop the dialogue with Jews because of the fear that this will be seen as breaking ranks with Muslims in the conflict over the question of Palestine. On the other hand, some see relations between Jews and Middle Eastern Christians in terms of separating Christians from the rest of the Arab people and even creating a common front against Muslims. What is still in its infancy is an overall understanding of how these two essential relationships—with Jews and with Muslims—can be coherently presented so that local Catholics can be both faithful to the Jewish roots of the Church and participate in the rich dialogue with the Jewish people as well as engage in an absolutely essential dialogue with Muslims, with whom Arab Catholics share a world, a history and an identity. § 96, quoting Pope Benedict, directly addresses this issue. How the Synod formulates this complex question will undoubtedly have an impact on how the Churches understand and present Christian identity and vocation in the midst of the interreligious reality that defines the life of the Catholic Churches in the Middle East.

The Deepening of an Awareness of Biblical and Jewish Roots
The *Instrumentum laboris* seeks to deepen the general Middle Eastern Christian awareness of the Jewish roots of the Church, the Jewish identity of Jesus and the ongoing fidelity of God to all God's children, including to the Jews.

The formulations strongly insist on these themes but the challenge is how to formulate this within the highly volatile political situation in the Middle East, and the Synod might indeed help in contextualizing the contemporary universal discourse of the Catholic Church about Jews and Judaism in the Middle Eastern Churches, helping them to move from a discourse of suspicion, bordering sometimes on contempt, to a discourse of respect.

For most indigenous Christians, Jews are seen uniquely within the context of the creation of the State of Israel, which resulted in the exile of the Palestinian people from their land. As the *Instrumentum laboris* states it is important, within the dialogue, to discern clearly between Biblical and contemporary political circumstances. The modern State of Israel is a political reality and should be treated as such. The Vatican Commission for Religious Relations with the Jews forcefully stated this in 1985: 'the existence of the State of Israel and its political options should be envisaged not in a perspective which is itself religious but in their reference to the common principles of international law.'[3] Furthermore, linking the modern State of Israel with the Biblical Israel (as some Western Christian groups insist on doing) makes it even more difficult for the Christians in the Holy Land and the rest of the Middle East to read the Old Testament and appreciate the 'shared heritage' of Christians and Jews because it would seem to involve a denial of the rights of Palestinians.

An important, ongoing theological project is the re-reading of the Bible, and in particular the Old Testament, within the context of contemporary Israel/Palestine with particular attention to the election of Israel and the giving of the Land. This could indeed be enriched by dialogue on these issues with Jews who are aware of the dangers involved in simplistically and fundamentalistically imposing Biblical texts on the volatile political situation. The *Instrumentum laboris* (§ 92) makes explicit mention of this danger.

A commitment to justice and peace

The *Instrumentum laboris* clearly presents the commitment of the Church to justice and peace in the Middle Eastern arena. The new insight that must become a coherent formulation is how the Church is firmly committed to dialogue with Jews and the Jewish tradition as well as to justice for the Palestinians. Pope Benedict XVI already went a long way in formulating this two-pronged commitment during his visit to the Holy Land in 2009.

3　Commission for Religious Relations with the Jews, *Notes on the Correct Way to Present the Jews and Judaism in Preaching and Catechesis in the Roman Catholic Church* (1985), § 25.

Deep fissures have marked the Church as various, often opposing, tendencies emerged with regard to dialogue with Jews and questions of justice and peace in Israel/Palestine. One tendency, strong in Europe and North America, was composed of the groups that saw with deep shame the role Catholics had played in promoting 'a teaching of contempt' for the Jewish people through the ages. This group is determined to push forward the dialogue with the Jewish people so that Catholics and Jews can enter a new age of reconciliation and collaboration. Often, this first group has been supported by those in the Church who study and teach the Bible. The increasing awareness that the Bible (both Old and New Testaments) is incomprehensible without a profound awareness of Judaism, the history of the Jewish people and the Hebrew language has strengthened the feeling that we have much in common with the Jewish people and that we have much to learn from them. Today it is not unusual for Catholic pastors, educators and lay leaders to travel to the land of the Bible and, reading the Biblical text there, become aware of the vitality and beauty of the Jewish tradition and those who practise it in Israel today. In this worldview, the Israelis are a courageous part of the Jewish people, struggling to be reborn after the traumatic and dramatic sufferings of the past. From this perspective, the Palestinians are barely on the radar screen.

However, alongside this tendency, another has emerged. Those Catholics committed to the work of justice and peace, determined to struggle against oppression and discrimination, have taken the Palestinians to their hearts. They see the Palestinians as a people struggling for their freedom and in some cases this struggle has become paradigmatic for understanding the struggles of so many marginalized and dispossessed peoples and groups in contemporary society. In this worldview, the Israelis are a powerful, militarized and oppressive majority who dominate the last of the Third World nations yet to achieve national independence through a cruel machinery of occupation. Those in the Church particularly concerned with the dialogue with Muslims also tend to see the Palestinian question as central. Muslims are often profoundly offended by Western support for Israel and they are sensitive to the mounting racism towards Muslims in many Western countries. Those Catholics in dialogue with Muslims cannot ignore the passionate concern for the plight of the Palestinians. To these is added the voice of those who are focused particularly on the plight of the Christians in the Holy Land and who blame the present instability in the Middle East on the establishment of the State of Israel in 1948.

247

The Holy Father's 2009 visit to Israel/Palestine illustrated to the Church that these two tendencies not only can but must be held together without confusion. The Church is obligated to continue the road of dialogue and reconciliation with the Jewish people. The Church is equally obligated to speak out for justice for Palestinians. These two positions will not always be accommodated among our partners in dialogue but they represent a Catholic position that integrates the Church's fundamental commitments. Commitment to dialogue with the Jewish people cannot be synonymous with support for the political options of Zionism and the State of Israel. Commitment to justice for the Palestinian people cannot be synonymous with acquiescence to anti-Jewish sentiment or the justification of violence. Pope Benedict XVI has reminded us that the Church must become more and more a presence that not only concretely manifests justice and peace but also pardon, reconciliation, love and hope. The way that the Church speaks about the land called to be holy and the people who reside there must ultimately open up new possibilities so that a radically different future can begin to take shape in our imaginations impregnated with the Gospel, in our discourse and ultimately in our praxis. The Synod might indeed carry on this important innovative work of the Holy Father, perhaps even formulating a position that can be adopted also by those Churches that are most active in dialogue with the Jewish people.

A Commitment to Relations inside Israel

The *Instrumentum laboris* explicitly mentions that the local Church in Israel today must prepare Christian leadership to fill the vacuum in Jewish-Catholic relations within the State of Israel (§ 83). Those who are active in this domain today are expatriates who are not always as sensitive as they should be to the local Church.

There is a positive side to engaging with a Jewish majority, confident and secure in a society defined by the mores of Jewish tradition. Today, in Israel there is a certain openness to Christianity as such, putting aside some of the more negative attitudes formed during the long centuries of traumatic history. This is particularly evident in the way Christianity is presented in history textbooks used in secular Israeli schools where Jesus, Paul and the early Church are discussed with objectivity and even respect. This is not true of textbooks used in religious schools and might not be true of the oral discourse in the classroom but there is a palpable change as Israelis see themselves less as victims and more as sovereign makers of history. In a survey of attitudes among the adult Jewish population in Israel regarding Christianity, Christians and the Christian presence in Israel, conducted by Dr Amnon Ramon for the Jerusalem Institute for Israel Studies and the Jerusalem Center for Jewish Christian Relations, published in February 2009, differences between secular and religious Jewish Israelis were clear.[4] According to this survey, for example, 80 percent of secular Jews believe they are allowed to enter churches, while 83 percent of religious Jews believe visiting churches is forbidden. 78 percent of religious Jews believe Christianity is 'idol worship', while 66 percent of secular Jews disagree. The most negative attitudes were expressed by the ultra-Orthodox. 51 percent believed that Christians should be encouraged to emigrate and 48 percent believed that Church activities should be restricted. Hamutal Bar Yosef, a Jewish Israeli professor of literature, points out:

> The State of Israel, though full of various tensions, enables a Jew to become interested in Christianity without ever experiencing anti-Semitism and without living in the midst of Christians. This is a completely new experience for the Jew (…) In a country where the visible manifestations of Christianity have a limited presence, there is no urgent need for Jewish-Christian dialogue, nor for the rehabilitation of Judaism in the eyes of Christians. The growing interest in Christianity (…) must therefore be explained by intellectual curiosity and emotional attraction, almost free from the burden of victim psychology, leaving blame and guilt to be cured through time.[5]

Israeli society is in a process of transformation with regard to Christianity and Christians. Large segments of Jewish society are more open than ever before to rethink attitudes towards Christianity and Christians. However, the Church, and in particular indigenous Catholic spokespeople, must take up the role of engaging those sectors in the society which are mediating change. From this vantage point unique theological perspectives on the dialogue might also develop.

I would suggest a number of important areas where relations must be developed more rigorously:

---

4   A Ramon, *Summary of a Public Survey of Attitudes among the Adult Jewish Population in Israel regarding Christianity, Christians and the Christian Presence in Israel*, Jerusalem Institute of Israel Studies, 2009. Cf. http://www.jiis.org/.upload/publications/attitude2christanity.pdf.

5   H Bar Yosef, *Jewish-Christian Relations in Modern Hebrew and Yiddish Literature*, Cambridge, 2000, p. 31.

1) Christians must be more resolute in protesting contravention of their rights, discrimination and acts of aggression within the Israeli socio-political system. The police and other civil authorities must be pressured to deal strictly with these events. These issues should be brought up in the forums of Jewish-Catholic dialogue, particularly those with official institutions in Israel. It is important to note that most aggression against Christians comes from religious circles. The dialogue with the Chief Rabbinate might be an appropriate forum to raise this issue.

2) Christians must speak out about the need for more education in the schools and other pedagogic institutions. Where possible Christians should be involved in the process of reading the educational material that is published (or, optimally, involved in the actual writing). This is particularly urgent in national religious schools where teaching about Christianity is almost non-existent.

3) As underlined by the *Instrumentum laboris* in § 83, Christians must be more engaged in Hebrew-speaking Israeli society, speaking about the Church, Christian faith, Church history and Jewish-Christian relations. Christians should be trained to take on the role of Hebrew language 'spokespeople' for the Church, the faith and the local community. This is particularly important in the formation of Jewish Israeli teachers and the Church should involve itself more fully in providing further education on Christianity, Church history, present-day Church attitudes, local Christians and Churches in the Holy Land. The Church can collaborate with the many organizations that are working for more tolerance and understanding within Israeli society, and who are constantly looking for Christian partners in their educational efforts.

4) The Church should sponsor the publication of more educational material in Hebrew. For this, a budget is needed as well as a team of writers and translators that able to produce the material that can be useful in these areas.

An Awareness of the New Catholic Populations

The Synod will certainly also take cognizance of a new reality in Israel and throughout the Middle East, the existence of large groups of non-Arab Catholics, mostly newcomers to the Middle East. In Israel, there are today not only Catholics of Jewish origin, who, together with committed Catholics of non-Jewish origin, have founded Hebrew-speaking communities in the country, but also tens of thousands of Catholic immigrants, foreign workers and refugees, whose children are already integrated into the Israeli Jewish school system. It is not uncommon today to hear Russian, Ukrainian, Filipino, Sudanese, Indian, Colombian and Lebanese children communicating fluently in Hebrew. They are living a dialogue with the Jewish people that is as yet unconscious and largely unrecognized. The Catholic foreign workers and refugees, being poor and mostly non-European, can and do witness to their faith in a simple and direct way that has already impacted positively on Jewish perceptions of Christianity. These groups constitute an enormous challenge for our Churches of the Middle East in general, and also for the Church of Israel. It has become more necessary than ever to promote the small Hebrew-speaking Church, that together with its much older Arabic-speaking sister can bear witness to the Risen Lord. However, the interesting theological perspective is to have these populations, living at the heart of majority Israeli Jewish society, formulate their own Jewish-Catholic dialogue, based upon the unique and new experience of a sovereign, empowered and self-confident Jewish population as a partner in the dialogue.

Conclusion

In conclusion, although Jewish-Catholic relations are not a central issue in the upcoming Synod, we can hope that there will be light shed on how these relations can be developed and how they can be integrated into the life of those Churches, particularly the Church in Israel/Palestine, that are part of societies that still live in conflict. The complex interreligious reality of the Holy Land and of the Middle East necessitate creative thinking and ongoing dialogue in order to facilitate the emergence of a prophetic voice and vision that will promote justice, peace, reconciliation and pardon in lands that are so torn by rivalry, violence and rejection.

THE THEOLOGICAL THOUGHT OF MICHEL SABBAH IN THE CONTEXT OF THE CHALLENGES TO THE CHRISTIAN PRESENCE IN THE HOLY LAND

Leonard Marsh

INTRODUCTION

This paper is an examination of the theological thought of Michel Sabbah, Latin Patriarch of Jerusalem and the Holy Land (1987-2008). It will explore how Sabbah's thinking, as shown in addresses, pastoral letters, and other commentary, is distinctive. We will also consider how it figures in the wider confluence of theological thought, and as a contribution to global Christian tradition. Finally, we will place Sabbah's work in a political and social context. Michel Sabbah was born in Nazareth in 1933. He began his studies for the Catholic priesthood at the Latin Seminary of Beit Jala in 1949, and was ordained a priest for the Latin Patriarchate of Jerusalem in 1955. After a short time in parish ministry, he went to the University of St Joseph in Beirut, studying Arabic language and literature, then becoming Director of Schools for the Latin Patriarchate until the Arab-Israeli war in 1967. Sabbah then moved to Djibouti where he taught Arabic and Islamic studies until 1973. He followed this with doctoral studies in Arabic philology at the Sorbonne. He became President of Bethlehem University in 1980.

In 1987, Michel Sabbah was appointed Archbishop and Latin Patriarch, the first native Palestinian to hold this office. Since 1999, he has been the international president of Pax Christi. Along with other prominent leaders in the region, he helped launch the Kairos Document in Bethlehem. In 2008, he resigned as Patriarch.

Michel Sabbah's patriarchal ministry has been shaped by the situation of the Holy Land, with a declining Christian population during the Israeli occupation; the complexities of Jewish, Muslim and Christian relations; and inter-Christian cooperation and tensions. This has been a difficult and daunting setting for Sabbah's thought and action. He was the first Arab head of the Church in the Middle East. The Israeli occupation and the two Palestinian intifadas have been special challenges, but Sabbah has also led his Church at more encouraging moments, as at the time of the Oslo Agreement (1993). The fundamental agreement between the Holy See and Israel, also in 1993, opened diplomatic relations—another pivotal event requiring careful handling by Patriarch Sabbah. The Jubilee Pilgrimage of John Paul II (2000) heightened the local Latin Church's visibility among Israelis and Palestinians as well as the rest of the world. Sabbah's position as a prominent Arab leader of the Church, within a society with Muslim and Jewish majorities, placed him in a unique position to develop Christian thought in the crucial contemporary reality of inter-religious dialogue.

Sabbah's work enabled him to address issues of terrorism and violence in a dynamic and even prophetic way. In addition, issues concerning the use of the Bible among Palestinian Christians featured profoundly in his contribution to the indigenous Christian Palestinian response to Christian Zionism.

Finally, Sabbah offered a new approach to the important area of ecumenical relations in Jerusalem and the Holy Land, where inter-church relationships and conflicts have been so damaging in the past.

I will consider Michael Sabbah's theological thought in the following contexts:

Peace and Justice Issues
The Church, Local and Universal
Christian-Muslim Understanding
The Bible in the Context of Palestinian Christianity
The Palestinian Christian Vocation

PEACE AND JUSTICE ISSUES

Michel Sabbah's commitment to peace and justice is a paramount feature of his theological thought. It is pervasive in both his statements and pastoral letters. In his Christmas message of 2001, he addresses the siege then taking place in the Church of the Nativity:

> In spite of bullets of death that reached as far as the Basilica and the Square of the Nativity, symbol of peace for humanity, we shall listen to the voice of the angel, and the song in the sky of Bethlehem, 'Glory to God in the Highest, and peace to men who enjoy his favour.' (Luke 2:14)

In a striking phrase, Sabbah states 'Peace is the weapon called for.'
This insistent demand for peace is taken up as a recurring theme. Sabbah's

Pentecost Homily in 2006 insists that Israel has a right to peace as well as the Palestinians.

The theme of violence is explored thoroughly in his essay, *Religions for Peace in the Middle East* (2003). Here, he states his conviction that, although religion and history have given rise to violence on many occasions, this is a contradiction of the true nature of religion which should be a factor of reconciliation. When religion becomes a matter of the individual's self-interest and property, the believer becomes his own god and fights for his own interests.

This concern for peace informs his theological work even more directly in *Reading the Bible in the Land of the Bible*—his fourth pastoral letter, 1993. It begins with a quote from the Epistle to the Ephesians, 'For He is our peace …' (Ephesians 2:14-16). Patriarch Sabbah expresses the hope that the message of his letter might be heard beyond the Christian community, by Muslims and Jews, and as a further contribution to co-existence and peace.

In emphasizing Sabbah's commitment to peace and non-violence, it is important to remember the context of his call for justice. In his homily, 'The Virgin Mary—Our Lady of Palestine', given on the Feast of Our Lady of Palestine, 29 October 2000, Sabbah states:

> In front of God, we pray through the Intercession of Our Lady, Mary. We ask God to have justice in us …

THE CHURCH, LOCAL AND UNIVERSAL

Sabbah's thinking about the Church stresses both its universal and local dimensions. He perceives its universal nature reflected in the fact that the Church's faith was proclaimed first in the Holy Land. But the role of the local Church is particular: the universal Church can be said to owe a huge debt to it, for bringing and maintaining the faith in this land.

Sabbah does accept a Catholic definition of the Church. In 'Faith', his first pastoral letter on the Feast of the Assumption (1988), he affirms being 'conscious of the faith, as the Holy Catholic Church defines it, in the situation in which we live, "the small flock of the Christian minority."'

There is the deep consciousness of being the Church of Jerusalem. As the inheritors of the apostolic faith, 'We too have to enrich it with our experience of life.'

This 'small flock,' Sabbah's phrase for the local Church, is not diminished by its smallness. The quality of its life and preservation needs to be transformed, from a faith merely inherited to a faith to which we give assent.

Although definitely a Latin Catholic, Sabbah acknowledges other Churches. In 'Christians in the Holy Land' (2006), a speech in Linz, Austria, he states that indigenous Palestinian Christians are Arabs, and belong to Arab culture and history. The new emergence of a Hebrew-speaking presence is recognised. All this is part of the richness that the Church of the Holy Land enjoys.

A sombre note is struck with the observation that the local Church seems to be in the stage of its final disappearance. However, the Church is still called to live, to grow and develop, as best it can.

The universal Church, born in Jerusalem and active throughout the world, remains present through the local Church, as Sabbah notes in 'Jerusalem: A Holy City and a Place for Living', a keynote address for the American-Arab Anti-Discrimination Committee.

Patriarch Sabbah acknowledges here again the various local Churches —Orthodox, Catholic and Protestant. Together, they make up the true Mother Church.

CHRISTIAN-MUSLIM UNDERSTANDING

Michel Sabbah has wished to emphasize the authentic nature of Palestinian Christianity as part of Arab culture. That culture has been profoundly affected by its relationship with Islam. Sabbah recognises that any future for Palestinian Christianity must be a future in co-operation with Islam.

In 2007, Sabbah played a formative role in the organization of the Council of Religious Institutions of the Holy Land, bringing together Jewish, Christian and Muslim leaders.

In 2008, he specifically addressed the subject of Christian-Muslim understanding, in a speech to mark the thirtieth anniversary of Bethlehem University. Here, he wanted to unite Palestinians, both Christians and Muslim, as people who believe. He acknowledged good relations, friendship and respect, but believed work is necessary to achieve 'a balance' in relationship and understanding to prevent tension and crises, and to avoid oppression.

Sabbah's first pastoral letter on faith (1988) had already laid the foundation for regarding the need for respect and dialogue, described thus:

> Dialogue, one of the characteristics of this diocese and this country, seen through the great variety of its religious and cultural communities.

Dialogue means 'to see the other one'. It does not mean sacrificing one's own faith for that of the other.

This is a foundation that will be necessary to build a new Palestinian society which will inspire trust and provide security for Muslims and Christians equally.

CHRISTIANITY AND JUDAISM

It is the case that in matters of inter-faith dialogue, Muslim-Christian understanding has featured more prominently than Jewish-Christian dialogue. Sabbah took part in the 1993 Synod, with participation by the Catholic and Oriental Churches, which reflected on the changes since Vatican II's *Nostra Aetate*. The Synod produced a document titled, 'Relations with Believers of other Religions'. It contained two sections, one devoted to Muslims and the other to Jews. The document states that the local Church does not see itself in the same position as its European counterparts, especially in their responsibility for the fate of European Jewry.

Patriarch Sabbah also hosted a monthly dialogue with local Jews which is noteworthy in the difficult context of modern Israel. In 'Religions for Peace in the Middle East', Sabbah commends the work of the Alexandrian group in furthering dialogue among the Abrahamic faiths, and sees it as a symbol and sign for the present and for the future.

THE BIBLE IN THE CONTEXT OF PALESTINIAN CHRISTIANITY

Patriarch Sabbah wrote a pastoral letter in November, 1993, entitled 'Reading the Bible today in the Land of the Bible'. In this, Sabbah notes that we have to struggle in order to maintain and build peace and justice. The word of God in the Bible is a difficult and delicate task, and the matters to be tackled are related to our daily lives. They even concern our very national and personal identity as believers, because unilateral, partial interpretations run the risk, for some people, of bringing into question their presence and permanence in their land, which is their homeland. Patriarch Sabbah points out that, for Palestinian Christians, the Bible is an integral part of their faith and religious heritage, whether this is meditated upon individually or realised in the community in liturgies and prayer groups. The fundamental questions raised in these prayer and reading groups have been numerous. These questions persist now: how is the Old Testament to be understood? What is the relationship between the Old and New Testaments?

The Bible narration includes stories of violence which have a striking resemblance to our present history, and which are attributed to God. How are these to be understood? And what is the relationship between ancient Biblical history and our contemporary history? Is Biblical Israel to be identified with the State of Israel? What is the meaning of the promises, the election, the covenant, and in particular the promise and gift of the land to Abraham and to his descendants? Does the Bible justify current political claims made on its behalf? Could we be the victims of our own salvation history, which seems to favour the Jewish people and condemn us? Is that truly the will of God to which we must inexorably bow down, demanding that we deprive ourselves in favour of another people with no possibility of appeal or discussion? Many Jews in Israel have differing views. Some of them, by what they say and sincerely believe, seem to confirm the fear and anguish of the Palestinians. They maintain that God has given the land to them alone; such implies their title and exclusive ownership of the whole of the Promised Land.

Some Christians would say the same thing. Certain fundamentalist Christians will go so far as to seek to directly link all of present history with the fulfilment of Biblical prophecy. They even accuse those Christians who do not ascribe to this idea of being unbiblical and not true believers.

Sabbah roots his pastoral letter in the Decree of Divine Revelation from the documents of the Second Vatican Council. In this Decree, it is asserted that the Bible is the divine and human Word revealed to a community. Its message is divine, spiritual, and eternal, but it comes to us clothed in linguistic, literary, cultural, historical and geographical terms which are human.

Sabbah reminds us that we cannot ask of the Bible what it is unable to give. He presents the Bible as a matter of progressive revelation, as noted at the Second Vatican Council, and notes the importance and value, for Palestinian Christians as well as anyone else, of Biblical criticism in understanding the meaning and value of the Bible.

THE PALESTINIAN CHRISTIAN VOCATION

Michael Sabbah's view of the Palestinian Christian vocation in many ways relates to the themes that have been outlined above.

In a homily on Pentecost Sunday, 2003, at the Benedictine Abbey Hagia Maria Sion in Jerusalem, titled 'The Mystery of the Palestinian Christian Vocation', Sabbah prays that the Spirit will help the Church to live its vocation in this land, to witness Jesus in his land, in all circumstances, difficult as they are today, and will remain so, in times of war and times of peace.

Witnessing is seen to be central to the Palestinian Christian Vocation, and this needs to be redefined.

The holiness of this land is affirmed, and the 'difficult birth' of peace and justice. According to the Christian faith, this is the land of the Cross. According to Sabbah, the hope lies in Jesus' promise to pray for us and to send his Spirit, who supports us throughout our life's journey to the Cross.

Palestinian Christians are called to be agents for reconciliation in intractable situations, where renewal needs enemies to be forgiven.

CONCLUDING THOUGHTS

In evaluating Sabbah's distinctive contribution to Christian thinking, it is necessary to look at material from pastoral letters, speeches, homilies, etc.— material of the sort not regarded as strictly academic in nature.

At very least, it is given its distinction because its source is a Palestinian holding the office of Latin Patriarch. It should also be pointed out that two areas owe their inspiration in part to decrees of the Second Vatican Council. Justice and peace issues have as a background *Pacem in Terris*; the latter is one of the most significant papal encyclicals of the twentieth century, issued by Pope John XXIII on 11 April 1963. This would establish major principles that featured in the documents of the Second Vatican Council. Four critical conditions for peace were outlined in Sabbah's 'Perspectives of a Peace between Israelis and Palestinians.' (*Pax Christi*, USA, 20 May 2003). These were:

—Acknowledgment of rights and duties.

—Respect for the rights of others and taking a responsible place in the world.

—A solidarity toward the needs of others.

—Decision-making and choices according to natural reason.

Sabbah applies these principles to the Israel-Palestinian situation, calling for a just peace, an end to occupation, and placing this conflict in the perspective of conflicts globally.

Sabbah's thinking regarding the Church is significant in regard to the role of the Latin Patriarchate. In a modern context, and with the receding of rival claims to be the only legitimate Church, the recognition of the Oriental rites by the Holy See might suggest the redundancy of the Latin rite. As a Palestinian and in his role as Latin Patriarch, Sabbah strengthened the Latin Patriarchate through having both links with the West and an authentic Arab identity. In a real sense, the Patriarchate shares power and authority with the Vatican, which in turn can express itself through him regarding regional and global questions.

In the area of Christian-Muslim understanding, Sabbah has promoted and shares with other Church leaders a commendable solidarity. Again, the links with the wider Catholic context provides added significance.

The most important theological document of Sabbah's period of office is his pastoral letter, 'Reading the Bible in the land of the Bible'. The application of principles regarding Biblical interpretation, rooted in the Vatican II decree on divine revelation, is an important contribution to addressing a particular problem in Palestinian Christianity. The appropriation of Old Testament narratives as a quasi-religious defence of Christian Zionism has been deeply troubling to thoughtful Palestinian Christians. Sabbah's insightful placing of these narratives in a wider context of progressive revelation, using authoritative Council documents, was unique. The Christ-centred hermeneutic embodied by this relativising of the Old Testament is shared by other Palestinian writers, including Naim Ateek.

Sabbah was able to put the Palestinian Christian vocation in the context of the Church in Jerusalem, with the Palestinian experience, in its smallness and vulnerability, enriching its life. This is a special expression of what it means to be the Church. The resilience of the Church in this experience of suffering provides a new dimension to its function and reality.

Ultimately, Patriarch Sabbah represented a remarkable change, as the first Arab to hold his position, and also as part of the wider confluence of Palestinian Christianity theology.

Sabbah's work emerged out of a multi-dimensional crisis for Palestinian Christianity. The Palestinian Christians have been a declining minority within a situation of oppression and expulsion following the establishment of the state of Israel. Their genuine Arab identity has been questioned by other Palestinians; their links with the West make them vulnerable to such accusations. Past internal divisions, and a troubled relationship with the Western Church, have compromised their loyalties and identity.

The specific difficulties in theological terms are well summed up by the Anglican scholar Kenneth Cragg:

> We need to grasp the mystique by which it is opposed, the divine mandate which—in the eyes of many in the West and in Christian quarters—its adversary commands and wields. This sense of what the Palestinians are up against in the massive yet elusive sanction Israel enjoys is no small part of their travail. How it may be demystified, how spiritually counterbalanced by more prosaic meanings of justice and peace, is a profound problem for the Palestinian soul—a problem that leads back into vexed areas of biblical interpretation and theology.
> (*The Arab Christian*, Mowbray, London, 1992, p. 235)

Sabbah's work is a significant response to the problem for the Palestinian 'soul'. His response has been both activist and pastoral, as well as theological, and is a truly remarkable achievement.

ARABIC CHRISTIAN RELATIONS WITH ISLAM: RETRIEVING FROM HISTORY, EXPANDING THE CANON

Sidney H Griffith

Prolegomena

Arabic-speaking Christians have been intimately in conversation with the Qur'ān and with Muslims from the very beginnings of Islam, up to and including the present day. Indeed one could make the case that already from the Qur'ān's point of view, as 'People of the Book', i.e., 'Scripture People', Jews and Christians are envisioned in the Islamic scripture as being virtual members of the 'Community of Believers',[1] whose views Muslims might profitably consult. In the Qur'ān, God advised Muḥammad, 'If you are in doubt about what We have sent down to you, ask those who were reading the scripture before you.' (X *Yūnus* 94) And in another important passage, the Qur'ān says, 'Do not dispute with the people of the Book save in the fairest way; except for those of them who are evildoers. And say: "We believe in what has been sent down to us and what has been sent down to you. Our God and your God are one and to Him we are submissive."' (XXIX *al-'Ankabūt* 46)[2] It was in this spirit that in their letter to Christian leaders on 13 October 2007/1428, entitled 'A Common Word between Us and You', Muslim world leaders cited another pertinent passage from the Qur'ān, which, according to traditional Muslim sources,[3] was revealed to Muḥammad on the occasion of the visit of

---

1   See Fred M Donner, 'From Believers to Muslims: Confessional Self-Identity in the Early Islamic Community', *Al-Abḥāth* 50-51 (2002-2003), pp. 9-53. The author has since somewhat improbably developed the ideas expressed in this article into the guiding principle of his view of Islamic origins. See Fred M Donner, *Muhammad and the Believers: At the Origins of Islam*, Harvard University Press, Cambridge, MA, 2010.

2   See Jane Dammen McAuliffe, '"Debate with them in the better way": The Construction of a Qur'ānic Commonplace', in Angelica Neuwirth *et al.* (eds), *Myths, Historical Archetypes and Symbolic Figures in Arabic Literature: Toward a New Hermeneutic Approach*, In Kommission bei Franz Steiner Verlag Stuttgart, Beirut, 1999, pp. 163-188.

3   See Abdelmadjid Méziane, 'Le sens de la *Mubâhala* d'après la tradition islamique', *Islamochristiana* 2 (1976), pp. 59-67.

a delegation of Christians from the south Arabian city of Najrān to Yathrib/ Medina in the year 631/10. The text records God's word to Muḥammad: 'Say, "O People of the Book, come to a common word between you and us, that we worship none but God, do not associate anything with Him and do not set up each other as lords besides God." If they turn their backs, say: "Bear witness that we are Muslims."' (III *Āl 'Imrān* 64)

After the Arab conquest and occupation of almost all of the territories of the Oriental Patriarchates of the Christians (Alexandria, Antioch, Jerusalem) in the course of the seventh Christian century, large communities of hitherto Greek, Syriac, Coptic, and Armenian-speaking Christians joined the already Arabic-speaking Christians of the original milieu of Muḥammad and the Qur'ān as 'People of the Book', living in the midst of the 'Community of Believers', with a guaranteed legal status of their own, albeit one that required them to pay a special poll tax and to adopt a low social profile as subaltern citizens in the World of Islam.[4] For in due course, and within about two centuries after the death of Muḥammad, the territories under Arab rule grew into the Islamic Commonwealth,[5] and became the World of Islam. As Albert Hourani memorably wrote:

> By the third and fourth Islamic centuries (the ninth or tenth century AD) something which was recognizably an 'Islamic World' had emerged. ... Men and women in the Near East and the Maghrib lived in a universe which was defined in terms of Islam. ... Time was marked by the five daily prayers, the weekly sermon in the Mosque, the annual fast in the month of Ramadan and the pilgrimage to Mecca and the Muslim calendar.[6]

The process of the enculturation of the several communities of Christians into this new world most notably involved the adoption of the Arabic language, not only as the idiom of public life in the caliphate, but as an ecclesiastical, even liturgical and theological language. It began as a project to translate the scriptures and other Church books into Arabic, and to write original theological and apologetic texts in the Arabic of Islamic religious

---

4   See Youssef Courbage and Philippe Fargues, *Christians and Jews under Islam*, trans. Judy Mabro, I B Tauris, London and New York, 1997; Yohanan Friedman, *Tolerance and Coercion in Islam: Interfaith Relations in Muslim Tradition*, Cambridge University Press, Cambridge, 2003.

5   See Garth Fowden, *Empire to Commonwealth: Consequences of Monotheism in Late Antiquity*, Princeton University Press, Princeton, NJ, 1993.

6   Albert Hourani, *A History of the Arab People*, Warner Books, New York, 1992, pp. 54-57.

discourse;[7] it culminated in a large Christian presence in the intellectual and cultural life of the classical period of the Islamic Commonwealth, extending well into the twelfth and thirteenth centuries.[8] During this half millennium of Jewish, Christian, and Muslim *convivencia* in the heartlands of the Arabic-speaking peoples after the Islamic conquest,[9] relations between Muslims and Christians were constant, often intellectually and culturally complementary, mutually comprehensible, but both confrontational and co-operative at the same time. In the end, from the thirteenth century onward, due to numerous disabling factors,[10] including developments in Islamic religious thinking,[11] the numbers of Christians living in the Islamic world gradually declined to

---

7   See Sidney H Griffith, 'The Monks of Palestine and the Growth of Christian Literature in Arabic', *The Muslim World* 78 (1988), pp. 1-28; 'From Aramaic to Arabic: The Languages of the Monasteries of Palestine in the Byzantine and Early Islamic Periods', *Dumbarton Oaks Papers* 51 (1997), pp. 11-31.

8   See Samir Khalil Samir, *Foi et culture en Irak au XIe siècle: Élie de Nisibe et l'Islam*, Collected Studies Series, 544, Variorum/Ashgate, Aldershot, 1966; Sidney H Griffith, *The Church in the Shadow of the Mosque: Christians and Muslims in the World of Islam*, Princeton University Press, Princeton, NJ, 2008; *idem*, 'Syrian Christian Intellectuals in the World of Islam: Faith, the Philosophical Life, and the Quest for an Interreligious Convivencia in 'Abbasid Times', *Journal of the Canadian Society for Syriac Studies* 7 (2007), pp. 55-73.

9   The Spanish term *convivencia* is normally used to describe the living situation of Jews, Christians and Muslims in al-Andalus in the medieval period. Some writers view the period somewhat romantically, envisioning a time of tolerance and enlightenment. See, e.g., María Menocal, *The Ornament of the World: How Muslims, Jews, and Christians Created a Culture of Tolerance in Medieval Spain*, Little Brown, Boston, 2002. The present writer views this account of affairs in Spain to be more legendary than real; see Griffith, *The Church in the Shadow of the Mosque*, 154-155. Nevertheless, *convivencia* is an apt term to suggest the modes of mutual accommodation of Jews, Christians, and Muslims in the wider world of Islam and particularly in reference to Baghdad and its environs from the ninth to the twelfth centuries. See Griffith, 'Syrian Christian Intellectuals', cited in the previous note.

10   See the accounts of difficulties, disabilities, and persecutions in Bat Ye'or, *The Decline of Eastern Christianity under Islam: From Jihad to Dhimmitude; Seventh-Twentieth Century*, Fairleigh Dickinson University Press, Madison, NJ, 1996. One must be aware of the extreme anti-Islamic prejudice of this and other recent publications by Bat Ye'or. Nevertheless, it is to this author's credit to have highlighted the need for systematic study of the cumulative effects over time of the Islamic legislation regarding the People of the Book on the factual diminution of Jewish and Christian communities in the world of Islam.

11   These developments are discussed with characteristic insight in Fazlur Rahman, *Revival and Reform in Islam: A Study of Islamic Fundamentalism*, (ed.) Ebrahim Moosa, Oneworld, Oxford, 2000/2003.

demographic insignificance in some areas, reaching crisis proportions in certain places by the dawn of the twenty-first century.[12]

Over the course of the long, early history of Arab Christian relations with Islam, extending roughly from the mid-ninth century to the mid-thirteenth century, in the environs first of Baghdad and then of Cairo, several areas of Christian intellectual and cultural accomplishment stand out. One might characterize them as points of historical reference, in consideration of which Christians in the early twenty-first century, might as it were expand the canon of Christian/Muslim relations, so that in the era of globalization, when Christians and Muslims live as neighbours to one another world wide, they may take advantage of the lessons to be learned from the accomplishments of the early Arabic-speaking Christians who lived among the Muslims in the Middle East from the very beginnings of Islam. These areas of Arab Christian accomplishment may the most usefully be discussed under three headings: translation and cultural assimilation; inter-religious colloquy; and the Islamochristian cultivation of philosophy, especially in Baghdad and its environs from the ninth to the eleventh centuries.

Although the study of Christianity in its Arabic expression is in its infancy, especially in Western academic circles, the landmark publication of Georg Graf's *Geschichte der christlichen arabischen Literatur*, completed by the middle of the twentieth century,[13] provided the impetus for a surge of international scholarly interest in Christian Arabic that by now has reached a point that allows the researcher to discern and discuss the main areas of Arab Christian intellectual and cultural accomplishment in the early Islamic period. While there is much yet to be done in the areas of text-editing, translation, and historical interpretation, and especially in the area of the study of the Bible in Arabic, just enough has been achieved to provide the first glimpses of a panoramic view of Christian/Muslim cultural and intellectual relations in the early Islamic period. The problem now is to

---

12   See Jean-Pierre Valognes, *Vie et mort des chrétiens d'Orient: Des origines à nos jours*, Fayard, Paris, 1994; Andrea Pacini (ed.), *Christian Communities in the Arab Middle East: The Challenge of the Future*, Oxford University Press, New York, 1998.

13   See Georg Graf, *Geschichte der christlichen arabischen Literatur*, 5 vols, Studi e Testi, 118, 133, 146, 147, 142; Biblioteca Apostolica Vaticana, Vatican City, 1944-1953. For subsequent general accounts of Muslim/Christian relations in Arabic see Bénédicte Landron, *Chrétiens et musulmans en Irak: Attitudes Nestoriennes vis-à-vis de l'Islam*, Cariscript, Paris, 1994; Jean-Marie Gaudeul, *Encounters and Clashes: Islam and Christianity in History*, 2 vols; rev. ed.; Pontificio Istituto di Studi Arabi e Islamici, Rome, 2000; David Thomas and Barbara Roggema (eds), *Christian-Muslim Relations: A Bibliographical History*, vol. I (600-900); Brill, Leiden and Boston, 2009.

bring this view to the attention of the present-day scholarly community, who seldom take notice of it.

The purpose of the present essay is briefly to give an account of the Arab Christian intellectual and cultural accomplishments under the three headings just mentioned, and then, building on the experience of Christians and Muslims together in the Islamic past, to suggest ways in which they might carry the lessons of that experience not only into the life of Muslims and Christians in the Middle East in the twenty-first century, where they face new and difficult challenges, but also to inform present-day efforts to bring about a meaningful *convivencia* of Jews, Christians and Muslims in inter-cultural and inter-religious dialogue for justice and peace worldwide.

ARABIC CHRISTIANITY IN 'ABBASID TIMES
Translation and Cultural Assimilation

Most of the earliest surviving Christian Arabic manuscripts contain translations of the Bible and other church books from Greek and Syriac into Arabic, the language of public life in the newly established Islamic caliphate. The translation movement got seriously underway in the second half of the eighth century, in early 'Abbasid times, just over a century after the death of Muḥammad. The earliest recorded date referring to a Christian text in Arabic is a note appended to the end of an Arabic version of an account of the martyrdom of the 'Fathers Who Were Killed at Mount Sinai', according to which the text was translated from Greek into Arabic in the year 772 AD.[14] This date is roughly compatible with the probable date of the earliest independent, original theological composition in Arabic, called by its modern editor, *On the Triune Nature of God*.[15] The date of its composition is inferred from a remark in the text to the effect that by the time it was written, Christianity had withstood Islam 'for seven hundred and forty-six years', that is, sometime between 737/738 and 770/771 AD, depending on the method of calculating the years one adopts.[16] For all practical purposes, one might conclude that the

---

14 See the discussion in Sidney H Griffith, 'The Arabic Account of 'Abd al-Masīḥ an-Naṣrānī al-Ghassānī', *Le Muséon* 98 (1985), pp. 331-374, esp. 337-342.

15 Margaret Dunlop Gibson, *An Arabic Version of the Acts of the Apostles and the Seven Catholic Epistles, with a Treatise on the Triune Nature of God*, Studia Sinaitica, VIII; C J Clay and Sons, London, 1899, pp. 74-107 (Arabic); 2-36 (English).

16 See Samir Khalil Samir, 'The Earliest Arab Apology for Christianity (c. 750)', in Samir Khalil Samir and Jørgen Nielsen (eds), *Christian Arabic Apologetics during the 'Abbasid*

surviving dated texts suggest that Christians living in the Islamic world began writing in Arabic in the second half of the eighth century. This is also the period to which on paleographical grounds scholars have dated the earliest translations of the Gospels and other portions of the Bible into Arabic.[17]

Albeit that the Christian Arabic translation movement had its origins in the late eighth century, it achieved its early, first flowering in the course of the ninth century; the earliest dated manuscripts bearing dates from the 850s through the 890s.[18] The translations included, in addition to the scriptures, saints' lives, patristic texts, popular theological works, and canonical and liturgical texts, translated mainly from Greek, Syriac, and Coptic.[19] In this early phase, the Christian Arabic translation movement paralleled in time the more narrowly focused, but much better known, Graeco-Arabic translation movement in the environs of Baghdad in early 'Abbasid times, also carried out largely by Christians, but with a much different set of texts and concerns.[20] The Christian Arabic translation movement continued well beyond the tenth century, reaching another highpoint in the region of Antioch in Syria in the eleventh century, exemplified in the translations and anthologies of the 'Melkite' scholar, Abū l-Fatḥ 'Abd Allāh ibn al-Faḍl al-Anṭākī.[21]

With the exception of the study of the Bible in Arabic, itself in its infancy,[22] the enormous numbers of Christian Arabic translation texts have hardly been studied at all in recent times. There are some studies of the earliest of them in connection with the academic exploration of the linguistic features of 'Middle Arabic'.[23] And a few studies by modern scholars have concentrated

---

Period (750-1258), E J Brill, Leiden, 1994, pp. 57-114.

17   See Sidney H Griffith, 'Les premières versions arabes de la Bible et leurs liens avec le syriaque', in F Briquel Chatonnet and Ph. Le Moigne (eds), *L'Ancien Testament en Syriaque*, Études Syriaques, 5; Geuthner, Paris, 2008, pp. 221-245.

18   See Griffith, 'The Monks of Palestine', and Sidney H Griffith, 'Arab Christian Culture in the Early 'Abbasid Period', *Bulletin of the Royal Institute for Inter-Faith Studies* 1 (1999), pp. 25-44.

19   See Graf, *Geschichte*, vol. I, 'Die Übersetzungen'.

20   See Dimitri Gutas, *Greek Thought, Arabic Culture: The Graeco-Arabic Translation Movement in Baghdad and Early 'Abbasid Society (2nd-4th/8th-10th Centuries)*, Routledge, London and New York, 1998.

21   See Graf, *Geschichte*, vol. II, pp. 52-64.

22   See Griffith, 'Les premières versions,' and Sidney H Griffith, 'The Bible in Arabic', forthcoming in Richard Marsden and Ann Matter (eds), *The New Cambridge History of the Bible: From 600-1450*.

23   See in particular, Joshua Blau, *A Grammar of Christian Arabic* (CSCO, vols 267, 276, 279, Peeters, Louvain, 1966-1967); *idem*, 'A Melkite Arabic Literary *Lingua Franca* from the Second Half of the First Millennium', *Bulletin of the School of Oriental and African Studies* 57 (1994), pp. 14-16.

on translations in a particular milieu,[24] or on particular translated texts, noticing the tendency of the translators, while remaining largely faithful to the texts in the original languages, to render them into Arabic with an eye to the special circumstances of the Islamic milieu.[25] But much work remains to be done in this field.

Translation of course had to do not only with the transfer of texts from one language or another into Arabic, but it also involved the carry-over into the Islamic milieu of the pre-Islamic theologies of the several, newly Arabic-speaking, Christian communities, along with their inter-communal quarrels and controversies. Concretely, this meant bringing the Church-dividing Christologies of the so-called 'Melkites', 'Jacobites', and the 'Nestorians', and their accompanying controversies, into this new realm of Christian discourse in Arabic and even into the sphere of Christian/Muslim encounters and controversies. Indeed it was under Muslim rule that these Churches came into their full ecclesiastical development.[26] In short, from the very inception of their response to the challenge of the Islamic critique of Christian doctrines, Arabic-speaking Christians spoke not in unison but from within the framework of their own internal controversies with one another, each community defending their defining Christological formulae, originally articulated in Greek, and continuing the polemic against their Christian adversaries in Arabic.[27] Only in a few instances in the early Islamic period do there seem to have been efforts

---

24 See, e.g., Samuel Rubenson, 'Translating the Tradition: Some Remarks on the Arabicization of the Patristic Heritage in Egypt', *Medieval Encounters* 2/1 (1996), pp. 4-14.

25 See, e.g., Jacques Grand'Henry (ed.), *Sancti Gregorii Nazianzeni Opera: Versio Arabica Antiqua*, Corpus Christianorum, vols 34, 43, 57 etc., Brepols, Turnhout, 1996-; Kate Leeming, 'Byzantine History in Arabic: Translations of Greek Hagiographies in a Ninth-Century Palestinian Manuscript (Vaticanus Arabicus 71)', (unpublished D.Phil. dissertation; Oxford University, Oxford, 1994). See also Sidney H Griffith, 'The *Life of Theodore of Edessa*: History, Hagiography, and Religious Apologetics in Mar Saba Monastery in Early 'Abbasid Times', in Joseph Patrich (ed.), *The Sabaite Heritage in the Orthodox Church from the Fifth Century to the Present*, Orientalia Lovaniensia Analecta, 98, Peeters, Leuven, 2001, pp. 147-169; Alexander Treiger, 'New Evidence on the Arabic Versions of the *Corpus Dionysiacum*', *Le Muséon* 118 (2005), pp. 219-240; *idem*, 'The Arabic Version of Pseudo-Dionysius the Areopagite's *Mystical Theology*, Chapter 1', *Le Muséon* 120 (2007), pp. 365-393.

26 See Griffith, *The Church in the Shadow of the Mosque*, pp. 129-140.

27 See the discussion of this 'problematic' in Kenneth Cragg, *The Arab Christian: A History in the Middle East*, Mowbray, London, 1992, along with the response of Sidney H Griffith, 'Theology and the Arab Christian: The Case of the "Melkite" Creed,' in David Thomas (ed.), *A Faithful Presence: Essays for Kenneth Cragg*, Melisende, London, 2003, pp. 184-200, and Bishop Cragg's response in K Cragg, 'A Strange Half-absence: Reflections on *A Faithful Presence*,' *Islam and Christian-Muslim Relations* 15 (2004), pp. 317-329.

toward what in our day would be called an ecumenical approach on the part of the Arabic-speaking Christians to the common challenge of Islam.[28]

But Arabic, the target language of the Christian Arabic translation movement, had in the meantime itself become the idiom of Islam's religious parlance; the tenor of the religious vocabulary had already been determined by the Qur'ān and early Islamic tradition. This development inevitably resulted in what one recent commentator on an early Christian Arabic translation from Syriac of an Old Testament book called a 'very noticeable Muslim cast to the language' of the translation.[29] This 'Muslim cast' to the language of the translated Christian texts was but the first trace of the enculturation of the Christians into the then burgeoning Islamic milieu. In due course, the cultural shaping reached such a pitch that to speak of the 'Islamicization' of Christian life and discourse in Arabic is not much of an exaggeration; the process is most notable in Christian theology in Arabic. One suspects that this shared cultural identity with Muslims has perhaps unwittingly been a determining factor in the long time it took Western Christians, from the time of the Crusades until virtually yesterday, effectively to recognize the so-called 'Oriental Christians' as their co-religionists.

Inter-religious Colloquy

From the very beginning, and even contemporary with the Christian Arabic translation movement, Christians have been writing theology, saints' lives and apologetic tracts in Arabic. And from the very beginning, the 'Muslim cast' of the undertaking has been in high profile. A striking case in point is evident in the earliest of the original Christian compositions in Arabic so far known, the aforementioned treatise, *On the Triune Nature of God*. The author quotes from the Qur'ān explicitly and in his work he uses both the vocabulary and the thought patterns of the Qur'ān to commend the credibility of the Christian doctrines that he is defending. In an important way, the Arabic idiom of the Qur'ān had become his religious lexicon. This feature of the work is readily evident throughout the text, but especially in the poetical introduction, which by allusion and the choice of words and phrases obviously evokes the diction and even the style of the Qur'ān.[30] Moreover, in the course of his

---

28   See Griffith, *The Church in the Shadow of the Mosque*, pp. 140-142.
29   See Richard M Frank, 'The Jeremias of Pethion ibn Ayyūb al-Sahhār', *The Catholic Biblical Quarterly* 21 (1959), pp. 136-170.
30   See Samir, 'The Earliest Arab Apology', esp. pp. 69-70. See also Mark N Swanson, 'Beyond Prooftexting: Approaches to the Qur'ān in Some Early Arabic Christian

text the author includes explicit quotations from the Qur'ān as testimonies to the truth, alongside the scriptural proof-texts he cites from the Law, the Prophets, the Psalms, and the Gospel, scriptures that he names as they are named in the Qur'ān.

The treatise, *On the Triune Nature of God*, is one of a kind. But the 'Islamic cast' of Christian theology in Arabic carried on in the later development of the Christian *kalām*, a style of apologetic theology that Christian writers patterned on the contemporary development of the *'ilm al-kalām* among the early Muslim apologists and theologians,[31] the *mutakallimūn* or 'religious controversialists and conversationalists' of the ninth and tenth centuries.[32] The most notable of the Arab Christian theologians of the early Islamic period whose names we know were the 'Melkite' Theodore Abū Qurrah (c. 755-c. 830),[33] the 'Jacobite' Ḥabīb ibn Khidmah Abū Rā'iṭah (d. c. 851),[34] and the 'Nestorian' 'Ammār al-Baṣrī (fl. c. 850).[35] Two important summaries of the Christian faith were also composed in the *kalām* style under 'Melkite' auspices in the second third of the ninth century; one now thought to have been written by Peter of Bayt Ra's (fl. c. 875),[36] while the other, sometimes attributed to Theodore Abū Qurrah, remains anonymous.[37] They were followed in the next century

Apologies', *The Muslim World* 88 (1998), pp. 297-319.

31 See Griffith, *The Church in the Shadow of the Mosque*, esp. pp. 75-105.

32 See W Montgomery Watt, *The Formative Period of Islamic Thought*, Edinburgh University Press, Edinburgh, 1973; Oneworld, Oxford, 1998; Richard M Frank, 'The Science of Kalām', *Arabic Science and Philosophy* 2 (1992), pp. 9-37; Josef van Ess, *The Flowering of Muslim Theology*, trans. Jane Marie Todd, Harvard University Press, Cambridge, MA, 2006; Tilman Nagel, *The History of Islamic Theology: From Muḥammad to the Present*, trans. Thomas Thornton, Markus Wiener, Princeton, NJ, 2000.

33 See John Lamoreaux, 'Theodore Abū Qurra', in Thomas and Roggema (eds), *Christian-Muslim Relations*, pp. 439-491. John Lamoreaux, *Theodore Abū Qurrah: Selections*, Brigham Young University, Provo, UT, 2005.

34 See Sandra Toenies Keating, 'Abū Rā'iṭa l-Takrītī', in Thomas and Roggema, *Christian-Muslim Relations*, vol. I, pp. 567-581; Sandra Toenies Keating, *Defending the 'People of Truth' in the Early Islamic Period: The Christian Apologies of Abū Rā'iṭah*, The History of Christian-Muslim Relations, vol. 4, Brill, Leiden, 2006.

35 See Mark Beaumont, ''Ammār al-Baṣrī', in Thomas and Roggema, *Christian-Muslim Relations*, vol. I, pp. 604-610; Sidney H Griffith, ''Ammār al-Baṣrī's *Kitāb al-burhān*: Christian *Kalām* in the First 'Abbasid Century', *Le Muséon* 96 (1983), pp. 145-181.

36 See Mark N Swanson, 'Peter of Bayt Ra's', in Thomas and Roggema, *Christian-Muslim Relations* vol. I, pp. 902-906.

37 See Mark N Swanson, '*Al-Jāmi' wujūh al-īmān*', in Thomas and Roggema, *Christian-Muslim Relations*, vol. I, pp. 790-798.

by the 'Jacobites' Yaḥyā ibn 'Adī (893-974)[38] and 'Īsā ibn Zur'a (943-1008),[39] the Copt Severus ibn al-Muqaffa' (c. 905-987),[40] and the 'Nestorians' Abū l-Faraj 'Abd Allāh ibn aṭ-Ṭayyib (fl. mid-eleventh century)[41] and Elias of Nisibis (975-1046).[42] In Egypt in the thirteenth century, the remarkable family of Arab Christian scholars, the so-called *awlād al-'Assāl*, aṣ-Ṣafī, Hibatallāh, and al-Mu'taman (fl. 1230-1260), reached the apogee of Christian theology in Arabic.[43] They re-copied and re-circulated many of the treatises of the earlier writers, irrespective of their denominations, and they composed their own comprehensive summaries of Christian faith. Finally, in the early fourteenth century, the Copt Shams ar-Ri'āsah Abū l-Barakāt, alias Ibn Kabar, (d. after 1321) composed his famous *Lamp in the Darkness and Elucidation of the [Divine] Service*,[44] a virtual encyclopedia of Christian faith and practice, complete with a retrospective list of Christian writers in Arabic from all of the denominations in the Islamic world. These are but a selection of the most notable names of the Christian Arabic theologians up to Mamluk times. Thereafter, until the dawn of modern times, most Christian Arabic theologians carried on in the traditions of their forebears in the formative period of both Muslim and Christian Arabic thought, explicating the principal Christian doctrines in language reflecting the influence of the methods, the vocabulary and the intellectual concerns of the dominant Muslim culture.

History too became an important area in which Christian Arabic writers in the early Islamic period strove both to express their Christian identity and to facilitate the enculturation of the lore of the Churches into the unfolding patterns of historical consciousness in the World of Islam. One of the earliest to do so was Sa'īd ibn Biṭrīq, who became the 'Melkite' patriarch, Eutychius of Alexandria (877-940), whose *Annals* seem to have had as one of their most important purposes to read local Christian history into the

---

38   See Emilio Platti, *Yaḥyā ibn 'Adī: Théologien Chrétien et philosophe arabe; sa théologie de l'incarnation*, Orientalia Lovaniensia Analecta 14, Katholieke Universiteit Leuven, Departement Orientalistiek, Leuven, 1983.

39   See Cyrille Haddad, *'Īsā ibn Zur'a: Philosophe arabe et apologiste Chrétien*, Pères et écrivains de l'église en orient, Dar al-Kalima, Beirut, 1971.

40   See Graf, *Geschichte*, vol. II, pp. 300-318; Sidney H Griffith, 'The *Kitāb miṣbāḥ al-'aql* of Severus ibn al-Muqaffa': A Profile of the Christian Creed in Arabic in Tenth Century Egypt', *Medieval Encounters* 2 (1996), pp. 15-42.

41   See Graf, *Geschichte*, vol. II, pp. 160-177; Samir Khalil Samir, 'La place d'Ibn aṭ-Ṭayyib dans la pensée arabe', *Journal of Eastern Christian Studies* 58 (2006), pp. 177-193.

42   See Samir, *Foi et culture en Irak au XIe siècle*.

43   See Graf, *Geschichte*, vol. II, pp. 387-414.

44   See Graf, *Geschichte*, vol. II, pp. 438-445; Samir Khalil Samir (ed.), *Ibn Kabar, Abū al-Barakāt, Miṣbāḥ al-ẓulma fī iḍāḥ al-khidma*, 2 vols, Maktabat al-Karuz, Cairo, 1971-1998.

on-going narrative of Arab history as it was being told in contemporary Muslim texts and traditions.[45] Similarly, the famous, multi-authored *History of the Patriarchs of Alexandria* limned the developing identity of the Coptic Orthodox Church in Islamic Egypt through carefully composed accounts of the multiple vicissitudes of the Church's life there under Muslim rule.[46] The tenth century 'Melkite' historian, Agapius of Manbij, Maḥbūb ibn Qusṭanṭīn, composed a universal history, the *Kitāb al-ʿunwān*, only part of which survives. The author seems to have used Muslim sources in some part and to have brought Islamic chronology into the narrative at the pertinent juncture.[47] In the Syrian Orthodox, 'Jacobite' community, the chronicle tradition continued in Syriac well into the thirteenth century,[48] culminating in the major historical compilations in Syriac such as the *Chronicle* of Michael the Syrian,[49] the *Chronicon ad annum Christi 1234 pertinens*,[50] the two-part chronicle, the *Chronicon Syriacum*, for political and secular affairs, and the *Chronicon Ecclesiasticum*, for ecclesiastical history, by the polymath, Abū l-Faraj Bar Hebraeus (1226-1286), who himself translated the former text into Arabic.[51] In these texts, the history of Muḥammad, the rise and spread of Islam and reports of Muslim/Christian encounters all find a place in the Christian accounts of the experience of the Churches in this milieu.[52] Similarly, in the Church of the East, the 'Nestorian'

45   See Sidney H Griffith, 'Apologetics and Historiography in the Annals of Eutychios of Alexandria: Christian Self-Definition in the World of Islam', in R Ebied and H Teule (eds), *Studies on the Christian Arabic Heritage*, Eastern Christian Studies 5, Peeters, Leuven, 2004, pp. 65-89.

46   See Johannes den Heijer, *Mawhūb ibn Manṣūr ibn Mufarrij et l'historiographie copto-arabe: Étude sur la composition de l'Histoire des Patriarches d'Alexandrie*, CSCO, vol. 513, Peeters, Louvain, 1989.

47   Robert Hoyland, *Seeing Islam as Others Saw It: A Survey and Evaluation of the Christian, Jewish and Zoroastrian Writings on Early Islam*, Studies in Late Antiquity and Early Islam 13, The Darwin Press, Princeton, NJ, 1997, pp. 440-442.

48   For the earlier period, see Witold Witakowski, *The Syriac Chronicle of Pseudo-Dionysius of Tel-Mahrē: A Study in the History of Historiography*, Almqvist and Wiksell International, Uppsala and Stockholm, 1987.

49   J B Chabot (ed. and trans.), *Chronique de Michel le Syrien*, 4 vols, Culture et civilisation, Bruxelles, 1963.

50   J B Chabot *et al.* (eds and trans.), *Chronicon ad annum Christi 1234 pertinens*, 4 vols, CSCO, vols 81, 82, 14, 15, 56, 154, J Gabalda, Paris, and Corpus SCO, Louvain, 1916-1974.

51   Jean Baptiste Abbeloos and Thomas J Lamy (eds and trans.), *Gregorii Barhebraei Chronicon Ecclesiasticum*, 3 vols, Paris and Peeters, Louvain, 1872-1877; Paul Bedjan (ed.), *Gregorii Barhebraei chronicon syriacum*, Maisonneuve, Paris, 1890.

52   See Lawrence I Conrad, 'Syriac Perspectives on Bilad al-Sham during the ʿAbbasid Period', in Muhammad Adnan Bakhit and Robert Schick (eds), *Bilād al-Shām during the ʾAbbasid Period, 132 AH/750 AD–451 AH/1059 AD: Proceedings of the Fifth International Conference*, 2 vols; Lajnat Tārīkh Bilā al-Shām, Amman, 1991-1992, vol. II, pp. 1-44;

Church, Elias bar Shinaya of Nisibis (d.1049), a theologian and religious controversialist of note who normally wrote in Arabic,[53] also produced a chronicle in Syriac and Arabic reaching the year 1018 and including a wealth of information about Biblical characters and chronological systems, along with a record of notable events up to the first quarter of the eleventh century.[54]

Philosophical Engagement

The crucial role of Christian translators in the Graeco-Arabic translation movement in Baghdad in early 'Abbasid times is widely recognized and it has been much discussed in the scholarly literature.[55] But from the perspective of the history of Christian cultural and intellectual life in the Arabic-speaking milieu of early Islam, the discussion has most often not included two important dimensions of the phenomenon. The first of these is the earlier Christian translation movement that one might describe as 'Greek thought, Syriac discourse' and the second is the Arab Christian participation not just in translating texts, but in actively cultivating the role of philosophy in public life in the cosmopolitan milieu of Baghdad as virtually a mode of inter-religious discourse.

As a prelude to their participation in the Graeco-Arabic translation movement in Baghdad, Syriac-speaking Christians had long been engaged in translating Greek texts into Syriac, beginning already with the Hebrew and Greek Bible from the mid-second century onward.[56] By the early fifth century, theological controversialists in Edessa, and subsequently in Nisibis, were translating the Greek works of their respective Christological authorities into Syriac, works by Cyril of Alexandria and Severus of Antioch for the proto-'Jacobites' and the Biblical commentaries of Theodore of Mopsuestia for the

---

Amir Harrak, 'Ah! The Assyrian is the Rod of my Hand!: Syriac View of History after the Advent of Islam', in J J Van Ginkel *et al.* (eds), *Redefining Christian Identity: Cultural Interaction in the Middle East since the Rise of Islam*, Orientalia Lovaniensia Analecta 134, Peeters, Leuven, 2005, pp. 45-66.

53   See Samir, *Foi et culture en Irak au XIe siècle.*

54   E W Brooks and J B Chabot (eds and trans.), *Eliae Metropolitae Nisibeni Opus Chronologicum*, 2 parts, CSCO, vols 62 and 63, E Typographeo Reipublicae, Paris, 1909-1910.

55   See Gutas, *Greek Thought, Arabic Culture.*

56   See Sebastian P Brock, *The Bible in Syriac Tradition*, 2nd rev. ed., Gorgias Press, Piscataway, NJ, 2006; F Briquel Chatonnet and Ph Le Moigne (eds), *L'Ancien Testament en syriaque*, Études Syriaques 5, Geuthner, Paris, 2008.

soon-to-be-called 'Nestorians'.[57] At the same time, and well into the sixth and seventh centuries, scholars in both communities were avidly translating a large corpus of Greek monastic literature into Syriac.[58] It was in this context, and very much in view of the on-going, soon to be Church-dividing Christological controversies, that Syriac translations of Greek logical and philosophical texts were made by a succession of scholars in the environs of Edessa and Nisibis, with ties reaching back to the philosophical circles of Alexandria in the sixth century.[59] In particular, the religious controversialists were interested in the logical works of Aristotle, Porphyry, and their commentators,[60] because these were the texts that dealt with the borrowed Greek terms enshrined in the rival Christological formulae, the proper definition and deployment of which in theological discourse were considered to be crucial. This Graeco-Syriac translation movement not only anticipated the subsequent Graeco-Arabic translation movement of early 'Abbasid times, largely accomplished by the Christian heirs of the earlier translators, but it uncannily featured an emphasis on Greek logic, concern for which would become a *cause célèbre* in the scholarly debates in Arabic among Christians and Muslims in the ninth and tenth centuries.

In the Graeco-Arabic translation movement of early Islamic times, Christians were not just translators, but important figures in inaugurating and developing the philosophical tradition in Arabic, including the promotion of philosophy and philosophical schools as the social means by which the several religious communities in the World of Islam might the most fruitfully discuss with one another the best conditions for fostering human happiness and the commonweal in society.[61] The concern begins already in the work of

---

57   See D S Wallace-Hadrill, *Christian Antioch: A Study of Early Christian Thought in the East*, Cambridge University Press, Cambridge, 1982; Griffith, *The Church in the Shadow of the Mosque*, esp. pp. 129-140.

58   The case of the translation of the works of Evagrius of Pontus from Greek into Syriac is the best studied. See Antoine Guillaumont, *Les 'képhalaia gnostica' d'Évagre le Pontique et l'histoire de l'Origénisme chez les grecs et chez les syriens*, Éditions du Seuil, Paris, 1962.

59   See John Watt, 'Grammar, Rhetoric, and the Enkyklios Paideia in Syriac', *Zeitschrift der deutschen morgenländischen Gesellschaft* 143 (1993), pp. 45-71; Griffith, *The Church in the Shadow of the Mosque*, esp. pp. 106-119.

60   See Henri Hugonnard-Roche, *La logique d'Aristote du grec au syriaque: Études sur la transmission des textes de l'Organon et leur interprétation philosophique*, Textes et Traditions, no. 9, J Vrin, Paris, 2004.

61   See John W Watt, 'The Strategy of the Baghdad Philosophers: The Aristotelian Tradition as a Common Motif in Christian and Islamic Thought', in Ginkel *et al.*, *Redefining Christian Identity*, pp. 151-166.

the best known translator of them all, Ḥunayn ibn Isḥāq (808-873),[62] whose ideas on the subject are put forward in a work attributed to him, but which in the form in which it has come down to us is certainly not all his, the *Ādāb al-falāsifah*.[63] In this work Ḥunayn is presented as offering a quick history of the seven schools of philosophy, beginning in ancient times and culminating in the schools of Socrates, Plato, Aristotle, and the Stoics. He suggests that after the Stoics and in the Muslim era, synagogues, churches, and mosques have taken over the role of the old philosophical schools in commending the pursuit of wisdom in society and fostering the development of a humane polity.[64] And in Baghdad in the ninth and tenth centuries, as Ḥunayn suggests, the pursuit of philosophy was certainly an inter-religious undertaking.

In the ninth century, the busy translation movement brought numerous works by Aristotle and his commentators into Arabic, along with many other texts, notably those of Galen and the Neoplatonists. The first notable Muslim philosopher, Yaʿqūb ibn Isḥāq al-Kindī (c. 800-c. 867),[65] who was a patron of the translators, was keen to take advantage of the potential of Aristotle's logic and philosophy 'to vindicate the pursuit of rational activity as an activity in the service of Islam.'[66] But it was the 'Nestorian' Christian, Abū Bishr Mattā ibn Yūnus (d. 940),[67] who was the real 'founder of the Aristotelian school in Baghdad early in the tenth century'.[68] He defended the universal validity of Aristotelian logic, albeit reportedly unsuccessfully, in a famous debate with a traditionalist Muslim scholar, Abū Saʿīd as-Sīrāfī, in the year 937/938 in the *majlis* of a high Muslim official in Baghdad.[69] But more importantly, Abū

---

62   Myriam Salama-Carr, *La Traduction à l'époque abbaside: l'école de Ḥunayn ibn Isḥāq et son importance pour la tradition*, Didier, Paris, 1990.

63   Abdurrahman Badawi (ed.), *Hunain ibn Ishâq: Âdâb al-Falâsifa (Sentences des Philosophes)*, Éditions de l'Institut des Manuscrits Arabes, Safat, Kuwait, 1985.

64   See Sidney H Griffith, 'Ḥunayn ibn Isḥāq and the *Kitāb Ādāb al-Falāsifah*: The Pursuit of Wisdom and a Humane Polity in Early 'Abbasid Baghdad', in George A Kiraz (ed.), *Malphono w-Rabo d-Malphone: Studies in Honor of Sebastian P Brock*, Gorgias Press, Piscataway, NJ, 2008, pp. 135-160.

65   See Peter Adamson, *Al-Kindī*, Great Medieval Thinkers, Oxford University Press, Oxford, 2007.

66   Gerhard Endress, 'The Circle of al-Kindi: Early Arabic Translations from the Greek and the Rise of Islamic Philosophy', in G Endress and R Kruk (eds), *The Ancient Tradition in Christian and Islamic Hellenism: Studies on the Transmission of Greek Philosophy and Sciences*, Research School CNWS, School of Asian, African, and Amerindian Studies, Leiden, 1997, p. 50.

67   See G Endress, 'Mattā b. Yūnus (Yūnan) al-Ḳunnāʾī, Abū Bishr', in *EI*, new ed., vol. VI, pp. 844-846.

68   Gutas, *Greek Thought, Arabic Culture*, p. 14.

69   See Gerhard Endress, 'Grammatik und Logik: Arabische Philologie und griechischer

Bishr was one of the two Christian teachers, the other one being Yuḥannā ibn Ḥaylān (d. 910), of Abū Naṣr al-Fārābī (c. 870-950), the famed 'second master', after Aristotle, as he came to be called.[70] Al-Fārābī in turn, along with Abū Bishr, was the teacher of the Christian 'Jacobite', Yaḥyā ibn Adī al-Manṭiqī (893-974), who in due course became the 'head of the Baghdad Aristotelians in the mid-tenth century',[71] and who was the teacher and centre of a whole circle of Aristotelians, both Christian and Muslim, reaching well into the next century.[72] Perhaps unfairly, they became the foil for the giant of Islamic philosophy in their day, Abū 'Alī Ḥusayn ibn 'Abd Allāh ibn Sīnā (980-1037), who reportedly had only disdain for those whom he regarded as the staid and un-adventuresome Aristotelians of Baghdad.[73]

This brief and inadequate account of social networking among the philosophers of Baghdad in the tenth century is nevertheless sufficient to show how intimately Christian thinkers were involved with the birth and practice of philosophy in Arabic. They also engaged with the Muslim thinkers of their day in conversations and debates about important issues in social and political philosophy, and about the spiritual exercises requisite for doing philosophy, such as the art of dispelling sorrows,[74] the cultivation of virtue ethics for the common good of the society as a whole,[75] and the role of sexual abstinence in the life of the philosopher and 'the perfect man' *(al-insān al-kāmil)*.[76] Philosophy and its concern for the cultivation of 'humane-ness'

Philosophie in Widerstreit', in Burkard Mojsisch (ed.), *Sprachphilosophie in Antike und Mittelalter*, Bochumer Studien zur Philosophie 3, Gruner, Amsterdam, 1986, pp. 163-299.

70   See Muhsin Mahdi, *Alfarabi and the Foundation of Islamic Political Philosophy*, University of Chicago Press, Chicago, 2001; Philippe Vallat, *Farabi et l'École d'Alexandrie: Des premises de la connaissance à la philosophie politique*, Études Musulmanes 38, Vrin, Paris, 2004. See too, in connection with present concerns, John W Watt, 'Al-Fārābī and the History of the Syriac *Organon*', in Kiraz, *Malphono w-Rabo d-Malphone*, pp. 751-778.

71   Gutas, *Greek Thought, Arabic Culture*, p. 101.

72   See Joel L Kraemer, *Humanism in the Renaissance of Islam: The Cultural Revival during the Buyid Age*, Brill, Leiden, 1986, esp. pp. 104-139.

73   See Dimitri Gutas, *Avicenna and the Aristotelian Tradition*, Brill, Leiden, 1988, pp. 64-72.

74   See Sidney H Griffith, 'The Muslim Philosopher al-Kindī and his Christian Readers: Three Arab Christian Texts on "The Dissipation of Sorrows"', *Bulletin of the John Rylands University Library of Manchester* 78 (1996), pp. 111-127.

75   See Yaḥyā ibn 'Adī, *The Reformation of Morals*, ed. Samir Khalil Samir, trans. Sidney H Griffith, Eastern Christian Texts, vol. I, Brigham Young University Press, Provo, UT, 2002.

76   See Sidney H Griffith, 'Yaḥyā ibn 'Adī's Colloquy on Sexual Abstinence and the Philosophical Life', in James E Montgomery (ed.), *Arabic Theology, Arabic Philosophy: From the Many to the One; Essays in Celebration of Richard M Frank*, Orientalia Lovaniensia Analecta, Peeters, Leuven, 2006, pp. 299-333.

(al-insāniyyah) in the body politic was undoubtedly the area in which Christians and Muslims in early Islamic times shared their thoughts and concerns most collegially; it happened in Baghdad in 'Abbasid times, particularly in the ninth and tenth centuries.[77]

EXPANDING THE CANON

As one looks back from the vantage point of the early twenty-first century over the course of Arabic Christian relations with Islam during the period of the growth and development of classical Islamic culture and intellectual life from the late eighth to the thirteenth centuries in the Middle East, one cannot fail to notice the mutually conditioning character of the *convivencia* of Jews, Christians, and Muslims in this era, prior to fall of Baghdad to the Mongols in 1258. These communities, with their subdivisions, very much constructed their intellectual culture in Arabic both in conversation with one another and over against one another, in a posture at once apologetic and polemical; yielding differently nuanced discourses in Arabic that in turn played an important, contrapuntal role in the processes of community self-definition within the larger Islamic polity.[78] A significant circumstance of this religiously polychromatic, socio-cultural situation was the fact that the hegemonic Muslim community was not yet demographically dominant. In other words, in all probability most people were still not Muslims until well into the thirteenth century.[79] When it came about that Muslims achieved the definitive majority of the population, and the centre of Islamic intellectual culture had shifted from Baghdad to Damascus and Cairo in the thirteenth century, the degree of Christian participation in over-all cultural formation

---

77 See Sidney H Griffith, 'Syrian Christian Intellectuals in the World of Islam: Faith, the Philosophical Life, and the Quest for an Interreligious Convivencia in 'Abbasid Times', *Journal of the Canadian Society for Syriac Studies* 7 (2007), pp. 55-73. See also Amira K Bennison, *The Great Caliphs: The Golden Age of the 'Abbasid Empire*, Yale University Press, New Haven, CT, 2009, esp. pp. 158-202.

78 It was the perception of this phenomenon that lay behind Wansbrough's insightful study of the early formulations of Islamic 'salvation history'. See John E Wansbrough, *The Sectarian Milieu: Content and Composition of Islamic Salvation History*, Oxford University Press, Oxford, 1978.

79 See Richard Bulliet, *Conversion to Islam in the Medieval Period: An Essay in Quantitative History*, Harvard University Press, Cambridge, MA, 1979; Nehemia Levtzion (ed.), *Conversion to Islam*, Holmes and Meier, New York, 1979. See also Richard Bulliet, *The Case for Islamo-Christian Civilization*, Columbia University Press, New York, 2004.

in the Islamic world gradually waned and strong anti-Christian positions were articulated in the works of major Muslim thinkers, such as Ibn Taymiyyah (1263-1328), whose book, *The Right Answer to those who Changed the Religion of the Messiah*, would prove to be definitive for later generations, reaching into the present day.[80] Meanwhile new challenges lay in wait for the Arabic-speaking Christian communities of the Middle East.

In Mamluk and Ottoman times, Christians from the West increasingly came into the purview of their Arabic-speaking co-religionists in the World of Islam and in due course they exerted a considerable influence on the cultural and intellectual life of Arab Christians, effectively turning their attention more to Athens, Rome, Paris, London, and Moscow, rather than to the centres of Muslim culture and scholarship. It began with the Crusades,[81] but by the dawn of the twentieth century, many, especially in the West, seem to have forgotten that Christianity was not just the religion of the West, but it was indigenous in the East and indeed in the World of Islam. Translation continued to be an important activity, but now, with the exception of the Bible and some liturgical texts, it most often concerned bringing Western philosophical and theological texts into Arabic; inter-religious colloquy became strongly affected by the missionary activities of Roman Catholics and Protestants;[82] and the Christian participation with Muslims in the cultivation of philosophy entered the realm of politics. These were also the times, especially in the Ottoman era and in the early colonial period, when the dwindling local Christian churches were further divided by significant numbers of their congregants coming

---

80 See Nancy N Roberts, 'Re-Opening the Muslim Christian Dialogue of the 13th-14th Centuries: Critical Reflections on Ibn Taymiyyah's Response to Christianity in *al-jawāb al-ṣaḥīḥ li man baddala dīn al-Masīḥ*', *The Muslim World* 86 (1996), pp. 342-366; Thomas F Michel, *A Muslim Theologian's Response to Christianity: Ibn Taymiyya's al-Jawāb al-Ṣaḥīḥ*, Caravan Books, Delmar, NY, 1984; Yahya Michot, *Muslims under Non-Muslim Rule: Ibn Taymiyya on Fleeing from Sin, Kinds of Emigration, the Status of Mardin, the Conditions for Challenging Power*, Interface Publications, Oxford, 2006.

81 See Johannes Pahlitzsch, *Graeci und Suriani im Palästina der Kreuzfahrerzeit*, Duncker und Humbolt, Berlin, 2001; *idem*, 'Georgians and Greeks in Jerusalem (1099-1310)', in K Ciggar and H Teule (eds), *East and West in the Crusader States III*, Peeters, Leuven, 2003, pp. 35-51; Christopher MacEvitt, *The Crusades and the Christian World of the East: Rough Tolerance*, University of Pennsylvania Press, Philadelphia, PA, 2008.

82 See, e.g., Valognes, *Vie et mort des chrétiens d'Orient*; John Joseph, *The Nestorians and their Muslim Neighbors: A Study of Western Influence on their Relations*, Princeton University Press, Princeton, NJ, 1961; *idem*, *Muslim-Christian Relations and Inter-Christian Rivalries in the Middle East: The Case of the Jacobites in an Age of Transition*, State University of New York Press, Albany, NY, 1983; J F Coakley, *The Church of the East and the Church of England: A History of the Archbishop of Canterbury's Assyrian Mission*, Clarendon Press, Oxford, 1992.

into union with the Roman Catholic Church, bringing the so-called 'Uniate' Churches into being.[83] At the same time, Protestant missionaries, many of whom had come to the Middle East with the intention of converting Muslims, stayed to convert local Christians instead, and established Arabic-speaking Protestant and Evangelical Churches in the area,[84] along with the foundation of such notable institutions as the American universities of Beirut (1866) and Cairo (1919).

In these circumstances, retrieval from the past for the purpose of energizing the future requires curing the historical amnesia about the first millennium of Arabic Christian relations with Islam. One late twentieth century author was still referring to the period between the death of Muḥammad and Napoleon's invasion of Egypt in the late eighteenth century as 'the dark millennium' and he characterized Napoleon's invasion as heralding a 'revival' of local Christianity.[85] Retrieving from the past what can help expand the canon of Christian/Muslim relations in the Middle East for the twenty-first century involves looking again at the 'Abbasid era and particularly at the historical points of reference we have heretofore reviewed and asking what lessons can be drawn from them for a time in which both the demographic circumstances and the Muslim posture toward Christian communities living in Muslim dominated lands are dramatically different from the circumstances that obtained prior to Mamluk and Ottoman times, and different too from the circumstances of the colonial and imperial experiences of the Arabic-speaking lands in the nineteenth and twentieth centuries.[86]

Translation and Cultural Assimilation

In 'Abbasid times, the translation of the scriptures into Arabic was a widespread undertaking in the Christian communities of the Middle East and it is an enterprise that continued into modern times, highlighted by the

---

83 See Robert M Haddad, *Syrian Christians in Muslim Society: An Interpretation*, Princeton University Press, Princeton, NJ, 1970; Bernard Heyberger, *Les Chrétiens du Proche-Orient au temps de la réforme catholique*, École Française de Rome, Rome, 1994; Joseph Hajjar, *Les Chrétiens Uniates du Proche-Orient*, new edition, Éditions du Seuil, Paris/Dar Tlass, Damascus, 1995.

84 See Julius Richter, *A History of Protestant Missions in the Near East*, Oliphant, Anderson and Ferrier, Edinburgh, 1910; Peter Pikkert, *Protestant Missions in the Middle East: Ambassadors to Christ or Culture*, CreateSpace, Scotts Valley, CA, 2008.

85 Robert Brenton Betts, *Christians in the Arab East: A Political Study*, John Knox Press, Atlanta, 1975/1978, esp. pp. 7-28.

86 See Eugene Rogan, *The Arabs: A History*, Basic Books, New York, 2009.

publication of the so-called Smith-Van Dyck Version, the Protestant Bible, in 1865, the Catholic Mosul Bible in 1875-1878, and the Jesuit Version of Beirut, completed in 1880.[87] Biblical translation has of course continued to the present day and Bible study is an integral part of the Christian life in every language community. Translation is in fact just the first step in interpretation, and interpretation is a process of cultural assimilation.

It is in this context that one recalls a suggestion included in Vatican II's document *Dei Verbum*. While the document does not speak of the Qur'ān, nor of dialogue with Muslims, toward the end there is a passage that suggests a way to 'expand the canon', so to speak, in the area of Bible study in the Islamochristian milieu. In connection with the discussion of the necessity for providing up-to-date translations of the Bible for Christians of the modern era, the document says, 'Furthermore, editions of the Sacred Scriptures, provided with suitable annotations, should be prepared also for the use of non-Christians and adapted to their situation. These should be prudently circulated, either by pastors of souls, or by Christians of any rank.'[88] Doubtless this suggestion originally envisioned the situation of evangelization and the proclamation of Christian faith, but such an edition of the Bible, perhaps in the Study Bible format, would also serve the purposes of Christian/Muslim dialogue. Given the wealth of Biblical traditions and scriptural stories that circulate among the Muslims, and the Qur'ān's own formal endorsement of the Torah, the Psalms and the Gospel, albeit on its own terms, the time seems to have come to take heed of *Dei Verbum*'s suggestion and to propose the preparation of an edition of the Bible specifically geared to Bible study within the horizon of the Qur'ān and of Islam,[89] in Arabic in the Middle East, but also in the languages of Western scholarship. It could prove to be an important step in the direction of promoting a measure of religious

---

87 See the comprehensive study by John A Thompson, 'The Origin and Nature of the Chief Printed Arabic Bibles', *The Bible Translator* (1955), pp. 2-12, 51-55, 98-106, 146-150.

88 Austin Flannery (ed.), *Vatican Council II: The Conciliar and Post Conciliar Documents*, Scholarly Resources Inc., Wilmington, DL, 1975, § 25, p. 765.

89 See the important initiatives in Muslim/Christian scripture study in Groupe de Recherches Islamo-Chrétien (eds), *Ces Écritures qui nous questionnent: La Bible and le Coran*, Bayard-LeCenturion, Paris, 1987; English translation: *The Challenge of the Scriptures: the Bible and the Qur'ān*, Orbis Books, Maryknoll, NY, 1989; Michael Ipgrave (ed.), *Scriptures in Dialogue: Christians and Muslims Studying the Bible and the Qur'ān Together: A Record of a Seminar 'Building Bridges' Held at Doha, Qatar, 7-9 April 2003*, Church House, London, 2004; idem, *Bearing the Word: Prophecy in Biblical and Qur'ānic Perspective: A Record of the Third 'Building Bridges' Seminar Held at Georgetown University, Washington, DC, 30 March-1 April 2004*, Church House, London, 2005.

rapprochement between the Christian and Muslim 'Scripture People' of the twenty-first century.

In 'Abbasid times, the translation of the Christian heritage into Arabic involved translating and importing the Church-dividing controversies over Christology into the new world of the Muslim caliphate and even into the religious conversations between Muslims and Christians. Indeed one could make the case that the denominational lines between the several Christian communities were drawn more definitively in Islamic times than previously. And when in modern times the Uniate and Protestant Churches came into being, the fissiparous state of Christianity in the Islamic Middle East reached a point that practically vitiated any measure of solidarity in Christian witness. Clearly the time for a meaningful commitment to ecumenism had arrived and the formation of the Middle East Council of Churches in 1974, with the seven member Catholic family of Churches joining in 1990, has been a step in the right direction.[90] One would like to see a full ecumenical participation in both the Bible translation and Bible study projects, and in the increasingly more important Christian/Muslim conversations.

In 'Abbasid times, Arabic-speaking, Middle Eastern Christians seem very much to have thought of themselves as well integrated into the socio-cultural fabric of the caliphate. With the turn to the West, and their increasingly common interaction with Western Christians from the thirteenth century onward, and especially in modern times, as Samir Khalil Samir has pointed out, a situation has developed according to which Arab Christians 'are considered foreigners by both worlds, even though they deeply belong to each of them.'[91] And in this situation, Samir goes on to say of the Arab Christians that it is their vocation now 'actually to serve as an inter-religious and intercultural bridge between East and West.'[92] Translation and assimilation has on this view yielded to the role of the inter-religious and intercultural interpreter, the Arab Christian has taken the place of the western *dragoman* in Christian/ Muslim relations.[93]

---

90 See the Middle East Council of Churches website for details: http://www.mec-churches.org/main_eng.htm.

91 Samir Khalil Samir, *111 Questions on Islam: On Islam and the West*, (ed. and trans.) Wafik Nasry, Ignatius Press, San Francisco, 2008, p. 215.

92 Samir, *111 Questions*, p. 215.

93 On the western dragoman, see Robert Irwin, *For Lust of Knowing: The Orientalists and their Enemies*, Allen Lane/Penguin, London, 2006, pp. 110-112.

Inter-religious Colloquy

In 'Abbasid times, unlike the practice in the inter-religious dialogues of the present day, the conversations between Christians and Muslims, be they only in writing or *viva voce* in an emir's or other dignitary's *majlis*,[94] were conducted with the expectation that the participants would argue in defense of the credibility and verisimilitude of their own community's doctrines and religious practices. The purpose was to demonstrate the reasonableness of one's own faith and to rebut the other's challenge to it. Christians confronted the Qur'ān's critique of their beliefs and practices and rebutted the challenges of Muslim polemics against them. In other words, the conversations were managed 'arguments about religion', an undertaking that is not deemed polite in the modern world and which even some Muslims in 'Abbasid times thought were outrageous.[95] But in ninth and tenth century Baghdad, Jewish, Christian, and Muslim intellectuals were expected to stand up for their own religion. Perhaps the lesson for the present day is to expect participants in inter-religious dialogue not to discount the tenets of their respective communities but faithfully to represent them, and respecting one another's integrity, in recognition of the right to freedom of religious expression, to be prepared to leave the judgment of the moral integrity and religious rectitude of their undertakings in the hands of God.[96]

Independently of the inter-religious debates, a readily observable feature of Christian Arabic theology in 'Abbasid times, as we noted above, is the obvious 'Muslim cast' not only of its language but of its methodology. As we have seen, theologians discussed the 'one-ness' and 'three-ness' of the one God in terms of the current Muslim conversations about the divine attributes; they discussed God's justice, God's foreknowledge and human freedom in terms of the largely Mu'tazilī conversations about these same topics. Similarly, Christian *mutakallimūn* discussed Christology and the doctrine of the Incarnation within the purview of the current Islamic prophetology

---

94   See Sidney H Griffith, 'The Monk in the Emir's *Majlis*: Reflections on a Popular Genre of Christian Literary Apologetics in Arabic in the Early Islamic Period', in Hava Lazarus-Yafeh *et al.* (eds), *The Majlis: Interreligious Encounters in Medieval Islam*, Studies in Arabic Language and Literature, vol. 4, Otto Harrassowitz, Wiesbaden, 1999, pp. 13-65.

95   See the report of a shocked Andalusī visitor to Baghdad, who attended a couple of inter-religious conversations in the caliph's city, in Griffith, *The Church in the Shadow of the Mosque*, pp. 63-64.

96   The Qur'ān offers a potential model for this position in *Āl 'Imrān* (III):68. See Griffith, *The Church in the Shadow of the Mosque*, pp. 160-162. See also Abdelmadjid Méziane, 'Le sens de la *mubāhala* d'après la tradition islamique', *Islamochristiana* 2 (1976), pp. 59-67.

and the discernment of the true religion. Christian philosophers like Yaḥyā ibn 'Adī addressed the topic of God 'one and three' in terms of the current philosophical discussions of the meaning of 'one' and 'one-ness' in the works of the Muslims al-Kindī and al-Fārābī; they discussed the role of Jesus vis-à-vis Muḥammad and how to discern the true religion in terms of the current philosophical discussions of the good life.

Not only is there the notable 'Muslim cast' of the language of Christian Arabic discourse in this era, but Christian thought *mutatis mutandis* became closely intertwined with Muslim thought. So much was this the case that from the perspective of traditional Christian thought, in most cases originally cast in Greek philosophical and logical terms, questions could readily be raised about the adequacy of the Arabic terms and concepts accurately to express the meanings of the traditional Christian *theologoumena* and confessional formulae. It was perhaps for this very reason that in Orthodox circles in Byzantium in the eleventh and twelfth centuries, heresiographers 'more and more had the tendency to tie the heretical phenomenon to linguistic and ethnic diversity.' And even 'if Christianity was recognized to be multilingual, a hierarchy of languages existed, and orthodoxy was exclusively Greek.'[97] Similar concerns about the adequacy of the Christian Arabic 'attribute apology' in Trinitarian theology have in recent times emerged among some Egyptian Christian thinkers.[98] But it is interesting to observe that so much has the by now traditional Arabic expression of Christian doctrine become part of the articulation of Coptic Orthodox doctrinal identity that officials in the Church seem to have rejected the ideas of those who propose to jettison the medieval Arabic idiom in favour of a return to the pre-Islamic, Greek and Coptic modes of religious thought and expression.[99] Contrariwise, in 2008 in the Arabic-speaking, Protestant communities of Egypt and Lebanon, scholars have published a systematic, evangelical, *Arabic Contemporary Theology*, a 500-page textbook in which the authors have presented a Bible-based approach to some of the major topics of theological concern to contemporary Christians

---

97 G Dabron, 'Formes et functions du pluralisme linguistique à Byzance (IXe-XIIe siècle)', *Textes et Memoires* 12 (1994), pp. 228-230.

98 See Mark N Swanson, 'Are Hypostases Attributes? An Investigation into the Modern Egyptian Christian Appropriation of the Medieval Arabic Apologetic Heritage', *Parole de l'Orient* 16 (1990-1991), pp. 239-250.

99 See Swanson, 'Are Hypostases Attributes?', p. 248. Something of the same attitudes may be seen in the present-day controversies between Pope Shenouda III and Mattā al-Miskīn. See Stephen J Davis, *Coptic Christology in Practice: Incarnation and Divine Participation in Late Antique and Medieval Egypt*, Oxford University Press, Oxford, 2008, pp. 272-278.

in the Arab world.[100] Needless to say, for all practical purposes it ignores entirely the elaborate Christian theologies of 'Abbasid times.

It is notable that in the second half of the twentieth century, after the appearance of Georg Graf's monumental history of Christian Arabic literature, Arabic-speaking, Middle Eastern Christian scholars have themselves been the leaders among the academics who retrieve the Christian Arabic heritage, who edit and translate the texts of the 'Abbasid era and write the histories of the Christians living among the Muslims. The most prominent scholar in this field has no doubt been Fr Samir Khalil Samir SJ (1938-),[101] who established the Centre de documentation et de recherches arabes chrétiennes (CEDRAC) at Beirut's Université Saint Joseph, along with many colleagues both in the Middle East and in Western universities. In present-day Iraq, the Chaldean Archbishop of Kirkuk has even published an interesting book in Arabic addressed to both Christians and Muslims on the Christian intellectuals of 'Abbasid times.[102]

The really intriguing question in connection with inter-religious colloquy concerns whether or not today's Arabic-speaking Christians in the Middle East, inspired by the accomplishment of their 'Abbasid forbears, could map their present-day theological undertakings on the thinking and writing of some current school of Islamic religious discourse? Many things have changed in the intervening hundreds of years between 'Abbasid times and now, most notably the Middle Eastern Christian turn to the West in intellectual matters, especially among the so-called 'Uniate' churches. In recent times, while many in the Roman Catholic Church have encouraged Christian/Muslim dialogue,[103] some have questioned the very possibility of a truly theological dialogue between Christians and Muslims in present circumstances,[104] let alone a new Christian theology in Islamic terms, even if only for apologetic purposes. Joseph Ratzinger, now Pope Benedict XVI, espouses a more fundamental

---

100 See: http//au.christiantoday.com/article/3892.htm.
101 See the bibliography of more than 500 publications in Arabic and several western languages up to 2003 published in the *Festschrift* in his honour: Rifaat Ebied and Herman Teule (eds), *Studies on the Christian Arabic Heritage: In Honour of Father Prof. Dr. Samir Khalil Samir SJ at the Occasion of his Sixty-Fifth Birthday*, Eastern Christian Studies 5, Peeters, Leuven, 2004, pp. 315-344.
102 Louis Sako, *Ḥawārāt masīḥiyyah-islāmiyyah: Muqāribāt lāhūtiyyah bi'l-'arabiyyah fī 'aṣr al-khilāfah al-'abbāsiyyah*, Chaldean Archbishopric, Kirkuk, Iraq, 2009.
103 See the carefully nuanced approach of Christian W Troll, *Unterscheiden um zu Klären: Orientierung im christlich-islamischen Dialog*, Herder, Freiburg, 2008.
104 See, e.g., the hesitating approach of François Jourdan, *Dieu des chrétiens, Dieu des musulmans: Des repères pour comprendre*, Éditions de l'Œuvre, Paris, 2007.

dialogue of cultures as a more comprehensive and a more immediately helpful undertaking for the day-to-day relations between Christians, Muslims and others, and as a better framework within which to approach inter-religious dialogue more properly so-called.[105] Perhaps it is a call for more inter-communal philosophical dialogue, which was a prominent feature of the Christian/Muslim conversation in 'Abbasid times, and which in both communities, historically played an important role in theological development.

Philosophical Engagement

Not unlike the situation in 'Abbasid times, in the area of political philosophy and thinking about the proper conditions for the promotion of a just society there has in fact in modern times been a considerable participation of Christians with Muslims in the Middle East, especially in the area of the philosophies that gave rise to the promotion of Arab nationalism and secular democracy in the area;[106] their influence extended well into the twentieth century.[107] But in more recent times Arab nationalism has given way for all practical purposes in most Arab countries, with the exception of Lebanon, to a more pervasive pan-Islamic political philosophy that provides no real opening for the participation of Christian discourse, or any other non-Muslim voice, in public conversation.[108] It may well be the first time in Islamic history that the Christian Arabic communities have had so small a part in public life. At the dawn of the twenty-first century, in many places in the Middle East, for the Christians, as for Jews and even for many Muslims, the sorrows of the *dhimmī* have given way to the fear of terrorism and of active persecution. In these circumstances, the public, inter-religious practice of philosophy has all but ceased. But it has been in philosophical discourse and philosophical dialogue in the Christian/Muslim encounter in the past that the discussions of inter-communal well-being were conducted.

---

105 See Joseph Ratzinger, *Truth and Tolerance: Christian Belief and World Religions*, trans. Henry Taylor, Ignatius Press, San Francisco, 2004.
106 See Rogan, *The Arabs*, pp. 277-354.
107 See Albert Habib Hourani, *The Emergence of the Modern Middle East*, University of California Press, Berkeley, CA, 1981; *idem, Arabic Thought in the Liberal Age, 1798-1939*, Cambridge University Press, Cambridge, 1983; Charles Habib Malik, *Man in the Struggle for Peace*, Harper and Row, New York, 1963; *idem, The Challenge of Human Rights: Charles Malik and the Universal Declaration*, Charles Malik Foundation, Centre for Lebanese Studies, Oxford, 2000.
108 See Rogan, *The Arabs*, pp. 397-482.

CONCLUDING REMARKS

A look back at the history of Christian Arabic theology, done inevitably in colloquy with Muslim *mutakallimūn* and philosophers alike in 'Abbasid times and later, raises the question about whether or not it represents a true development of Christian doctrine, or even a distinctive Christian theology, or has it been merely a disadvantaged exercise in apologetics, polemics, and scriptural proof-texting, that gradually gave way after the thirteenth century to a retreat on the part of Arabic-speaking Christians into their traditional, pre-Islamic, religious discourses in some cases, or who turned to Western thought in other instances. The fact is that Christian Arabic theology scarcely features at all in the great essays in comparative, Christian/Islamic theology done in the past by either Protestant or Catholic, Western authors. One thinks in particular in this connection of works composed in the mid-twentieth century by the Catholics, Louis Gardet (1904-1986) and Georges Anawati (1905-1994),[109] and the Protestant, James W Sweetman (d. 1966).[110] In both works, which are professedly exercises in comparative theology, the theologies compared are those of the major Muslim thinkers and the classical, Western Christian theologians; there is scarcely a mention of Christian Arabic theologians in either work. Even some present-day Western scholars, whose work has focused on Christian Arabic texts, seem to discount their independent theological significance.[111]

It must first of all be said that Christian theology in Arabic in its origins is derivative, importing into Arabic previously Greek, Syriac, or Coptic discourses, as described above in the discussion of the Christian Arabic translation enterprise. The works were addressed to a primarily Christian, Arabic-speaking audience, one's own community and one's Christian adversaries. But in Arabic in the Islamic milieu, the need to defend Christian teachings against challenges from Muslims would be pressing as well, especially

---

109 Louis Gardet and M M [Georges C] Anawati, *Introduction à la théologie musulmane: Essai de théologie comparée*, Études de Philosophie Médiévale, XXXVII, Librairie Philosophique J Vrin, Paris, 1948.

110 James W Sweetman, *Islam and Christian Theology: A Study of the Interpretation of Theological Ideas in the Two Religions*, 2 parts in 4 vols, James Clarke and Co., Cambridge, UK, 1945-1967, reprint 2000.

111 See Mark N Swanson, 'Are Hypostases Attributes?'; *idem*, 'Beyond Proof-Texting: Approaches to the Qur'ān in Some Early Arabic Christian Apologies', *The Muslim World* 88 (1998), pp. 297-319; *idem*, 'Beyond Prooftexting (2): The Use of the Bible in Some Early Arabic Christian Apologies', in David Thomas (ed.), *The Bible in Arab Christianity*, The History of Christian-Muslim Relations, vol. 6, Brill, Leiden, 2007, pp. 91-112.

in an effort to forestall Christian conversions to Islam. Furthermore, in this same milieu, and due to the shared, Arabic language, Muslim readership is not to be excluded, and in fact in some instances Muslim readers of Christian Arabic texts can be identified; in some cases they even responded with treatises of their own in refutation of the Christian texts.[112]

In Arabic the first task of the Christian authors was the apologetic one of presenting the traditional *theologoumena* of the several ecclesial communities in a new language, in a way that commended their credibility. This apologetic undertaking in turn gave rise to a certain polemical imperative that was conditioned by two factors; the need on the one hand, and often in the same text, to discount the effectiveness of the arguments of one's Christian theological adversaries, and on the other hand to rebut the pertinent Islamic critique of Christian thought or practice. Then the task was convincingly to present one's own case. In the end, it was never a matter of simple translation; it was always a matter of re-articulating the *theologoumena* in the new Arabic idiom. And this new idiom was by the late eighth century, when Christians first started seriously to employ it, already definitively Islamicized. This circumstance is what conditioned the Christian presentation of the core doctrines of their faith, the Trinity and the Incarnation, already criticized in the Qur'ān, in terms of the concurrent Islamic discussions of the ontological status of the divine attributes and of the signs and proofs of prophecy, even in Arabic texts intended primarily for Christian readers. They correlated their discussion of the two topics both with the discussion of the two articles of the Islamic testimony of faith, and with the themes and structure of the earliest Muslim *kalām* texts, a step taken already by Patriarch Timothy I (727/8-823) in Syriac.[113]

Christian Arabic theologians in the 'Abbasid era, even the most systematically philosophical of them, accordingly came to be reckoned among the *mutakallimūn* of the era, a denomination that many of them would vigorously have rejected,[114] but one which nevertheless vividly betokened

---

112 On the subject of the audience for Arab Christian texts see Griffith, *The Church in the Shadow of the Mosque*, pp. 99-103.
113 See Sidney H Griffith, 'The Syriac Letters of Patriarch Timothy I and the Birth of Christian *Kalām* in the Mu'tazilite Milieu of Baghdad and Baṣrah in Early Islamic Times', in Wout Jac Van Bekkum, Jan Willem Drijvers and Alex C Klugkist (eds), *Syriac Polemics: Studies in Honour of Gerrit Jan Reinink*, Orientalia Lovaniensia Analecta, 170, Peeters, Leuven, 2007, pp. 103-132.
114 Yaḥyā ibn 'Adī, for example, would have been appalled to know that Moses Maimonides named him as one of those from whom the Muslims learned the arts of the *'ilm al-kalām*. See Pines (trans.), *Moses Maimonides: The Guide of the Perplexed*, 2

their acculturation into the ways of doing theology in the Islamic milieu. Inevitably in this situation their discourse came to have a 'Muslim cast' and could be accurately described as in some way Islamochristian. In its formal dress this Christian discourse in Arabic was in its style and methodology, and even in the definition and understanding of its technical terms, distinctively different from any other Christian discourse, in any other language, albeit that the Christian Arabic agenda was to present traditional Christian thinking in Arabic, in an idiom accessible to the Islamicized mentality of the milieu.[115] It arguably marked a theological development, if not a development of doctrine in John Henry Newman's (1801-1890) sense of the term.[116] Amid the welter of apologetic and polemic tracts composed in Christian Arabic in 'Abbasid times, the distinctive, Islamochristian theological profile is most visible in the summary presentations of Christian faith, elicited by the challenge of Islam, which were composed in the new Arabic idiom. The way was prepared for them by earlier summary presentations of Christian theology composed against the Islamic background in Greek and Syriac, works such as John of Damascus' *Pēgē Gnoseōs* in Greek[117] and Theodore Bar Kônî's *Scholion* in Syriac.[118] The most notable *summae theologicae* composed in Arabic in 'Abbasid times are the still unpublished and anonymous *Summary of the Ways of Faith*,[119]

---

vols; University of Chicago Press, Chicago, 1963, vol. I, pp. 177-178.

115 One may illustrate the importance of this point by recalling that when Christian thinkers like Yaḥyā ibn 'Adī discuss the *hypostases/aqānīm* of the Trinity in terms of the *ṣifāt Allāh*, they are not equating or correlating *hypostases* and 'attributes' in the western senses of these terms. In this context, the translation term 'attribute' is itself highly problematic. In *Kalām*, the horizon within which the matter must be understood, the term *ṣifah* ontologically bespeaks a reality, an actual 'referent' *(ma'nā)*, truly predicated of the divine essence in virtue of an actual state *(ḥāl)* of that essence. For the proper understanding of these technical terms in *Kalām*, see Richard M Frank, *Beings and their Attributes: The Teaching of the Baṣrian School of the Mu'tazila in the Classical Period*, State University of New York Press, Albany, NY, 1978.

116 See the ground-breaking discussion of the notion of doctrinal development in John Henry Newman, *Essay on the Development of Christian Doctrine* (2nd ed., J Toovey, London, 1846), many times reprinted.

117 See Sidney H Griffith, 'John of Damascus and the Church in Syria in the Umayyad Era: The Intellectual and Cultural Milieu of Orthodox Christians in the World of Islam', *Hugoye* 11, no. 2 (Summer, 2008): http://syrcom.cua.edu/Hugoye/Vol11No2/HV11N2/Griffith.html.

118 See Sidney H Griffith, 'Theodore Bar Kônî's *Scholion*: A Nestorian *Summa contra Gentiles* from the First 'Abbasid Century', in N Garsoïan, T Mathews and R Thomson (eds), *East of Byzantium: Syria and Armenia in the Formative Period*, Dumbarton Oaks, Washington, DC, 1982, pp. 53-72.

119 See Thomas and Roggema, *Christian-Muslim Relations*, vol. I, pp. 790-798.

the *Kitāb al-burhān*, now attributed to Peter of Bayt Ra's,[120] the monumental work of the Copt, al-Mu'taman ibn al-'Assāl, called *Majmū' uṣūl ad-dīn wa masmū' maḥṣūl al-yaqīn*,[121] and finally, the fourteenth century, retrospective work, Ibn Kabar's *Lamp in the Darkness*.[122] These works present the Christian faith in a theological profile that would be virtually unfamiliar in the West. The question of their theological adequacy from a Western perspective is another matter. What is unmistakable is their Islamochristian character, a feature that seems to have prevented comparative theologians from taking them seriously.

Against this background, one more topic comes to the fore. The Christian *kalām* of 'Abbasid times is a Christian theology keyed to the modes of Islamic religious thought. In the Qur'ān, and in Islamic religious thinking more generally, especially after the time of Ibn Taymiyyah and his influential book, *al-Jawāb aṣ-ṣaḥīḥ 'alā man baddala dīn al-masīḥ*, it is clear that there is a coherent Islamic account of Christianity in Islamic terms, albeit that Christians would quarrel with the sense of most of those terms, as not being adequate expressions of actual Christian beliefs. Nevertheless, on the basis of their own faith commitments, Muslims do have an Islamic theology of Christianity. The question then arises, is it possible, with the help of a retrieval of the Christian Arabic theology of 'Abbasid times, for Christians of the twenty-first century, and especially those living in the Middle East, to compose an adequate and useful Christian response to the religious challenge of Islam, utilizing for that purpose, as some Muslim thinkers have done for their view of Christianity, the very idiom and paradigms of the religiously other, in this instance, Islamic religious thought in its classical expression? It is true that it would be in part a theology of 'why one is not a Muslim', but that would seem to have been precisely the stance of Christian Arabic thought in 'Abbasid times, just as one might view the Islamic *kalām* of that era and even later as in part a theology of 'why one is not a Christian'. Such may well be the stance that each member community in a religiously plural *convivencia* must inevitably assume, respecting the good-will of one's dialogue partners, and leaving the judgment between them in the hands of God.

---

120 See Thomas and Roggema, *Christian-Muslim Relations*, vol. I, pp. 902-906.
121 See al-Mu'taman ibn al-'Assāl, *Summa dei principi della religione*, 7 vols, (ed.) A Wadi, trans. B Pirone, Franciscan Printing Press, Cairo and Jerusalem, 1997-2002.
122 See Samir, *Miṣbāḥ al-ẓulma*, n. 44 above.

THE VATICAN, THE CATHOLIC CHURCH, ISLAM AND CHRISTIAN-MUSLIM RELATIONS SINCE VATICAN II

Anthony O'Mahony

The *Instrumentum laboris* (§ 95-99) for the Synod of Bishops Special Assembly for the Middle East creatively engages with Catholic theological and ecclesiological thought on Christian relations with Muslims in the Middle East. This paper seeks to give context in historical and religious terms to the encounter between Christianity and Islam; to explore the tradition that emerged at the Second Vatican Council, especially the document *Nostra Aetate*, for Catholic engagement with Islam; and some final reflections on the Christian-Muslim relations in the modern world.

JUDAISM, CHRISTIANITY AND ISLAM: THEOLOGICAL CONFRONTATION

The 'Clash of Civilizations' has in recent years been posited as the global framework for relations between the different nations and religions of the world.[1] The theme has been taken up to describe the encounter between Islam and Christianity as 'The Clash of Theologies'.[2] Roger Arnaldez has reminded us:

> Moses, Jesus and Muhammad: three messengers of the one, the only God! And yet: three different messages, three religions standing against one another in their dogmas, sometimes in their spirit and in their conceptions of the One who sent their founder! How do we understand and justify such divergence if the God whom they invoke is the same?[3]

---

1 David Camroux, 'Le choc Huntington', *Études*, no. 6, 1996, pp. 735-746.
2 Emilio Platti, 'Islam et Occident: "Choc de theologies"', *Mélanges de l'Institut dominicain d'Études Orientales au Caire*, Vol. 24, 2000, pp. 347-379. See also Daniel W Hardy, 'The Church after September 11: A Study of Social Forms', *International Journal for the Study of the Christian Church (IJSSCC)*, Vol. 3, no.1, 2003, pp. 5-28.
3 R Arnaldez, *Three Messengers for One God*, trans. Gerald W Schlabach, with Mary Louise

Echoing Arnaldez, the Church's relations with the Muslim world, and the Christian encounter with Islam has been summed up, according to Jean Aucagne, as 'an affirmation of the unicity of God and the division of his people'.[4]

The historical study of the relationship between Muslims and Christian communities, between Islam and Christianity, is still in its beginnings.[5] It cannot be otherwise, since Islamic history itself, as well as the history of those Christian communities that have been in contact with Islam in different times and places, is still being enacted.[6] Christian-Muslim relations are as old as Islam. In the course of thirteen centuries of history they have been manifested in the most varied and even contradictory ways. There have been hard and painful periods. But there have also been periods of frank and fruitful collaboration and even moments of sincere friendship, which have not been overcome in conflict. We can find elements in describing this relationship in the account given by the Jesuit Paul Nywia (1925-1980) who grew up in northern Iraq, in a mixed Christian-Muslim village. Reflecting on his childhood, he remembered his first contacts with Muslims:

> Searching far back in my memory, I rediscovered my first impression of my contacts with Muslims. Those contacts were frequent, for many Muslim religious leaders used to visit my family. But despite the real friendship on which these relations were based, I had a strong feeling that, in the eyes of these Muslim friends, we were and remained *strangers*: people who because of their religion were fundamentally different. What awakened this feeling in me was the superior attitude which these friends adopted, an attitude that only their religion could justify. They regarded themselves as followers of the

Gude and David B Burrell, University of Notre Dame Press, Notre Dame, Indiana, 1994, p. 1.

4   J Aucagne SJ, 'L'Islam par rapport à l'unicité et à la division du peuple de Dieu', in J M Garriques, (ed.), *Approaches chrétiennes du Mystère d'Israël*, Criterion, Limoges, 1987, pp. 170-209.

5   Hugh Goddard, *A History of Christian-Muslim Relations*, Edinburgh University Press, Edinburgh, 2000; Ian Richard Netton, *Islam, Christianity and Tradition: A Comparative Exploration*, Edinburgh University Press, Edinburgh, 2000; Jacques Jomier OP, *How to Understand Islam*, SCM Press, London, 1989.

6   The Eastern Churches had early contact with the Muslim faith, and the theological reflection which emerged during this period still is essentially the 'canon' of Christian perspectives on Islam, see Sidney H Griffith, *The Church in the Shadow of the Mosque: Christians and Muslims in the World of Islam*, Princeton University Press, Princeton, 2007; 'The Eastern Christians and the Muslims: The Past as prelude to the present', *Bulletin of the Royal Institute for Inter-Faith Studies*, vol. 7, no. 2, 2005, pp. 225-241.

true religion and manifested this conviction with such self-satisfaction and such contempt for others that they were the living image of those whom the Gospel describes as men with pharisaical traits. Many of them were very brave and their attitude towards us was often only unconsciously superior, but we always remained strangers in relation to them. This fact did not bother them; on the contrary, it made them feel that they were all the more faithful to their religion.[7]

Even as a child, Nwyia was sensitive to the tensions between Christianity and Islam.[8] Not only is Islam different from Christianity; it sees itself as positively abrogating Christianity. Muhammad is the 'seal of prophets'; the revelation accorded to him supersedes all that came before.[9]

As Hugh Goddard has reminded us, the relationship between Christians and Muslims over the centuries is a long and tortuous one. Geographically the origins of the two communities are not so far apart—Bethlehem and Jerusalem are only some 800 miles from Mecca and Medina—but, as the two communities have grown and become universal rather than local influences, the relationship between them has sometimes been one of enmity, sometimes one of rivalry and competition, sometimes one of mutual influence, sometimes one of co-operation and collaboration.[10] Different regions of the world in different centuries have therefore witnessed a whole range of encounters between Christians and Muslims.

Since the earliest period in their history, the Islamic tradition has been conscious of the religious diversity of humanity and considered it an issue of importance. Muslim tradition maintains that diversity of religions has been

---

7   Paul Nwyia, 'Pour mieux connaître l'Islam', *Lumen vitae*, Vol. 30, 1975, pp. 159-171.
8   This response to Islam is found in a wide range of Christian thought. 'It is not a question whether Islam is judged with greater or lesser sympathy, but whether it is judged correctly or incorrectly', said Dr Hendrik Kraemer, the Dutch Reformed scholar of comparative religion, in a report on Indonesian missions written between the wars but re-published in 1958. See Norman Daniel, 'Some Recent Developments in the Attitude of Christians Towards Islam', *Re-Discovering Eastern Christendom*, (eds) A H Armstrong and E J B Fry, Darton, Longman and Todd, London, 1963, pp. 154-166, p. 155.
9   Jane Dammen McAuliffe, 'The Abrogation of Judaism and Christianity in Islam: A Christian Perspective', *Concilium*, no. 4, 1994, pp. 116-123.
10   Hugh Goddard has set out six dimensions of Christian-Muslim Relations—The Theological Dimension; The Philosophical Dimension; The Historical Dimension; The Social Dimension; The Political Dimension; The Cultural Dimension, in 'Christian-Muslim Relations: Yesterday, Today and Tomorrow', *International Journal for the Study of the Christian Church*, Vol. 3, no. 2, 2003, pp. 1-14.

the hallmark of human society for a very long time, but it had not been its primordial condition.[11]

Yohannan Friedman has reminded us that 'We can learn from this that according to the Islamic tradition Islam is not only the historical religion and institutional framework, which was brought into existence by the Muslim prophet Muhammad in the seventh century, but also the primordial religion of mankind, revealed to Adam at the time of his creation.'[12] For Muslims, Islam is not simply God's final revelation but also God's first.[13]

Christianity nevertheless has a significant, if negative, rôle in Muslim self-understanding. Muslim writers have always been quick to claim that Islam's abrogation of Christianity mirrors the Christian relationship with Judaism.[14] A Christian might respond that this is not a correct since Christianity does not understand itself as abrogating Judaism.[15] The Christian tradition continues to acknowledge Judaism as a source of its identity; it at least claims to be constantly revisiting Judaism, and it continues to use—in its own fashion—the Hebrew Scriptures. Islam, by contrast, sees itself as the restoration of what Judaism and Christianity would have been, had they not become corrupted *(tahrīf)*, especially with regard to their Scriptures.[16] This doctrine has supported an overall concept of Islam abrogating both Judaism and Christianity.[17] The concept of corruption, especially scriptural, is key to Muslim self-understanding and the Islamic tradition's relations with the religious Other.[18]

---

11   J Aucagne, 'L'Islam par rapport à l'unicité et à la division du people de Dieu', pp. 170-209.

12   Yohanan Friedmann, *Tolerance and Coercion in Islam: Interfaith Relations in the Muslim Tradition*, Cambridge University Press, Cambridge, 2003, p. 14.

13   Guy Monnot, 'L'ideé de religion et son evolution dans le Coran', in *The Notion of Religion in Comparative Research*, (ed.) Ugo Bianchi, L'Erma di Brettschneider, Rome, 1994, pp. 97-102.

14   For a Jewish scholar's view of the relationship between Judaism and Islam see, Hava Lazarus-Yafeh: 'Some differences between Judaism and Islam as Two Religions of Law', *Religion*, Vol. 14, 1984, pp. 175-191; H Lazarus-Yafeh: 'Jerusalem and Mecca' in *Jerusalem: Its Sanctity and Centrality to Judaism, Christianity and Islam*, (ed.) Lee I Levine, Continuum, New York, 1999, pp. 287-299.

15   Jane Dammen McAuliffe, 'The Abrogation of Judaism and Christianity in Islam', p. 119.

16   Frederick Mathewson Denny, 'Corruption', in *Encyclopedia of the Qur'an*, (ed.) Jane Dammen McAuliffe, E J Brill, Leiden, 2001, pp. 439-440. On the relationship between the Bible and the Qur'an see, Jane Dammen McAuliffe, 'Is there a connection between the Bible and the Qur'an', *Theology Digest*, Vol. 49, no. 4, 2002, pp. 303-317; and 'The Qur'anic Context of Muslim Biblical Scholarship', *Islam and Christian-Muslim Relations*, Vol. 7, 1996, pp. 141-158.

17   Jane Dammen McAuliffe, *Qur'anic Christians: An Analysis of Classical and Modern Exegesis*, Cambridge University Press, Cambridge, 1991.

18   The concept of misdeeds and corruption has a strong presence in modern Islamist

The Quranic presentation of Christianity can be subdivided into three themes—Jesus and Mary, Scripture, and the Christians. Christian practices (for example monasticism) and Christian doctrines (for example the Trinity), are also categories in the Muslim sacred text. On reading of the Quranic text, what constitutes a Quranic reference to Christians as a social (religious-communal) group ranges from the unequivocal to the ambiguous.[19]

Christian response to the assertion of abrogation *(naskh)* has been a straightforward rejection of the Islamic understanding of Christianity. Christian apologists have repeatedly insisted that the Quranic and post-Quranic assessment of Christian doctrine is flawed. The Quranic account of Jesus' crucifixion and death; the doctrine of the Incarnation; and the Christian understanding of God as Trinity[20] do not match with mainstream Christian self-understanding.[21] As Goddard has reminded us, 'The facts remain, however, that although some modern Christians, and indeed medieval Christians too, have suggested that the Quran is denying heretical Christian beliefs rather than mainline ones, Muslims have almost without exception taken the Quran to be denying mainstream Christian ideas too.'[22] In his study *The Muslim Jesus*, Tarif Khalidi has written, 'Jesus is a controversial prophet. He is the only prophet in the Qur'an who is deliberately made to distance himself from the doctrines that his community is said to hold of him.'[23]

thought. The equation between the misbehaviour of ancient Jews, particularly in Medina, and the Islamist description of the modern misbehaviour of 'Zionist Jews' in Palestine, Israel and Jerusalem has became an important paradigm for some. See Ronald L Nettler, 'Early Islam, Modern Islam and Judaism: The *Isra'iliyyat* in Modern Islamic Thought', *Muslim-Jewish Encounters Intellectual Traditions and Modern Politics*, (eds) Ronald L Nettler and Suha Taji-Farouki, Harwood Academic, Amsterdam, 1998, pp. 1-14.

19   David Marshall, 'Christianity in the Qur'an', *Islamic Interpretations of Christianity*, (ed.) Lloyd Ridgeon, Curzon, Richmond, 2001, pp. 3-29.

20   The Christian doctrine of one God in three persons is directly mentioned three times in the Qur'an. Muslim disregard for the Trinity is linked to the questioning of Christian belief in the humanity and divinity of Christ. Christians from an early age have questioned the description of the doctrine in Muslim sources and what is meant there. See David Thomas, 'Trinity', *Encyclopedia of the Qur'an*, 2006, pp. 368-372. See also Michael Ipgrave, *Trinity and Interfaith Dialogue: Plenitude and Plurality*, Peter Lang, Bern, 2003.

21   Jane Dammen McAuliffe, 'The Abrogation of Judaism and Christianity in Islam', p. 120.

22   H Goddard, *Muslim perceptions of Christianity*, Curzon, London, 1996, p. 16. Kate Zebiri has developed this idea: 'Most Western scholars regard the Qur'anic material on Christianity as reflecting or responding to the heterodox forms and divided state of Christianity in contemporary Arabia and the surrounding areas,' *Muslims and Christians Face to Face*, Oneworld, Oxford, 1997, p.16.

23   Tarif Khalidi, *The Muslim Jesus; Sayings and Stories in Islamic Literature*, Harvard University

Christian accounts of Islam vary, but they nevertheless generally draw attention to how Islam is expressive of a kind of natural law, given with the creation. Louis Massignon, who is considered by some the greatest modern influence on the Christian-Muslim encounter writes, for example, as follows:

> The goal of Qur'anic revelation is not to unveil and justify previously unknown supernatural gifts but, by calling back intelligent beings in the name of God, to make them rediscover the temporal and eternal laws—natural religion, primitive law, the simple worship that God has prescribed for all time—that Adam, Abraham and the prophets have always practised in the same way.[24]

Jacques Jomier, another great Christian Islamicist, complements this account

> Islam is a natural religion in which the religious instinct which is present in the heart of each person is protected by a way of life, with obligations and [religious] observances imposed in the name of One who is, for the Muslim, the [source of the] Qur'an revelation. It is a patriarchal religion, spiritually pre-dating the biblical promise made by God to Abraham, but which conserves the episodes of the life of the Patriarch involving his struggle against his fathers' idols and his voluntary submission to God, even his sacrifice of his own son. Islam re-presents Abraham (Father of the Prophets) as its great ancestor.[25]

As Charles Malik, a thinker in the Eastern Christian tradition has reflected, the historic break caused by Islam did not influence in the slightest the internal development of Christianity, one can study that development today as a completely autonomous whole, as though Islam did not exist. Christianity is wholly intelligible without any reference to Islam. By contrast, Islam is not so intelligible unless reference is made to Christianity. Historically and

---

Press, Cambridge, MA, 2001, p. 12.

24 Louis Massignon, *Examen du 'Présent de l'Homme Lettré' par Abdallah ibn Torjoman*, Pontifical Institute of Arabic and Islamic Studies, Rome, 1992 (following the French translation published in *Revue de l'Histoire des Religions*, 1886, Vol. XII), with a preface by Daniel Massignon, introduction by Père Henri Cazelles and observations by Père Albert (M J) Lagrange, Collection 'Studi arabo-islamic del PISAI', No. 5, PISAI, Rome, 1992. For the wider context for Massignon's thought see S H Griffiths: 'Sharing the Faith of Abraham: the "Credo" of Louis Massignon', *Islam and Christian-Muslim Relations*, Vol. 8, no. 2, 1997, pp. 193-210.

25 Jacques Jomier, 'Le Coran et la Liturgie dans l'Islam', *La Maison-Dieu*, 190 (1992), pp. 121-127, here p. 121.

theologically, however, Christianity inevitably challenges and disturbs Islam; and Islam inevitably challenges and disturbs Christianity. Neither religion can ignore the other, happy in its own conviction and simplicity.[26]

According to Malik the Christian is disturbed and challenged by the Islamic refutation of Christianity: that the Trinity is *shirk* (polytheistic blasphemy); that the crucifixion was only an apparition; that the stories about Christ and his mother in the Qur'an are the authentic ones, rather than those in the four Gospels. Similarly, a Muslim must be disturbed by what Christianity at least implies about Islam: that Christianity has not in fact been abrogated by Islam; that God became flesh in Jesus of Nazareth without ceasing to be God; that this same Jesus actually died and rose from the dead on the third day; that the Church, as a distinct historic body, makes absolute claims about itself. And this mutuality of disturbance is not confined to the order of theory: it expresses itself in the growth of distinct historic communities, with conflicting norms, laws and *mores*.

For Malik, the central question is whether the Word of God is literally a word, or rather a living person. On this issue, Christianity and Islam diverge, and all the other differences relate to this one. Whatever affinities between Christianity and Islam there may be, arising from their common links with Abraham, this question about the nature of revelation remains. Thus according to Malik any dialogue which avoids it remains sentimental and superficial. The Qur'an has the highest respect for Christ and his mother, *Nostra Aetate* has reminded us of this, and speaks of him as a Word of God; nevertheless, the authoritative Muslim doctrine is that *the* Word of God is the Qur'an itself. The Muslim claim that Islam constitutes 'the essence of truth and religion' implies a sharp judgment on other religions. It is saying, for instance, that Christianity's true essence is found in Islam—'But if that is so, then normal Christians ought to find themselves wholly at home in Islam. This is manifestly not the case.' [27]

Paul Nwyia may have sensed the conflict between Islam and Christianity even as a child. But he was also aware, even then, that a Christian could not rest content with this situation. The passage quoted at the beginning continues as follows:

---

26 Charles Malik, 'Introduction', *God and Man in Contemporary Islamic Thought*, (ed.) C Malik, American University of Beirut, Beirut, 1972, p. 90. Charles Malik: Greek Orthodox of the Patriarchate of Antioch; Professor of Philosophy at the American University of Beirut; Lebanon's Minister and Ambassador to the United States, 1945-55; Rapporteur of the Commission on Human Rights at the United Nations; three times President of the Security Council and President of the General Assembly.

27 *Ibid.*, p. 91-92.

One could easily have been tempted to react like them, to regard
them as 'strangers' to transform the difference into indifference,
or to meet their contempt with even deeper scorn. But this is
precisely what my faith forbade me to do. To react thus would
have meant doing away with the difference and, by that very fact,
disowning my Christian identity. Hence I came to ask myself:
'How can I turn these strangers into the *neighbours* of which
the Gospel speaks? How can I resist the temptation to react as
they do, so that my way of seeing them may be different from
the way they look upon me?' I understood that to achieve this
I would have to discover, beyond the image they projected of
themselves, certain things in them or in their religion which
could help me regard them as neighbours whom one must love.

This quest for understanding and for the love of neighbour led Nwyia to
study and reflect on Islam throughout his life until his tragic death in 1980.[28]
Trained in France by Louis Massignon, Nywia became a widely renowned
and celebrated scholar in the field of Islamic mysticism. His contributions
included an edition of letters on spiritual direction by Ibn 'Abbad of Ronda,
who was chiefly responsible for putting forward an understanding of Sufism
as a spirituality available to all who put their trust in God. He also wrote
on Islamic mysticism and Christianity, with special reference to the *Spiritual
Exercises* of Ignatius of Loyola, and on the monastic character of early Muslim
spiritual life.[29]

Nwyia reflected on the different ways in which Islam characterized the
religious other, and what these revealed about Muslim self-understanding. For
Nwyia, Islam's relations with other faiths are shaped by the tension between
two antagonistic principles: mutabilities and immutability, between the diverse,
changing forms in which religious commitment is lived on the one hand, and
the unchangingness of 'Allah' on the other. This tension has been operative
since Islam began; it reflects the complex attitude of Muhammad towards the

---

28 Nywia's theme here 'Love of Neighbour' is an important element in the Muslim
document: '"A Common Word Between Us and You", An Open Letter and Call
from Muslim Religious Leaders to His Holiness Pope Benedict XVI and Other Major
Christian Leaders', 13 October 2007.

29 Among his numerous academic studies see, 'Ibn 'Abbad de Ronda et Jean de la Croix:
à propos d'une hypothèse d'Asin Palacios', *Al-Andalus*, 22 (1957), pp. 113-130; *Ibn-
'Abbad de Ronda (1332-1390): un mystique prédicateur à la Qarawiyin de Fès*, Imprimerie
catholique, Beirut, 1961; *Exégèse coranique et langage mystique: nouvel essai sur le lexique
technique des mystiques musulmans*, Dar el-Machreq, Beirut, 1970.

religious other: polytheists, Jews and Christians. Islam is faced with a crucial dilemma of how to find 'the synthesis between historical and spiritual truth'.[30]

Within the Qu'ran, there are also discussions of how Muslims should relate to Christianity. According to the Anglican Islamicist Kenneth Cragg these vary in tone from unequivocal rejection to ambivalent co-existence. We find warnings to Muslims not to make friends with Christians, as well as more positive calls for interreligious understanding. A dictum in the Qu'ran placed on Muhammad's lips, 'to you your religion and to me mine' (109:6), can be interpreted in both these ways. It might suggest a gentle tolerance, honouring the diversities of culture and experience. Alternatively, it could be taken as expressing an exasperated weariness with how the differences in belief and ritual can never be resolved.[31]

Christianity's encounter with Judaism following the *Shoah* raises questions touching very deeply on the core identity of the Christian. Similar questions arise from its encounter with Islam, particularly as regards mission. The Jesuits Henri Sanson and Christian Troll, have suggested that Christians should reflect on their missionary vocation towards Muslims 'in the mirror of Islam'. This means that we should take into account at every step the fact that our Muslim partners are convinced in faith that they have a missionary vocation towards us, that they too are called, individually and collectively, to witness to the Truth. Only in this light can we discern with any sensitivity what a Christian missionary vocation towards Islam might amount to, and how it might appropriately be lived out.[32]

30 Paul Nwyia, 'Mutabilités et immutabilité en Islam', *Recherches de sciences religieuses*, Vol. 63, 1975, pp. 197-213.
31 Kenneth Cragg, 'Islam and Other Faiths', *Studia missionalia*, Vol. 42, 1993, pp. 257-270, here p. 257.
32 Henri Sanson: *Dialogue intérieur avec l'Islam*, Centurion, Paris, 1990; Christian W Troll, 'Witness Meets Witness: The Church's Mission in the Context of the Worldwide Encounter of Christian and Muslim Believers Today', *Vidyajyoti Journal of Theological Reflection*, 62/3 (March 1998), pp. 152-171, reprinted in *Encounters*, 4/1 (March 1998), pp. 15-34.

CHRISTIAN THEOLOGICAL PERSPECTIVES ON ISLAM:
THE SECOND VATICAN COUNCIL

One of the most important elements of Christian reflection on Islam in contemporary times has been a need to speak on Christian-Muslim relations with the highest level of authority or 'magisterium'. The Roman Catholic Church was the first to undertake this ecclesial reflection. In creating this leading 'original', this 'ecclesial-turn' in the Christian encounter with Islam,[33] other Christian Churches have acknowledged *Nostra Aetate*, as a common document, or fashioned their own based upon this originating theological position.[34] This desire to locate the precise point of authority for interreligious relations has had a profound impact upon all religious traditions in the modern world. We have recently seen the Muslim community seek to respond to endeavours of the Second Vatican Council, John Paul II and Benedict XVI to engage with Islam by setting out its own response, in the form of what one might call a Muslim *Nostra Aetate*—'*"A Common Word Between Us and You", An Open Letter and Call from Muslim Religious Leaders to His Holiness Pope Benedict XVI and Other Major Christian Leaders'* ,13 October 2007.

---

33   'Always be ready to make a defence to anyone who asks for a reason for the hope that is in you, and make it with modesty and respect' [1 Peter 3: 15b-16a]. Since the Middle Ages, this biblical text has been considered to state the fundamental charge given to the theologian. One could say that four fundamental features of theology thus appear: it is an articulation of the ground of one's hope; it arises as a response to questions about the way Christians live their lives; the norm for that hope and practice in Jesus Christ; and reasons may be given for that hopeful practice, whether those addressed are fellow Christians or others. Taking the text of First Peter as a fundamental challenge, theology may be conceived thus as a mediation of the Christian gospel within a cultural context. Addressing two not entirely distinct audiences, those who have already accepted the gospel and those who have not, theology faces two tasks, one primarily *ecclesial* and the other primarily cultural. How these tasks are conceived and interrelated is a basic question for the conception of theology. For most of the Catholic tradition both dimensions and roles of theology have been visible. See Joseph A Komonchak, 'Defending Our Hope: On the Fundamental Tasks of Theology', *Faithful Witness: Foundations of Theology for Today's Church*, (eds) Leo J O'Donovan and T Howland Sanks, Geoffrey Chapman, London, 1989, pp. 14-26.
34   See Christian Troll, 'Catholic Teachings on Interreligious Dialogue. Analysis of some recent official documents with special reference to Christian-Muslim relations', *Muslim-Christian Perceptions of Dialogue Today: Experiences and Expectations*, (ed.) Jacques Waardenburg, Peeters, Leuven, 2000, pp. 233-276.

On 20 October 1965, the Second Vatican Council[35] (October 1962-December 1965), after many long discussions and emendations of the original text, promulgated a declaration on the relations of the Church with non-Christian religion. Of Vatican II's sixteen promulgated statements, a total number of one hundred thousand words, by the far the shortest is the 'Declaration on the Relation of the Church to Non-Christian Religions', also known by the first words of the Latin text, *Nostra Aetate*. Thomas Stransky has characterized *Nostra Aetate* as follows:

> It began with an introduction to the objective unity of the human family, a unity of origin, pilgrimage and ultimate destiny that is reflected in universal questions seeking, 'answers to the profound riddles of the human condition'. This was followed by sections on various religious (Primitive, Hinduism, Buddhism), on Islam and on Judaism. The schema concluded with a condemnation of every kind of discrimination and harassment because of race, colour, condition of life or religion.[36]

In short, the Catholic Church spoke to the whole of humanity, not as 'believers or non-believers', but on the basis of our common humanity.

A part of the declaration was dedicated to Islam, marking the first time in history that the Roman Catholic Magisterium had formulated an official position toward Islam as a major religion.[37] The texts of Vatican II concerning Islam consist of a single sentence in the Dogmatic Constitution on the Church, *Lumen Gentium*, and a full paragraph in the Declaration on the Relations of the Church with Non-Christian Religions, *Nostra Aetate*. Several fundamental theological principles are said to be underlying the Church's approach to other

---

35 The Second Vatican Council was one of the most significant events in the history of the modern Roman Catholic Church, which, after centuries, gathered all its bishops together from across the world to discuss and implement reforms and chart new directions for the church. The Second Vatican Council, especially the document *Nostra Aetate*, has been of great influence on other Christian denominations.

36 Thomas Stransky, 'The Genesis of *Nostra Aetate*', *America*, 24 October, 2005, pp. 8-12, p. 8. See also, Michael L Fitzgerald and John Borelli, *Interfaith dialogue: A Catholic View*, Orbis Books, Maryknoll, New York, 2006. For a commentary on *Nostra Aetate*, see G M-M Cottier, 'L'Historique de la déclaration', *Vatican II. Les relations de l'Église avec les religions non-chrétiennes*, Collection Unam Sanctam, Éditions du Cerf, Paris, 1966, pp. 37-78.

37 For the commentary on the text concerning Islam, cf. R Caspar, 'La religion musulmane', *Vatican II. Les relations de l'Église avec les religions non-chrétiennes*, Collection Unam Sanctam, Éditions du Cerf, Paris, 1966, pp. 201-36; Guy Harpigny, 'L'Islam aux yeux de la théologie catholique', *Aspects de la foi de l'Islam*, Publications des Facultés universitaires Saint-Louis, Bruxelles, Vol. 36, 1985, pp. 199- 235.

religions: the universality of God's salvific will and the sacramental nature of the Church; and a third principle, lying between these two and connecting them, namely the necessary mediation of Jesus Christ.

During the second session of the Council, when the project of a text about Judaism was presented, the Catholic Eastern patriarchs and bishops living in Muslim countries asked for 'balance', in other words, that justice should be done not only to the reality of Judaism but also to Islam. Hence the origins of *Nostra Aetate* are complex and still an open historical question. John XXIII died on 3 June 1963 and was succeeded by the Archbishop of Milan, Giovanni Battista Montini as Paul VI.[38] The new pope had for a long time expressed an interest in ameliorating relations between Catholics and Jews; however it was his predecessor who in 1960 gave the task of preparing an initial document on Judaism to Augustin Cardinal Bea. Bea was a German Jesuit who had been at one time the rector of the Pontifical Biblical Institute and also the confessor of Pope Pius XII, and so a commission under the Secretariat for Unity was set up specifically to deal with this sensitive subject.

Other Council members brought up the point that if the question of the Church's relationship to Judaism was taken up then its relationship with other non-Christian religions should necessarily be discussed as well. It was clear that a definite impasse was arising between those who believed that the Jewish religion should have a unique position in a document all by itself and those who regarded a treatment of Judaism in an official conciliar document as inopportune and detrimental to the apostolate and presence of the Church in the Muslim world.[39] Between the founding of the commission to draft a document in 1960 and its completion as a separate conciliar decree in 1964, there was a constant struggle not just over the details of the document but also over its very existence. When it finally appeared and was approved in November 1964, significantly after Paul VI's pilgrimage to Jerusalem in January 1964, it included not only material on the Church's relationship with Judaism but also, albeit much shorter, sections on the Church's relationship to Islam and two other major world religions, Buddhism and Hinduism.[40]

---

38   Michel Lelong, 'Paul VI', in *Les papes et l'Islam*, Éditions Alphée, Monaco, 2009, pp. 39-58.

39   Recognizing the sensitivity of this issue, in his presentation of the text of *Nostra Aetate* to the general congregation on 25 September 1964, Cardinal Bea made a specific disclaimer that the sections of the document on Judaism were entirely of a religious and not a political nature. See *Council Daybook: Vatican II, Session 3*, (ed.) F Anderson, National Catholic Welfare Conference, Washington, 1965, pp. 62-63.

40   See the following studies on the legacy of *Nostra Aetate*: John McDade, 'Catholic Christianity and Judaism since Vatican II'; A O'Mahony, 'Catholic Theological

However, it would be too negative an evaluation to suggest that *Nostra Aetate* emerged solely in relation to a controversy over a document on the Catholic Church's relationship with Judaism. The theology which informed and grounded the conciliar document had been developing in the mind of Catholic thinkers for some decades, especially in such groups as the Cercle du Saint Jean-Bapiste and in the thought of Louis Massignon, Jean Daniélou SJ, and Jules Monchanin.[41]

It is well to record here, that the Council's concern with Islam arose incidentally, out of a desire for a declaration concerning the Jewish people. There was no intention of providing a full discussion of Islamic beliefs and practices, nor for that matter, of those of any other religion. Thus it has often been commented that the Second Vatican Council spoke about Muslims but not about Islam. This is true, insofar as the Council did not intend to give a full description of Islam, entering into a comprehensive theological assessment of the tradition; for that the Council left open for a future consideration of the Church.

Muslim belief as presented in Lumen Gentium

The demand for the inclusion of Islam in the conciliar documents resulted in two relatively short but important and decisive texts. Although they are primarily concerned with the Catholics' practical attitude towards Muslims, they imply elements of a fresh Christian theological view of Islam. §16 of the 'Dogmatic constitution on the Church' *Lumen Gentium* declares:

> But the plan of salvation also embraces those who acknowledge the Creator, and among these the Muslims are first; they profess to hold the faith of Abraham and along with us they worship the one merciful God who will judge humanity on the last day.[42]

Perspectives on Islam at the Second Vatican Council'; Michael Barnes, 'Expanding Catholocity: the Dialogue with Buddhism'; Martin Ganeri, 'Catholic Encounter with Hindus in the Twentieth Century'; *New Blackfriars*, Vol. 87, no. 1016, 2007, pp. 367-432.
41 See the important studies by Françoise Jacquin, 'L'abbé Monchanin et l'Islam', *Islamochristiana* (Rome), Vol. 23, 1997, pp, 27-42; 'Louis Massignon et l'abbé Monchanin', *La vie spirituelle*, no 694, 1991, pp, 175-183; *Histoire du Cercle Saint Jean-Bapiste. L'enseignement du père Daniélou*, Éditions Beauchesne, Paris, 1987. See also Michel Lelong, 'De la chrétienté médiévale au concile Vatican II', pp. 11-38.
42 Norman Tanner, *Decrees of the Ecumenical Councils*, Sheed, London/Georgetown, Washington, 1990, see vol. 2, p. 861. Some Islamic opinion objects to the statement of *Lumen Gentium*—'with us they worship the one merciful God'; as there are Muslims who counter the Christian claim to monotheism. The origins of this might be that the Qur'an

The study of the proceedings of the Council makes it clear that it did not want to state an objective link between Islam, Ishmael and the Biblical revelation. The reference to Abraham is put on the subjective level: 'they profess ...'[43]

Some decades before the Council there were influential currents in Catholic thought which attempted to reconcile Islam and Abraham in Christian theology. Louis Massignon (1883-1962), Islamicist, Catholic priest of the Greek Catholic Melkite Church and mystic who, having recovered his own Christian faith through contact with Islam, devoted his life to presenting the faith of Islam to the West. He was no theologian and never systematized his thought but presented it in flashes of an intuitive nature.[44] His position has been summarized as:

> Islam, according to Massignon, is the heir of Hagar and Ishmael, the 'excluded', driven into the desert but enjoying a special blessing (Gen. 16:11-20; 21:17-20; 25:12-18). Muhammad receives this blessing of Ishmael 'at the providential and symbolic hour': exiled from his homeland, Mecca, like Abraham from Ur and Ishmael driven into the desert, he claims inheritance of Abraham against Israel (the Jewish people) unfaithful to their Covenant and against the Christians unfaithful to Jesus.[45]

---

contains a reference to a Trinity consisting God, Jesus and Mary (Q 5:116). Christians may reply that the Qur'an is denying a false Trinity; but they will still be considered by some Muslims to be *mushrikūn* (associators), *kāfirūn* (unbelievers). This critique has roots in early Islam, where the question of the unity or diversity of the polytheistic world is discussed; see Yohanan Friedmann, *Tolerance and Coercion in Islam: Interfaith Relations in the Muslim Tradition*, pp. 76-80.

43 Christian Troll, 'Changing Catholic Views of Islam', *Islam and Christianity* ..., pp. 23-27.

44 A O'Mahony, '"Our Common Fidelity to Abraham is What Divides": Christianity and Islam in the Life and Thought of Louis Massignon', *Catholics in Interreligious Dialogue: Studies in Monasticism, Theology and Spirituality*, (eds) A O'Mahony and Peter Bowe, Gracewing, Leominister, 2006, pp. 151-190; A O'Mahony, 'The Influence of the Life and Thought of Louis Massignon on the Catholic Church's Relations with Islam', *The Downside Review*, [Special issue on 'Catholic Encounters with Islam'], Vol. 126, no. 444, 2008, pp. 169-192.

45 Robert Caspar, *A Historical Introduction to Islamic Theology*, Pontifico Istituto di Studi Arabi e d'Islamistica, Rome, 1998, p. 97. See also Sidney H Griffith, 'Sharing the Faith of Abraham: the "Credo" of Louis Massignon', *Islam and Muslim-Christian Relations*, Vol.8, no. 2, 1997, pp. 193-210. Massignon's influence has been felt widely in Catholic circles. See S H Griffiths, 'Thomas Merton, Louis Massignon and the Challenge of Islam', in *The Merton Annual: Studies in Thomas Merton, Religion, Culture, Literature and Social Concerns*, Vol. 3, 1990, pp. 151-172; Agnes Wilkins, 'Louis Massignon, Thomas Merton and Mary Kahil', *Aram: Society for Syro-Mesopotamian Studies*, Vol. 20 (2008) pp. 355-373.

Islam's role is thus, as it were, to goad Jews and Christians to return to the correct understanding of their own religions. It could be considered almost as an:

> Abrahamic schism, prior to the Ten Commandments, the foundation of Judaism and to Pentecost, the foundation of Christianity.[46]

According to Louis Massignon's 'theological' vision, Muhammad possessed the faith of Abraham, he did not experience mystic union, for the night when he was transported from Mecca to Jerusalem and thence to heaven he stopped short of the 'Lotus of the Limit' (Q 17:1; 53:9-17). By abstaining from crossing the threshold and not daring to intercede for all sinners, he excluded himself from understanding the inner workings of the divine life. Hence the Quranic denials of the Incarnation and Christ's death on the cross. Muslim faith, although authentic, therefore needs to be completed by Christian charity. Nevertheless, in Massignon's view, it is evident from the lives of Muslim saints that the Holy Spirit is at work bringing about this completion from within Islam. This is nowhere more apparent than in the case of al-Hallāj.[47] Massignon maintains that al-Hallāj's death, in ecstatic participation in the Christ, summons Islam to admit the truth of the crucifixion. The rift between the three faiths, Judaism, Christianity and Islam, will not finally be healed until Christ returns and, as Muslims themselves believe, Jerusalem once more becomes the direction of prayer (initially the *qiblah* oriented the faithful towards Jerusalem). In the meantime, the Qur'an may be regarded as a truncated Arab Bible, the scriptural rule of the 'Abrahamic schism', and given the conditional authority conceded to the decisions of the anti-popes.[48]

Massignon, who died on the eve of the opening of the Second Vatican Council, certainly helped to bring about a new vision of Islam in Catholic circles, though his own position was not adopted by the conciliar texts.[49]

---

46 Robert Caspar, *A Historical Introduction to Islamic Theology*, Pontifico Istituto di Studi Arabi e d'Islamistica, Rome, 1998, p. 98.

47 Al-Hallāj was executed in Baghdad in 922 having scandalized the authorities by claiming to have achieved union with God and uttering the words *anā' l-Ḥaqq* ['I am the Truth']. He went to the gibbet willingly, declaring God's love to the last. Massignon set out in his classic work to prove beyond reasonable doubt not only that al-Hallāj was innocent of heresy, but also that his miracles and mystical experiences were as well-documented as those of any Christian saint. The second edition was translated into English by Herbert Mason, *The Passion of al-Hallāj: Mystic and Martyr of Islam*, Bollingen Series XCVIII, Princeton University Press, Princeton, 1982, 4 Vols.

48 Neal Robinson, 'Massignon, Vatican II and Islam as an Abrahamic Religion', *Islam and Christian-Muslim Relations*, Vol. 2, no. 2, 1991, pp. 182-205.

49 Andrew Unsworth, 'Louis Massignon, The Holy See and the Ecclesial Transition from

The figure of Abraham is a difficult figure in the encounter for Christianity and Islam.[50] Some two hundred and forty-five verses in twenty-five sūras of the Qur'an make reference to Abraham (Ibrāhīm), the 'progenitor of the nation of Israel'. Among the Biblical figures, only Moses[51] receives more attention in the Qur'an. Abraham and Moses are the sole prophets explicitly identified as bearers of scriptures (Q. 53:36-7; 87:18-9). Although, according to Reuven Firestone, the Islamic Abraham shares many characteristics with the figure in the Bible and later Jewish exegetical literature, the Qur'an especially emphasizes his rôle as a precursor of Muhammad and the establisher of the pilgrimage rites in Mecca.[52]

For Jews, Abraham's special covenantal relationship with God established him as 'the authenticator and founder of Judaism'. It was natural that when Christianity established itself as related but independent of Judaism, Christians would associate with the figure of Abraham (Rom. 4:9-25; 9:7-9; Gal. 4:21-31).[53] Similarly, Abraham's role in the Qur'an includes a related but more polemical aspect, as he appears as neither a Jew nor a Christian but as a *ḥanīf muslim* (Q 3:65-70). Like the New Testament citations, the Qur'an stipulates that the divine covenant established with Abraham does not automatically include all his progeny (Q 2:124; 4:54-5; 37:113; 57:26). In as much as the religion of Muhammad is the religion of Abraham (Q 22:78), those Jews who reject Muhammad and the religion he brings are, in fact, rejecting their own religion. The Jews further deny the religious sanctity of Mecca, despite Abraham's intimate association with it (Q 3:95-8) as outlined in the Islamic tradition.

"Immortale Dei" to *"Nostra Aetate"*: A Brief History of the Development of Catholic Church Teaching on Muslims and the Religion of Islam from 1883-1965', *Aram: Society for Syro-Mesopotamian Studies*, Vol. 20. (2008) pp. 299-316.

50 Y Moubarac, 'Abraham en Islam', *Cahiers Sioniens: 'Abraham, père des croyants'*, Vol. V, no. 2, 1951, pp. 104-120.

51 Y Moubarac, 'Moïses dans le Coran', *Cahiers Sioniens, 'Moïses, l'homme de l'alliance'*, Vol. 8, no. 2-3-4, 1954, pp. 373-393.

52 One series of Abrahamic references in the Qur'an finds no parallel in either the Bible or later Jewish traditions. These associate Abraham, and often Ishmael, with the building of the Kaʻba, with Arabian cultic practice and with terminology of Islamic religious conceptions. I am indebted to the account given by Reuven Firestone, 'Abraham', *Encyclopedia of the Qur'an*, Vol. 1, pp. 5-11; 'Abraham's association with the Meccan sanctuary and the pilgrimage in the pre-Islamic and early Islamic periods', *Le Muséon*, Vol. 104, 1991, pp. 365-393; *Journeys in Holy Lands: The evolution of the Abramic-Ishmael Legends*, State University of New York Press, Albany, 1990.

53 Jean Daniélou, 'Abraham dans la tradition chrétienne', *Cahiers sioniens: 'Abraham, père des croyants'*, Vol. V, no. 2, 1951, pp. 69-87.

Abraham in Islam also has a defining rôle in the abrogation *(naskh)* of Judaism and Christianity. For Yohanan Friedmann this is intimately related to the notion that Abraham/Ibrāhīm was a Muslim in a metahistorical sense. At some point Judaism and Christianity deviated from their pristine condition and became hopelessly corrupt *(taḥrīf)*, especially in the scriptural transmission. A prophetic mission would have been required to ameliorate this situation—no prophets were sent to accomplish this task between Jesus and Muhammad and, consequently, true religion ceased to exist. Only with the emergence of Islam in the seventh century was the situation transformed.[54]

Thus throughout the centuries since the rise of Islam, Muslim/Christian relations have revolved around this double axis of familiar, Biblical appeal and strenuous, religious critique. It was against this background that the Second Vatican Council sought to give account of Islam.

Both texts of Vatican II link Islamic faith with Abraham. *Lumen Gentium* says that Muslims 'profess to hold the faith of Abraham'. *Nostra Aetate* states that Muslims submit to God 'just as Abraham submitted himself to God's plan, to whose faith Muslims eagerly link their own.' It must be admitted that these references to Abraham remain somewhat vague. Abraham's faith is recognized, but it is not said how he exemplified this faith. Muslims see Abraham as a champion of monotheism and attribute to him the rebuilding of the Ka'ba, the shrine in Mecca that has become the direction of Muslims' prayer. Christians insist on Abraham's response to God's call to leave his country for a promised land. By both religions Abraham is given as a model of submission to God's mysterious decrees. There is silence above all on the question of descent from Abraham. Quite apart from the historical question of the descent of the Arabs from Abraham through Ishmael, a question which remains disputed, the silence on this point is quite consistent with the Christian position with regard to Abraham. Physical descent is unimportant; it is faith that counts.[55] As long as there is a readiness to respect the different interpretations, the figure of Abraham provides common ground, albeit limited, for the followers of Judaism, Christianity and Islam.[56]

54   Friedmann, *Tolerance and Coercion in Islam,* p. 16.
55   On Abraham, see, R Caspar, 'Abraham in Islam and Christianity', *Encounter: documents for Christian-Muslim understanding,* no. 92, 1996, pp. 1-17; Jean-Louis Ska, 'Abraham dans le Coran ou le prototype du, "musulman"', *Abraham et ses hôtes. Le patriarche et les croyants au Dieu unique,* Éditions Lessius, Bruxelles, 2001, pp. 61-84.
56   Michael L Fitzgerald, 'From Heresy to Religion: Islam since Vatican II', *Encounter: documents for Christian-Muslim understanding,* no. 296, 2003, pp. 1-13.

Islam in the conciliar declaration Nostra Aetate

The second text of the Council which refers to Islam is longer and more substantial. It constitutes §3 of the 'Declaration of the Church's relation to the non-Christian religions' *Nostra Aetate*, in which were put together the schemata about Judaism, Islam and the other religions. The declaration begins with the assurance that the Catholic Church regards her Muslim brothers 'with esteem'. It proceeds to detail the essential elements of Islamic doctrine, stressing those features that are common to the two religions; for example, Muslims are conceded to 'adore the one God, living and enduring, merciful and all-powerful, Maker of heaven and earth'. Further, without actually accepting the revealed character of the Qur'an, the declaration observes that Muslims recognize that God 'has spoken to men', and affirms that Muslims are anxious to submit themselves with all their souls to God's decrees even though the decrees be hidden, just as Abraham, 'with whom the Muslim faith is pleased to associate itself,' submitted himself to them.[57]

A radical divergence, however, is the person of Jesus: 'Though they [Muslims] do revere Him as a prophet.' Reference is made to the exalted place occupied by Mary in Muslim doctrine: 'They also honour Mary, his virgin mother; at times they call on her, too, with devotion.' Concerning the last things, eschatology: 'Muslims await the day of judgment when God will give each man his due after raising him up'. A brief allusion is made to Muslim morality: 'They prize the moral life and give worship to God especially through prayer, almsgiving, and fasting.' The radical novelty of the declaration is obvious.

The Council document states in full:

> The Church also looks upon Muslims with respect. They worship the one God living and subsistent, merciful and almighty, creator of heaven and earth, who has spoken to humanity and to whose decrees, even the hidden ones, they seek to submit themselves whole-heartedly, just as Abraham, to whom the Islamic faith readily relates itself, submitted to God. They venerate Jesus as a prophet, even though they do not acknowledge him as God, and they honour his virgin mother Mary and even sometimes devoutly call upon her. Furthermore they await the day of judgement when God will require all

---

57   See Jacques Jomier's profound meditation, *Dieu et l'homme dans le Coran: L'aspect religieux de la nature humaine joint à l'obéissance au Prophète de l'Islam*, Cerf, Paris, 1996, a further reflection of the intuitions found in Islam.

people brought back to life. Hence they have regard for the moral life and worship God especially in prayer, almsgiving and fasting.[58]

Two characteristics of this text are immediately evident: first, it highlights the common or related points between Islam and Christianity, noting at the same time the essential difference: the Christian profession of the divinity of Jesus. Second, it opens up the possibility of collaboration between the two religions, at the service of the most pressing needs of contemporary humanity.[59]

The opening sentence of the paragraph constitutes a unique statement and an absolutely new beginning insofar as it is an official declaration about Islam issued by the highest teaching authority of the Church.[60] John Paul II[61] took up this theme on 19 August 1986, when addressing young Moroccans gathered in the Casablanca stadium, he did not hesitate to tell them: 'We believe in the same God, the one God, the living God, the God who creates the worlds and brings the worlds to their perfection.'[62] This is an indubitable affirmation of the existence of one and the same creator God. But one also has to add that Christians and Muslims who worship the same God have very different conceptions of God's unity. One could even say that the monotheism, which is a common heritage of all children of Abraham, has at the same time divided them for centuries.[63]

One would do well to listen to the warning of Roger Arnaldez:

> Hence, the problem of the diverse messages stubbornly remains. There is no way of reducing it to a common core so long as we situate ourselves within one of the three religious families [Judaism, Christianity, Islam]. One must be Jewish, Christian, or Muslim, adhering to a faith that excludes the other two. If we want to extract some monotheism-in-itself, a monotheistic

---

58   Norman Tanner, *Decrees of the Ecumenical Councils*, pp. 969-970.
59   Robert Caspar, *Traité de Théologie Musulamne*, Pontifico Istituto di Studi Arabi e d'Islamistica, Rome, 1987, pp. 83-87.
60   This analysis owes much to Christian Troll, 'Changing Catholic Views of Islam', *Islam and Christianity* ..., pp. 23-27.
61   Andrew Unsworth, 'John Paul II, Islam and the Christian-Muslim Encounter', in (eds) A O'Mahony, Wulstan Peterburs and Mohammed Shomali, *Catholic-Shi'a Engagement: Faith and Reason in Theory and Practice*, Melisende, London, 2006, pp. 200-249.
62   'The Speech of the Holy Father John Paul II to Young Muslims, Casablanca, Morocco, 19 August 1985', *Encounter: documents for Christian-Muslim understanding*, no. 128, 1986, pp. 1-12. See also Claude Geffre, 'The One God of Islam and Trinitarian Monotheism', *Concilium,* 2001, no1, pp. 85-93.
63   Roger Arnaldez, *Three Messengers for One God*, 1994, p. 3.

theology or morality as such, we must simultaneously depart from the three monotheistic religions and place ourselves outside or above them. To put it most forcefully, we would have to neglect the particularities of their messages, ignore the characteristics of each, and repress the very notion of a Messenger.

Muslims cannot accept Christian monotheism as Trinitarian monotheism, and that is a direct consequence of their rejection of the divine Sonship of Jesus.[64] So we should remember how, by its radical nature, Islamic monotheism differs from Christian monotheism, and note that in Muslim eyes the sin par excellence, that of idolatry, is committed not only by pagan polytheists but also by Christians themselves.[65]

Muslims and Christians, whilst they adore together the one God, they do not always give him the same 'names', nor do they give the same meaning to apparently similar 'names'. Therefore the Council mentions explicitly some of these 'names', those especially important to Islam, mentioned repeatedly in the Qur'an, and common to both religions. An annotation to the text of the Council refers to the letter of Pope Gregory VII to al-Nasir, the eleventh-century amir of Mauritania, where the Pope greets the ruler as his 'brother in Abraham' and as a believer in God, One and Creator.[66]

Although the Council refused to add 'through the prophets' to the phrase 'who has spoken to humanity',[67] because of the ambiguity of the reference to the prophets, who are not always the same, do not always have the same 'face' nor play the same role,[68] in Islam and Christianity. This phrase is of

---

64   Robert L Fastiggi, 'The Incarnation: Muslim objections and the Christian response', *The Thomist*, Vol. 57, 1993, pp. 457-493.

65   Robert Caspar, 'The Permanent Significance of Islam's Monotheism', *Concilium*, no. 177, 1985, pp. 67-78.

66   The letter was written in AD 1076. See C Courtois, 'Grégoire VII et l'Afrique du Nord', in *Revue Historique*, CXCV (1945), pp. 97-122; 193-226.

67   In Islamic tradition the Qur'an teaches that prophets have been sent by God to all peoples giving the same guidance and warning. As a result, all the prophets recognized in the Qur'an are accorded equal status. Muhammad is regarded as the 'Seal of the Prophets' because Muslims believe that his teaching has been preserved without corruption. He is given the title *rasūl* or 'the one whom God sends' and this reflects the Muslim belief that the scriptures were given to him as a universal revelation. Every community has received a *rasūl*, but Muhammad was sent to a people who had not previously received one. Muslims regard a *rasūl* (prophets such as Noah, Moses or Jesus) as being free from sin. See Jacques Jomier, 'The Idea of the Prophet in Islam', *Bulletin: Secretariatus pro non-Christianis* (Rome), no. 18, 1971, pp. 149-163.

68   One of the essential differences between Islam and Christianity is that of their understanding of the revelation from God and, therefore, a major difficulty in Christian-Muslim dialogue is the fact that while Muslims accept Jesus as a genuine prophet and

the greatest importance as to Christian qualification of the Muslim faith: the Muslim faith does not relate to a God invented by human reason. Muslim faith relates to the transcendent God who has made himself known by his Word entrusted to humanity, to the prophets—even if this is not the same Word nor are they the same prophets as for the Christian faith.

The Muslim faith is essentially *islām,* active submission to the Will of God, to 'whose decrees, even the hidden ones, they seek to submit themselves whole-heartedly.' Thus is noted the 'mysterious' aspect which this faith comprises: reasonable without being rational, in line with the Qur'an which demands of the believer the acceptance of the Will of God, even if it appears paradoxical to the eyes of reason. It is as type and model of this faith of submission that Abraham finds his true role in the Muslim faith.

Jesus and Mary are among the most venerated persons in the Qur'an. The text indicates the refusal to see in Jesus more than a great prophet.[69] This will be taken positively by Muslims who glory in this refusal which is born from the desire to respect the transcendence of God. Mary is also respected as the virgin mother of Jesus according to Islam, which has never hesitated on this point. [70]

Muslim eschatology is briefly indicated. The resurrection of the body and the judgement which follows it are one of the essential points of the Muslim and the Christian faith. The modalities and the criteria of this judgement can differ from one theology to the other. It remains that, according to the Qur'an as well as according to the Gospel, everyone will be judged by their actions and that, for the Christian as well as for the Muslim, 'the world which comes from God, returns to God,' to find there its fulfilment.

They have regard 'for the moral life' is the phrase that remained, after the Council had discussed a proposed, fuller text: 'for the moral life, individual as

messenger of God, Christians do not accord the same status to Muhammad. See Jacques Jomier, 'The Problem of Muhammad', *How to Understand Islam,* SCM Press, London, 1989, pp. 140-148. Maurice Borrmans, in Louis Gardet and J Cuoq, *Guidelines for Dialogue between Christians and Muslims,* Ancona, Rome, 1969, states, 'Christians are inclined to perceive that Muhammad was a great literary, political and religious genius, and he possesses particular qualities which enabled him to lead multitudes to the worship of the true God. But, at the same time, they find in him evidence of mistakes and important misapprehensions. They also discern in him marks of prophethood' (pp. 57-58). See also, 'Muhammad's Prophetic Office and the inspired nature of the Qur'an', Robert Caspar, *A Historical Introduction to Islamic Theology,* Pontifico Istituto di Studi Arabi e d'Islamistica, Rome, 1998, pp. 89-134.

69   David Marshall, 'The Resurrection of Jesus and the Qur'an', *Resurrection Reconsidered,* (ed.) Gavin D'Costa, Oneworld, Oxford, 1996, pp. 168-183.

70   David Marshall, 'Mary in the Qur'an', *A Faithful presence: essays for Kenneth Cragg,* (eds) David Thomas with Claire Amos, Melisende 2003, London, pp. 155-165.

well as familial and social'. The Council refused to refer explicitly to family and social morality because of the Qur'an's passages on polygamy.

The Muslim faith is described by its three foremost manifestations: ritual prayer, the alms-tax and fasting. Of the profession of faith only its first part, the faith in the One God, was mentioned at the beginning of the text. The pilgrimage could have been mentioned but it is far from being practised by all Muslims, and the Council did not intend in any way to present a complete exposition of Islam.

The document continues:

> Although considerable dissensions and enmities between Christians and Muslims may have arisen in the course of the centuries, this synod urges all parties that, forgetting past things, they train themselves towards sincere mutual understanding and together maintain and promote social justice and moral values as well as peace and freedom for all people.[71]

The second part of the text concerns the present and future perspectives of understanding and collaboration between Christians and Muslims. The past of hatreds and wars must be forgotten, i.e. not ignored but overcome. Mutual understanding—objective and respectful—will require much effort and progress on both sides. But the dialogue itself must be surpassed in order to arrive at collaboration between believers towards one objective: to confront together the challenges of modern thought and civilisation, not only in order to save faith in God.[72]

There can be no doubt that the Council's statements regarding Islam, in the light of history, represent a radical novelty. However, soon after the closure of the Council, the Dominican scholar of Islam and Christian-Muslim Relations, George Anawati (1905-1994), in a critical analysis of these statements pointed out their remarkable silence regarding the figure of Abraham and Islam's, possible historical as well as, spiritual link with him through Ishmael and, above all, concerning Muhammad, and hence the prophetic character of Islam. In 1967, Anawati stated: 'One can say that the Declaration summarizes with a minimum of words Muslim *theodicy* but not what is essential to the Muslim *faith* of which the belief in the mission of Muhammad is one of the most important elements.'[73] The silence of the Council concerning the second part

71 Norman Tanner, *Decrees of the Ecumenical Councils*, pp. 969-970.
72 Robert Caspar, *Traité de Théologie Musulmane*, Pontifico Istituto di Studi Arabi e d'Islamistica, Rome, 1987, pp. 87.
73 Georges Anawati, 'Exkurs zum Konzilstext über die Muslim', *Lexikon für Theologie und*

of the Muslim profession of faith *(shahāda)* doubtless represents the most sensitive point for the Muslims. The Council chose to deal with it by—silence.

What the Second Vatican council said on Islam can be summed up in the words of Robert Caspar:

> The Council affirms positively the minimum which is to be accepted, Islam is in the first rank of non-Christian monotheistic religions. If further studies concerning the theology of religions and in particular regarding the theological status of Islam allow one to say more, the Conciliar texts are not opposed.[74]

THE CATHOLIC CHURCH AND ISLAM IN A GLOBAL CONTEXT

How do we give context to Christian-Muslim relations today? We experience Christian-Muslim engagement at many levels: theological, political, cultural and global. Today, looking at the world as a whole, Christians and Muslims together make up over half of the global population. Statistics are almost inevitably estimates, however Christians make-up 33 percent (approximately 2.3 billion) and Muslims 18 percent (1.5 billion).[75]

Christian-Muslims relations increasingly must be set within a context of global religious resurgence. This religious-political context is opening up dynamic encounters, which go far beyond the classic historic relationship between Europe and Islam across the Mediterranean or in the Balkans. It also goes substantially beyond the discussion on the relationship between church and state and religion and politics in the public square. The state of Christian-Muslim relations has world significance.

Today these relations take place in a multiplicity of contexts. The Middle East has a majority Muslim population; however, there are significant Christian communities in Egypt, Iraq, Lebanon and Syria, which were present some six hundred years before the arrival of Islam. The Middle East is the historic homeland of Christianity, Judaism and Islam. Jerusalem is central to Jewish and Christian religious identity and is of importance in Islam. Eastern Christian

---

Kirche, Herder, Frieburg, 1967, Vol. 2, pp. 485-487, quoted in Christian Troll, 'Changing Catholic Views of Islam', p. 27.

74 R Caspar, 'La religion musulmane', *Vatican II. Les relations de l'Église avec les religions non-chrétiennes,* p. 215.

75 H Goddard, 'Christian-Muslim Relations: Yesterday, Today and Tomorrow', *International Journal for the Study of the Christian Church,* Vol. 3, no 2. (2003), pp. 1-14.

experience of living with Islam in the Middle East is of great importance for global Christian tradition in widening and giving historical maturity to its religious encounter with Islam.

We also witness a reconfiguration of Christian-Muslim relations in Russia. Little understanding of the political and religious encounter between the Eastern Orthodox Churches and Islam, as majorities in Russia and some Balkan states, or as minorities in the Middle East, such as the Patriarchates of Antioch, Constantinople, Alexandria or Jerusalem, is given in Western Christian circles. The Christian Churches of the West, also generally have little knowledge and understanding of the Oriental Churches, Armenian, Coptic, Ethiopian, Syrian, and their contribution to understanding the Islamic tradition that they have experienced historically over many centuries.[76]

For sustaining a more robust historical and theological reflection of the Christian-Muslim encounter Churches of the West must expand the 'canon' of knowledge, experience and understanding. One of the main features, not often commented upon, of Benedict XVI's reflection on 'Faith, Reason and Violence' in the modern world at Regensburg in August 2006, was his emphasis on Eastern Christian experience of Islam and its religious thought on the nature of Christian-Muslim engagement.[77]

Christian-Muslim relations also have a global context: in Africa large numbers of Christians and Muslims are found in the four regions West, East, Central and South Africa. Africa is also a continent associated with ancient Christianity—Egypt, Nubia (Sudan) and Ethiopia. According to Lamin Sanneh Professor of Christianity at Yale University, (USA) it is estimated that in Africa in the year 2025 there will be 600 million Christians and 500 million Muslims.[78] Asia has largest concentration of Muslims in the world (Indonesia, located in Southeast Asia, being the largest Muslim nation by population followed by Pakistan, India and Bangladesh). Christianity is undergoing tremendous growth in Asia. The Philippines and South Korea have Christian majority

---

76 H Goddard, 'Challenges and Developments: Christian-Muslim Relations in the Middle East', *IJSCC*, Vol. 3, no 2. (2003), pp. 15-35.
77 Andrew Unsworth, 'John Paul II, Islam and the Christian-Muslim Encounter', pp. 253-302; Barbara Wood and Andrew Unsworth, 'Pope Benedict XVI, Interreligious Dialogue and Islam', *One in Christ: a catholic ecumenical review*, Vol. XLI, no. 4, 2006, pp. 89-108; Peter Gallagher, 'What dialogue with Islam adds to Christianity: Reflections on the Thought of Benedict XVI', *The Downside Review*, Vol. 126, no. 444, 2008, pp. 219-228.
78 Lamin Sanneh, 'Religion's Return', *The Times Literary Supplement* (London), 13 October 2006. See also Klaus Kock, 'Christian-Muslim Relations in the African Context', *IJSCC*, Vol. 3, no 2. (2003), pp. 36-57.

populations. It is now estimated that China, with over 10 percent of its population Christian (which is estimated to grow by 5 to 10 percent each year), is rapidly making it one of the largest Christian concentrations in the world.[79] In contemporary Europe today there are sizeable Muslim communities whereas the Americas (North and South) have dominant Christian societies with extremely small Muslim populations.[80] What is certain is that how Christians respond to Islam has a global significance and, as we have seen, it is an encounter located in history and theological tradition.[81]

In this context, the Catholic Church has developed a wide range of encounters with Islam on a number of significant issues, and at many different levels of engagement, including: theological issues, religious freedom, the rights of the person, the rights of religious minorities and conflict resolution through religious exchange.[82] However the challenge remains,[83] as Louis Gardet, a great Thomist, scholar of Islam and follower of Charles de Foucauld reminded Christians and Muslims many decades ago, to create a City, 'where the temporal remains charged with religious values', seen 'to participate in the same humanity'.

79 Thomas Michel, 'Implications of the Islamic Revival for Christian-Muslim Dialogue in Asia', *IJSCC*, Vol. 3, no 2. (2003), pp. 58-76.

80 Philip Lewis, 'Christians and Muslims in the West: From Isolation to Shared Citizenship?', *IJSCC*, Vol. 3, no 2. (2003), pp. 77-100.

81 David Marshall, 'Heavenly Religion or Unbelief? Muslim Perspectives on Christianity', *Anvil*, Vol. 23, no. 3, 2006, pp. 89-100.

82 Andrew Unsworth, 'The Vatican, Islam and Muslim-Christian Relations, in: *Christian responses to Islam: Muslim-Christian relations in the modern world*, (eds) A O'Mahony and Emma Loosley, Manchester University Press, Manchester, 2008, pp. 54-65; Christian W Troll, *Dialogue and Difference: Clarity in Christian-Muslim Relations*, Orbis Books, Maryknoll, New York, 2009.

83 The Church in the Middle East has renewed and rearticulated its developed understanding on Church-State relations in the contemporary Middle East, especailly in relation to religious freedom see Rafael Palomino Lozano, 'The Role of Concordats promoting Religious Freedom with Special Reference to Agreements in the Middle East', *Congregazione per le Chiese orientali, 'Ius Ecclesiarum, Vehi culum Caritatis', Atti del simposio internazionale per il de cen nale dell'entrata in vigore del Codex Canonum Eccle sia rum Orienta lium, Città del Vaticano, 19-23 novembre 2001*, Libreria Editrice Vaticana, 2004, pp. 893-901.The origins of religious freedom as an ecclesial engagement has deep roots; however, the role of Paul VI should be highlighted in particular, Gianpaolo Salvini, 'La "Dignitatis Humane": La Libertà religiosa in Paolo VI', *La Civiltà Cattolica* (Rome), no. 3784, 2008, pp. 338-348. The Chaldean Archbishop of Kirkuk, Louis Sako, in his recent interventions has developed doctrine, this theological idea, with in Iraq since 2003.

IS A NON-VIOLENT INTERPRETATION
OF THE QUR'AN POSSIBLE?

Michel Cuypers

The *Lineamenta* for the Middle East Synod give a great deal of importance to the difficulties which Islamic political extremism presents not only for the Christians of the Middle East but also for Muslims themselves. Consequently, the *Lineamenta* call for Christians and Muslims to work together to combat these religious deviations which lead to the perpetration of violence in the name of God. During the last few years, many initiatives have been taken by Christians and Muslims to denounce this resort to religion to justify the killing or exclusion of others. Their arguments are based on philosophy, theology, law, spiritual wisdom and, of course, for Muslims, the Qur'an. In the latter case, there is an attempt to highlight those verses which call for attitudes of respect and tolerance towards 'the others'; such an approach was used in the famous 'Letter of the 138', 'A Common Word between Us and You'. These arguments have their validity but, all the same, leave a certain malaise, in so far as they do not satisfactorily resolve the problems of those Qur'anic verses which do, in fact, incite violence against non-Muslims and which the fundamentalists use to justify their acts of violence. A rigorous exegesis of these verses has yet to be done.

Moreover, quite a few Muslim intellectuals realize the necessity of a new hermeneutic of the Qur'an.[1] Some of them even want to apply to the Qur'an the exegetical techniques which Christians have successfully been using for the Bible for over a century.[2] This is what I have also been trying to do for the last fifteen years.

The objection may be raised that a Christian is not qualified to undertake Qur'anic exegesis. There are several ways of responding to this objection:

—In the actual context of globalization, the Qur'an is, more

---

1   See, for example, Adnane Mokrani, *Leggere il Corano a Roma*, Icone ADV, 2010, p. 66.
2   Among others, this is the case of the Iranian philosopher and theologian Mohammad Mojtahed-e Shabestari.

than ever, part of the universal cultural and religious patrimony; consequently, it can be studied by everyone.

—Since the violence of Islamic extremists affects both Muslims and non-Muslims, especially Christians, Christians have the right to question the Qur'an—the source which the Islamic extremist use for the religious justifications of their acts.

—Finally, a Christian knowledgeable in Biblical exegesis is certainly better prepared than a Muslim for the application of Biblical exegetical methods to the Qur'an.

Initially, my research did not centre on the question of violence or intolerance in the Qur'an but rather on a purely literary question: is there a unity and coherence which can be found behind the apparent disorder of the Qur'anic text? If such is the case, what would such a discovery mean for the interpretation of the text? This process progressively led me to the conviction that a specific scientific exegesis could resolve not only the question of the apparent disorder of the Qur'anic text, but also the question of violence and intolerance in the Qur'an as well as its opposite—the Qur'an's acceptance of the existence of other religions and their followers.

My presentation will consist of two parts. First, I want to describe certain classical exegetic mechanisms revived by present-day fundamentalists and then propose other exegetical procedures, borrowed from Biblical studies, which open new possibilities for a hermeneutic of the Qur'an. In brief, it is a question of two manners of 'returning to the Qur'an'. The fundamentalists do this naively and literally, as though the Qur'anic text conveyed its message directly, by simply reading it. The other manner is to return to the text of the Qur'an using technical and scientific tools which have already been proven useful in Biblical exegesis.

SOME PROCEDURES OF CLASSICAL EXEGESIS
USED BY MODERN-DAY FUNDAMENTALISTS

The classical commentaries of the Qur'an are characterized, among others, by the following procedures:

1) The text is commentated verse by verse without considering the immediate literary context of the verse. A Muslim researcher (Mustansir Mir) rightly named this procedure 'linear atomistic':

the verses are studied as small independent units, as if they were 'atoms', one after the other. It is well known what happens when a verse is taken out of context: it can be interpreted in any manner.

2) The verse is interpreted not by its literary context but by its historical—or supposed historical—context. In Qur'anic exegesis this technique is called the 'occasions of revelation' *(asbāb al-nuzūl)*: the verse is referred to an event in the life of the Prophet or of his first Companions as an explanation of why the verse had been revealed. Sometimes the verse clearly makes reference to an event (a battle, the conclusion of a treaty etc.) and this justifies the use of these historical explanations. Very often, however, nothing in the text refers to any precise historical event and, in these cases, the historical explanations appear artificial, expressly invented in order to give a particular meaning to a more or less obscure verse. But if the verse is placed in its immediate literary context, its meaning often becomes apparent without any necessity of another historical explanation.

3) In order to resolve apparent contradictions between the verses, Qur'anic commentators have recourse to the method of abrogation *(naskh)*: certain verses of the Qur'an are considered as abrogating others; the former are obviously considered of later date than the latter. The classical example is the prohibition of wine: a first verse (16:67) refers to wine as an intoxicating beverage but does not forbid it. Verse 2:219 states that wine has its good aspects and bad aspects but the bad ones prevail. In verse 4:43 it is forbidden to pray while intoxicated and finally, in verses 5:90-91, wine is totally forbidden as something evil and diabolic. Since the two verses of sura 5 are chronologically later, they abrogate the preceding verses. In general, the commentators and jurists have judged that the verses which are more lenient legally or more tolerant in religious matters have been abrogated by the verses which are stricter or more intolerant. This is, however, an *a priori* ideological option. There is no reason why the opposite would not be true: that the milder verses mitigate the harsher verses.

319

Fundamentalists use this abrogation method to claim that the violent verses—such as verses 5 and 29 of the ninth sura—abolish up to 130 verses which are milder and more tolerant. Here is verse 9:29: 'Fight those of the People of the Book who do not believe in God and the Last Day and do not forbid what God and his messenger have forbidden and do not practise the religion of truth, until they pay the tax and agree to submit.' By making it abrogatory, they decide (as do a certain number of classical authors) that this sura must necessarily be, chronologically, the final sura of the Qur'an—a claim which is very dubious. I believe that I have demonstrated in my book *The Banquet* that the fifth sura appears as a text-testament which closes the Qur'anic revelation in the framework of the farewell pilgrimage of the Prophet shortly before his death, which occurred in the tenth year of the Hegira[3]—whereas the quoted verses of the ninth sura are situated in the context of on-going wars (namely the battle of Tabuk, against Christian tribes) which took place in the ninth year of the Hegira, a year earlier.

This question of abrogation is so important in our present context that it merits closer study.

> —The abrogation method does not date from the beginnings of Islam: no hadith (prophetic tradition) mentions it. It was created by the first jurists who, at the time when Muslim law *(fiqh)* was being drawn up, wanted to put some sort of order in the Qur'anic prescriptions, which sometimes diverged and even contradicted themselves.

> —This method was not unanimously adopted by the commentators. Some rejected it completely, others allowed for the abrogation of a small number of verses (5), others used it more extensively, judging that hundreds of verses (up to 564!) were abrogated by others.

The partisans of abrogation base their theory on an interpretation of three Qur'anic verses (16:101, 13:39 and 2:106). Verse 2:106 is the verse used most frequently to justify the principle of abrogation: 'For whatsoever verse We cancel or cause to forget, we bring a better or the like' (trans. R Bell).

The commentators use the following 'occasion of revelation' to explain this verse: the Prophet would have received a revelation during the night and

---

3   See Michel Cuypers, *The Banquet. A Reading of the fifth Sura of the Qur'an*, Convivium Press, Miami, 2009, pp. 122-23, pp. 481-87. English translation by Patricia Kelly of *Le Festin. Une lecture de la sourate al-Mâ'ida*, Lethielleux, Paris, 2007.

forgotten it the next morning.[4] Others explain it according to a different anecdote: the pagans complained that Muhammad would sometimes give an instruction and then another which contradicted the first. This was taken as a proof that the word did not come to him from God but was the fruit of his own imagination; in the face of this accusation, God sent down the verse in question.[5]

But if this verse is read in its literary context, it can be seen that it is part of a very long polemic with the Jews who refuse to believe that God could send a prophet and a revelation outside of the sole chosen people—the Jewish people. Not only did Muhammad pretend to be a prophet, but he also claimed authority to quote the Torah and modify it. Thus it is that God, in verse 2:106, backs up his prophet by affirming that he can very well abolish or ignore certain passages of the Torah, because something better will be sent down, i.e. the verses of the Qur'an. Thus it is that abrogation does not mean replacing one verse from the Qur'an by another verse from the Qur'an but rather replacing certain verses of the Torah by those of the Qur'an.

The other two verses which are invoked to justify the abrogation method are in a similar situation; their context is that of a polemic with the Jews, regarding the Torah and they do not refer to the Qur'an. Several Muslim commentators of the late nineteenth century (Sayyid Ahmad Khan) and the twentieth century (Muhammmad 'Ali, Muhammad Asad, Yusuf 'Ali and even Maududi—one of the founders of modern political Islam) denounced the misinterpretation of this verse … but in vain. This doctrine continues to circulate as a quasi-dogmatic certitude. A Muslim researcher by the name of Ahmad Hasan published an article in 1965 in which he expresses his astonishment: 'In view of the evident context of the verse under reference [2:106] … it looks strange that some of the most eminent authorities of *tasfir* have missed the central point of this verse.'[6]

The abrogation theory has no foundation in the Qur'an; it is the invention of the jurists *(fuqahā')*.

The example of verse 2:106 demonstrates the weakness of interpreting a verse in isolation, without considering its literary context, and also the shortcomings of many of the 'occasions of revelation'; those invoked to explain verse 2:106 are obviously artificial.

If the abrogation theory should be put aside as a method of exegesis,

4   See al-Suyūṭī, *Lubāb-al-nuqūl fi asbāb al-nuzūl*, Cairo, 1966, p. 32.
5   Al-Wāḥidī al-Nīsābūrī, *Asbāb al-nuzūl*, Cairo, 1991, p. 25.
6   Ahmad Hasan, 'Theory of *naskh*', *Islamic Studies*, IV, 1965, p. 189.

the problem of the verses propagating violence or an intolerant exclusivist position remains unsolved. How should these verses be integrated into a modern reading of the Qur'an, in the context of a pluralistic global society where different religious and non-religious communities have to try to live together peacefully and constructively for the good of all mankind?

SEMITIC RHETORIC IN THE QUR'AN

Alongside the method of historical criticism which seeks to reconstruct the history of texts, some Biblical scholars have developed another way of approaching Scripture. This process began near the middle of the eighteenth century and is known today as 'rhetorical analysis'. Rhetorical analysis does not deconstruct the texts according to their different chronological layers but rather takes the text such as it is, in its final canonical version, and tries to decipher its structure and interpret it in function of this structure.

The Pontifical Biblical Commission, in an important document, *The Interpretation of the Bible in the Church*, published in 1993, describes the rhetorical analysis as follows:

> Rooted in Semitic culture, [the Biblical literary tradition] displays a distinct preference for symmetrical compositions, through which one can detect relationships between different elements in the text. The study of the multiple forms of parallelism and other procedures characteristic of the Semite mode of composition allows for a better discernment of the literary structure of texts, which can only lead to a more adequate understanding of their message.

Rhetorical analysis is thus a method of analysis of the text of the Bible which takes into account characteristics of Semitic literary culture, leading to 'a more adequate understanding of the message of the texts'.

The study of 30 Qur'anic suras, has enabled me to verify that they all obey the same rules of Semitic composition that were originally discovered in the texts of the Bible.

The term 'rhetoric', as we use it here, should be understood as 'the art of arranging the parts of a discourse among themselves' in such a way that they form a coherent whole. According to the tradition of Greek rhetoric, which we have all received as a heritage, the discourse should begin with an introduction and continue with a continuous and progressive linear development in view of arriving at a clear and convincing conclusion. The texts of the Semitic world, however, which include the Bible and the Qur'an, do not function like this. They obey the laws of a rhetoric totally different from Greek rhetoric. They are constructed, in their entirety, on the basis of the principle of symmetry. This symmetry can appear in three forms or three 'figures of composition':

> *parallelism* where the textual units with a two by two semantic relationship are arranged in the same order: ABC//A'B'C':

> *mirror composition* or reverse parallelism where the units which are in relationship reappear in reverse order: ABC//C'B'A';

> *concentric composition* where a central element is inserted between the two sides of the symmetry: ABC/x/C'B'A' or, sometimes, just A/x/A'.

These figures of composition are found at different levels of the text; at the elementary level of two parallel *members* (e.g. two short verses) which would constitute a *segment*, then at the level of a group of two or three symmetrical segments constituting a *piece* and continuing with more complex arrangements known as *parts, passages sequences* and *sections*. A long text, such as the lengthy suras of the beginning of the Qur'an, can include as many as ten levels, each of which is composed according to one or another of the three figures of composition. The most common figure of composition by far, on the higher levels (a collection of several long verses), is concentric composition. The centre of these compositions have a certain number of characteristics which differentiate them from the surrounding text.[7] I will only mention two of them that will be useful to our presentation:

> —At the centre there is often a change in the trend of thought and an antithetical idea is introduced. After this the original trend is resumed and continued until the system is concluded.

> —The centre is frequently occupied by a quotation, a question or a sentence (wisdom, moral or theological sentence) drawing the attention of the reader-listener to an important point and inviting him to reflect on it. Often the key to the interpretation of the whole system can be found in the centre.

The long fifth sura, which I studied in detail in my book *The Banquet*, includes a number of central verses constructed concentrically which take

---

7   See 'Lund's laws' in *The Banquet, op. cit.*, p. 36.

the form of universal proclamations in contrast to the surrounding verses which have a more limited and circumstantial scope and which are often very polemical.[8] In this paper, I will only examine two of these cases which could have an important significance in the relationships between Islam and the other religions. The first example is often evoked in Islamic-Christian meeting—the second example less so, I believe.

The ensemble of the fifth sura is made up of 2 sections, including 8 sequences.

The two verses which I would like to analyze more thoroughly are symmetrically positioned in the last two sequences of the first section. Each of these sequences is, moreover, made up of 3 passages; the two verses we are dealing with are both in the centre of the 3rd passage.

The passage 5:48-50

> [5.48a] And *WE HAVE SENT DOWN TO YOU THE SCRIPTURE* with truth, [b] confirming what of the Scripture was before it, [c] and preserving it. [d] **SO JUDGE BETWEEN THEM ACCORDING TO WHAT GOD HAS SENT DOWN,** [e] **AND DO NOT FOLLOW THEIR PASSIONS,** [f] far from what has come to you of the truth.

> +[48g] For each of you we have made *a way and a path*,
>> = [h] and if *God* had wanted, he would have made you a single community.
>>> – [i] But he tests you in what he has given you
>>> – [j] – surpass yourselves in good works.
>> = [k] Unto *God* shall you return, all together;
> + [l] he will tell you of *that in which you have been differing*.

> [49a] **AND MAY YOU JUDGE BETWEEN THEM ACCORDING TO WHAT GOD HAS SENT DOWN,** [b] **AND DO NOT FOLLOW THEIR PASSIONS.** [c] And beware of them, do not let them tempt you away [d] from any part of *WHAT GOD HAS SENT DOWN TO YOU*. [e] And if they turn away, [f] know that God only wants to strike them for some of their sins [h]—surely, many people are perverse. [50a] Do they wish for judgment of Ignorance [times]? [b] What judgment is better than God's [c] for a people who truly believe?

---

8   See *The Banquet*, 'From rhetoric to universal wisdom', pp. 464-470.

This text forms a *passage* made up of three *parts* arranged concentrically. There is a correspondence between the outer parts of the passage which frame a central part.

In the two outer parts, the Prophet is exhorted to judge between the People of the Book in the same terms: 'according to what God has sent down, and do not follow their passions (48d-e, 49a-b). The synonymic sentences 'We have sent down to you the Scripture' (48a) and 'what God has sent down to you' (49d) are repeated in the same parts. Thus the two outer parts can be read in continuity. But the flow of thought is brusquely interrupted by the central part (48g-l); an eschatological and theological part on why God allows differences between religions appears in the centre. This verse 48g-l is especially emphasized by its chiastic form and its situation at the centre of the passage. In addition, it contrasts semantically with the parts which frame it—we jump suddenly from legal questions about judging the People of the Book to a universal theological principle aimed at shedding the light of wisdom on the problem under discussion.

The reformist scholar Fazlur Rahman (d. 1988) saw the second part of v. 48 (48g-l) as the Qur'an's final answer to the problem of a multi-cultural world. 'The positive value of different religions and communities is, therefore, that they might compete with each other in goodness ['Surpass one another in good works'].[9]

We do not need to emphasize the contemporary importance of this verse. The great classical commentator, Fakhr al-Dīn al-Rāzī, only gives a few short lines of commentary to this verse;[10] Mawdūdī, one of the fathers of political Islam, sees it as a parenthesis.[11] On the other hand, however, a recent Islamic-Christian conference on multi-culturalism emphasized this verse several times to confirm the Qur'anic foundation of religious plurality not only as a fact, but as a necessity for human development in mutual emulation for the good.[12]

---

9   Fazlur Rahman, *Major Themes of the Qur'an*, Minneapolis, Chicago, 1980, p. 167.
10   Fakhr al-Dīn al-Rāzī, *Al-Tafsīr al-kabīr*, Beirut, 1986, XII, p. 13.
11   Abū al-A'lā al-Mawdūdī, *The Meaning of the Qur'an*, Islamic Publications, Lahore, 1991, III, p. 49.
12   See *One World for All: Foundations of a Social-Political and Cultural Pluralism from Christian and Muslim Perspectives*, A Bsteh (ed.), Delhi, 1999, esp. pp. 26, 29, 86, 102, 149, 359.

^{65a} If **THE PEOPLE OF THE BOOK** had believed and been pious, ^b we would have wiped out from them their bad actions, ^c and we would have let them enter to the gardens of delight. ^{66a} And if they had followed the Torah and the Gospel ^b and what has BEEN SENT DOWN TO THEM from their Lord, ^c they would have eaten of what is above them and of what is under their feet. ^d Among them is **A MODERATE COMMUNITY**, ^e but [for] *MANY AMONG THEM, WHAT THEY DO* is bad!

------

^{67a} Prophet, communicate what has been sent down to you from your Lord!
^b And if you did not do this, ^c you would not communicate his message!
^d And God will protect you from men. ^e Surely, God does not guide the unbelieving people.

------

^{68a} Say, 'O people of the Book, you do not rely on anything ^b as long as you do not follow the Torah and the Gospel ^c and what HAS BEEN SENT DOWN TO YOU from your Lord.' ^d And certainly makes *MANY AMONG THEM* grow ^e what has been sent down to you from your Lord, ^f in rebellion and unbelief. ^g And do not torment yourself for unbelieving people.

^{69a} Surely, those who believe, ^b and **THOSE WHO PRACTICE-JUDAISM, AND THE SABIANS AND THE CHRISTIANS,** ^c whoever believes in God and the Last Day ^d and does good works ^e —there is no fear for them, ^f and they will not be afflicted.

^{70a} Surely, we have received the covenant of the **CHILDREN OF ISRAEL,** ^b and we have SENT TO THEM messengers. ^c Each time CAME TO THEM a messenger ^d with what their souls did not want, ^e some they treated as liars, ^f and some they killed.

------

^{71a} They reckoned there would be no test, ^b and they became blind and deaf. ^c Then God CAME BACK TO THEM. ^d Then became blind and deaf *many among them*. ^e But God is well-seeing *WHAT THEY DO*.

As was the case in the preceding text, these verses form a *passage* of three *parts* where the outer parts, which are in correspondence, frame a central part.

The 'People of the Book' appear at the start of each part; in 65a as the People of the Book; in more detail in the central part (69b) and, finally, reduced to the 'children of Israel' in the third part (70a).

In the outer parts, the People of the Book and the children of Israel are the ungrateful beneficiaries of God's care. In the first part, God sends down the Qur'an to them (66b, 68c); in the third part he sends messengers (70b-c) and he himself 'came back to them' after their first act of infidelity (71c). But they have not responded to the divine benevolence but rather rebelled and not believed (65a, 68f-g), treated the prophets as liars and killed them (70e-f).

The outer parts of the passage end with the words 'what they do'—the way the People of the Book act is condemned (66e) for God knows well what they do and sees it is wrong (71e).

However, the outer pieces as well as the outer parts have the words 'many among them' (66e, 68d, 71d) as their last or penultimate terms. Not all the People of the Book or the children of Israel, therefore, are rebels, but *only* many of them. There are some who are a faithful 'moderate community' (66d). This is what the central part will vigorously affirm.

The declaration in verse 69 is a theological, trans-historical one, while the parts which frame it allude to particular situations and attitudes based on the contingency of history: 'If the People of the Book had believed ... if they had followed the Torah and the Gospel ... for many among them what they do is bad ...,' the Qur'an stirs up the rebellion and unbelief of many of them, treating the prophets as liars and killing some of them etc.

The same verse 5:69 is also found in sura 2:62. According to the classical commentators,[13] 2:62 has been abrogated by verse 3:85: 'And whoever desires a religion other than Islam, it will not be received by him, and in the hereafter he will be among the losers.'

Rhetorical analysis, however, demonstrates the opposite by pointing out the importance of this verse due to its central situation in 5:69.

Once again, the Muslim reformist Fazlur Rahman strongly rejects the traditional interpretation:

> In both these verses (2:62, 5:69) the vast majority of Muslim commentators exercise themselves fruitlessly to avoid having to admit the obvious meaning: that those—from any section

---

13   See Ibn Kathīr, *Tafsīr*, Beirut, 2000, p. 74.

of mankind—who believe in God and the Last Day and do
good deeds are saved.[14]

It is evident that there is a frequent tendency in classical exegesis to
minimize the importance of verses which seem to contradict those which
frame them—or even to abrogate these verses. But the fact that they are
found at the centre of concentric compositions, gives them, on the contrary,
enhanced importance. These are the central verses meant to explain the
others —and not the other way around!

Since the Medinan suras are later than the Meccan verses, the Medinan
verses are thought, according to abrogation theory, to abrogate the Meccan
verses. However, the Sudanese reformist Mahmud Muhammad Taha has
proposed turning things around; since the Meccan verses have a more
universal, theological and broad-minded perspective, these verses should
abrogate the Medinan verses which are profoundly influenced by the very
special historical context of the foundation of the first Muslim state. He
certainly was right in giving the more far-reaching verses precedence over
more circumstantial verses. But it can be seen that both types of verses are
found in the Medinan suras, such as the 5th sura, which is, indisputably, the
final word of the Qur'anic revelation. Textual analysis, according to Semitic
rhetoric, enables us to distinguish the different semantic levels in the suras:
certain verses have a universal ethical or theological significance and a timeless
value. These verses are at the centre of the concentric rhetorical compositions.
The peripheral verses have a more limited significance and are marked by
concrete historical circumstances—those surrounding the foundation of the
first Muslim community—and have a cultural context extremely different
from our times. These verses should not be 'abrogated' but they should
be understood in the historical context of the foundation of the Muslim
community and not be given an absolute and permanent validity. This is the
opinion of Professor Nasr Abu Zayd: 'The confusion between what is dated,
whose meaning is linked to a specific historical event, and what is stable and
permanent in religious texts always leads to aberrations.'[15]

---

14 F Rahman, *Major Themes of the Qur'an*, p. 166, quoted in J D McAuliffe, *Qur'anic
   Christians*, p. 121. The same interpretation by the contemporary Pakistani legal scholar,
   Nasira Iqbal, of salvation granted equally to Muslims, Christians, Jews and 'Unitarians'
   (Sabians) is found in *One World for All*, *op. cit.*, p. 148.
15 Nasr Abou Zeid, *Critique du discours religieux*, Sinbad—Actes Sud, Paris, 1999, p. 72
   (quotation translated from French edition).

CONCLUSION

I am not the first to propose that all the verses of the Qur'an should not be put on the same semantic level. Even in the classical tradition, certain suras —such as the first one, the *Fātiḥa*, or the sura 112, *al-'Alaq*—are considered as more important than all the others because of their theological scope. However, in the context of contemporary Islam which gives an exaggerated importance to certain violent verses and, on the contrary, abrogates verses which are more tolerant and open, the use of rigorous instruments of literary investigation such as rhetorical analysis can be very useful in restoring balance, and demonstrating that the very structure of the text stresses the more far-reaching and universal verses, those at the centre of concentrical or ring compositions, in contrast with the peripheral and circumstantial verses linked to the particularities of the epoch of the foundation of Islam and which do not have a permanent value.

CHRIST IN ISLAM AND MUHAMMAD, A CHRISTIAN EVALUATION: THEOLOGICAL REFLECTIONS ON TRADITION AND DIALOGUE

John Flannery

I CHRIST IN ISLAM
Introduction

There can be no doubt that Jesus ('Isa) is an important figure in the Qur'an, which devotes a total of ninety-three verses in fifteen *suras* to him, and refers to him either as 'Isa, *Masih* (Messiah), or *Ibn Maryam* (Son of Mary) some thirty-five times.[1] The majority of these *suras* date from the Medinan period, reflecting the increasing contact of Muhammad with Christians.[2]

Fully two-thirds of the material relating to Jesus is concerned with the two lengthy and partly duplicated nativity accounts of suras 3 and 19, leaving little room for a detailed portrayal of the person and work of Jesus: as Cragg points out, if the New Testament Gospels can fairly be described as passion narratives with extended introductions, then the Jesus cycle in the Qur'an can be described as a nativity narrative with an attenuated sequel.[3] This limited Qur'anic Christology, which for Islam is always outside theology,[4] has been built on by numerous traditions drawing on a variety of sources, including the apocryphal gospels and mystic or gnostic writings. The classical[5] exegesis of the Qur'anic texts hardened into fixed positions under the effect of Islamo-

---

1 G Parrinder, *Jesus in the Qur'an,* Sheldon Press, London, 1965, p. 18.
2 N Robinson, *Christ in Islam and Christianity: the representation of Jesus in the Qur'an and the classical Muslim commentaries*, Macmillan, London, 1991, pp. 26-30 gives a summary of the chronology of the revelations.
3 K Cragg, *Jesus and the Muslim: an exploration,* One World, Oxford, 1999, p. 26.
4 *Ibid.*, p. 67.
5 The classical period spanned some 350 years from the turn of the fourth/tenth century until the fall of Baghdad in 656/1258 cf. Robinson, *Christ in Islam and Christianity,* p. 60. Robinson argues that the classical commentaries are often mistakenly neglected by those engaged in contemporary Muslim/Christian dialogue as they underestimate the important part they play in maintaining the Muslim worldview, *ibid.*, p. 191.

Christian polemic and these are to be found unchanged in many modern Muslim writers.[6]

The first part of this contribution will consider some aspects of the portrayal of Jesus in the Qur'an and the classical commentaries, suggest the context in which 'negative' Qur'anic portrayals of Jesus are made, examine support in the Qur'an for speaking of the 'surpassing greatness' of Jesus, and finally ask whether Christians and Muslims can find common ground for dialogue in the person of Jesus.

ISLAMIC PORTRAYALS OF JESUS
The annunciation, conception and birth of Jesus

The Qur'anic version of the Annunciation has strong echoes of the Gospel account. Having withdrawn into the Temple in order to serve God, Mary is visited by the Spirit of God (19:17, but by angels in 3:45), who tells her that he is God's messenger who has come to give her a holy son.

Mary asks how it is possible for her to bear a son as she has never known a man or been unchaste. The reply echoes that to Zacharias' question about the possibility of his having a son when his wife is barren (19:8): God tells her 'That is easy enough for me … Our decree will come to pass' (19:21). Both Qur'an and Gospel make clear the willing submission of Mary to God's will.

It appears that the Qur'an makes no precise differentiation between the annunciation and conception, 'Thereupon she conceived him' (19:22). Although the insufflation of the Spirit is not mentioned here but at 21:91, the classical commentaries reflect varying understandings of the identity of the divine messenger and the way in which conception occurred. Tabari assumes that the messenger is the angel Gabriel and other commentators agree that this is the correct interpretation, while still recording the alternative view that the messenger is the Messiah himself (Robinson notes that this interpretation appears in the apocryphal *Epistola Apostolorum*). Baidawi, on the basis of an alternative reading of the messenger appearing as a 'shapely' human being, suggests that the perfect human form in which Gabriel appeared aroused Mary's desire, thus facilitating the descent of the maternal fluid into her womb. Razi lists a number of mechanisms by which the breath of Gabriel gives

---

6   Robinson, *Christ in Islam and Christianity*, p. 60.

rise to conception, and even considers the possibility that Gabriel himself is endowed with creative power.[7]

The classical commentators accept the literal truth of the virginal conception while rejecting any suggestion that it is proof of Jesus' divinity. Rather, as the Qur'an emphasises, the conception of Jesus was a creative act of God. The creation of Adam from the dust of the earth by God's *fiat* was perhaps even more remarkable than that of Jesus from a virgin's womb, but the 'revelation' and 'wise admonition' (or 'reminder') of 3:59 insists that 'Jesus is like Adam in the sight of God.' While it can be argued that this linking of Jesus to Adam may suggest that he has universal significance,[8] there is no suggestion in the Qur'an of the Pauline notion of the second or last Adam; Islam rejects the doctrine of original sin as contrary to the supremacy of God's justice. There is, however, a tradition that both Mary and Jesus are unique in having been preserved from contact with Satan at the moment of their birth.

Mary gives birth after retiring to a 'far-off place' (19:21) and on returning to her family it is the baby Jesus himself who defends her from criticism. The following verses insist that the account given of the conception and birth of Jesus is indeed the whole truth of the matter, in confutation of Christians 'who still doubt'. Any idea of Incarnation is rejected: 'God forbid that He Himself should beget a son' (19:36) (the alternative reading, that God does not 'take to Himself offspring', also rejects the Christian heresies of Sabellianism and Adoptionism).[9] The title Son of Mary *(Ibn Maryam)*, which the Qur'an frequently applies to Jesus, serves as a reminder that he has no father, and, in contrast to the Christian title Son of God, stresses the humanity of Jesus.

Jesus as Prophet

Speaking from the cradle in defence of the purity of his mother, the infant Jesus declares that God has ordained him as a prophet (19:31). Jesus is seen as being in the succession of the Hebrew prophets and patriarchs to whom were given the Torah *(Tawrah)* and the Psalms *(Zabur)*, but he receives a new book, the Gospel *(Injil)*. The prophetic office of Jesus is confirmed by his miraculous birth, and also by the proofs *(bayyinat)* of the miracles he

---

7   See Robinson, *Christ in Islam and Christianity,* ch. 15.

8   Cragg, *Jesus and the Muslim,* p. 32, see also pp. 21, 91, which support this idea.

9   Parrinder, *Jesus in the Qur'an,* p. 80. (There is evidence of 'adoptionist' theories in early Islam. See J W Sweetman, *'Islam and Christian Theology: a Study of the Interpretation of Theological Ideas in the Two Religions,* 2 vols in 4 parts, Lutterworth Press, London, 1945-1967, pp. 110ff.).

performed. These included breathing life into clay models of birds (3:43),[10] curing the blind and leprous (5:110), and the bringing down of a Table from heaven (5:122-115). While these 'signs' serve to confirm his prophetic office, Jesus is not, as Christianity would argue, qualitatively different from the prophets who preceded him. Jesus as prophet also serves to legitimate the prophecy of Muhammad. Sura 61:6 has Jesus announcing the good tidings of the messenger who will come after him, bearing the name Ahmad. On the basis that Muhammad derives from the same root, Muslim commentators have commonly identified the two, making Jesus prophesy the coming of Muhammad. The fact that the Christian Bible does not foretell the coming of Muhammad is seen as evidence of Christian falsification or misinterpretation of the Gospel *(tahrif)*. Tabari identified the Paraclete with the person of Muhammad.[11] Robinson draws attention to the affinities between Jesus and Muhammad depicted in the Qur'an, claiming that these similarities serve to legitimise Muhammad by giving the impression that he was doing what Jesus had done before him.[12]

The death, crucifixion and return of Jesus

Two questions need to be asked on the subject of the death of Jesus in the Qur'an, was Jesus actually crucified and died on the cross, or, if not, did he

---

10   A clear borrowing from accounts in the apocryphal gospels, cf. Parrinder, *Jesus in the Qur'an*, p. 84.

11   A Muslim scholar who produced a Persian translation of the Gospels at the end of the seventeenth century feels able to argue: 'Thus the three meanings of Fâraqlît fit the Lord of Messengers'. See Franco Ometto (Karen Cristenfeld tr.), 'Khatun Abadi: the Ayatollah who translated the Gospels', *Islamochristiana* 28 (2002), pp. 55-72. See also Hava Lazarus-Yaffe, *Intertwined Worlds. Medieval Islam and Bible Criticism*, Princeton, 1992, esp. ch. 4; L Bevan Jones 'The Paraclete or Mohammed', *Muslim World* 10 (1920), pp. 112-125; A Guthrie and E F Bishop 'The Paraclete: Almunhamma and Ahmad', in *ibid.*, 51 (1951), pp. 251-256; W Montgomery Watt, 'His Name is Ahmad' in *ibid.*, 43 (1953), pp. 110-17. Curiously, in a medieval Muslim tract, it is said that the Emperor Constantine's 'canonical advisers' deliberately chose to identify the Paraclete with the Holy Spirit, lest the project for the Christianisation of the empire be delayed by Constantine awaiting the promised appearance. The emperor is said to have been open to this suggestion of 'spiritual forces' in view of his connection to the Sabians of Harran: see Rifaat Y Ebied and David Thomas (eds), *Muslim-Christian Polemic during the Crusades: The letter from the people of Cyprus and Ibn Ali Talib al-Dimashqi's Response*, Leiden, 2005, p. 185, also citing S M Stern, ''Abd al-Jabbar's account of how Christ's religion was falsified by the adoption of Roman Customs', *Journal of Theological Studies* 19 (1968), pp. 128-185.

12   Robinson, *Christ in Islam and Christianity*, p. 36-38.

die a natural death? The answer to the first seems clear enough in 4:156-7 which states that although the Jews claimed to have killed the son of Mary 'they did not slay him, neither crucified him, only a likeness of that was shown to them' (or as Robinson has it 'a semblance was made to them') and later 'they slew him not of a certainty—no indeed: God raised him up to Him.' Muslim tradition interpreted 'a semblance was made to them' *(shubbiha la-hum)* as meaning that someone other than Jesus died on the cross, after having been made to resemble him. Tabari records two early interpretations; in the first all the disciples are made to look like Jesus and one of them is killed by the Jews, in the other Jesus asks his companions for a volunteer on whom his appearance is projected and who dies in his place. Various candidates have been proposed for this substitutionary role, including Judas, Simon of Cyrene, Satan, a Jewish rabbi or a Roman soldier. Schirrmacher credits the Gospel of Barnabas (a medieval Spanish forgery) for the current popularity of the idea that it was Judas who died on the cross.[13] While Docetism may have influenced the Qur'anic rejection of the crucifixion,[14] such rejection is perfectly consistent with the internal logic of the Qur'an. The Biblical stories recorded there, as well as episodes relating to the emergence of Islam, clearly demonstrate that it is God's practice to make faith finally triumph over adversity, 'so truly with hardship comes ease' (94:5). The death of Jesus on the cross would have meant the success of his persecutors, but the Qur'an insists on their failure: 'assuredly, God will defend those who believe'(22:49).[15] He is well able to confound the plots of Jesus' enemies (3:54).

If Jesus did not die on the cross, then how should texts referring to the death of Jesus, such as 19:34, 'Blessed was I on the day I was born, and blessed I shall be on the day of my death, and on the day I shall be raised to life', be interpreted. The key text here is 4:155-7, which envisages a special resurrection for Jesus, separate from the general resurrection foretold in 19:84. Later tradition taught that only after the return of Jesus at the end of time would he die the natural death referred to in 19:34.

Robinson lists no less than ten interpretations given by the classical commentators. He argues that the most likely intention is to convey the idea that, despite appearances to the contrary, 'the human life or prophetic mission was brought to completion by God,' and such a reading is in accord with

---

13   See p. 2 of Christime Schirrmacher, 'The Crucifixion of Jesus in View of Muslim Theology', http://www.contra-mundum.org/schirrmacher/crucifixion.pdf.
14   Cf. Parrinder, *Jesus in the Qur'an*, pp. 109-110.
15   Cf. M A Merad, 'Christ according to the Qur'an', *Vidyajyoti*, Vol. XLV, No. 7, August 1981, pp. 306-320.

4:155-7.[16] The Qur'anic sequence, then, is apparent death, ascension, second coming, natural death, general resurrection.

On the basis of a reading of 43:61, declaring that he is 'knowledge for the hour', and the prediction that all the People of the Book will believe in him before his death (after his return) in 4:159, there is support for an eschatological role for Jesus in the Qur'an.[17] A remarkable amount of traditional material has been built on this slender base, and some flavour of it can be had from Baidawi's claim that Jesus would return to earth in the Holy Land, kill the Antichrist, go to Jerusalem and pray there, kill all pigs and those who do not believe in him, reign in peace for forty years, before dying and being buried in Medina. While these notions have no Qur'anic basis, such opinions have remained popular, although modern opinions vary, and Parrinder quotes the Rector of Al-Azhar university as saying 'Any person who denies his [i.e. Jesus'] bodily ascent and his continuance in physical existence in the heavens, and his descent in the latter days, does not deny a fact that can be established by clear conclusive arguments.'[18] Certainly neither the Qur'an nor the commentators allow any element of atonement or vicarious satisfaction to be associated with the crucifixion.

From a Christian viewpoint, however, Cragg sees Jesus as fulfilling a necessary eschatological function in Islam, a role for which he, as a result of his rapture to heaven, is available to fulfil in a way which Muhammad, now dead and buried cannot: 'the hope of history is the final triumph of the prophetic, as culminated in Muhammad but assigned to his nearest predecessor.' As Cragg points out, we have the paradoxical situation of a Jesus in final espousal of Islam, and a Muhammad in ultimate accomplishment only through the agency of Jesus. Here, strangely, neither figure triumphs in the way their faiths assume: Jesus prevails through the Qur'an, not the Cross and Resurrection, and Muhammad is final not by *jihad* but through the heavenly Jesus. It is not clear what benefit for inter-faith dialogue this curious eventuality may provide.[19]

---

16   Robinson, *Christ in Islam and Christianity,* p. 125.
17   On Muslim apocalyptic thought and the return of Jesus and his role, see Larry Poston, 'The Second Coming of 'Isa: an Exploration of Islamic Premillenianism', *Muslim World*, 100 (January 2010), pp. 100-116. From a modern Muslim perspective, see Tim Winter, 'Jesus and Muhammad: New Convergences', *Muslim World* 99/1 (2009), pp. 21-38.
18   In *Islamic Review* September 1961, pp. 11ff.
19   Cragg, *Jesus and the Muslim,* p. 59.

Jesus as Messiah and Servant of God

The use of the term Messiah *(Masih)* may at first sight suggest a Christian understanding of Jesus, but the term is used in a different sense in the Qur'an. The historical development of the understanding of Jesus as Messiah in the Gospels is lacking there. The term is applied to him from the moment of his birth, but the Qur'an remains firmly opposed to any understanding of Jesus the Messiah as the Son of God and in 9:30-31 Christians are criticised for their perversity in saying the Messiah is the son of God, and accused of making not only the Messiah but also their clerics and monks 'Lords besides God; though they were ordered to serve one God only.'

While for Christianity the self-emptying by which the Messiah fulfils his servant-hood (Phil. 2:6ff.) by complete expenditure of himself in the service of God, even to death on the Cross, is exactly what leads to the justification of Christ's Sonship in the resurrection, the Qur'anic description of Jesus as one who 'does not disdain to be a servant of God' (4:172) confirms his very creatureliness. As Cragg puts it, 'The logic by which, for the Qur'an, Jesus can never be "Son" to God is precisely the logic by which, for Paul and the New Testament, he is.'[20]

Our brief survey of Jesus in the Qur'an is nevertheless sufficient to reveal fundamental differences with respect to Christian belief about him. We turn now to ask what it is in Islam that gives rise to the negative statements about the central figure of Christian faith.

Jesus and the Unity of God

The modern Algerian Muslim author Ali Merad lists five negative statements in the Qur'an referring to Christ, or rather, statements of what he is not, most of which have been referred to at least implicitly in our previous section; Christ is not God, or rather God is not Christ himself, Christ is not a divinity outside of (or below God), Christ is not the third person of a triad, Christ is not the Son of God, and Christ did not die a human death on the Cross since God through an exceptional act of his Goodness raised him to himself.[21]

Arising in the milieu of Arabian polytheism, Islam is characterised by an absolute insistence on the unity and supremacy of God *(tawhid)*. It is against this background of uncompromising monotheism that we must understand the negative statements which the Qur'an makes about Jesus. Set against

---

20   *Ibid.*, p. 30.
21   Merad, 'Christ according to the Qur'an', pp. 308-9.

this standard it is clear that any idea of Incarnation, Trinity or filial adoption is anathema to Islamic orthodoxy, and indeed associationism *(shirk)* is the most serious charge which it levels against Christianity. The Christological controversies between the Christian groups with whom Islam was first in contact simply served to confirm for them the falsity of Christian claims.

It may well be that the Qur'anic view of genuine Christian doctrine is in some cases rather wide of the mark: Christianity also rejects any idea of physical paternity in connection with Jesus as Son of God, nor do Christians recognise a portrayal of the Trinity as consisting of a family triad of God, Mary, and Jesus, although this may reflect pagan Arab beliefs or heretical Christian Mariolatry. For Christians to say that Jesus is Son of God means that he is God in self-revelation, the Father begets the Son only in the sense that his 'will' to be revealed is translated into act.[22]

Such misunderstandings of Christian thought as the Qur'an may demonstrate, however, do not detract from the fact that at the basis of the difference between the portrayal of Jesus in Islam and Christianity is a different understanding of God. As Tracey points out, 'Among the three historical radically monotheistic religions, Islam has been the most insistent on the oneness of God.' This monotheism 'is not only a soteriological monotheism but a profoundly dogmatic one. Indeed ... the central dogma of Islam.[23] The God of Islam is utterly transcendent, and the only proper human response is total submission *(islam)*. While there has long been within Christianity, especially in the mystical tradition, an apophatic strand which also stresses the unbridgeable ontological gulf between God and creature, even to the extent of asserting that nothing positive can be said about God,[24] the mainstream tradition speaks about God in the language of analogy. While Islam sees itself as the primeval religion given to mankind, Christianity sees the historical engagement of God in a process of revelation culminating definitively in the person of Christ.

Some Christological Reflections

The fact that Christian understanding of the relation of Christ to God, and the way in which the triune God is revealed as Father, pre-existent Word,

22   Cragg, *The Call of the Minaret,* Oxford University Press, Oxford, 1956, pp. 290ff, 315.
23   D Tracey, 'The Paradox of the Many Faces of God in Monotheism', *Concilium* 1995/2, pp. 30-39, see pp. 32-33.
24   An assertion also present in Muslim speculative theology, cf. Robinson, *Christ in Islam and Christianity*, p. 43.

and Spirit, came to be expressed in the language of a Hellenistic philosophy foreign to Semitic thought,[25] no doubt added to the difficulty which Islam experienced in its contact with orthodox Christianity. Talk of a Divine-human *hypostasis,* and of Trinitarian 'processions' continue to baffle the vast majority of Christians today, as evidenced by the prevalence of a frankly docetic Christology, and by an emphasis in personal devotion to one 'person' of the Trinity to the exclusion of others, reflecting a tendency to tritheism. It is important to understand, however, that while the ideas behind the early credal formulations must retain their validity, the language in which they are expressed can, indeed should, be subject to a continual process of interpretation and reformulation in order to remain meaningful for other times and cultures.[26] A renewed emphasis on the person of the historical Jesus in much modern Christology certainly benefits attempts to explain the Christian understanding of Jesus to those of other faiths (although it must be admitted that the current trend in Trinitarian theology, which is relatively comfortable with speaking of the 'persons' in the modern sense of the term, is rather less helpful to dialogue than the quasi-modalism of Barth and Rahner).

The suggestion by Hans Kung, among others, that a low, Jewish Christian Christology influenced the Qur'anic view of Jesus and may provide a fruitful way to initiate dialogue appears unsatisfactory on two counts; firstly, there is little if any historical evidence for the presence of such Jewish Christian groups where Islam arose, and secondly, such a Christology is inadequate as an expression of Christian belief in Christ as it has developed within the mind of the Church. This second objection can equally be applied to modern 'Spirit' Christologies which speak of Jesus as indwelt by the Spirit in a quantitatively, but not qualitatively different way to the rest of humanity.

I would argue that an adequate Christology requires three elements; that the Christ event is an initiative purely from the side of God, that in his life Jesus serves as a supreme exemplar of relationship to God and neighbour, and that he has *continuing* significance in the lives of people in bringing them to God (explicitly so in the case of Christians).[27]

---

25 Although I would not wish to deny the evidence of acculturation to Hellenism which is evident in inter-testamental Judaism.

26 This notion is accepted as legitimate by the Catholic Church in the document of the Congregation for the Doctrine of the Faith, *Mysterium Ecclesiae* (1973).

27 This is a necessarily brief summary of the approach suggested by Anthony Baxter, unpublished course notes—'Christology', Heythrop College, University of London, 1999.

We have seen how negative statements in Islam about Jesus must be understood in the context of a concept of God which differs from that in Christianity, we now move on to ask whether positive statements about him may provide for a degree of common ground between the two religions.

The surpassing greatness of Jesus in the Qur'an

Warning that there are difficulties in interpreting the Qur'anic references which appear to connect Jesus with the Word of God *(kalima* cf 4:171; 3:45) or the Spirit of God *(ruh,* cf 4:171), Merad argues that 'they bear an exceptional message: for in the Qur'an no other being is said to be *kalima* of God, *ruh* of God.' Admitting that the evidence this provides for the 'surpassing greatness' of Jesus is intuitive rather than discursive, he finds many other Qur'anic texts which support such a claim; the Envoys of God differ in status (2:253), the Qur'an makes particular mention of Moses, and of Jesus to whom God gave 'clear signs' *(bayyinat,* cf. 2:253; 43:63) and strengthened by the holy spirit *(ruh al-kudus)* cf. 2:87, 253); Jesus is an Envoy on whom God has conferred an eminent privilege *(wajih)* in this world and the next, implying holiness and the grace of intercession; he is among those intimate associates of the Lord, 'near-stationed'; only he is credited with the ability to create life *(yakhluq)* and to bring the dead to life *(yuhyi)*—always, of course, by the leave of God. For Merad, it is particularly the possession of these latter attributes not accorded to the other prophets, which 'places Christ above the ordinary condition of the 'Envoys of God', and raises him to a level never attained by other men'.[28]

While there can be no question for Merad of Jesus having a share in the sovereign freedom of God, participation in his omniscience, or any association with God in his work in the world, his reading of the Qur'an enables him to state 'that a mission has been confided *(taklif)* to him—an extraordinary mission, without precedent in the history of mankind,'[29] and this affirmation of the surpassing greatness of Jesus finds its highest point in his rapture to God. Even though Islam rejects the idea of the death of Jesus, this is to safeguard both the honour of God and the dignity of man: 'for in Jesus mankind attains its supreme dignity.'[30]

Without attempting to force on the Qur'anic texts a purely Christian understanding of Jesus which does not belong there, it is nevertheless possible

---

28   Merad, 'Christ according to the Qur'an', 1981, pp. 315-316.
29   *Ibid.,* p. 316.
30   *Ibid.,* p. 318.

to argue that it certainly presents Jesus as an initiative from the side of God: as 'a sign to all beings' (21:91), one raised by God to a level never attained by other men, whose life and teachings are therefore significant:[31] and as one 'near-stationed' to God who has the continuing power of intercession on behalf of humanity. As we have seen, the internal logic of the Qur'an demands a denial of the death of Jesus on the cross, but there is no doubt that human rejection of his message, a message to which he nevertheless holds fast, brings him to the point of death, and only by the intervention of God is he saved. While in Christianity the obedience of Jesus 'even to death on a cross' is vindicated by his resurrection, in Islam the same purpose is served by his rapture to heaven. Two relevant points of clarification of the Christian position should be made here; the Anselmian notion of the necessity of the crucifixion as atonement for sins, or as substitutionary sacrifice, is only one way of understanding the death of Jesus: and while the Creed says simply that Jesus rose from the dead *(resurrexit),* the New Testament witness insists that he was raised from the dead *by God.*

Having surveyed some important elements of the Islamic representation of Jesus, noting the context in which negative statements about him must be understood, and balancing them with the remarkably positive understanding of him which can be derived from the Qur'an, we now consider how Jesus may be a sign both to Christians and Muslims rather than a stumbling-block between them.

I have endeavoured to show that a careful reading of the Qur'anic text shorn of some of the fanciful excesses of the *ahadith* can permit us to recognise there something of the Christian Jesus, especially if he is understood in the light of the New Testament, rather than the rarified language of Hellenistic neo-Platonist philosophy (to this extent Kung is quite correct to call for a return to the roots of Christianity). While the Qur'anic view of Jesus is, from a Christian perspective, limited by Islamic insistence on the absolute unity of God, stressing the transcendence of God over mankind, it can nevertheless be argued that, like Christianity, it accords him a unique status. While fundamental doctrinal differences will continue to affect the understanding of Jesus in the two religions, the great esteem in which he is held in each, when properly understood, must provide a basis for dialogue, and a recognition that he is truly 'a sign for all beings'.

---

31   This reflection on the life of Jesus has developed strongly in the Sufi tradition (cf. Cragg, *Jesus and the Muslim,* pp. 59ff.), but the classical commentaries also incorporate numerous sayings of Jesus from the Gospels, cf. *ibid.,* pp. 46-51.

II In what sense can Christians call Muhammad a prophet?

The question 'What say you of Muhammad', addressed long-ago to the Assyrian patriarch Timothy (d. 823), is one which Islam has asked of other religions from its earliest times, and which it continues to ask today. In the contemporary context, Jacques Jomier sees two issues in the mind of the enquirer; why, if Muslims accept Jesus as a prophet, Christians are unwilling to afford the same respect to Muhammad, and the slanderous medieval attacks on the character of the Prophet of Islam.[32]

Thankfully, Christians today have no truck with the calumnies heaped on Muhammad as a result of earlier polemic and military conflict. Such are the theological issues raised by the former issue, however, that Christianity has largely elected to remain silent on the status of the founder of Islam. The Second Vatican Council was able to speak of the high esteem of the Church for Muslims who worship the same, one, creator God and 'strive to submit themselves without reserve to his decrees' (*Nostra Aetate* §3). Among those who have not yet received the Gospel, Muslims are among those accorded first place in the plan of salvation (*Lumen Gentium* §16). As the Council elsewhere acknowledges that salvation for individuals takes place within their cultural milieu, including their religion, we can see here an acknowledgement of the part played by Islam in the salvation of its adherents. What is lacking is any reference either to Muhammad or to the Qur'an.

Space does not permit an in-depth discussion of all the theological issues raised for Christians by the question of the status of the Prophet of Islam, We will begin by looking at early Christian response to Islam in the region in which it arose, before turning to a consideration of recent attempts by theologians to give a positive response to our question, and finally attempt some tentative conclusions.

Historical Christian responses to the emergence of Islam
According to Goddard, there were three main strands of Christian interpretation of Islam during the initial period of interaction of some two centuries: fulfilment of God's promise to Abraham and his son, Ishmael;

---

32   J Jomier, 'The Idea of the Prophet of Islam', *Bulletin,* Secretariatus pro non-Christianis (Rome), Vol. 6/3 no. 18, pp. 149-163, see p. 140.

judgement from God on those who accepted Chalcedonian Christology; and a Christian heresy.[33] We will look briefly at each of these.

The book of Genesis tells of the two sons of Abraham; Ishmael, the first-born, was born to Abraham's concubine, Hagar, and Isaac, born later to Abraham's wife Sarah and declared his heir. The text in Genesis states that certain promises were made by God to Ishmael '... I will make a nation of the son of the slave woman also, because he is your offspring' (Gen. 21:12-13), and later, 'I will make him a great nation' (Gen. 21:18). When the descendants of Abraham are listed in Genesis 25, the sons of Ishmael precede those of Isaac, and the fact that they are twelve in number, like the tribes of Israel, has traditionally been interpreted as signifying that they make up some kind of sacred unit.[34] The Armenian bishop Sebeos declared that Muhammad, 'Being very learned and well-versed in the Law of Moses, he taught them [the Arabs] to know the God of Abraham,' and also stated that he told his hearers that in them the promises made to Abraham and his descendants would be realised.[35] (It should be noted, however, that the description 'sons of Hagar' when used by later Christian apologists was in the more derogatory sense of Gal. 5:25.)[36]

This early Christian understanding of Islam rapidly changed as it became apparent that Islam saw itself not just as the fulfilment of ancient prophecy but as a corrective to or fulfilment of the Christian message. Eastern Christians who rejected Chalcedon soon came to see Islam as God's judgement on those who accepted that Council's teaching.

Those Eastern Christians who remained loyal to Chalcedon, however, developed a different view, represented by the attitude of John Damascene. As a result of his long contact with Muslims, supplemented by theological reflection, John included Islam as the one hundred and first Christian heresy in his work *De Haeresibus*. He sees Islam as a Christological heresy created

---

33 H Goddard, *A History of Christian-Muslim Relations*, Edinburgh University Press, Edinburgh, 2000, p. 41.

34 G von Rad, *Genesis: a Commentary*, SCM, London, p. 258.

35 J Moorhead, 'The Earliest Christian Theological Response to Islam', *Religion,* Vol. 11, 1981, pp. 265-266, see pp. 245-246.

36 S H Griffith, 'The Prophet Muhammad his scripture and his message according to the Christian Apologies in Arabic and Syriac from the First 'Abbasid Century' in *Arabic Christianity in the Monasteries of Ninth-Century Palestine* (Collected Study Series, CS380), Study 1, Ashgate, Aldershot, 1992, p. 122. See also the important study by the same author, *The Church in the Shadow of the Mosque: Christians and Muslims in the World of Islam*, Princeton University Press, Princeton, NJ, 2010.

by Muhammad with the aid of an Arian monk. John describes Islam as 'a deceptive superstition of the Ishmaelites'.[37]

For the early Christian apologists, writing in Syriac and Arabic, the life of Muhammad is discussed only in order to discredit those claims about him put forward by Muslims.[38] These authors completely rejected Muslim claims that he had received a revelation from God, that he was the Paraclete of the New Testament, or even that he should be considered a genuine prophet.[39] Griffith sees as a common refrain running through the Christian apologies of the first 'Abbasid century the contention that miraculous signs are the only sufficiently reasonable warranty for accepting anyone claiming divine inspiration. These apologists believed that people accepted Islam and the prophetic status of Muhammad, not on the base of evidentiary miracles but because of a number of unworthy motives; al-Basri lists possible motives as 'tribal collusion', 'the sword', 'wealth, dominion and power', 'ethnic bigotry', 'personal preference', 'licentious laws', and 'sorcery'.[40] It is remarkable that something of this approach has continued through medieval Spanish polemic to contemporary Christian apologetics: the motives which led Muhammad to opt for political power are still seen as a politicisation of prophethood that nullified his theologically valid role in Mecca.[41]

While Christians living within *dar al-Islam* were familiar with the Qur'an and with Muslim traditions, this was not so in the case of those Christians of other lands who produced later polemical works against Islam in Latin and Greek containing hostile fantasies, often betraying Muhammad as possessed by the devil, as an agent of the Antichrist, or as morally depraved. The military expansion of Islam into Christendom ensured that this vitriolic polemic continued for centuries to come.[42]

---

37   Goddard, *A History of Christian-Muslim Relations*, p. 39.
38   Griffith, 'The Prophet Muhammad', p. 132.
39   *Ibid.*, p. 131.
40   *Ibid.*, p. 143.
41   D Kerr, 'Muhammad: Prophet of Liberation—a Christian Perspective from Political Theology', *Studies in World Christianity*, 6/2, 2000, pp. 139-174, proposes that this line is taken by both Kraemer and Cragg, although each attributes different motives to Muhammad, see p. 160.
42   For a survey of Muslim/Christian confrontation and interaction in East and West respectively during this period, cf. Goddard, *A History of Christian-Muslim Relations*, Chs. 4 and 5. A shorter summary of the history of Christian thinking on Islam is given in R Caspar, *A Historical Introduction to Islamic Theology: Muhammad and the Classical Period*, Pontifical Institute of Arabic and Islamic Studies, Rome, 1998, p. 89ff.

This negative portrayal of Islam and its prophet, however, should not be allowed to eclipse a better informed and more irenic attitude which began to emerge in the Christian West during the twelfth century. Writers such as Peter of Malmesbury and Otto of Freising recognised that Muslims worship one God, that they respect Christ and the apostles, and that Muhammad is venerated only as the prophet of God. Peter the Venerable, abbot of Cluny, proposed a study of Islam from its own sources, and set up a comprehensive translation programme, much of which was undertaken in Toledo by scholars including Robert of Ketton and Herman of Dalmatia. On the basis of this Toledan collection, Peter wrote two works on Islam. The first purported to set out the beliefs of Islam, and although free neither from factual error or a tendency to polemic, it represented a tremendous advance on what had gone before. Peter's second work was a refutation of the 'errors' of Islam, remarkable nevertheless for the genuine spirit of Christian charity which he evinces towards his Muslim audience: he aims to convince them ' … by words, not by force, but by reason; not in hatred but in love'.[43]

The humanism of the Renaissance saw attempts at achieving a 'concord' between religions, including that of Nicholas of Cusa (1401-1464) in his *De pace fidei*, but, alongside these somewhat syncretic attempts, anti-Muslim polemic continued, and the Protestant reformers were hostile to Islam, always seeing Muhammad as a false prophet.

Some Enlightenment thinkers saw in Islam a natural and reasonable religion, contrasting it with the 'religion' of Catholicism. Voltaire describes Islam simply as a religion centred upon faith in the one God and for the Arabs' good.[44] The rationalism of the eighteenth century was followed by the exotic romanticism of the nineteenth. Napoleon spoke of 'our prophet Mahomet'; for Goethe, Muhammad exhibited the type of genius; while Robert Carlyle sees him as one of the greatest heroes of humanity. However, the theological interpretation of Islam by a Catholic Church engaged in the missionary expansion of the nineteenth century, and with an insistence on the need for membership of the Church for salvation, remained largely negative.

The twentieth century, by contrast, was characterised by a sea change in the Christian understanding of Islam, moving, as Caspar puts it 'from an almost totally hostile and negative attitude to impartiality and a positive appreciation

---

43   Quoted in Goddard, *A History of Muslim-Christian Relations*, p. 95.
44   Caspar, *A Historical Introduction to Islamic Theology*, n. 13, p. 95.

almost without nuance.'[45] Foremost among those responsible for the change was the remarkable Louis Massignon, whose views considerably influenced the new approach to Islam shown by the Second Vatican Council.

The Prophethood of Muhammad— *some recent approaches in Christian Theology*

We turn now to a consideration of the approach taken by four Christian scholars, the French Islamicist, Louis Massignon, the Anglican Professor of Islamic Studies, William Montgomery Watt, the German Catholic theologian, Hans Kung, and David Kerr, Professor of Christianity in the non-Western World at Edinburgh University.

In an interview given in 1948, Massignon's primary point was to defend Muhammad from the charge of being a false prophet. In his definition of Muhammad's genuine prophethood he introduced the term 'negative prophecy' which he saw as opposed to 'positive prophecy'. While Massignon saw positive prophecy, which challenges and reverses human values, as accounting for much of Muhammad's career as a social reformer, he went further in describing him as a negative prophet in the sense of bearing witness to 'the final separation of good and evil'.[46] For Massignon, negative prophecy is an eschatological category, bearing witness to the Last Day when God will disclose 'the transcendent secret of the glory of the just God', Massignon used the phrase 'the Marian sign' to express his belief that Muhammad's 'negative' prophethood in Medina consisted essentially of his witnessing to the secret of the virginity of Mary—an eschatological truth for all mankind that the Second Coming of Jesus the Messiah will reveal the freedom of God's glory in salvation, and in judgement of those who may have sought to 'domesticate' the Messiah with a physical genealogy, or to have 'carnalized' the Incarnation.[47] Just as Mary bore Jesus in Bethlehem, so Muhammad's 'Marian sign' witnessed the Second Coming. This equivalence between Mary and Muhammad at least implies the finality of the latter: as Mary was unique in remaining immaculate, so Muhammad was the definitive negative eschatological prophet. Furthermore, while Muhammad follows chronologically the first coming of Christ, it is his very anticipation of the

---

45   *Ibid.*, p. 96.
46   L Massignon, 'Le Signe Marial', *Rhythmes du Monde*, Vol. 3/1, Paris, 1948, pp. 7-16, see p. 9.
47   *Ibid.*

Second Coming that, for Massignon, can be said to recommend him to Christians as an authentic eschatological prophet.

Known primarily as a historian of Islam, and particularly of the life of Muhammad, Montgomery Watt's later thought concentrated on Christian-Muslim relations. In a recent work he unequivocally states that 'I consider Muhammad was truly a prophet' and that Christians should recognise him as such on the basis of the principle that 'by their fruits you shall know them,' Islam having produced many good and saintly people.[48] In a much earlier work, Watt described the nature of a prophet as 'a religious leader who brings religious truth in a form suited to the needs of his society and age.'

The prophet presents a vision which requires action, and exhibits sufficient coherence for his ideas to become 'the basis of a systematic world-view, that is, a dogmatic system.' For this to be true, Watt argues, following Jung, the prophet must be in intuitive touch with 'the collective unconsciousness or the movement of Life'. It is this that enables the ideational synthesis of a prophet to function as 'the core of the religious ideation of vast civilisations'. Watt recognises both Jesus and Muhammad as examples of such transformative ideational synthesis. He accepts the problems involved in extending a prophet's teaching from one culture to another, proposing that we ask the simple question as to whether religions in history work for the general moral well-being of their followers.[49] It is by the ethics of what it does that a religion may be judged 'true'.[50] Watt sees the fruits of Islam in the Qur'anic virtue of *sabr*—'patience'—resulting from obedience to God's command, with its reward of 'the great success' on the Last Day. In this Watt sees the mark of Muhammad's prophetic message, which he equates in Muslim experience with 'the attainment of a supremely meaningful life'.[51] On this basis he concludes that, as Islam has enabled countless numbers of people to enjoy a quality of life which has been generally satisfactory for its members, and helped many to attain saintliness of life, 'the view of reality presented in the Qur'an is true and from God, and that therefore Muhammad is a genuine prophet.'[52]

---

48 W M Watt, *Muhammad's Mecca: History in the Qur'an,* Edinburgh University Press, Edinburgh, 1988, p. 1.

49 W M Watt, *Truth in the Religions: A Sociological and Psychological Approach,* Edinburgh University Press, Edinburgh, 1963, see pp. 149-151.

50 A similar stress on the importance of the 'fruits' of a religion, from the perspective of social anthropology, is apparent in T W Overholt, *Channels of Prophecy: the Social Dynamics of Prophetic Activity,* Fortress Press, Minneapolis, 1989.

51 Watt, *Truth in the Religions,* p. 21.

52 *Ibid.,* p. 135.

Hans Kung differs from the previous two scholars in that he is not a specialist of Islam. Addressing the relationship between the two religions in his *Christianity and the World Religions*, he lists the similarities between Muhammad and the Hebrew prophets. In summary, for Kung, Muhammad's prophethood was based not on appointment by his community but on a special relationship with God, which caused him to see himself as totally permeated by his divine calling and led him to challenge the socio-religious environment of his time with a message not his own, but solely that of God, the one, kind and merciful creator and judge, who rejects idolatry and demands social justice of all those who submit to the divine will. In view of this, Kung asks whether Christian acceptance of Amos and Hosea, Isaiah and Jeremiah, as prophets, but not Muhammad, is merely dogmatic prejudice. Kung does not ignore the tension between similarity and difference; however, in his view 'Muhammad is discontinuity in person, an ultimately irreducible figure, who cannot simply be deduced from what preceded him, ... as he establishes permanent new standards.'[53] These 'permanent new standards' are apparent in Islam, which shows an ability to enhance the human condition 'against the background of the Absolute'.[54] Kung is equally convinced that 'Muhammad has functioned as a religious archetype for a large part of the human race.'[55]

Kung points out that the office of prophecy continues to have New Testament authority, which anticipates prophets after the time of Jesus, and does not reject them if their teaching is in basic agreement with his. Applying this to Muhammad, Kung argues that the Vatican II references to Muslims should be extended to include recognition of Muhammad, the Prophet of Islam, who alone led them to pray to the one God, who has spoken to mankind through him.[56] This acknowledgement of Muhammad's prophethood is required not only in respect of what Muhammad has been and continues to be for Muslims, but also subjectively in terms of the inner needs of the Church. Christianity continues to need the prophetic corrective of not only the prophets of the Church but also prophets outside the Church. Kung suggests that Islam, in preserving the Servant of God Christology of Syrian-Semitic Christianity challenges the Church to retrieve insights which were obscured by its Hellenistic development. In support of Kung, Kerr believes that the

---

53   H Kung, *Christianity and the World Religions*, Doubleday, New York, 1986, pp. 25-27.
54   H Kung, *Theology for the Third Millennium*, Doubleday, New York, 1988, p. 255.
55   Kung, *Christianity and the World Religions*, p. 25.
56   *Ibid.*, p. 27.

lack of historical evidence for this influence of a Semitic low Christology on Islam is less important than the theological point that Kung wishes to make. Rather than arguing for a return to the origins of Christianity, he wishes to retrieve 'an original perception of Jesus that in its contextual difference from Western Christianity can encourage new contextual thinking about Jesus among Arab, African, and Asian Christians.'[57]

Such an approach, Kung believes, enables Muhammad to be valued by Christians as 'a witness for Jesus', and Islam as 'interwoven' with Christianity.[58]

It is interesting to note that Kung's understanding of Islam as reminding the Church of an earlier, lower, Christology appears to be in direct opposition to Massignon's view of it as a warning against 'carnalizing' the Incarnation. Kung also differs with Massignon in rejecting claims of 'finality' for Muhammad (as, indeed, he does for Christ).

The new contextual thinking called for by Kung is echoed by the Palestinian Christian theologian Mitri Raheb,[59] who argues that Arab Christians should attempt to build bridges of contextual theology with progressive Muslim theologians who are reading the Qur'an contextually. Kerr believes that political theology offers such a bridge for Christians to understand Muhammad as prophet 'that includes him in the liberative process of transforming human history into the Kingdom of God ... '[60]

Political theology, drawing on the ideas of European political thinkers, particularly the Frankfurt school, developed first in contexts where Christianity was the dominant religion. The best known example is the Liberation Theology of South America, which later gave an impetus to the development of black, feminist, gay, and other versions of Liberation Theology. Space does not allow us a full exposition of political theology here, but Kerr sums it up well by saying that it 'arises where oppressed persons or groups analyse injustice in the light of biblical analogies, and counter the causes of injustice through biblically-inspired political action.'[61] It may also be said that the marginalised are seen as the preferred locus for 'doing' theology.

While political theology as such originated within Christianity, the phenomenon to which it refers is also present in other religions. Kerr claims that Islam represents a political theology *par excellence,* going back to the time of Muhammad's preaching of ethical monotheism in Mecca, which culminated

---

57   Kerr, *Muhammad: Prophet of Liberation*, p. 155.
58   Kung, 1985, p. 116.
59   Kerr, *Muhammad: Prophet of Liberation*, p. 139.
60   Kerr, *Muhammad: Prophet of Liberation*, p. 141.
61   *Ibid.*, p. 142. The 'hermeneutical circle' of liberation theologies—see, judge, act.

in the creation of a new socio-political community in Medina. The Qur'anic account of the stories of the prophets, particularly Moses, consistently emphasises the connection between belief *(iman)* in God and the struggle for social justice *(jihad)*.[62]

As an example of a modern Islamic political theology, Kerr draws attention to the work of the South African scholar Farid Esack, who develops a new way of reading the text of the Qur'an, based on hermeneutical principles arising from Moses' confrontation with Pharaoh and his leading of the exodus from Egypt.[63]

He concludes that 'A commitment to humankind and active solidarity with the *mustad'afun* (the oppressed, those afflicted by injustice perpetrated by people or institutions) results in a re-reading of both social reality and the text from their perspective.'[64]

Having established that there are clearly parallels in contemporary Islam to Christian political theology, Kerr goes on to consider how this bridge between the traditions may help Christians to make theological sense of Muhammad. He suggests that the renewed understanding of prophecy among liberation theologians may provide the key. As Guttierez puts it, 'The prophets announce a kingdom of peace, but peace presupposes the establishment of justice ... the liberation of the oppressed.'[65] This approach allows Christians to re-evaluate the long-held view we referred to above, that the Medinan career of Muhammad represented a politicisation of his ethical teaching at Mecca which forfeits any claim to true prophethood. In fact, the Medinan Constitution which he established between diverse religious and tribal groups, should be seen as an attempt 'to build a radically new society that would observe in socio-political terms the ethical standards by which God judges human communities.'[66] The Constitution links faith with the practice of justice *('adl)*: the peace of Medina united the migrants *(muhajirun)*, who had been oppressed in Mecca, with the new converts in Medina in a system of fraternity that established social justice. On this basis, Christians should have no difficulty in recognising Muhammad as a prophet 'who was clearly

---

62   *Ibid.*, p. 143.
63   The centrality of the Exodus theme to Christian theologies of liberation can hardly be over-emphasised. On this topic see the important collection of articles in *Concilium* 1987/1.
64   Kerr, *Muhammad: Prophet of Liberation*, p. 104.
65   G Guttierez, *A Theology of Liberation*, SCM, London, 1974, p. 167.
66   Kerr, *Muhammad: Prophet of Liberation*, p. 162.

part of the liberative process by which the Kingdom of God becomes a transformative socio-political reality in history.' Questions still remain over the differing Christologies of Islam and Christianity, the finality of the Prophet, and the validity of Islam as a religion, but the stress on orthopraxis rather than orthodoxy, so characteristic of Liberation Theology, enables Christians and Muslims who commit themselves to a dialogue of the poor/*mustad'afun* to see themselves as allies rather than competitors in the liberative mission of Jesus and Muhammad.[67]

To the extent, then, that Muhammad fulfilled the function of eschatological prophet who worked to advance the process of liberation and making real the Kingdom of God, and was inspired to establish a way of life which continues to bring countless people to knowledge of and submission to the one, true God, it would seem that Christians should have no difficulty in accepting the prophethood of Muhammad. A note of caution must be sounded, however.

Resulting largely from the demands of Muslim-Christian dialogue, the ideas put forward by the four thinkers we have briefly reviewed must be seen as principally intra-Christian in nature, their Christian theological criteria give little consideration to Muslim understandings of prophecy and prophethood, it can also be argued, with the possible exception of David Kerr, that they tend to emphasise the historical Muhammad rather than giving full weight to the Muhammad of Islamic doctrine, piety, prayer and politics.[68]

We must ask whether Muslim and Christian theologies of prophecy are in fact compatible—Jomier warns that they are not and points out that, for many Muslims, Christian acceptance of the prophethood of Muhammad in the strict sense would be understood as making them *de facto* Muslims.[69]

The understandings of prophethood themselves depend on theories of revelation, and only by further study of this question by Christians and Muslims will it be possible to arrive at a new statement of the nature of revelation which may allow, as Kerr puts it 'a fuller mutual acceptance of

---

67 *Ibid.*, p. 170.

68 D Kerr, 'He Walked in the Path of the Prophets; Towards Christian Theological Recognition of the Prophethood of Muhammad' in Y D and W Z Haddad (eds), *Christian Muslim Encounters,* University of Florida Press, Gainesville, FL, 1995, pp. 426-446; see p. 441.

69 Jomier, 'The Idea of the Prophet in Islam', p. 161.

their normative human personifications of faith'.[70] It must be said, however, that progress in this endeavour will likely be minimal until Muslims are able to accept the same kind of historico-critical reading of the Qur'an which Christians have come to apply to the Bible.[71]

---

70   D Kerr, 'He Walked in the Path of the Prophets', p. 442.
71   A move in such a direction can be seen in the work of scholars such as Farid Esack, and Mohammed Talbi (cf. R L Nettler, 'Mohammed Talbi: "For Dialogue Between All Religions"' in Nettler and Taji-Farouki [eds], *Muslim Jewish Encounters Intellectual Traditions and Modern Politics*, Harwood Academic Publishers, Amsterdam, 1998, pp. 171-199, see p. 181) but neither can be said to represent mainstream thought.